Screen Printing

A Contemporary Approach

Screen Printing
A Contemporary Approach

Samuel Hoff
Rochester Institute of Technology

Delmar Publishers

an International Thomson Publishing company

Albany • Bonn • Boston • Cincinnati • Detroit • London • Madrid
Melbourne • Mexico City • New York • Pacific Grove • Paris • San Francisco
Singapore • Tokyo • Toronto • Washington

Printed in the United States of America

For more information, contact:

Delmar Publishers
3 Columbia Circle, Box 15015
Albany, New York 12212-5015

International Thomson Publishing Europe
Berkshire House 168-173
High Holborn
London, WC1V7AA
England

Thomas Nelson Australia
102 Dodds Street
South Melbourne, 3205
Victoria, Australia

Nelson Canada
1120 Birchmount Road
Scarborough, Ontario
Canada M1K5G4

Cover and Text Design: Stillwater Studio, Stillwater NY

Delmar Staff
Publisher: Robert D. Lynch
Senior Administrative Editor:John E. Anderson
Development Editor: Michele Canistraci
Production Manager: Larry Main
Cover Design Coordinator: Nicole Reamer

International Thomson Editores
Campos Eliseos 385, Piso 7
Col Polanco
11560 Mexico D F Mexico

International Thomson Publishing Gmbh
Königswinterer Strasse 418
53227 Bonn
Germany

International Thomson Publishing Asia
221 Henderson Road
#05-10 Henderson Building
Singapore 0315

International Thomson Publishing – Japan
Hirakawacho Kyowa Building, 3F
2-2-1 Hirakawacho
Chiyoda-ku, 102 Tokyo
Japan

1 2 3 4 5 6 7 8 9 10 XXX 02 01 00 99 98 97

Library of Congress Cataloging-in Publication Data

Hoff, Samuel.
Screen printing: a contemporary approach / by Samuel Hoff.
p. cm.
ISBN 0-8273-7128-4
1. Screen process printing. I. Title
TT273.H64 1996
667' .38–dc20

96-36589
CIP

Dedication

Whenever one commences a major venture such as writing a book, it soon becomes apparent that outside assistance is essential in reaching the final goal. I've been assisted by so many individuals and companies that it is impossible to list them all here.

The two people that I wish to acknowledge are my parents, Claude and Martha Hoff. I remember them as people of strong character, who practiced their beliefs in their daily lives. They instilled in me important values that have assisted me in establishing my personal identity. I learned from them the work ethic and the importance of contributing your best effort in life. The greatest value is the belief in God and the importance of a personal relationship with Him through his son, Jesus Christ.

The Bible verse that has inspired me throughout my life is found in the book of Philippians 4:13. "I can do all things through Christ who gives me strength." This verse has inspired me to reach the greatest achievements in my life.

Samuel Hoff
February, 1997

CONTENTS

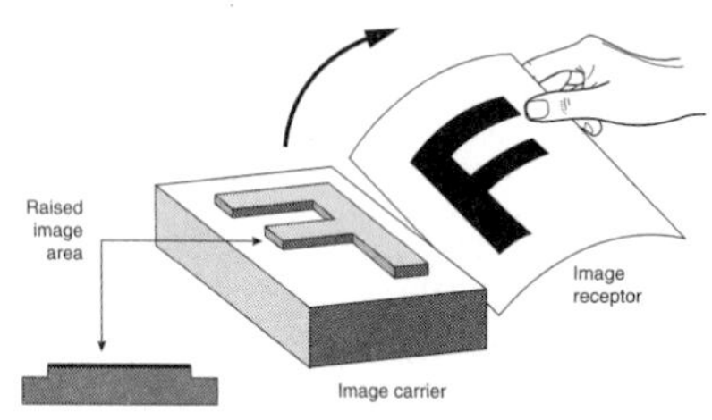
Raised image area
Image receptor
Image carrier

myrrh
A Division of Word, Inc., Waco, TX
AMY GRANT
SAVED BY LOVE
4:39
Amy Talks About "SAVED BY LOVE"
3:17

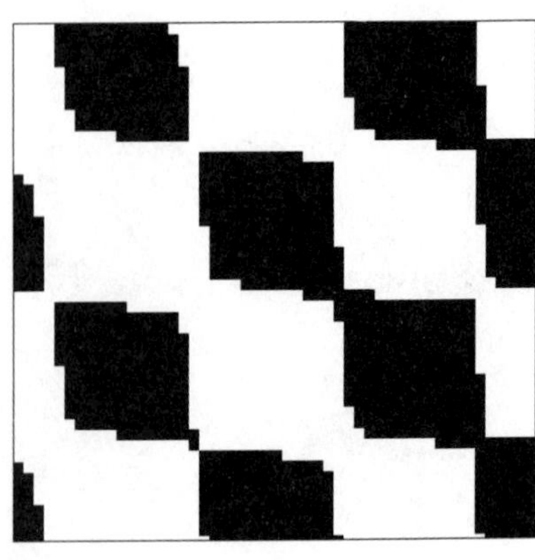

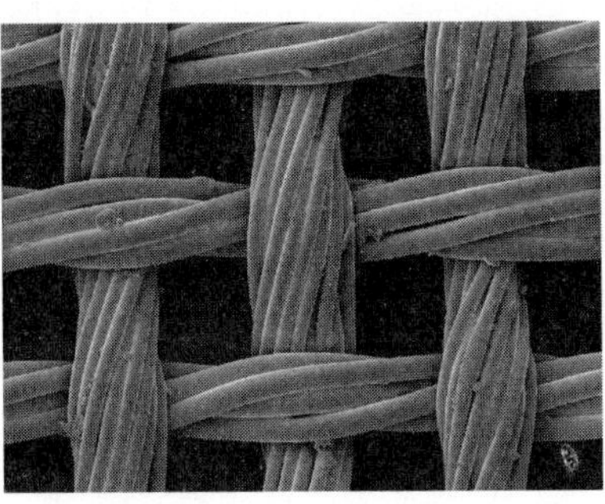

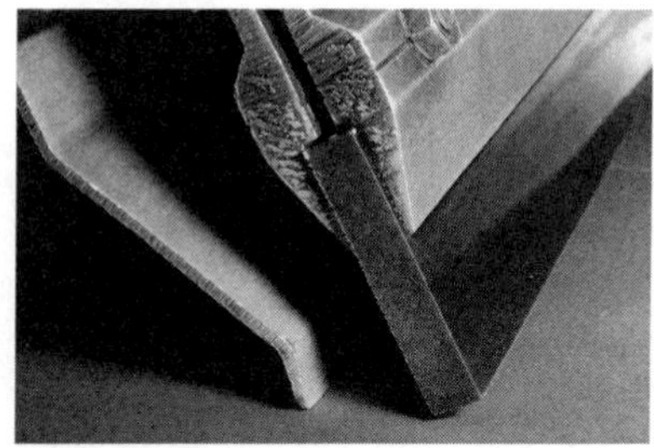

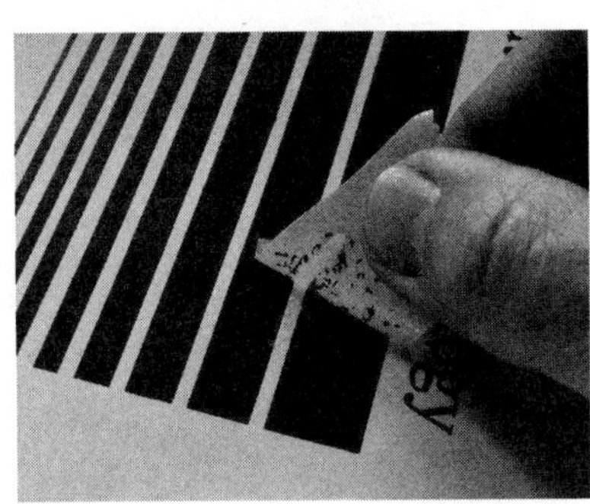

Foreword

I first visited the School of Printing at Rochester Institute of Technology in the early 1970's. Although there already was an active graphics curriculum, RIT was still building the reputation of excellence it now enjoys.

After that visit, a three-way effort was initiated by RIT, screen printers in Rochester, and the Screenprinting & Graphic Imaging Association International to acquire new, state-of-the-art equipment to enhance the screen printing educational offerings.

For the succeeding twenty-five years, RIT's screen printing classes have helped to develop young men and women for careers in our industry. Since 1987, when Professor Sam Hoff assumed the mantel of responsibility for the screen printing courses, they have grown in popularity as well as in technical education excellence.

The publication of *Screen Printing: A Contemporary Approach* is a new milestone in sharing concise and detailed specifications of the intricacies of the unique screen printing medium.

While screen printing is often called the "print anything process," this text, graphically and in words, depicts the characteristics and production requirements for screen printed decals, posters, textiles, nameplates, glassware, ceramics, electronic components, displays, signage, and hundreds of other products.

The liberal use of photographs, charts, and diagrams contribute immeasurably to the educational value of this manual. Materials from leading industry authorities, major suppliers & manufacturers, industry trade publications, the Screen Printing Technical Foundation and the Screenprinting & Graphic Imaging Association International contribute to the variety and authenticity of the material compiled by Sam Hoff.

Screen Printing: A Contemporary Approach is a testament to the diversity, production quality, and modern technology of today's screen printing industry.

Students, industry practitioners, serigraphers, and anyone interested in an in-depth analysis of screen printing, will gain from studying this text. It will be an important element putting you on the road to a career in the graphics.

John M. Crawford
President
Screenprinting & Graphic Imaging Association International

PREFACE

Over the years I have often been asked to recommend an up-to-date textbook on the screen printing process. I have found books that covered a number of stages aspects of the process, but none that were sufficiently comprehensive and in-depth. Covering all stages aspects of the process in depth in one book would be a monumental task. A more realistic goal would be to address major stages aspects of the process in as much depth as could reasonably be accommodated. While visiting plants and doing consulting work over the years, I have seen a wide range of different screen printing operations. One observation that I have made is that nearly all technical problems can be traced back to problems with basic principles of the screen printing process. . This book was written after a comprehensive review of a wide range of up-to-date resources on the screen printing process, and it stresses the basic principles of each stage of the process.

This textbook is comprehensive in nature and covers the entire screen printing process, which allows the interaction between each stage aspect of the process to be examined. This book takes a technical approach, applying theory to actual practice. Up-to-date technical advancements are emphasized to reflect the latest trends in the industry. The text uses the following methods to present the material in a thorough, clear manner.

- Photographs are used to show various technical details.
- Illustrations and diagrams are used to display technical information such as squeegee angle, durometer, and so on.
- Graphs are used to show technical data such as fabric usage trends over the past few years.
- Charts are used to make comparisons between two elements such as monofilament versus multifilament mesh count.

The intended audience for the textbook is as follows:

- Educators and students in graphic arts programs at the high school, college, trade, or technical school level.
- Technical personnel in the screen printing industry.
- Artists with an interest in the technical aspects of the process.

This book contains current trade practices of the screen printing industry as well as cutting edge technology. It emphasizes screen printing as a technical process rather than an artistic craft process.

Each of the nine chapters has key technical terms highlighted and includes study questions to enhance learning of the chapter content. The final chapter of the text is a comprehensive glossary of screen printing terms taken from the Screenprinting and Graphic Imaging Association (S.G.I.A.) Glossary. This will assist the reader in becoming familiar with technical terms used in the industry.

The chapters are organized into sections aspects of the screen printing process. The first chapter introduces screen printing and compares it to traditional and new printing processes. The second chapter discusses various materials and products that are commonly screen printed. Each chapter introduces various phases aspects of the process, starting with design and film production. Other items aspects such as screen fabric, fabric tensioning and frames, stencil selection and production, squeegees, inks, and finishing with press and dryers are also covered.

ABOUT THE AUTHOR

Samuel Hoff graduated from California State University, Los Angeles, with B.A. and M.A. degrees, and has been involved in various aspects of the screen printing industry for over twenty years. He Samuel Hoff is currently an associate professor in the School of Printing Management and Sciences at Rochester Institute of Technology. He is a tenured member of the graduate and undergraduate faculty in charge of the screen printing program.

He has served on the Educational and Vocational Development Committee of the Screenprinting and Graphic Imaging Association International (S.G.I.A.) since 1988 and makes presentations at its annual conventions. He has recently been elected to the Screenprinting and Graphic Imaging Association International Board of Directors.

He has written numerous articles for screen printing publications. He has been a regular columnist for Screen Graphics Magazine since its initial issue in September of 1994.

Professor Hoff has recently completed the most comprehensive textbook on traditional and cutting edge technology for the screen printing industry.

He has presented seminars around the country for graphic arts professionals and educators on various topics related to screen printing.

He serves as a consultant to the industry testing new products, equipment and materials, and developing specialized training programs. He strives to maintain close contact to stay abreast of industrial trends through visits to various printers, as well as to manufacturers of equipment, materials, and supplies.

Professor Hoff graduated from California State University, Los Angeles with B.A. and M.A. degrees. He has been involved in various aspects of the screen printing industry for over 20 years. His early beginnings were during early college years when he ran his own screen printing business to pay his way through college. These experiences brought him to a practical hands on approach with his seminars and industry involvements.

The author and publisher wish to thank the following reviewers for their valuable contributions to the manuscript:

Joseph Schickel
Department of Industry and Technology
California University of Pennsylvania

James Miekle
The George Brown College
Toronto, Ontario, Canada

Ken Daley
Department of Art
Old Dominion University
Norfolk, VA

Introduction to the Screen Printing Process

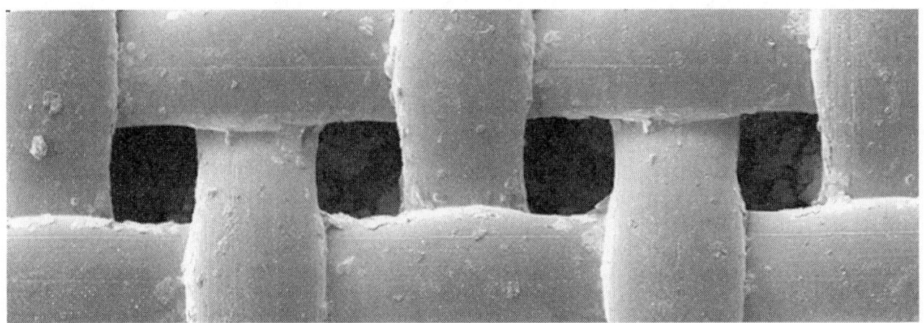

Printing is defined as the reproduction of an image from a printing surface by contact impression that causes a transfer of ink. A number of copies are printed in one continuous operation. Screen printing is just one of several printing processes. Before we take an extensive view of the screen printing operation it would be beneficial to discuss the most significant printing processes and establish the strengths and weaknesses of each. There is no ideal printing process that will work in every circumstance; it is a matter of determining which process will achieve the desired results in the most efficient, cost effective manner.

THE PRIMARY PRINTING PROCESSES

There are four dominant printing processes in use today. These processes are classified according to the action of the image carrier used in creating the image. The basic fundamentals can be classified as: **relief, intaglio, planographic** and **stencil.** The terms used today for these processes as presented in Figure 1-1 are: flexography, gravure, lithography and screen printing. There are a number of other processes used for printing applications which are too numerous to discuss at length in this context. One such process which has a significant impact on screen printing is known as pad

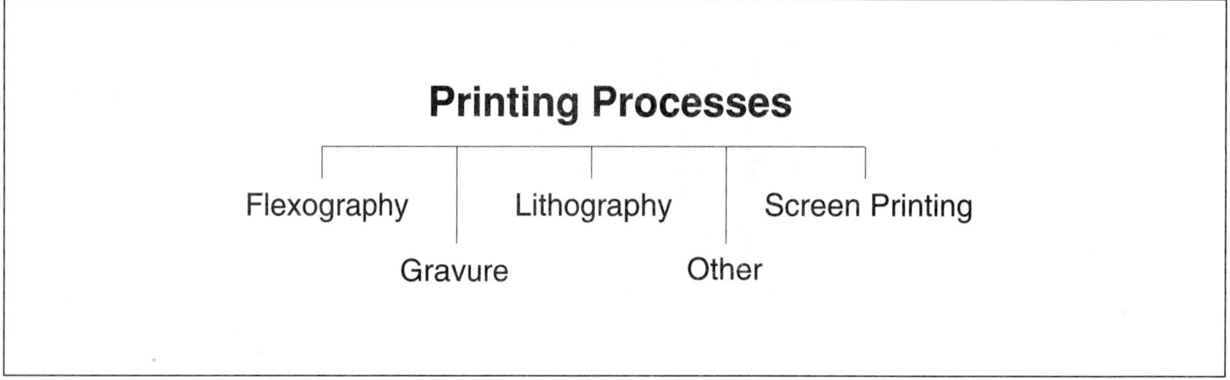

Figure 1-1

transfer printing. There are other electronic printing processes that are used when small quantities are needed. We will introduce them later in this chapter.

Flexography/ Letterpress

Flexography and letterpress are relief processes; that is, raised areas form image areas. The raised areas are inked and the image is transferred to paper when pressure is applied between image carrier and paper. Letterpress image carriers can be of lead, wood type or photo engravings. In principle flexography is the same as letterpress. The primary difference between the two is the flexible nature of the flexographic image carrier due to its polymer composition. Its flexible nature makes it suitable to print on rough surfaces such as brown kraft paper bags or market plastic bags. See Figure 1-2.

Flexography is a form of rotary web letterpress using a flexible rubber or photopolymer image carrier with fast drying solvent or water-based inks fed by an Anilox inking system. Flexography is the principle method of relief printing in use today, printing from a raised image. The roller configuration, type of ink, and the image carrier make flexography considerably different from conventional letterpress. See Figure 1-3.

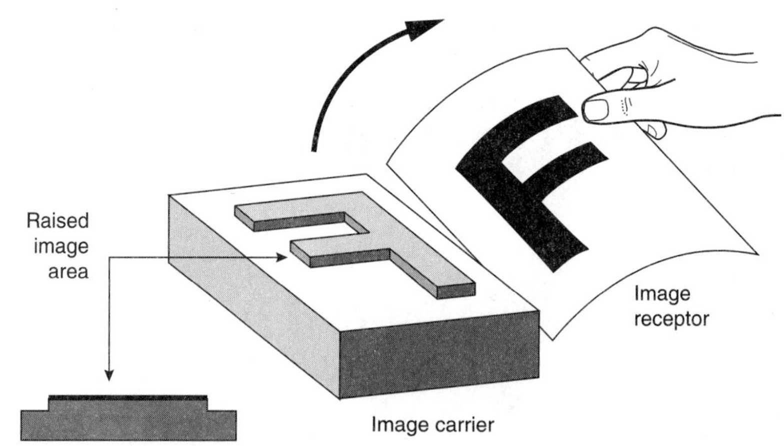

Figure 1-2 Relief

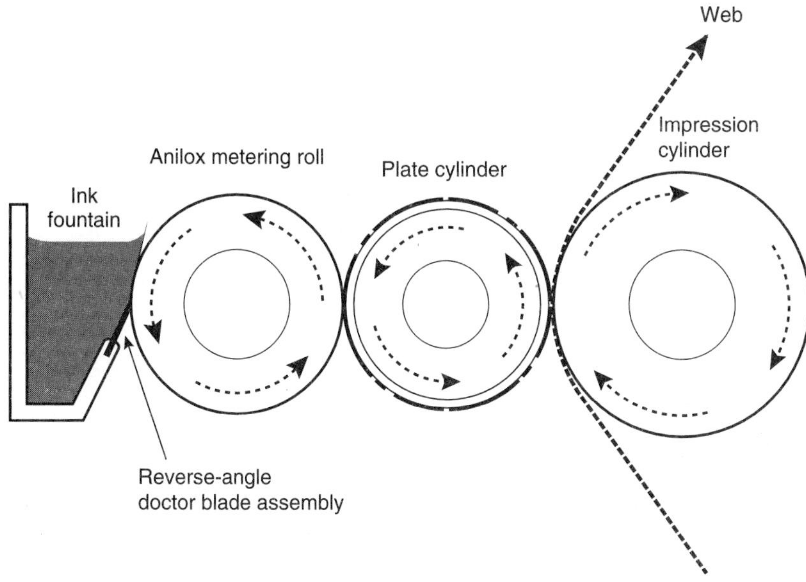

Figure 1-3 Flexography

Figure 1-4 Flexographic press

The flexographic process was first developed at the beginning of the twentieth century. Recent technical advancements in inks and photopolymer plates have improved its accuracy, versatility, speed economy and print quality. It was once limited to relatively low quality printing, but is now capable of halftone and four color process reproduction. The ink distribution system begins by flooding the surface of the Anilox roller with ink. The surface of the Anilox roller is made up of a large number of cells or cavities that hold ink. The Anilox roller averages about 100,000 cells per square inch of surface area.

The angle, shape, and depth of the cells affect ink deposit and print quality much the same as the effect that screen fabric has on screen printing. A reverse angle doctor blade wipes the surface of the Anilox roller leaving ink in the recessed areas of the cells. The Anilox roller is brought in contact with the flexographic image carrier. This delivers a uniformly metered ink film on the surface of the plate which maintains ink density regardless of press speed. See Figure 1-4.

The growth of flexography has occurred in concert with the growth of the packaging industry. Some of the products printed by flexography are flexible packaging materials, paper and plastic films, multi-wall bags, corrugated containers, envelopes, pressure sensitive labels, gift wrap and paperback books.

Gravure

This printing process is the opposite of relief printing; here the image areas are recessed. **Gravure** is an example of intaglio printing. The term intaglio is derived from *intagliare* (Italian) meaning to engrave and *tagliare* (Latin) meaning to cut. It uses a sunken or depressed surface for image areas. The image areas consist of cells or wells etched into a copper cylinder; the non-etched surface of the cylinder represents the non-printing areas. The typical gravure cell (for a 150 line screen) is 35μ **(microns)** deep by 125μ square with 22,500 per square inch.

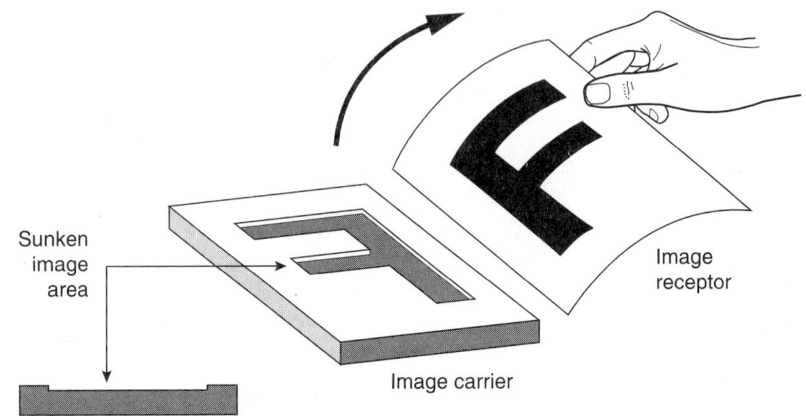

Figure 1-5 Intaglio

The image cylinder rotates in an ink supply filling the cells with ink. Ink is wiped off the surface of non image areas with a flexible doctor blade. Ink remains in the thousands of recessed cells to form an image; it is transferred to the paper as it passes between the plate cylinder and the impression cylinder. The printing cylinder has a copper surface which is engraved either chemically or mechanically to form image areas. The size and depth of each dot can be modified to give gravure the widest tonal range of all printing processes. See Figure 1-5.

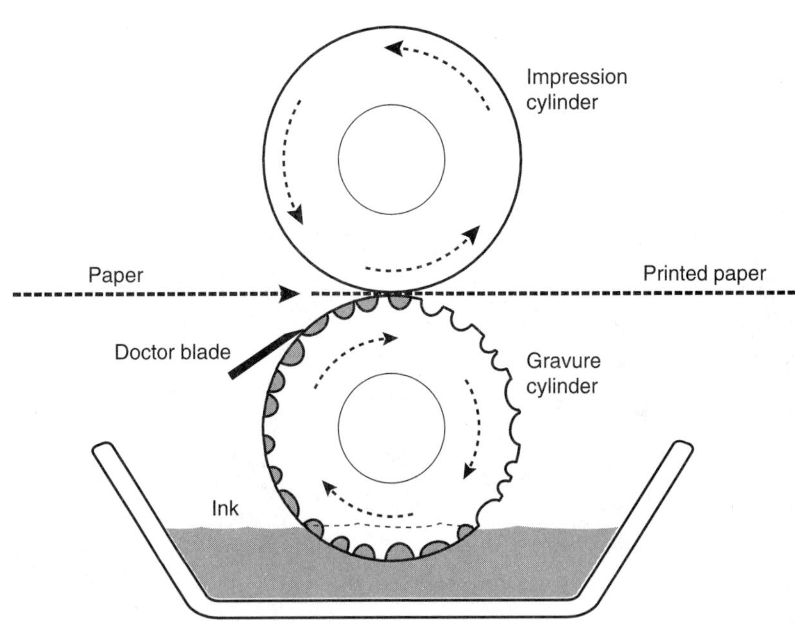

Figure 1-6 Gravure

Gravure printing is considered to be excellent for reproducing photographs, but the high cost of cylinder making limits its use primarily to large runs. Gravure is able to print at high speeds with the ink drying at low temperatures due to the high speed solvents that compose the inks, and the simplicity of the inking system. This makes the inks highly volatile, yet produces high quality results on a wide range of substrates. See Figures 1-6 and 1-7.

Gravure is used in printing and coating operations. Gravure markets can be broken down into three

Figure 1-7 Gravure press

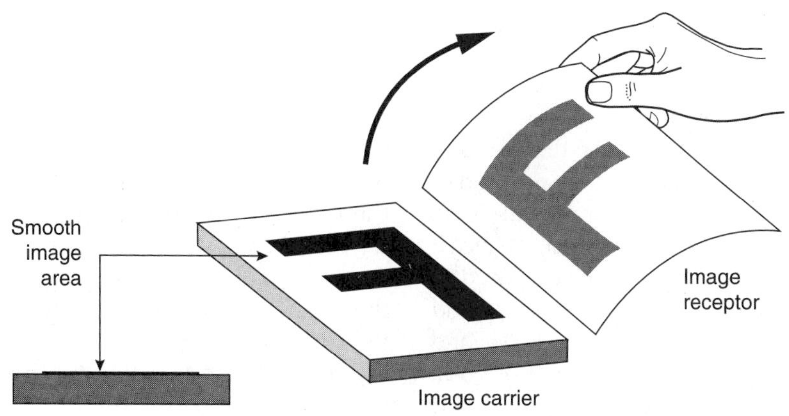

Figure 1-8 Planographic

groups: publications, packaging, and specialities. Publications category includes magazines, catalogs, newspaper supplements, comics and other commercial printing. Packaging uses include folding cartons, flexible packages such as soap cartons, ice cream cartons, flip top cigarette packages, frozen food wraps, and polyethylene bread bags. Specialty includes wall and floor coverings, decorated household paper products such as paper towels, cigarette filter tips, vinyl upholstery, wood grains and plastic laminates.

Lithography

Lithography is a planographic process. The term planographic is derived from *planus* (Latin) meaning flat, smooth, or level. Therefore, lithography uses an image carrier that is flat. Image areas are neither raised nor recessed as with other printing processes. See Figure 1-8. Lithography is made up of two root words, *lithos* meaning stone and *graphein* meaning writing. This term literally means stone writing. The earliest form of lithography used a flat stone for the image carrier. Lithography is a chemical process based on the principle that ink and water do not mix. A special marker was used to produce image areas on the stone. The stone was then dampened, after which ink was applied allowing ink only in image areas. Modern production methods employ metal plates that are imaged using a photographic process.

Image areas are ink receptive on the lithographic plate, causing ink to stick. Nonimage areas are water receptive which repels ink. A balance between these two elements is essential to produce black image areas with no signs of ink in nonimage areas. Pressure is used to transfer the ink to the substrate. But unlike other print processes ink transferal does not occur directly from the image carrier. The image carrier transfers ink to an intermediate rubber blanket cylinder which then prints the image on paper. This indirect method of image transferal from the image carrier to paper is known as offset lithography. Nearly all lithography (except fine arts lithography) is printed using the offset principle. The principle of offsetting the image has been applied to other printing processes, including screen printing in specialized situations. See Figure 1-9.

Figure 1-9 Lithographic press

Current and future applications for lithography include the following: brochures, maps, books, magazines, newspapers, catalogs, annual reports, business forms, stamps, labels, coupons and inserts.

Screen Printing

Screen printing is entirely different from other printing processes for many reasons. The most distinctive characteristic is its versatility, the ability to print on virtually any surface. Although it is a simple process in concept it can be used for complex jobs such as four color process. A second attribute is its ability to vary ink film deposit ranging from thin to thick. Additionally, screen printing is often used when a heavy ink film is needed to achieve a durable result. Screen printing is often used for adverse situations where abrasion is a factor or exposure to sunlight for extended periods of time is possible.

This process can be used by the novice or a commercial printer. Silk screen printing has been used as a term to describe this printing process; this term is outmoded today for two reasons. Silk is no longer used in this process, since it is inferior in quality compared to modern synthetic fabrics and costs ten times more. The second reason is one of perception. Silk screen denotes a craft process for printing. Modern screen printing is a merging of science and technology working together to produce better quality printing at lower costs.

Screen printing can be used in two different settings. It can be used as a commercial/industrial printing technique or for artistic purposes. The artistic use of the screen printing process is called serigraphy. The term **serigraph** is derived from two terms, *sericum* (Latin) meaning silk and *graphein* (Greek) meaning write or draw. Literally serigraphy means writing on silk, or is defined where the stencil is manually produced on the silk by the artist. One such technique of imaging directly on the screen mesh is called tusche and glue.

A second attribute of serigraphy is that prints are printed by hand in limited numbers. Each print may vary slightly since each is printed by hand. Yet this is not a problem since they are often numbered, each considered a unique print in itself. In contrast to serigraphy, commercial screen printing produces stencils using photo mechanical techniques with film, requiring no artistic talents. A second point is that printing is normally done using a press to maintain consistent quality, to be certain each print is identical. A third point is that quantities can be large or small since the processs is done by machine. See an example of heavy ink deposit in Figure 1-10.

Although it is uncertain as to the first use of the screen printing process, there is some evidence of its early beginning. A simple stencil process was used in several early cultures. Evidence of its use in China dates back to the construction of the Great Wall and its use in Egypt dates to the time of the pyramids. It was used for decoration on pottery, fabrics and buildings. Early results were crude due to the materials used. Stencils were prepared from papyrus, skins or fabrics with holes cut or punched. Stencils were strengthened by applying animal fats or shellac. Stencils were also used in the Fiji Islands to produce designs on fabric for apparel. Stencils were made by cutting openings in banana leaves. Vegetable dyes were rubbed through the stencil openings onto cloth. The Chinese also used a stencil process to decorate apparel. The Japanese used strands of hair on silk to hold small details in place on stencils.

Silk was woven into a mesh for the first time in the 1830s. It was used to sift flour in the milling industry. For the first 100 years sifting or filtering was the sole use for mesh. After this time its potential for use by screen printing was discovered and it was developed for that market up to the present day. We now have mesh that is specifically designed for screen printing use.

Figure 1-10 Heavy ink deposit

Some sources feel the first commercial screen printing company in the U.S. was founded in the early 1900s in California. Screen printing spread throughout the country through the early 1940s primarily in the sign industry. Screen printing continued to grow during World War II due to the need for signs and posters to assist the allied war effort. After the war's end, with military personnel returning to civilian life, many started screen printing companies. The primary products were signs and point-of-purchase advertising. Due to the rapid growth of this new industry the Screen Process Printing Association was formed in 1948. The association continued to grow in response to the needs of this new industry. In 1968 the name was changed to Screen Printing Association International to reflect its growth on a worldwide scale. In January 1995 the name was changed once again to reflect technological changes in the industry. The Digital Printing and Imaging Association joined the association and the name changed to the Screenprinting and Graphic Imaging Association International.[1]

The first production stage of any printing process is the design process. Image generation is the stage where images are produced based on the design as specified in the layout provided for the job. Both these stages can be done by an outside firm or at the printing facility itself. Films then need to be generated. Often this is best done by the printer as this gives the best control of quality of the job. Fabric is selected based on job specifications and it is tensioned in preparation for selection and application of the stencil.

The press is selected based on substrate and quantity of run. There are a wide range of presses designed for printing on the wide range of substrates such as bottles, T-shirts, flat or shaped objects. Presses can range from manual presses for low quantities up to fully automatic presses for larger quantities. Once printed the job is ready for any bindery operations that may be required such as trimming, die cutting, and so on. The job is then ready to be shipped to the customer.

Pad Transfer Printing

Pad transfer printing is a method for transferring images to irregular surfaces with little distortion. It uses a cliché that is inked with a silicon rubber pad to transfer the image to any irregular surface. The **cliché** is an intaglio image carrier etched to create recessed image areas. Ink is applied to the cliché and a doctor blade wipes across to clear the surface of ink leaving ink only in recessed areas. The silicon pad is placed in contact with the cliché and when removed it pulls ink from the recessed image areas. The pad is then placed in contact conforming with the surface to be printed. Once in contact the ink is transferred to the surface. See Figure 1-11.

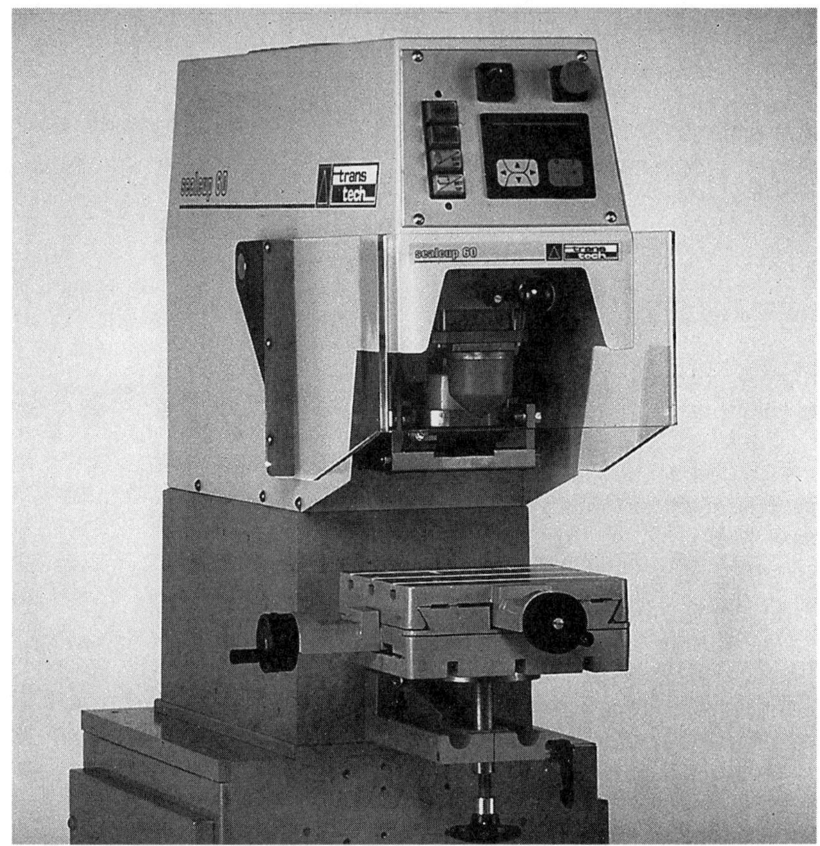

Figure 1-11 Pad transfer press *(Trns Tech America Inc.)*

There are advantages of using pad transfer over screen printing. Due to the nature of the silicon pad it conforms to nearly any surface. Also, it is possible to print in recessed areas that would be difficult for the screen printing process. More than one color can be printed wet-on-wet without drying between colors with pad transfer. It is possible to print designs using pad transfer that wrap around cylindrical three dimensional shapes which cannot be screen printed.

There are also limitations to the pad printing process. Due to the use of the silicon pad in transferring ink, this process is limited to small images based on the size of the press and pad. Since it transfers ink using pressure, this limits ink deposition. It does not deliver ink with the same thickness and impact as screen printing. It may not achieve the durability, wear or fade resistance of the screen printing process.

"Moreover, pad printing is a thin-film process. It starts with an etch depth in the cliché of just 25 microns, and only about half of that ink film is picked up by the pad. Of this wet ink, 60% is a solvent that evaporates, leaving only a 5-micron dry ink deposit."[2] See Figures 1-12 and 1-13.

Figure 1-12 Cliché image carrier *(Trans Tech America Inc.)*

Figure 1-13 Syringe pad printing *(Trans Tech America Inc.)*

Other Print Processes

New printing technologies have emerged in recent years that are different than the primary printing processes. They are having a significant impact on the printing industry. The primary advantage of electronic printing over other printing processes is no press make-ready time. This makes it less costly at low numbers in spite of its high production time. We will explore three electronic printing processes: electrophotographic (electrostatic), ink-jet and thermal transfer.

Electrophotographic Printing

Electrophotographic printing is based on xerography. This is called electrostatic or laser printing. It prints without pressure but is based on the principle that electrostatically charged powders are attracted to a surface with an opposite charge. A laser places a charge on an electrostatic photo conductor creating image areas. A computer sends a digital signal using a page description language such as Postscript. A dry or liquid toner is attracted to the image areas, and then transferred

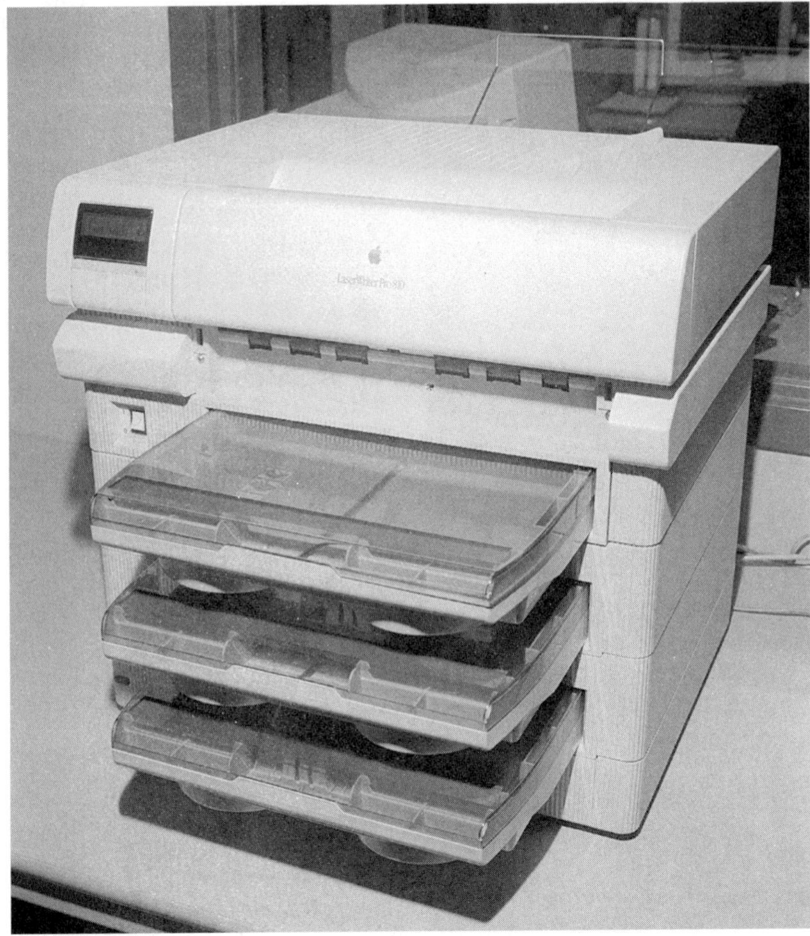

Figure 1-14 Electrostatic printer

to paper. The paper is then located to fuse the toner onto paper. See Figure 1-14.

Electrostatic printers are used for the low-end, short run, throw away promotional market. It offers fast printing speeds, but is high in cost with greater environmental control compared to an ink-jet printer. It can be used to print images as large as 4.4′ by 50′ in length. It is compatible only with media that is especially coated for application of toner. One method allows the image to be transferred to a range of materials such as banner vinyl, foam board, poster board, and styrene. Although toners have improved significantly they are vulnerable to weather and abrasion. To address these limitations a protective topcoat or laminate is required. This extends durability but is not equal to a screen printed product.

Ink-jet Printing

It is important to understand the basic principle of the **ink-jet printer.** Ink is forced through a nozzle and converted by vibrating piezoelectric crystals to produce uniform droplets that are electrostatically charged. These droplets are transported across a slight air gap and controlled by a computer or other digital image generating device to place each into a precise position. As the droplets come into contact with the print media, they combine to form an image. This is a noncontact process since only the ink comes in contact with the print media. Ink-jet printing uses an ink that is composed of a dye in a solution (either water, alcohol or solvent). See Figure 1-15.

There are two types of ink-jet systems. The simplest type uses a single nozzle that alternates across the page in a back and forth motion. The second approach uses a bank of nozzles instead of only one. The ink-jet process is especially effective for printing a limited number of copies for variable printing such as addressing, or bar coding. Ink-jet printing is often used for personalized direct mail advertising. Ink-jet is also used for digital color proofing.

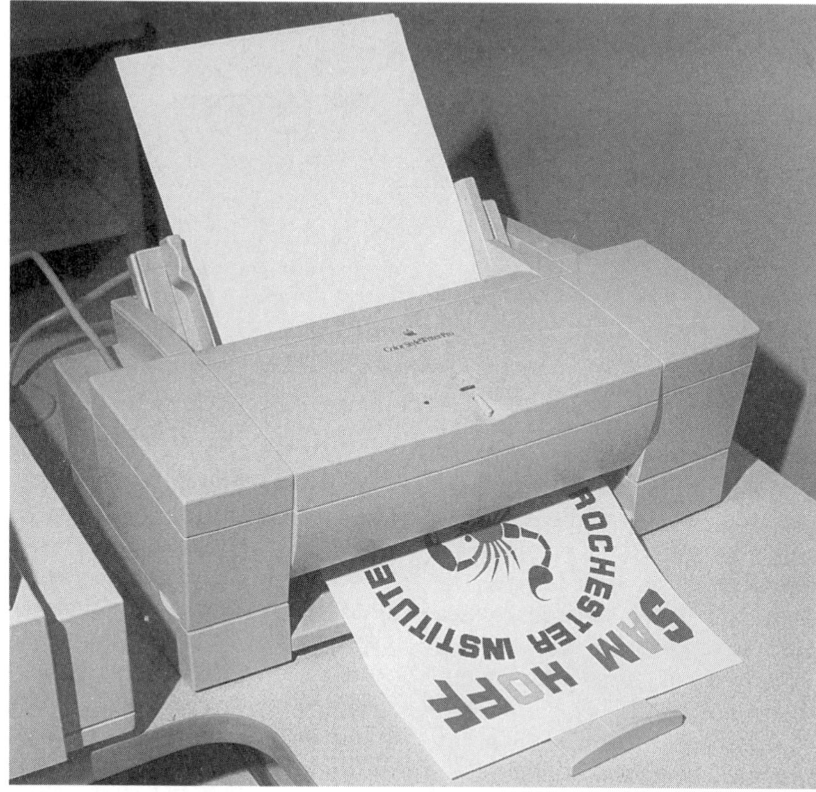

Figure 1-15 Ink-jet printer

Figure 1-16 Gerber SR 1500 *(Gerber Scientific Products Inc.)*

Ink-jet can be used to produce good quality four color process. It provides reliable performance and can be used to print images as large as 52" x 90". It can be used with a number of top coated materials such as polyester film, silver foil, translucent film, pressure sensitive materials and paper. The water based inks will adhere only to top coated substrates.

The greatest problem with ink-jet ink is its poor fade resistance. The ink must pass through small openings that restrict the use of more highly pigmented inks. Fade resistance is problematic with ink-jet ink for outdoor applications and even in indoor use. Lamination must be used to improve its poor fade resistance.

Thermal Transfer

A **thermal imaging** head is used with resin based color ribbons to print on vinyl and a range of other materials. There are two manufacturers of these systems, which offer faster prepress of graphics for short run printing. The Gerber SR1500 Digital Printing System, as shown in Figure 1-16, uses 11.8-inch wide cassette ribbons to print on 15-inch wide punched materials. It produces virtually any length graphic. Another manufacturer has a printer that uses 2″ ribbon cassettes with a maximum output size of 24"x 40".

These systems function basically the same as a thermal printer as explained in chapter 3. The computer tells the thermal imaging head which areas to heat. The ribbon is placed on top of the substrate so that when heat is applied the color is transferred from the ribbon to the substrate below. Each color is printed separately and the proper color cassette must be place in the printer until all colors are printed. Ribbon cassettes are available in the process colors in addition to a wide range of spot colors. With the Gerber system the process colors are warranted for three years for outdoor applications and five years for the spot colors.

An added part of the Gerber system which makes it well suited for production of labels, decals, and so on, is the HS 15 Plus Plotter. It die cuts individual decals, labels, and the like without setup time. It takes the sprocket fed printed material and the same computer file to cut out desired shapes on the plotter. Cutting can be done using a tangentially steered blade or a swivel knife to achieve greater productivity in a wide range of situations. It offers simple, unattended operation. After cutting is complete, undesired areas of the substrate may be manually weeded away to leave decals precut to the desired shape ready to apply.

Comparison of Ink Deposit

Due to the differences in the image carriers of the printing processes, each produces a different wet ink film thickness. We will compare each process in its ability to print a full solid on coated paper. Sheet fed offset prints a wet ink film deposit of only 5µ (microns) while web offset is capable of a deposit of 7.5µ. Web letterpress (relief) is able to print a slightly heavier deposit of 10µ. Due to the ink cells of the gravure cylinder it is capable of wet ink deposits up to 30µ. Screen printing is capable of printing wet ink film deposits from 25µ up to 125µ.[3] See Figure 1-17.

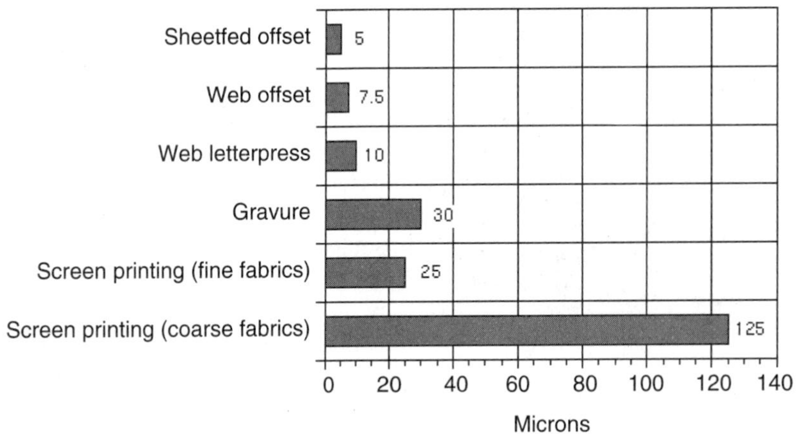

Figure 1-17 Image carrier ink deposit comparison

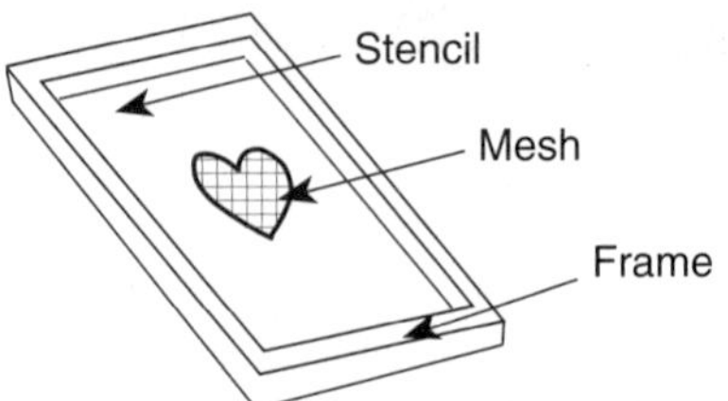

Figure 1-18 Image carrier

SCREEN PRINTING BASICS

The frame, fabric and stencil work together form the image carrier for the process. The squeegee is used to force ink through image areas onto the substrate. By making changes in the fabric, stencil or squeegee, ink deposit can be adjusted to produce anything from a thin deposit to very thick deposit as needed by the job requirements. For example, a T-shirt job may require a heavy ink deposit, while a high quality four color process job may desire a thin ink deposit.

Essential Components

The screen printing process is based on six basic components: stencil, screen fabric, screen frame, squeegee, ink, and substrate. Each plays a distinctive role in the process. Other secondary factors, such as the press, also play a role in the process. Each of these components will be discussed in length in later chapters.

Image Carrier

The **image carrier** is a physical device that causes ink to form in image areas, then transfers the

Figure 1-19 Screen fabric

image onto the substrate or to an intermediate surface that will transfer ink to the substrate. The image carrier for screen printing is made up of three components: the screen fabric, the frame, and the stencil. See Figure 1-18.

The stencil determines image areas, but is incapable of acting independently as an image carrier due to its fragile nature. Screen fabric provides support for the stencil, giving it the durability to print the desired number of prints. The frame allows the fabric to be tensioned to the proper tension level for the desired quality of work.

STENCIL The stencil is one component of the image carrier (printing screen) which directly impacts the design to be printed. It is made up of image and non image areas. Nonimage areas are formed on the screen after the stencil is transferred to the screen mesh. The stencil may be produced using mechanical or photographic techniques.

SCREEN FABRIC Many textiles that we use in everyday life are produced by a weaving process, including clothing, furniture and a wide range of other products. During the weaving process fibers are linked at right angles to each other. The warp threads are kept taut on a loom while the cross threads are interlaced. Threads are densely placed with a tight weave for textiles used for clothing. See Figure 1-19.

Screen printing fabrics are woven using a similar technique, yet not placing fibers densely. They are placed at some distance apart to allow openings in the mesh much like those in a window screen. Fabric of this type is used for sifting or filtering. It allows particles of a given size or smaller to pass, and stops larger particles. This screen fabric may also be used in screen printing applications. It is composed of silk, stainless steel, or synthetics such as polyester or nylon. Mesh types are selected to make them suitable for different purposes. For instance, a coarse mesh such as a 75T monofilament polyester should be used when printing metallic inks with large pigments or when printing heavy ink deposits.

SCREEN FRAME A screen frame is a frame or device used to support screen fabrics, as two components of the image carrier. There are two types of frames: rigid and retensionable. With a rigid frame, fabric is tensioned separate from the frame and then attached using an adhesive. After fabric is attached to a retensionable frame (using rods or plastic strips), tension is applied to the screen fabric through a built in mechanism.

SQUEEGEE A squeegee is a tool used to force ink through openings in the screen printing image carrier during the printing process. As shown in Figure 1-20, it is made of a flexible plastic blade supported

Figure 1-20 Squeegee

in a handle. There are different squeegee blades and handles used for different purposes.

INK Ink is a dispersion of pigment or a solution of a dye in a carrier vehicle with a fluid or pastelike consistency that can be applied to a substrate and dried depending on the nature of the ink. Inks can perform various functions. Ink may be used for aesthetic purposes with a printed poster. Inks may be conductive or resistive compounds for use in printing electronic circuitry.

SUBSTRATE A substrate is a surface or base material to which an image may be applied. Materials or substrates printed by the screen printing process may be rigid such as glass, metal or wood. They also may be semi-rigid (such as paper, cardboard and certain plastics), or flexible (such as textiles).

Aspects Affecting Screen Printing Quality

The screen printing process is simple in concept. Yet looking at the basic elements of the process in greater depth there are a total of 53 variables that control those basic elements. The variables are classified into eight categories: the film image; stencil; screen fabric; squeegee/flood bar; ink; substrate; press/dryer; and environmental factors. We introduce these variables in this chapter and address them at greater depth in the appropriate section of the text.

FIFTY-THREE SCREEN PRINTING VARIABLES

Film

- image density
- film base density
- image resolution

Screen

- mesh fiber composition
- thread structure
- mesh count
- thread diameter
- mesh opening
- weave structure
- mesh color
- screen tension
- frame stability

Squeegee/Flood Bar

- blade hardness
- blade shape
- blade angle
- stroke speed
- squeegee pressure
- flood bar edge shape
- flood bar angle
- flood bar stroke speed
- flood bar pressure

Ink

- particle size/distribution
- pigment dispersal
- viscosity
- tack
- flow characteristics
- adhesive properties
- dry/cure rate

Environmental Factors

- airborne contamination
- ambient temperature
- ambient humidity

Stencil

- mesh preparation
- stencil thickness
- stencil characteristics
- stencil durability
- moisture content
- exposure intensity
- exposure distance
- exposure duration
- stencil processing

Press/Dryer

- off-contact distance
- peel-off adjustment
- press bed evenness
- press bed to screen parallelism
- color sequence
- curing temperature
- U.V. lamp intensity
- curing duration

Substrate

- surface texture
- surface porosity
- color
- thickness consistency
- static effect

Controlling Ink Deposit

Earlier in the chapter the statement was made that screen printing could deliver wet ink film deposits ranging from 25µ up to 125µ. The question remains of the relationship of the basic screen printing elements and their role in determining ink deposit.

"Among the factors which determine the thickness of the ink deposit in screen printing, the mesh is without doubt the most important. If the pressure, durometer, sharpness and printing angle of the squeegee are so vital as may not be neglected, these factors affect not more than 30% of the ink deposit, and must be compared with the influence of the stencil (20%) and with the choice of meshes (50%)."[4] See Figure 1-21.

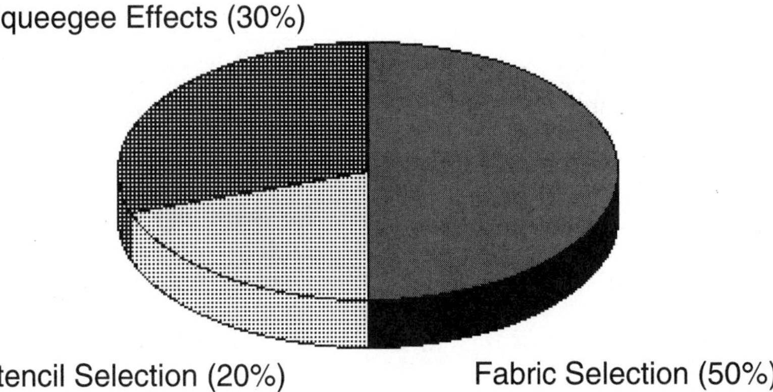

Figure 1-21 Factors determining thickness of ink deposit

It is important to realize that 70% of the ink deposit is controlled by the image carrier (screen fabric and stencil). This emphasizes the importance of job planning and screen making in delivering the desired ink deposit for a job. Yet, a pressman can regulate 30% of the ink film deposit to achieve the desired result.

KEY TERMS

cliché
electrophotographic printing
flexography
gravure
ink-jet printing
image carrier
intaglio
lithography
microns
pad transfer printing
planographic
relief printing
serigraph
stencil
thermal transfer

REVIEW QUESTIONS

1. What are the four major printing processes in use today?
2. How do the image carriers for the four printing processes differ?
3. Why is the term "silk screen printing" outmoded for describing the screen printing process?
4. In which instances is pad printing better to use than screen printing?
5. What are the differences between electronic printing methods of electrophotography, ink-jet, and thermal transfer?

NOTES

[1] John Crawford, letter from the president of S.G.I.A., April 1995.

[2] Peter Kiddel, "Pad Printing: Controlling Ambient Conditions for Better Quality," *Screen Printing Magazine* 116 (July 1994): 94–97.

[3] Nelson R. Eldred and Terry Scarlett, *What the Printer Should Know About Ink* (Pittsburgh: Graphic Arts Technical Foundation, 1990).

[4] Michel Caza, *The Theory and Practice of UV Screen Printing Part 3* (Fairfax: Technical Guidebook of the Screen Printing Industry, Screenprinting and Graphic Imaging Association International, March 1981).

Screen Printed Products and Substrates

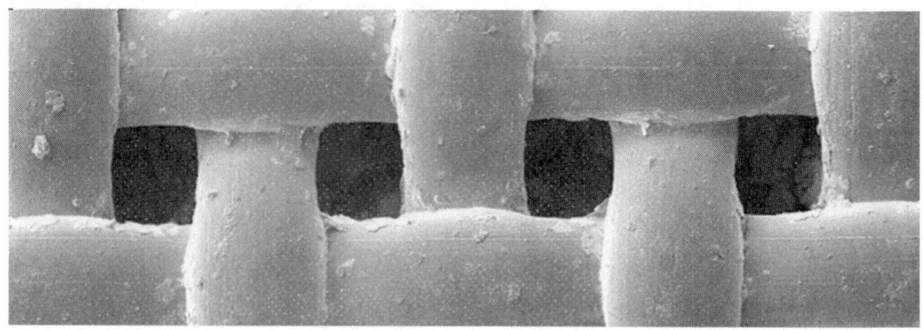

The primary strength of the screen printing process is its ability to print on virtually any surface. Due to the widespread use of the screen printing process, it is very difficult to identify every product and substrate used by the screen printing process. This chapter will explore the largest market applications and substrates for the process.

SCREEN PRINTED PRODUCTS

The Screenprinting and Graphic Imaging Association has established the top ten screen printed products (See Figure 2-1) in a 1994 Industry Profile Study. The top ten listed in order of importance are: textiles, pressure sensitive decals, plastic sheet products, single or multisheet posters, banners, POP displays, advertising specialities, panel fronts or face plates, metal signs, and heat applied transfers. We will arrange screen printed products into eight categories. The categories are: ceramics, decals, electronic/electrical, large format, display/signage,textiles, three dimensional objects, and miscellaneous.

Ceramics

Ceramics are materials that are hard and brittle, with heat and corrosion-resistant properties. They are made from nonmetallic, inorganic minerals that are fired at

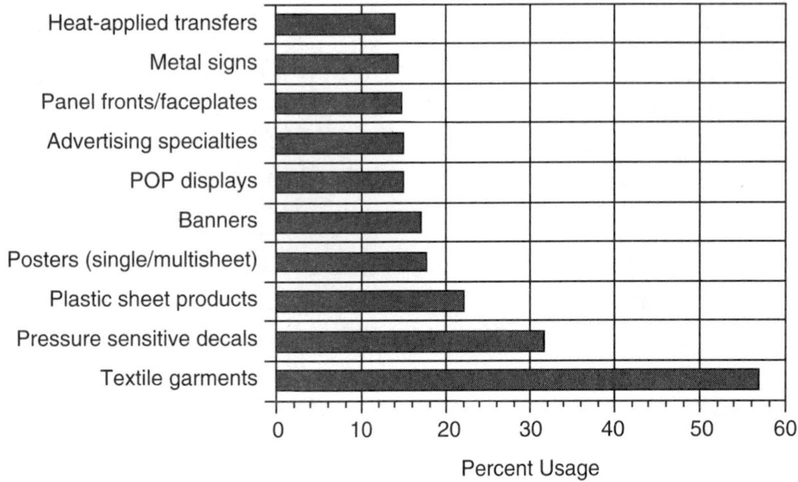

Figure 2-1 Top ten screen printed products *(The Screenprinting and Graphic Imaging Association)*

circuit. The Duracell battery checker is another screen printed item. This device uses a number of inks. It uses graphic inks, conductive and liquid crystal display (LCD) inks. This device translates the battery voltage into a color scale: green is full capacity, yellow is partial capacity, and red indicates depletion.

Screen printing is important in the automotive industry. Rear window defrosters are produced by screen printing. A silver conductive ink is screen printed in a high temperature. Ceramics include china, stoneware, ceramic tiles, and decorated glassware. Ceramic can be printed on directly, or water slide off decals may be used.

Decals

There are three types of **decals**: pressure sensitive, water slide off, and static cling. Pressure sensitive decals are based on a peel-and-stick principle. They are easily applied and are used in a wide range of applications. They can be printed on face stock with either permanent or temporary adhesive on a liner. Water slide off (simplex and duplex) decals are the oldest type of decal. Once soaked in water the decal may be slid off the gummed paper onto the desired surface. They have been used for a number of uses such as with model airplane kits. Static cling are the third type of decal. They are self-adhering to smooth surfaces such as glass. They are used for applications such as holiday window decorations and automobile maintenance reminders. See Figures 2-2 and 2-3.

Electronics/Electrical

There are a wide range of electronic or electrical devices that are produced by the screen printing process. **Membrane switches** are screen printed for use in electrical appliances such as microwave ovens. They are momentary contact pressure sensitive switches used to activate circuits. A more complex device is a **force sensing resistor.** It interprets the amount of force applied to the device into a resistance value and acts as an electronic throttle to regulate the amount of electricity flowing in a

Figure 2-2 Static cling decal example

Figure 2-3 A bumper sticker

grid pattern and fused into the glass after it is fired at high temperature. A similar procedure is used to produce the embedded radio antenna for some car windshields. Screen printing is used to print the black border on front windshields for decorative and functional purposes.

Large format

These are large scale items not printed at full size. The billboard, as shown in Figure 2-4, falls into this category. There are three basic sizes: 24 sheet (the smallest), 30 sheet (the standard), and 30 sheet bleed. The 30 sheet size is printed in eight sections, and the 30 sheet bleed in 10 sections. Each section is printed in a 60" x 66" size. The 30 sheet is 117" x 225.5", and the 30 sheet bleed is 125" x 272". A smaller size is known as the junior billboard and is printed in 2 sections and is 60" x 132". Fleet marking is another example of large format screen printing. Large trailers used in the trucking industry are often decorated with graphics. They are printed in sections using pressure sensitive vinyl.

Figure 2-4 A billboard *(Vincent Printing Company)*, is an example of a large format item.

Transit advertising is another form of large format screen printing. This is advertising placed on the sides of buses, taxis, and other forms of transportation. See Figure 2-5. Large banners also fall into this category. They are used for various marketing campaigns for businesses or fast food restaurants. Banners are printed on reinforced vinyl, polyethylene and polypropylene.

Figure 2-5 Transit advertising is an example of a large format item

Figure 2-6 Political signage is often screen printed

Display/Signs

Points of purchase (POP) displays, as shown in Figure 2-7, bring attention to an individual product. They are used as self standing or hanging displays for markets or other stores. Back lit displays are used in a variety of ways, such as vending machines. Real estate signage is often screen printed due to the low quantities needed and outdoor weatherability. Political signage is often screen printed due to the low quantities needed with designs having heavy ink coverage. See Figure 2-6. Screen printing is ideal since a typical election campaign will call for 1,000 18" x 24" yard signs for average situations.

Figure 2-7 POP display example

Textiles

This category is broken down into three subcategories: apparel, household goods, and miscellaneous. Apparel includes such items as t-shirts, nylon jackets, football jerseys, caps, and ties. Household goods includes items such as towels, bed sheets, table linens, and carpeting. Miscellaneous items includes flags, umbrellas, and pennants, among a vast number of other items. See Figure 2-8.

Three Dimensional

This includes items that are dimensional in nature such as containers, dinnerware, and cigarette lighters. They are often glass, metal, plastic or wood in composition.

Miscellaneous

This encompasses items that do not fit into any other category. This is a diverse group including such items as credit cards, vinyl binders and compact discs. It also includes advertising specialties such as key chains, refrigerator magnets, and many items too numerous to identify. See Figures 2-9 and 2-10.

FLAT SUBSTRATES

The versatility of the screen printing process makes it possible to print on nearly any surface. Yet, a majority of screen printed products are flat materials. The most commonly used materials are: papers, plastics, ceramics, metals, textiles and wood.

Figure 2-8 A pot holder is an example of a textile

Figure 2-9 Audio compact disk

Figure 2-10 Advertising specialties

Paper Products

Paper is composed of cellulose fibers which are derived from the cell walls of plants. Various fibers such as bamboo, cotton, hemp, jute, sugar cane, wheat and rice straws can be used to make paper. Wood is the most common source of paper-making fibers in North America. The paper-making process begins by combining cellulose fibers with water and then placing the mixture on a special wire screen. The fibers intertwine to form chemical bonds between the molecules of the paper fibers as the water drains off. The paper achieves its greatest strength once dry. Paper has a wide range of properties based on its composition. It may be flexible or rigid, fragile or durable, transparent or opaque, soft or coarse. It may absorb or repel water. There are a number of different types of paper. In screen printing there are two classes of paper materials that are most often printed: paper and cardboard.

PAPER Papers can be classified into four basic types: bond papers, book papers, text papers, and cover papers. Bond papers are strong, durable papers designed for business use such as stationery or letterheads. Book papers are for use in printing books or advertising and are available in different finishes and thicknesses. Text paper is a fine quality paper with unique surface textures, colors or finishes for use with announcements, annual reports, or booklets. Cover paper is a heavy weight paper for use with brochure covers, folders, and other special applications.

CARDBOARD Cardboard is a stiff paper or paperboard 0.006" or greater in thickness. It is used for a wide range of products such as boxes, signs, or printed materials. Index or bristols are heavy weight papers used in business. They are solid or laminated in construction, and are treated to permit writing or erasing. They are used for index cards, folders, postcards, and other record-keeping materials. Tagboard, as the name implies, is used for making tags and is extremely strong.

Chipboard, or news board, is a basic type of cardboard. It is a multipurpose paperboard used when strength and quality are not essential. It is a board made up of low density waste papers as a basic raw material. The lowest grade is often made from recycled newsprint and can be identified by its gray color. It is used as a core or backing material for other board products. It is often used for packaging (in cereal boxes, for example).

Several cardboards can be classified as paste boards. A paste board is made by pasting paper to conceal an inner core. There are several types of paste boards. **Blanks** are a type of paste board used for display purposes. They can be produced as a single ply on a Fourdrinier machine, multiply cylinder board or multiply by laminating. The most important traits are stiffness, smooth surface quality, and good printability. It is available in white or colors, coated or uncoated, and in thicknesses of 15 to 48 point (0.012" to 0.078").

Another type of paste board is **railroad board.** It is manufactured on a cylinder machine in four or 6 ply (0.018" to 0.024"). It uses an inner core of news board with white or colored outside liners. It is available coated or uncoated. Its uses include signs, displays or advertising.

Tough check is a strong paper board made on a cylinder machine from extra strong unbleached chemical wood pulp which may be blended with rope stock. It may be coated on one or both sides and comes in a variety of colors. Thicknesses available are 3, 4, 6, or 8 ply (12, 18, 24 or 30 point). It is used where toughness is needed, such as in tickets or shipping labels.

Plastics

Plastics are high molecular weight materials with either synthetic or a semi-synthetic organic ingredient formed by polymerization, condensation, or chemical treatment. They can be molded, cast, extruded, drawn, or laminated into objects of all shapes and sizes or into filaments or films. Each formulation has unique properties based on its composition.

Plastics can be broken down into two categories: thermoplastics and thermosetting. Thermoplastics can be shaped or formed after application or heated any number of times. A large number of plastics used in the screen printing industry, such as back lit displays, are thermoplastics. Thermosetting plastics cure as they set up after being formed. A chemical change causes the plastic to permanently retain the new shape and does not allow it to be reformed at a later time.

Acrylic

Acrylic (Plexiglas or Lucite™) has the appearance of glass, with outstanding transparency and ten times its strength. Its outstanding weatherability makes it ideal for outdoor signs and window applications. Acrylic is available clear,

Figure 2-11 Plastic signage

Figure 2-12 Back lit display

slightly tinted, or opaque. It is made from acrylic acid or methacrylic acid. It may be cast or extruded. Extruded acrylic is less expensive but less durable and optically inferior to cast acrylics with good surface integrity. Acrylic has the following properties: high tensile and impact strength, good compressive strength and electrical insulative properties, fair resistance to heat and chemical resistance. Its resistance to scratching is poor. It is a thermoplastic material and may be vacuum formed. For the best results inks must be formulated to use with acrylic products.

Cellulose Derivatives

Cellulosics were the earliest form of plastics produced. They are produced from natural cellulose. Cellulose nitrate was the first of the commercially important cellulose derivative as well as the first synthetically produced plastic. It was produced in 1865 under the name of celluloid. Cellulose acetates are thermoplastic in nature. Acetates may be used for pressure sensitive labels due to their low cost but they are not suitable for use in adverse situations, such as outdoor use. Lacquer inks have been used with cellulose acetates for a number of years although there are several other formulations that may work as well. Testing must be done to find the best ink to use. See Figure 2-13.

CELLULOSE ACETATE This is one of the most widely used cellulose derivatives. It is synthesized from acetic acid. Cellulose acetate is combined with plasticizers, dyes and pigments to achieve its composition. Its properties include dimensional stability and strength, moisture resistance, and low flammability, and it can be used for molding plastics. It is often used as a printing material due to its receptivity to ink. It dissolves in solvents such as acetone. It is inexpensive and can be identified by the smell of the softeners used in its manufacture.

CELLULOSE ACETATE BUTYRATE This is an esther of cellulose formed by a result of a mixture of acetate acid, butyric acid and their anhydrides on purified cellulose. A plasticizer is added to give the required properties. It is tough and weather resistant with a high clarity and luster. It has low water absorption and flammability with good electrical properties. It can be injection or vacuum molded or extruded.

Figure 2-13 Banner

Polycarbonate

Polycarbonate (Lexan®) is synthetic resin made from bisphenol and phosgene which form a plastic material that is the least prone to breakage. Due to its highly transparent nature it is effective for back lit signage and second surface graphics. Its glossy appearance is attractive but abrasion resistance is less than optimum. It is thermoplastic and may be formed to achieve embossing or three dimensional molding effects, which can be a problem with polyester. It can be die-cut to various shapes.

Polycarbonate has the following properties: high impact strength and clarity, good resistance to weathering, heat and electrical insulating properties; and fair chemical resistance. It is often used as a substitute for glass bottles or containers due to its low moisture absorption. It does not need to be pretreated before printing as there are several inks that work well with Polycarbonate. Vinyl and acrylic inks may be used in addition to UV curing inks. Polycarbonate may be used in applications such as signage, membrane switch overlays, name

Figure 2-14 Automobile instrument panel

plates, instrument panels (see Figure 2-14), decals and product information labels.

Polyester

Polyester (Mylar) resins are produced by a reaction of dibasic acid with glycol. Polyester is an extremely versatile material. It can be used to mold into objects or blown to form bottles, extruded to form fibers that are woven into garments, or formed into film or sheets. All of these applications are produced from the same polymer resin. It has the following properties: excellent compressive strength, resistance to chemicals, water and weatherability, good scratch resistance, electrical insulative properties, and fair heat resistance.

Polyester used by the screen printing industry is produced in two classes: non oriented and oriented. Non oriented polyester is often used in the packaging industry. It is extruded and produced in a wide range of thicknesses. It may be screen printed although it lacks stability compared to oriented polyester. It is available in a wide range of colors.

Oriented polyester is stretched at the final stage of the film extrusion process. This produces a stronger, more dimensionally stable product. Oriented polyester is the most common polyester used by the screen printing industry. It is available in clear, translucent, white or opaque in color with a smooth finish. Polyester may be used for pressure sensitive film applications in thicknesses from 1.0 to 7.0 mils thickness. The maximum thickness that polyester can be produced is 14 mils.

Polyester's physical characteristics make it ideal for decal applications. It is resistant to most industrial solvents and chemicals in addition to being abrasion resistant. This makes it well suited for use in product identification where it may be used in many adverse environments. Its high tensile strength makes it resistant to wear and tear but it is more difficult to die cut. Ink must be specially formulated for use with polyester in its untreated state to achieve adhesion. It is also available with a top coating that modifies the surface for printing other screen printing inks. Pretesting polyester for ink compatibility is important before printing.

Applications where polyester is used in the screen printing industry include instrument panels, name plates, product identification labels, membrane switch overlays, POP displays, signs, and advertising specialty items.

Polyolefins

Polyolefins are a group of plastics that are polymers of alkenes or olefins. The two most common polyolefins are polyethylene polymerized from ethylene and polypropylene from propylene.

POLYETHYLENE **Polyethylene** is produced from a polymer which is a whitish translucent color, high in toughness and moderate in strength. It is available either flexible or slightly rigid. It has a waxy feel and ranges from translucent to opaque in appearance. It is lightweight and is resistant to very low temperatures, weather, and water. It has the following properties: excellent electrical insulating properties; good resistance to chemicals and water; fair heat resistance, tensile strength and scratch resistance.

It can be printed by dry offset, hot stamping or screen printing. With screen printing of dry offset, it must be first surface treated or top coated to achieve ink adhesion. It is often used for molded squeeze bottles or containers. It can be used for pressure sensitive labels. It has the appearance of vinyl with improved dimensional stability at a lower cost.

POLYPROPYLENE **Polypropylene** is similar to polyethylene but is tougher and is able to withstand higher temperatures. It maintains its strength even after repeated bending. It is translucent white or may be colored. Its properties are: excellent resistance to chemicals, abrasion and stress cracking; good heat resistance and electrical insulating properties. It is often used for food containers and squeeze bottles. It is a viable alternative to polyester for pressure sensitive labels due to its dimensional stability, resistance to tearing, abrasion, moisture, and chemicals with excellent clarity and conformity. It is also available at a lower cost than polyester. It must be surface treated before it can be screen printed.

POLYSTYRENE **Polystyrene** is a clear white glassy polymer that is rigid and may be injection molded or extruded in sheet form. It is often smooth in finish and may be colored brightly. It can be used for indoor and outdoor signs, POP and other displays and other applications. Polystyrene resins are produced from ethylene and benzene. It is thermoplastic and may be vacuum formed. It has the following properties: good compressive strength, heat resistance and electrical insulating properties; fair tensile strength and resistance to chemicals; poor scratch resistance and impact strength. It has low moisture absorption.

Figure 2-15 Pressure sensitive decal

Adding rubber to styrene produces high impact styrene (HIPS). Certain grades are available, depending on the screen printing project. Less additives have been used that interfere with screen printing. Printing grades have a matte finish on both sides of the sheet. It is best to use inks formulated for styrene although other formulations may be used in some instances. Printability may be compromised in using lower grades of styrene. For best results it is important to test for ink compatibility.

Polyvinyl Chloride

Polyvinyl Chloride (PVC) is a strong, tough, low cost thermoplastic polymer with excellent properties. It is used in a wide range of products ranging from floor tiles to upholstery. PVC resin is a product of vinyl chloride gas. Its properties are: excellent chemical and electrical insulating properties; good tensile strength; fair compressive strength and resistance to heat. It is abrasion and flame resistant. Vinyl may be flexible, semi-rigid or rigid. Addition of a plasticizer increases elasticity of the vinyl for use in applications such as shower curtains. In its rigid state it is used for products such as pipe or house siding.

Vinyl films come in a wide range of thicknesses, grades, colors and finishes. They are tough, long wearing, unbreakable and low in cost. They can be transparent, translucent or opaque in appearance. They soften at temperatures of about 130°F and harden at very low temperatures. Flexible vinyls are often used for pressure sensitive labels such as the one shown in Figure 2-15. Cling vinyl is used for static cling decals. These vinyls and other low-cost vinyls use monomeric plasticizers that migrate to the surface and affect printing quality. A topcoat can be used to improve adhesion of the ink to vinyl.

CALENDERED VINYL **Calendered vinyl** is produced by heating the raw materials, resins, pigments, plasticizers, and so on. This heated resin is then fed into a calendaring machine made up of a series of rollers. These rollers are used to produce a film of a given thickness and surface finish. Calendered vinyl film is produced in a continuous web. This places stress on the film in the direction of the web as it travels through the rollers. This results in film that is dimensionally unstable. Due to this effect the calendered vinyl is more difficult to apply to uneven surfaces. Calendered films are thicker than cast films ranging from 3.0 to 10.0 mils in thickness. Durability of calendered film is significantly less than with cast vinyls. The number of rollers required for the calendaring process makes the machinery quite large. This large size machine necessitates very large batches of vinyl film to be produced. It results in an economical process that permits calendered vinyl to be made at low cost. But these large batches limit the number of colors produced. See Figure 2-16.

Figure 2-16 Fleet marking

CAST VINYL Another method of manufacturing vinyl film is by coating a liquid compound onto a substrate, usually a polished chrome plated sheet, where it is allowed to set up forming a sheet of **cast vinyl.** Using this process, very little stress is applied to the film since casting sheets support the film. As a result cast films have much less shrinkage than calendered films. This makes them better suited for long term exterior applications. They are manufactured in thicknesses from 1.5 to 3.0 mils thickness. The machine required for cast films is smaller than for calendered films. This allows for smaller batches and permits a wider range of colors to be produced. The raw materials used give cast films improved performance over calendered films and make them more expensive to produce. Extended exterior durability, short run capacity and better conformity are produced at an increase in price of two to three times over that of calendered vinyls.

Tyvek

Tyvek is a spun bonded olefin that makes up a family of tough durable sheet products. Although synthetic in nature it has an appearance of a paper like product. Fibers of continuous strands of high density polyurethane are formed. These fibers are then bonded together using heat and pressure to form durable sheets. This product combines a good surface for printing or coating with high toughness and capacity that is unique over other sheet products. It is used for tags, labels, maps, fishing licenses, wall coverings, bags, envelopes, signs, banners, and disposable and novelty apparel.

There are three types of Tyvek: Type 10, Type 14, and Type 16. In the Type 10 series products, fibers are bonded to form tough, dense, somewhat stiff paper-like sheets. The dense bonding of fibers produce a smooth surface with a naturally white opaque sheet. It is a stable, abrasion resistant sheet that retains enough mobility to have high tear strength in all directions. Types 14 and 16 restrict fiber bonding to produce a sheet with high fiber mobility to achieve a fabric-like product.

Type 10 Tyvek is best suited for screen printing or any other printing process due to its structure. The softness and flexibility of Types 14 and 16 make it less suited for printing. Ink selection is important with Tyvek since solvents will swell and distort the sheet. Tyvek is also sensitive to heat since it shrinks at about 250°F and melts above 275°F. It should not be dried at temperatures above 175°F.

There are five different styles of Type 10 Tyvek produced. Style 1056 and 1058 are 6 mils in thickness. Style 1073 is 8 mils thick; styles 1079 and styles 1085 are 9 mils in thickness. Tyvek can be cut using a conventional guillotine cutter. For best results, stock should be slip sheeted every 25-50 sheets with waxed paper before cutting. The blade should also be lubricated with a silicone spray. It can be die cut using male-female dies although steel rule dies are usually preferred. Tyvek can be embossed using either cold or heated embossing rollers as long as the rollers do not exceed 225°F. Tyvek can be sewn using a conventional sewing machine. For best results the manufacturer should be consulted for sewing recommendations. Tyvek is resistant to most chemicals other than solvents and nitric acid. It is resistant to aging unless it is placed in direct exposure to UV light. It can be improved by applying a UV resistive coating.

Other Flat Materials

There are so many materials used in screen printing operations that is impossible to identify all of them. There are two, however, that have unique properties that make them applicable in certain applications. They are foam board and corrugated board.

Foam Board

A family of rigid, foam-cored sheets and boards are made from a variety of laminate materials. Foam board is available in a range of thicknesses. The center core is styrofoam with paper or board outer liners to enclose the core. It provides a strong board that is very lightweight. It provides a uniform surface consistency for printing over a similar thickness corrugated board. It is less apt to be affected by changes in moisture and humidity than a board composed entirely of paper fibers.

Corrugated Plastic Board

Corrugated plastic board is a durable lightweight material that is formed by an extrusion process. It is composed of polyethylene or polypropylene. It is available in sizes up to 48" x 96" weighing less than 6 pounds with a cost of about $7.00. It can last outdoors for several years due to its extruded construction. One of the uses for this product is political signage.

Corrugated plastic boards are available in 14 colors. To assist the screen printer in attaining ink adhesion they are surface treated by the manufacturer using corona discharge. This permits use of a range of ink types: solvent, water based, or UV curing inks. Yet the corona treatment is effective for only about thirty days before it drops off in effectiveness. If the product is not used within this period, ink adhesion will be affected.

Ceramics

Ceramics are one of the most important synthetic engineering materials. Equally important are metal and plastic. Originally the term ceramics referred to products made from natural earth and exposed to high temperatures. Ceramics include brick, cement, glass and porcelain.

Ceramic

Ceramics are made from minerals such as clay, felspar, silica and talc. Silicates form most of the earth's crust. Clay is an important silicate, but it is not used in all ceramic materials. Dinnerware is a ceramic product made from clay, felspar and quartz. It produces excellent containers for food and drink. It does not absorb liquids, and it

Figure 2-17 Ceramic china *(Syracuse China Company)*

Figure 2-18 Glassware

resists acids, detergents and changes in temperature.

Ceramics are often screen printed prior to being fired. Ink must be formulated specifically to be used with this application. It can be directly printed on the surface of the ceramic or printed as a water slide off decal. The water slide off decal is often used with china and dinnerware, cups, saucers, and plates. After the decal is applied the surface of the ceramic is coated with glazing material. Once the piece is fired a hardened surface is achieved which protects the printed design. See Figure 2-17.

Glass

Glass is a hard brittle material that is transparent in nature. It is produced from silica sand, soda ash and limestone. After heating the ingredients, glass is formed and shaped. It is one of the most useful materials in the world. In a flat state it is useful for windows or shaped as a container or bottle for food storage. It has a smooth, nonporous surface that is resistant to chemical attack. It is resistant to weather, compression and most acids. It is an efficient electrical insulator but a poor conductor of heat.

It can be decorated by a number of methods. Application of hydrofluoric acid will etch into the surface of the glass producing a frosted effect. Decoration can also be fired into the glass. Ink selection is crucial to its performance if screen printing is done. Screen printed ink will remain on the surface of the glass and not penetrate. When dry or cured the ink must reach a state of hardness to endure resistance to abrasion. Several ink types may be used to achieve the proper performance. See Figure 2-18

Metal

Although screen printing may print on a number of metal surfaces, aluminum and sheet metal are often screen printed for permanent signs. Its smooth nonporous hard surface is similar to glass. Ink selection is important to

Figure 2-19 Metal signage

achieve durability needed by the application. Many of the inks that may be used with glass can also be used on metal. For best results an ink durability test is recommended. See Figure 2-19.

Textiles

Fabrics may be produced by weaving, felting, knitting, braiding or netting from natural or synthetic fibers. Cotton is a natural fiber that is commonly used. Polyester, nylon, rayon or acetates are a few of the synthetic fibers that are also used in textiles. Textiles can be classified into two categories. The largest share of textile production is apparel textiles. This includes ready to wear clothing and yard goods for homemakers' use. The second largest category is household or domestic textiles. This includes such items as bed sheets, table linen, draperies, towels, blankets and carpets.

Textiles for many of these uses require decoration. A significant amount is done directly at the mill as a final operation to the fabric production. It can be decorated by a number of methods based on the decoration desired. It can be done by either a relief method or intaglio process as well as by heat transfer. It can also be screen printed using either a flat or rotary screen based on the type of equipment used. After fabric has been manufactured and decorated it can be converted into piece goods (garments, table linen, pillow cases, and so on). In other cases the garments are decorated after being converted into piece goods. This is commonly done with screen printed T-shirts and towels. See Figures 2-20 and 2-21. With very large orders, T-shirt decoration is done at the mill prior to converting to individual garments. With smaller quantities it makes more sense to screen print after the garment has been converted.

As with any substrate, ink compatibility is important. Cotton is very absorbent and allows ink to soak into the fibers more easily. However, other formulations such as rayon or nylon may require a special formulation to achieve the required durability. Some ink types remain on the surface and bond to the fibers, while other are dyes that change the composition or bleed into the fibers. Pretesting is important to determine the proper ink match.

Wood

Screen printing may be used to print a design or image on wood. The rough porous surface will allow a number of inks to be used since they will be absorbed by the substrate. If other inks or sealers are to be used it is important to select an ink that is compatible. Also a screen fabric and stencil should be selected that will conform to the irregular surface structure.

Figure 2-20 Towels may be decorated after conversion into piece goods

Figure 2-21 Golf ball printing *(Trans America Inc.)*

THREE DIMENSIONAL OBJECTS

In addition to flat substrates screen printing is often used to print three dimensional objects. It is often selected as a last resort when other processes are not able to print the job. Pad transfer printing has its greatest usage in printing three dimensional objects.

Containers

Containers can be used to hold various products. They can be used to hold liquids such as chemicals or beverages. They can be also used for foods, or products such as toner for office copiers. The containers may be glass, plastic or some other material. Ink must be formulated with properties to adhere to the material used. In some cases special ink is required to prevent it from dissolving when in contact with chemicals stored in the container. This necessitates an ink such as an epoxy that will endure exposure to very strong chemical agents.

The decoration can be printed directly on the container or printed flat on pressure sensitive labels with a high speed press. See Figures 2-22 and 2-23. After the labels are printed and die cut they are applied to the container. This is the approach most often used with items such as shampoo bottles. Direct container printing requires a press that rotates the container under the screen to facilitate transfer of ink to the cylindrical shaped object. Other unusually shaped containers may be printed in a similar fashion as long as the shape is not too extreme.

Lighters

Lighters are often screen printed since their surface is flat or slightly curved. When the surface is curved in shape, nylon screen fabric will conform more readily to the irregularity. See Figure 2-24.

Figure 2-22 Direct container decoration

Figure 2-23 Labeled container decoration

Figure 2-24 A cigarette lighter is an example of a three dimenional object

Figure 2-25 The textured surface structure of T-shirt fabric can cause difficulties in printing

Figure 2-26 Fabric weave structure

PRINTING FACTORS

Screen printing is used to print on virtually any material. Yet different techniques must be employed to achieve success in each situation. Differences in surface structure make ink transfer more challenging.

Surface Consistency

Surface structure varies between different substrates that are screen printed. It can be smooth or irregular. Surface consistency can be defined as the degree of difference in surface texture.

Smooth Surface

A smooth surface is much easier to achieve ink transfer than irregular surfaces. The smooth surface will achieve complete contact with the image carrier (screen) during the printing process. This will make it possible for the stencil to achieve a seal with the substrate to keep ink within the desired image areas. This is important when printing fine line designs or halftones. It prevents the ink from spreading to create dot gain with halftones. A smooth surface is essential to achieve high quality printing with fine line designs.

Textured or Irregular Surface

Due to the surface structure of irregular surfaces there are several levels to print. One surface is raised and other areas are recessed. It is relatively easy to transfer ink to the raised areas since they come in direct contact with the image carrier (screen). But it is more difficult to get ink to transfer into the recessed areas in a controlled manner. One of the primary difficulties in printing on textiles is due to the textured surface structure caused by the manufacturing process (weaving, knitting, and so on), as shown in Figures 2-25 and 2-26. The design is to be transferred to the surface structure makeup of fibers or threads. It can be most problematic with fine details that will not transfer in these recessed areas. Also the coarseness or weave of the textile material can lead to dif-

Figure 2-27 Antique and laid finish papers

ficulties. Knit fabrics are one example of this problem and carpet is an extreme case. Fortunately, with carpet small details are not needed, only bold designs or patterns. The problem of printing on a textured surface is also a factor with various types of cardboard and paper. Text, for instance, is available with different surface finishes such as laid or antique textures. See Figure 2-27.

In order to get this to occur the screen must conform to the surface structure. A monofilament nylon will more readily conform than any other fabric due to its elastic nature. In addition the stencil must be flexible enough to adjust to the changes in elasticity. Since indirect stencils are the least flexible of stencils they would be poorly suited to this task. And lastly the squeegee can assist in forcing ink into these recessed areas. By selecting a beveled shape this will conform to the surface irregularities more readily than a standard square shape. A hard blade will also have more difficulty in conforming to the irregularities than a soft blade.

Surface Absorbancy

Ink will react differently based on the **absorbancy** of the substrate surface. Ink must be selected based on this factor. The ink will either soak into the substrate or it will lay on top of the substrate. With an absorbent substrate the ink will spread as it soaks in. This adversely affects fine details and causes dot gain with halftone images. The use of nonabsorbent stock is essential for printing halftones or fine line images. Nonabsorbent substrates such as metal or glass do not allow ink to soak into its structure. Additional attention must be taken to print on absorbent substrates such as paper or pasteboard. By selecting coated stock this problem can be prevented.

Surface Coatings

At times various substrates may be given a surface coating. These coatings may assist or interfere with ink adhesion to the substrate. With substrates such as polyester a top coat may be applied by the manufacturer to make it more receptive to inks. In other instances coatings may be applied to make paper stock more durable which makes them less receptive to inks. Testing of ink to substrate is important to find the best results in different situations.

Substrate Color

Although the substrate color has little effect on the transfer of ink, it does affect how the color is perceived. For instance, yellow appears different when printed on a white substrate than printed on a red substrate. This is problematic with the use of proofs in screen printing. A proof is commonly made using a white background. Yet a job printed on a red substrate will not appear the same as a proof made on a white background.

KEY TERMS

absorbancy
acrylic
blanks
calendered vinyl
cast vinyl
chipboard
decal
force sensing resistor
membrane switch
polycarbonate
polyester
polyethylene
polypropylene
polystyrene
polyvinyl chloride
railroad board
tough check
tyvek

REVIEW QUESTIONS

1. Which basic paper is suited for use with most screen printing jobs?
2. What is the difference between thermoplastics and thermosetting plastics?
3. What are the differences between cast and calendered films?
4. What is the difference in composition between foam board and corrugated plastic board?
5. What are the two methods used to apply decoration to containers?
6. Why is a textured surface more difficult to print on than a smooth surface?

Producing Films for Screen Printing

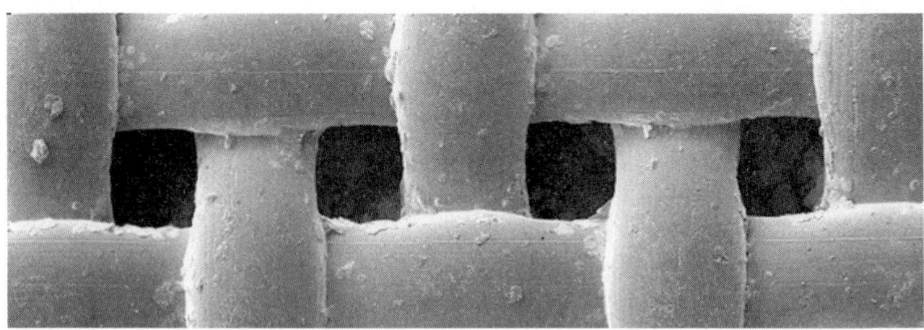

Films have been an integral part of each of the printing processes for a number of years. Their function is transfer of the image to the image carrier. Since each printing process uses different image carriers film requirements vary based on the process. The image carrier for the lithographic process requires a "wrong" reading film negative, while the screen printing process requires a "right" reading film positive. The image carrier for the screen printing process is produced by causing nonimage areas to harden and image areas to remain in a nonhardened state that may be removed during washout.

Traditionally the processing of an image carrier required the use of films for all printing processes. Recent technological advancements have resulted in changes in this approach. Lithographic plates are now imaged directly from the computer, eliminating the need for films. This approach is also beginning to find its way into the screen printing process. With the advent of direct imaging systems films will not be needed in the future.

"The silver halide **film emulsion** remains the finest image capture system yet devised; even the best digital image capture system can produce only a fraction of the resolution, per area, that film can."[1]

For the present time these systems are very expensive or may not achieve the same quality standards of films. For these reasons films will continue to be an important aspect of the screen printing process for the foreseeable future.

TRADITIONAL METHOD OF FILM PRODUCTION

Using a traditional approach in preparing film positives a number of operations are required. Each operation requires different types of equipment with specific skills for each. This makes film production complex and time intensive in nature. Revisions are also time consuming since they require repeating portions of the process. Producing films traditionally is inefficient by design in some cases. For example, handset type is set to customer specifications and then printed. See Figure 3-1. This copy then must be photographed to convert to film. At least three steps are needed to produce a film. Modern methods have resulted in a more direct, efficient approach of producing a final film. The five stages of film production by the traditional method are: layout/design, copy generation, copy pasteup, film generation, and proofing.

Layout/Design

The designer takes the customer's specifications and devises a printed piece to achieve those needs. The artist determines what is needed for the design—type, illustrations or photographs. Other important considerations include size of printed piece, colors printed, substrate color and type. The designer in essence decides how to best communicate the message through the printed piece. A **layout** is prepared showing how the finished piece should appear. It gives specifics on type style, size and other information on the job. This guides all aspects of the production process in making the proper decisions to achieve the final printed result to meet the customer need. See Figure 3-2.

Figure 3-1 Handset type

Copy Generation

Copy is generated using the designer's layout as a blueprint. The typesetting method must be de-

Figure 3-2 Layout vs printed result

cided. Methods might include handset type, photo typesetting, or dry transfer to name a few. Type is prepared at the desired size and placement. Handset type must be proofed on paper, or phototypesetting is imaged on photographic paper. Illustrations must be provided by an artist as needed. If they need to be resized this can be done using diffusion transfer on the reproduction camera. See Figure 3-3.

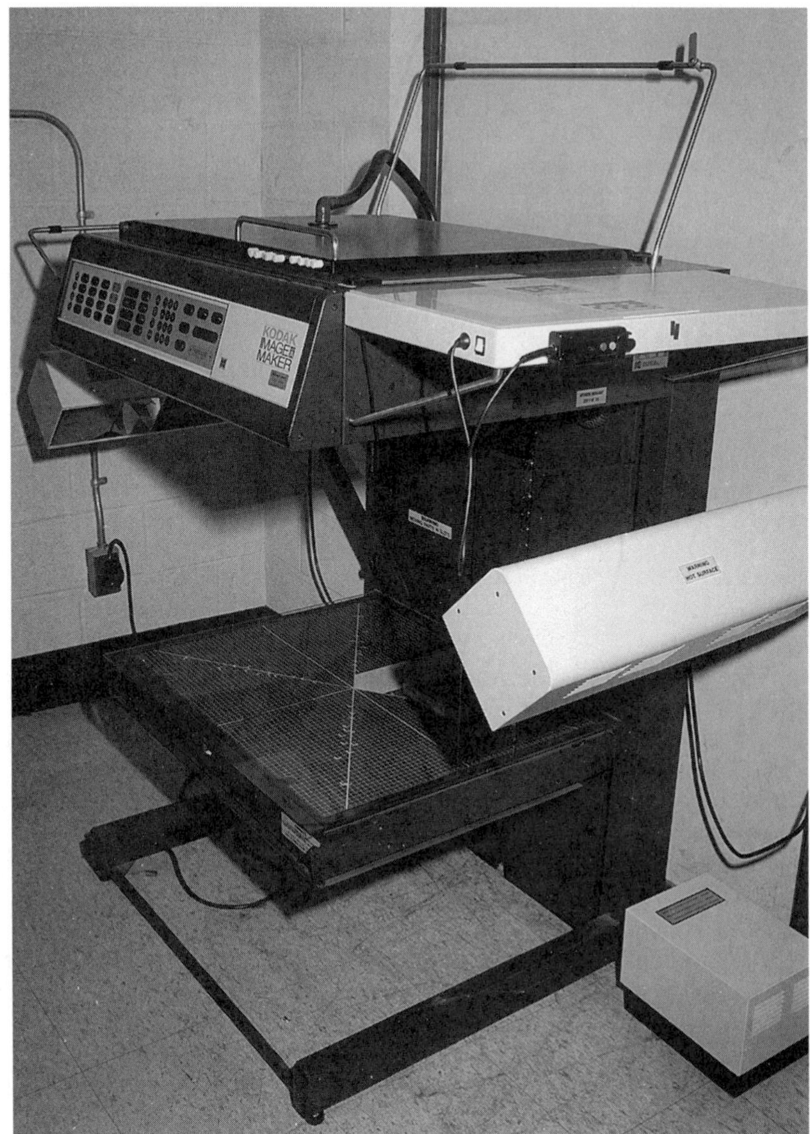

Figure 3-3 Repro camera

Copy Pasteup

Once all copy is prepared it must be pasted into position on a pasteup board as specified by the artist's layout. Type, illustrations or other elements are placed in exact position with trim or register marks. For best results images on **pasteup copy** should be dense black in color on a white background. This assists in producing high quality film negatives. Reproduction of color can be more complex and avoided with the exception of color photographs. The final pasteup should be clean and free of dirt, smudges or dust.

Film Generation

Films can now be produced from the pasteup copy using the artist's layout as a guide. There are three primary methods of generating films: mechanically, photographically using diffusion transfer films, or photographically on a reproduction camera using litho films and chemistry. The selection of method used is based on quality, copy requirements and the most efficient way to achieve those ends.

Mechanical Method

The simplest approach in preparing a film positive is to mechanically cut one using **ruby** (or

Figure 3-4 Mechanical positives

amber) **knife-cut film.** This can be easily done if the design is composed primarily of straight lines. This is often the approach used for sign cutting operations. It can produce sharp, clean results. But if the design is more complex with either curves or small details this method may not be reasonable unless the person is a highly skilled cutter. A modern improvement is a computerized cutting device which will be discussed at a later time.

A second method of mechanically reproducing a positive is by applying an opaque ink to vellum or acetate. See Figure 3-4. TrueGrain is a textured translucent polyester drafting film from Autotype International which is made for use by artists for this purpose. Due to its base and image densities stencil exposure with this product is critical. This will be discussed further at a later point in the chapter.

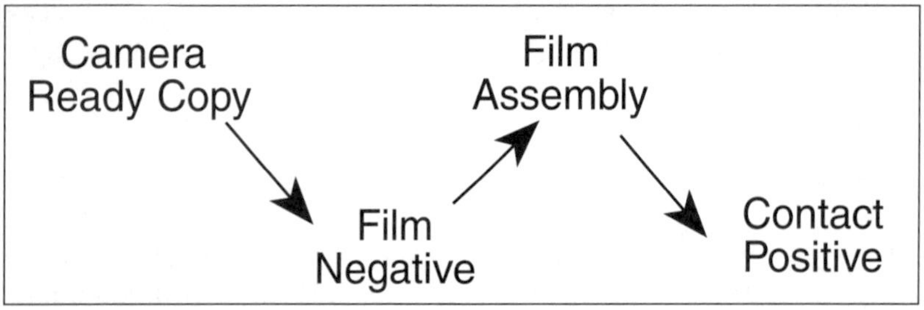

Photographic Method Using Diffusion Transfer

Diffusion transfer is a simple photographic method of producing a positive in one easy step. It is a photographic material that is used to produce film or paper positives on a reproduction camera. Diffusion transfer film made by Kodak is PMT which stands for photo mechanical transfer. It uses two elements: negative paper and receiver (either film or paper).

Camera ready copy is placed in the copyboard and set to achieve the final size desired. After the negative paper is exposed on the camera it is sandwiched together with the receiver paper or film and placed into a processor. It is allowed to develop for the recommended time, usually 90 seconds. The receiver is peeled apart from the negative paper to reveal a finished film positive or paper print. The diffusion transfer print is often used to enlarge or reduce illustrations to be pasted up. This method is a simple way to create a film positive ready to expose the stencil in a very short amount of time.

Camera Ready Copy → Film Negative → Film Assembly → Contact Positive

Figure 3-5 Repro camera film production

Figure 3-6 Film negative

Photographic Method Using Litho Film

This common method for film production is described in Figure 3-5. Copy is placed on the copy board **litho film** and exposed and processed yielding a film negative, as shown in Figure 3-6. Camera work is a simple procedure when the copy is basic line art.

The camera operation becomes more complex with black and white or color photographs. Black and white photographs are continuous tone images made up of an infinite range of shades of gray from white to black. Continuous tone images must be converted into dots through a halftone conversion process. To achieve this effect several exposures must be made on the reproduction camera making this more complex.

After the film is exposed on a reproduction camera it may be tray processed or processed through an automatic processor. Processing requires four steps: development, fixing, washing and drying. See Figure 3-7. Manual tray processing is less consistent and convenient than a processor. This process takes several minutes since it requires specific time intervals in each stage for proper processing to occur. Once the film comes out of the processor it is ready to use.

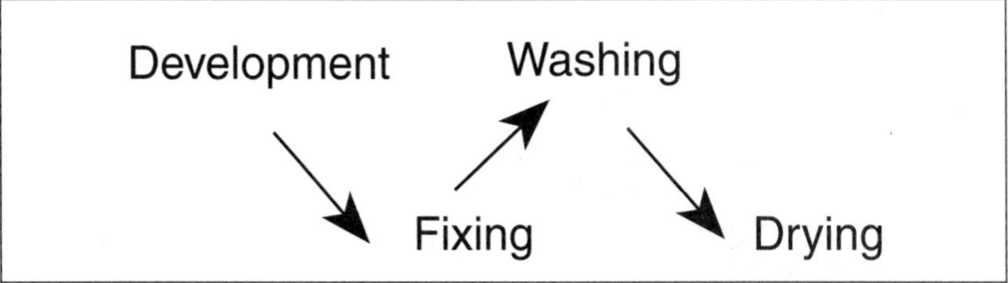

Figure 3-7 Lithographic film processing

Film Assembly

Once all the films (either line or **halftone** images) for a job are complete, film assembly may proceed. Film assembly is required when combining multiple images such as halftone and **line art**. It is also essential for precise alignment of multiple images. It is useful when adding various quality control marks such as color bars, trim marks and register marks. It also assists when using pin registration for exposing multiple screens for multicolor work in register. Film assembly comprises positioning and taping films based on the artist's layout onto a goldenrod masking sheet. Once films are in place and quality control marks are added, opaquing is done to eliminate pinholes in the films. See Figure 3-8.

Figure 3-8 Film assembly

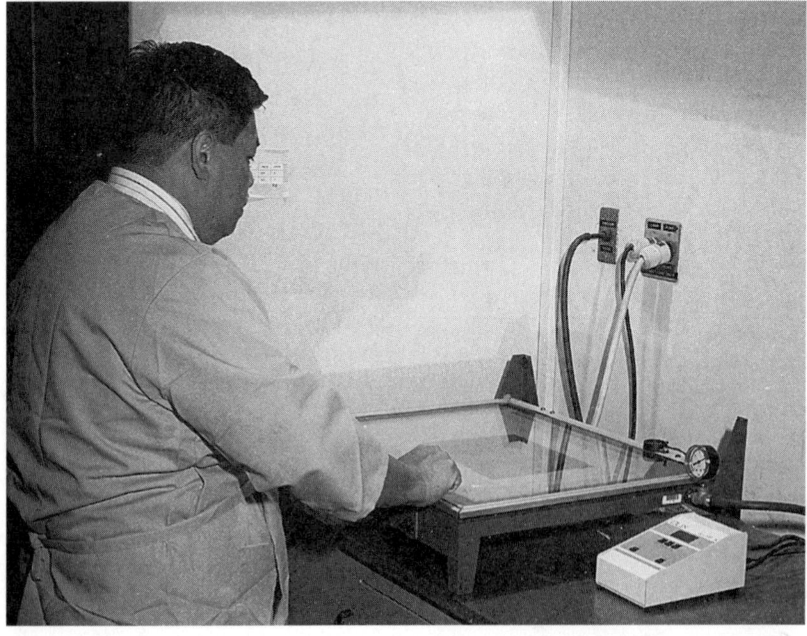

Figure 3-9 Film contacting

Proofing

A **proof** is an important quality control step to check position and other details to simulate final printed results. Proofing is done by exposing the proofing material using films and then processing the proof. It is used as a customer sign off as a quality control step before further production. If changes are requested by the customer the operation may have to be repeated based on how much change is requested.

Film Contacting

Positives may be produced once negatives have been assembled on flats, based on the job layout and proofs which have been approved by the customer. Flats should be assembled using pin registration where registration is critical or when more than one exposure is needed to make a film positive. The negative flats will be exposed with contact film which results in a positive. This is done by placing the contact film under the negative flat in a vacuum frame as shown in Figure 3-9. After it is exposed to a point light source for the proper time the film is placed in a film processor. Once dry it can be inspected and corrected with opaque as needed.

COMPUTER FILM GENERATION

The number of operations to achieve a final film is simplified over the traditional method since a large portion of the job is done on a computer. It eliminates multiple operations on different pieces of equipment, each requiring specialized skills. It streamlines workflow and is more responsive to changes along the way.

Computer Film Generation Workflow

The three stages of computer film generation are: layout/design, proofing and film generation.

Layout/Design

The role of the designer has not changed from the traditional method of film production. Today, however, many designers use the computer as a tool to achieve the layout to meet the customer's needs. See Figure 3-10. Once the layout is complete it does not need to be transferred to other operations or departments as a significant portion of the work is already done.

Figure 3-10 Computer design

Proofing

The job can be proofed prior to making films using a digital color proofing device. This allows a proof to be shown for customer approval without spending time and money making films, thus allowing for changes to be more easily made. See Figure 3-11. Once the customer approves the proof, production can proceed.

Figure 3-11 Digital proof, right

Film Generation

Films may be output by one of a number of devices. As with traditional film production the output method is based on quality and copy characteristics selecting the most efficient and cost effective method to produce the films needed. Output methods are: computer assisted film cutting, ink-jet, electrostatic, imagesetter using litho film or imagesetter using dry process film.

Figure 3-12 C.P.U. and monitor

Computer Hardware Requirements

There are two general elements to a computer. Hardware are the physical components that are needed for a computer system. These components are the Central Processing Unit (C.P.U.), the monitor, input devices, storage devices and output devices. The second requirement for a computer system is software. Software is the information or instructions that assist the user in getting the hardware to accomplish actions needed.

C.P.U. and Monitor

The central processing unit is the principal component making up a computer system. It provides the circuitry where arithmetic and logical operations are performed and instructions are decoded and executed. It controls operation of the computer. The monitor displays information from the computer on the screen. See Figure 3-12.

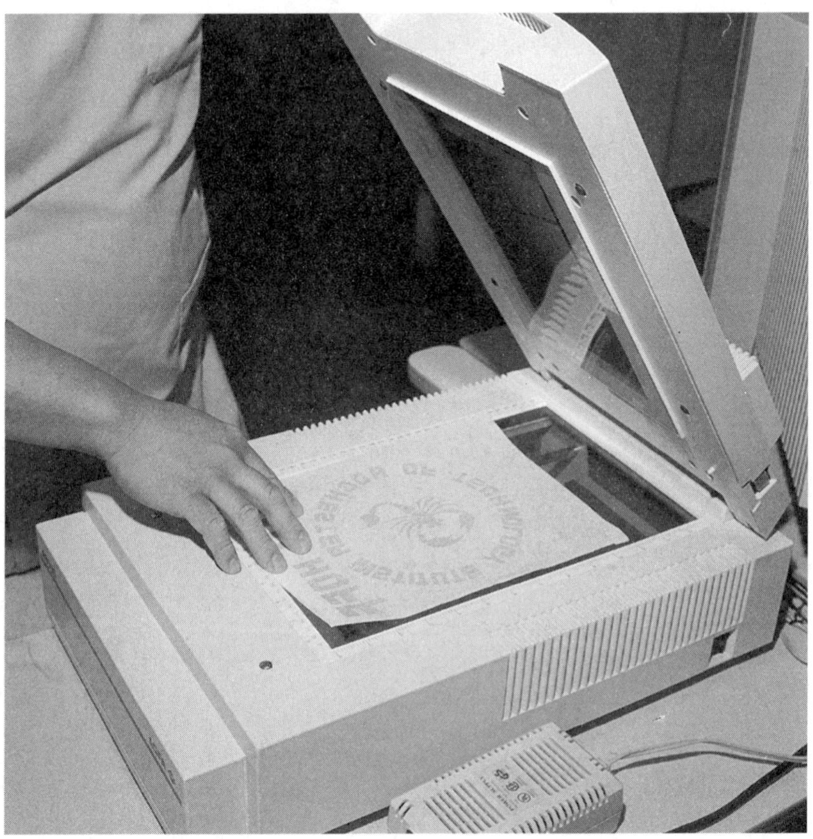

Figure 3-13 Input scanner, right

Input Devices

Input devices are components used to furnish information to the C.P.U. The keyboard and mouse are simple input devices, with scanners, digital cameras, and modem being more complex devices. See Figure 3-13.

Storage Devices

Storage devices, as shown in Figure 3-14, are components for storing data from the C.P.U. for use in the future. Storage devices include hard disks, removable disks such as floppy disks, optical disks and compact disks (CDs).

Output Devices

At some point it becomes necessary to obtain hard copy of the information on the C.P.U. This output can be printed on paper in black and white or color depending on the device, as a proof or camera ready copy. It can also output on film to image the image carrier.

COMPUTER ASSISTED FILM CUTTING Since handcut mechanical stencils are time consuming and skill dependent, automation can make this process more efficient. The job design is set in the computer and a plotter is then used to do the cutting. Even though it still requires a significant amount of time to cut the film, the operator is free to do other work while the plotter does the cutting. If the stencil needs to be recut for any purpose at a later time the design can be stored in the computer for retrieval. It is limited in the type of designs much like handcut stencils. It is best suited for bold line art such as type, lines and simple graphics. Intricate designs or halftones are not suited for this approach.

The computer is connected to the film plotter for output. A plotter, as shown in Figure 3-15, is a device that draws pictures on paper following directions given by the computer. A film plotter uses a knife blade instead of a pen

Figure 3-14 Storage devices

Figure 3-15 Film plotter *(Gerber Scientific Products Inc.)*

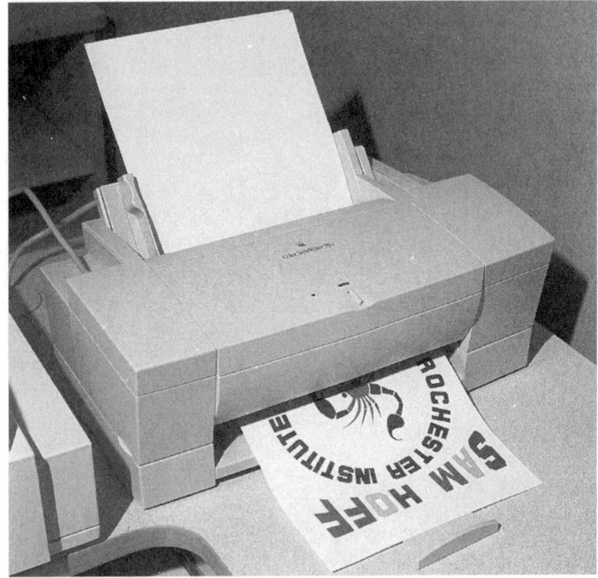

Figure 3-16 Ink-jet printer

Figure 3-17 Electrostatic printer

to cut film. A roll of film is used in the plotter instead of paper. The roll of film has holes on both sides of the material to assist in transporting into the tractor feeding mechanism of the plotter. The computer provides data in vector-graphics format as a series of point to point lines for the plotter to follow. After cutting is complete unwanted areas on the film must be manually stripped away using a dull knife or removal tool. This part of the operation is not automated and is a time consuming manual process. If a knife cut stencil is produced image areas must be removed. Ruby film may be used to make positives for use with photostencils. It is cut the same but nonimage areas must be stripped away. This film may be used a number of times as needed.

INK-JET PRINTER The principle of the ink-jet printer, as shown in Figure 3-16, is quite simple. Ink is drawn into the print head where heating elements cause the ink to boil. As the ink boils it expands, forming a bubble, causing a droplet of ink to be forced through a nozzle onto the paper. Hence another term for this device is bubble jet. Resolution is the same as low end electrostatic printers, 300 dots per inch (d.p.i.). Some of the newest ink-jet printers have a higher resolution of 720 d.p.i. Ink-jet printers are normally used to print on paper. There are ink-jet printers designed to produce film positive for use with screen printing. They come in widths up to 36 inches and can output unlimited lengths. Conventional halftones are difficult to produce using ink-jet printers due to their low resolution. It is important the check the minimum (d-min) and maximum (d-max) film densities for proper exposure of the stencil. This is discussed later in the chapter.

Due to differences in design and operation, the ink-jet printer has certain limitations in quality and use. Ink-jet output is unique when compared to either electrostatic or digital imagesetter. When viewed under magnifications a lack of sharpness of detail is noted due to the ink spraying. When printing on paper further loss of detail occurs due to the ink's penetration into the paper fibers.

ELECTROSTATIC PRINTER Electrostatic printers, like copiers, are based on the principle of electrophotography. There are two types. One causes image areas to be selected and created on a cylinder using a laser. Toner powder is attracted to these charged areas and is fused on the paper by a heating element. A second type uses thousands of liquid-crystal shutters that open and close, allowing light from a halogen lamp to illuminate the cylinder to form image and non-image areas. The resolution of electrostatic printers are from 300 up to 2400 d.p.i. They are available in sizes as large as 24" x 36". See Figure 3-17.

There are several ways that an electrostatic printer can be used to produce films for screen exposure. A traditional approach would involve taking its printed output and producing a film using a reproduction camera. There are guidelines for photographing electrostatic or ink-jet output on a reproduction camera that will be discussed later in the chapter.

Another approach is to use the electrostatic printer to directly output a positive using either a special vellum or matte-finish Mylar film. See Figure 3-18. This eliminates the production steps and cost of producing a film. It is important to understand that this approach produces a film that is different than a conventional film. Its minimum (d-min) and maximum (d-max) densities will be different so stencil exposure will be affected. Various points on the use of these films will be discussed later in this chapter.

Figure 3-18 Electrostatic positive

THERMAL PRINTER Thermal is derived from the word *thermë* which is Greek for heat. This device uses heat to produce an image. It is classified as a non-impact printer. Areas of the media are heated by an array of fast acting heat elements. This is accomplished by one of two methods. A print head made up of an array of resistive elements moves across the sheet sequentially (from one side to the other) to heat each spot in that line, until all image areas are created on the sheet. Another configuration uses the array of elements to heat all areas of an entire line at one time as the media moves past. Small localized areas of the sheet are heated by small pin like areas of the thermal imaging head. After an area is heated the corresponding area of the media darkens. Resolution is low (300 to 400 d.p.i.) with this device due to the mechanical aspects of this process. Very inexpensive thermal printers are used with devices such as calculators. This device images in one operation, unlike conventional films that require multiple steps to expose and process before they can be used.

Special films have been developed by several manufacturers for use with a thermal printer to produce films. These films, when heated, have a molecular change which causes image areas to darken. There are some limitations with these films. The minimum (d-min) and maximum (d-max) densities of these films are not the same but are relatively close to silver films. For the best results it is important to test d-min and d-max of the film to insure the best results during stencil exposure. Due to the low resolution its use is very limited when printing halftones. There can also be problems with registration since heating of the films during imaging may cause films to change in size. The largest film width that may be produced with this device is forty-four inches. These devices can image at the speed of four seconds per lineal inch.

Figure 3-19 Imagesetter

POSTSCRIPT IMAGESETTER USING LITHO FILMS An imagesetter, as shown in Figure 3-19, is a device that exposes film using laser diode technology or a helium neon laser. It is connected to the computer and is operated like any printer. Information is sent from the computer to a raster image processor (RIP). This device converts the information into pixels to be printed. Each of these tiny pixels combine to form the desired graphic or typographic image. Once the conversion is complete the information is relayed to the printer and the laser images the film. The exposed film is fed into a film cassette to allow transfer into the film processor under total darkness. See Figure 3-20. After

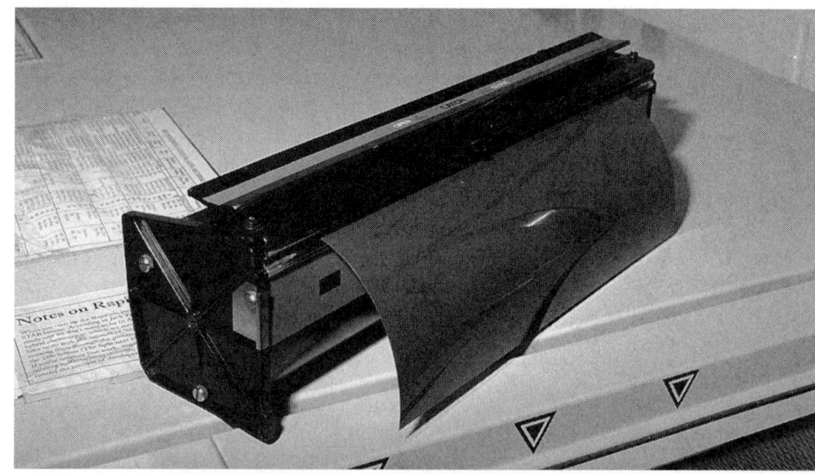
Figure 3-20 Film cassette

Figure 3-21 Film processor

being placed in the processor it emerges dry and ready to use for stencil exposure. See Figure 3-21.

Resolution of imagesetters ranges from 635 d.p.i. up to as high as 6,000 d.p.i. A common resolution that is used is 2500 d.p.i. Imagesetters can output films as large as 55" by 67". These large size imagesetters are the most expensive costing up to $500,000. Imagesetters can output on either film or resin coated (RC) typesetting paper. Output can be in the form of either negative or positive as set up by the software. The imagesetter allows resolution to be changed through settings in hardware or software. Some of the manufacturers of these devices include Linotype, Agfa Compugraphic, and Varityper, in addition to others.

IMAGESETTER USING DRY PROCESS FILMS A new direction in film generation is the use of dry processing films, as shown in Figure 3-21. These films are also called thermal films. They are produced by a number of companies at the present time. They eliminate wet processing of film minimizing environmental problems due to chemical disposal. Expensive film processing units are eliminated. Films are exposed much the same as with litho films on an imagesetter (although the unit must be set up to use these films). After exposure the film is fed into a thermal processor that heats the film to temperatures over 200°F. Heat causes the exposed areas to become opaque. The films requires no further processing.

The downside of these products at the current time is achieving the high maximum image density and minimum density of nonimage areas. Resolution is less desirable with some of these products. It requires an imagesetter designed to operate with these new films. Last, film costs with dry process films are no less expensive than current film costs.

OTHER FILM OPERATIONS

There are special circumstances which require a different approach to film making due to the nature of the printing. We will address two of these operations. These are step and repeat where multiple images are printed at once, and large formats requiring large films.

Step and Repeat

This is the technique of repeating a single image or more than one image onto photosensitive material using a film negative or positive. This is often done when screen printing decals, instrument or thermometer dials. Various commercial materials that may be

Figure 3-22 Computer

used include film (either contact or dupe films), proofs (one color or full color) or litho plates.

There are three primary methods of accomplishing the step and repeat technique. A traditional approach is to assemble multiple films onto a single **flat,** or carrier. This flat is then used to expose the image carrier. An important note! If multiple film positives are assembled on a clear carrier sheet using tape, problems will result due to the multiple layers created. This will be discussed further in the chapter. A better approach is to assemble multiple film negatives on a flat and then produce a contact positive. This will result in a one piece film positive.

A second approach is a step and repeat machine. This machine can be used to create multiple images on one film or plate. The machine mechanically moves into exact position and exposes the desired number of images. This method is known as photo imposition since it photographically positions each image onto a photosensitive material. This machine is capable of greater precision and also is less labor intensive than through manual imposition methods. Once job planning is complete the machine will place each image into position photographically. This can be most advantageous when changing press sheet sizes. Instead of entirely restripping a job, job planning can be redone in a few minutes on the computer for the new size. Then, using existing intermediate films in the step and repeat machine, the images will be photographically imposed in the new layout. Generally there is a greater hourly cost due to the equipment expense over manual imposition techniques.

There are two units that make up a step and repeat unit: the job planning computer (See Figure 3-22) and the step and repeat output device (See Figure 3-23). Planning is done on the computer, using a dedicated software program. Basic job information is input first. This information includes sheet size (press and trim sizes), output media to be exposed (film, plate or proof), and size and placement of each image element needed for the job. Placement of each element can be viewed by changing magnification of the view on screen. The data can be then sent to the exposure device.

After job planning is complete intermediate films flats must be prepared. Each film to be exposed must be stripped on the center of a clear carrier sheet using pin registration. It is taped in place, emulsion up, and a knockout flat must be prepared to cover all non-print areas of the intermediate film flat. Each film must be placed on a separate flat to be exposed separately.

With job planning and intermediate films complete, the step and repeat exposure device can be prepared for operation. The light sensitive material (film, proof or plate) is loaded onto the bed using

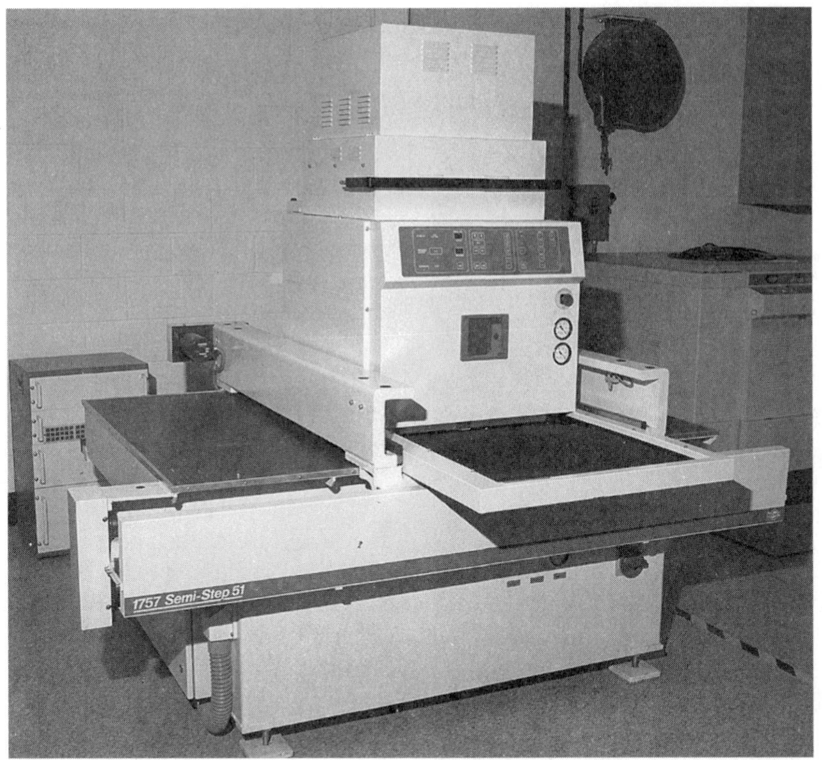

Figure 3-23 Step and repeat unit

pin registration. The vacuum bed is activated to hold the material in place. Intermediate films are placed in the chase based on the burn sequence as established by the job planning procedure. Now the start sequence is activated. The step exposure device will expose each film the prescribed placement and time as set up by the job planning computer. It will also change films as needed. After the entire exposure sequence is complete film can be developed in the film processor unit.

A third approach is to electronically step and repeat the image using a digital imagesetter and software. When digital films are produced the imagesetter can be given instructions to repeat the image multiple times using software. This approach is limited to the maximum film size of the imagesetter. Thus, one may not be able to step and repeat large size images.

Large Format

Producing large graphics poses a challenge due to the large size of the product. It is often difficult to secure the needed supplies and materials for a large size. It is more difficult to make and print a large screen. Producing a film and imaging the large screen is no exception. There are several approaches that may be used in film production of a large film size. These methods are: knife-cut mechanical films or stencils, photographic enlargement, projection screenmaking, thermal films, large format imagesetters and tiling of films.

Knife-Cut Films or Stencils

One approach is to knife cut mechanical films or stencils. Knife-cut films are available in rolls. This allows a long length to be made into a cut stencil or a knife-cut mechanical film positive. It is limited by the width of the roll purchased up to 60". This is discussed in Chapter 6.

Photographic Enlargement

Traditionally a film negative is contacted to produce a same size positive film. Large size films may be produced by photographically enlarging a small size film negative. A photographic enlarger or reproduction camera capable of producing large size films is required. These may be available through color separation houses. It is important that the original film negative is produced at the highest resolution since enlargement of the image reduces its resolution. If you begin with a low resolution image that is enlarged in size the resultant loss of sharpness can erode the final image

Figure 3-24 Projection screenmaking

quality. An example is the customer that brings in a design on a matchbook and wants it enlarged to poster size. This issue will be covered in the recommendations section at the chapter's end.

Projection Screenmaking

An alternate approach in dealing with large format images is projection screenmaking. As shown in Figure 3-24, it is similar to photographic enlargement but instead of projecting the image onto an intermediate film it is projected directly onto the light sensitive coated screen. This eliminates a step in the procedure and also reduces film use considerably since only a small size film negative is needed. There are several projection screen exposure devices available. They must be placed at a distance from the screen to enlarge to the desired image size, which causes the light intensity to drop off significantly in spite of the large wattage bulb used. This results in rather lengthy exposure times. There are high speed emulsions that are designed for projection use that reduce exposure time. As with photographic enlargement a loss of resolution will occur. It is essential that the original film negative should be of high resolution. With large format graphics such as billboards, resolution is not critical since it is viewed from a distance and not close up.

Thermal Films

These are films that are imaged using a thermal printer ranging in size up to 15 feet in length. At the present the largest width is 44 inches. Details of thermal printers have been discussed earlier in the chapter. This is one method of generating long films suitable for printing banners. Larger widths would present a problem with this approach.

Large Format Imagesetter

Films can be produced from a computer using an imagesetter as an output device. Imagesetters are being produced in larger sizes which will allow greater use in larger screen printing applications. At the present the largest size film that may be produced on an imagesetter is 55" x 67". They are also very expensive, costing up to $500,000. If you need a large size film, it is possible to have a service bureau produce large films from your electronic files rather than purchasing the unit yourself.

Film Tiling

Another approach that can be used in producing large films is to break it down into sections that may be output using conventional methods. This can easily be done when producing images using a computer and is known as tiling. This method will be difficult to use if halftones are split between two sections or if a noticeable "seam" will be evident. After each film section is produced it may be lined up with all the other sections to form a complete film positive at actual size. Clear tape may be required to hold sections together but will produce undesirable results if used. If the films overlap, problems may occur in making the stencil. This method has limited applications for use. One situation that would be appropriate for tiling is the production of a large graphic where it is printed in sections such as a billboard. In this situation it doesn't matter if halftone images are split on two sections since they are pieced together after they are printed to form the fill size image.

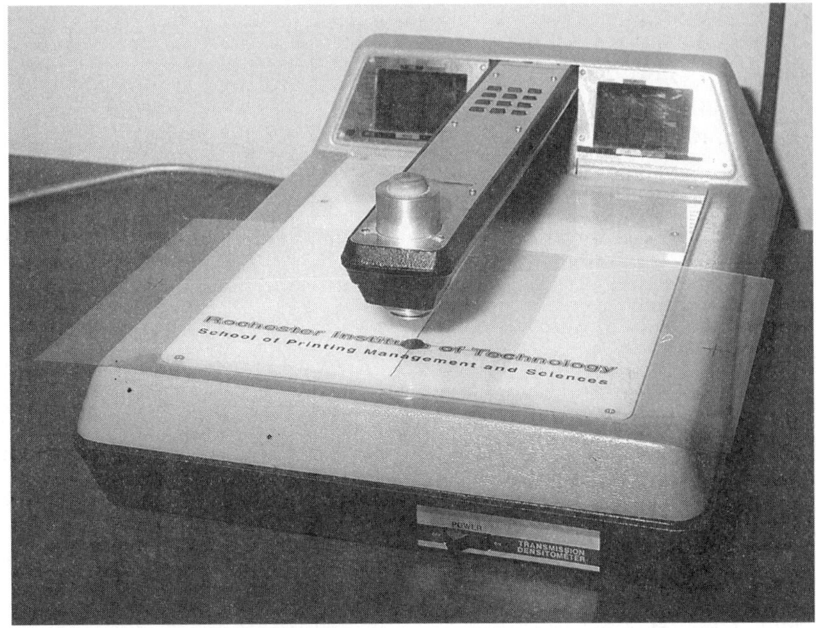

Figure 3-25 Transmission densitometer

EVALUATING FILM QUALITY

The significance of having the highest quality films cannot be overemphasized. The expression "garbage in, garbage out" applies very well here. One can only attain a final printed quality as good or less than what one begins with. It is unrealistic to think that one can produce a printed result better than the film. Therefore, the better the quality of the film, the higher the quality of the printed product will be.

We are going to address several issues in producing films for use in making the image carrier (screen). These are film image density, film base density, image resolution, film emulsion orientation, film layering, and film inspection.

Film Image Density

Density is the light-stopping ability of the darkened area of a photographic film image. The density must be sufficient to block burn-through of UV light during the stencil exposure process. This is often referred to as d-max or maximum density of the film. If burn-through occurs portions of these areas may not print. Density is measured using a densitometer, which translates the density into a numeric value. There are several types of densitometers which measure either reflected or transmitted light. A densitometer can be used to measure a photographic transparency (transmitted light) or a photographic print (reflected light), or printed ink density on press. Transmission refers to the light-passing ability through the film. See Figure 3-25.

As the density of film increases its transparency decreases and the ability for light to pass declines. With a density of 0.0, transmission or transparency is 100%. As the density increases to 0.3 its transparency decreases to 50%. At a density of 1.0, transparency decreases to 10%. At a density of 2.0, transparency is 1%, down to a 4.0 density where transparency is 1/100%.

The higher the maximum density (d-max), the less likely that burn-through will occur. At the highest density of 4.0 it is very difficult for burn-through to occur where nonimage areas become image areas. In looking at the numbers it may seem that the difference between a d-max of 3.0 and 4.0 (0.1% verses 0.01% transmission) may not make a significant difference in the "real world." Yet a 3.0 density allows ten times more light to pass than a 4.0 density. This may be a problem since screen printing uses a high intensity light source at relatively long exposure times (based on the speed of the stencil material used). With a d-max of 4.0, burn-through is the least likely to occur.

Processing or exposure factors of litho films will directly affect d-max. For instance if exposure or development is short the desired d-max of 4.0 may not be achieved. The device used to produce the film will affect image density. For instance another method of producing a film positive is tracing vellum with an electrostatic printer. Electrostatic printers create image areas using toner. Tracing vellum has a better affinity for toner with electrostatic printers and will achieve better results than using a clear base material. Toner tends to have lower density than silver halide used in litho film. This lower density causes the toner to have low resistance to actinic light during exposure of the stencil emulsion. A vellum positive produced on an electrostatic printer will typically have a maximum density of 2.8, considerably less than film at 4.0. At a density of 2.8 transparency is 0.0016 and at a density of 4.0 transparency is 0.0001. This means that a density of 2.8 will allow 16 times more light to burn through image areas. This means that exposure times must be kept low to minimize burn-through of image areas. A second problem is that individual toner particles may not result in a uniform density throughout the image areas. This may result in areas that the UV light is able to burn through. Refer to Figure 3-26.

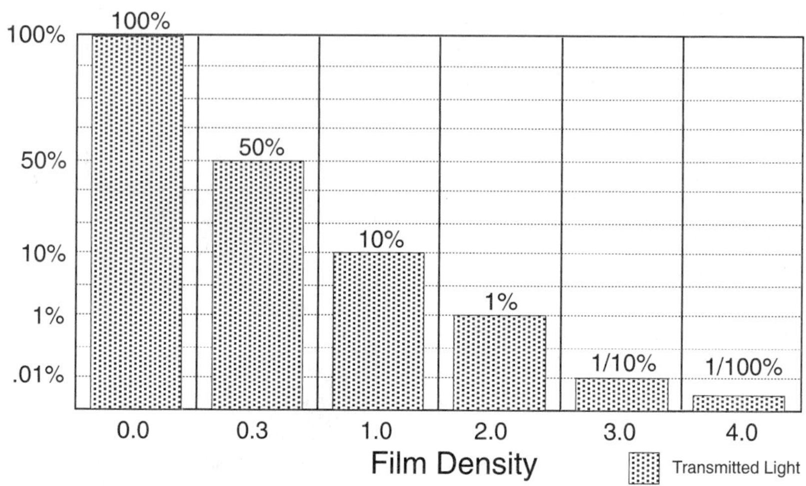

Figure 3-26 Light transmission

Film Base Density

The **film base density** known as d-min. determines how easily light passes through nonimage areas during the stencil exposure

Film Base Density Readings

	Film Base Density	Transmission Value
Polyester Film Base (0.004")	0.05	89%
Film Base + Clear Tape	0.06	87%
2 layers Polyester Film Base (0.004")	0.11	77%
Film Base (2 layers) + Clear Tape	0.12	75%
Tracing Vellum	0.19	65%

Figure 3-27 Film base density readings

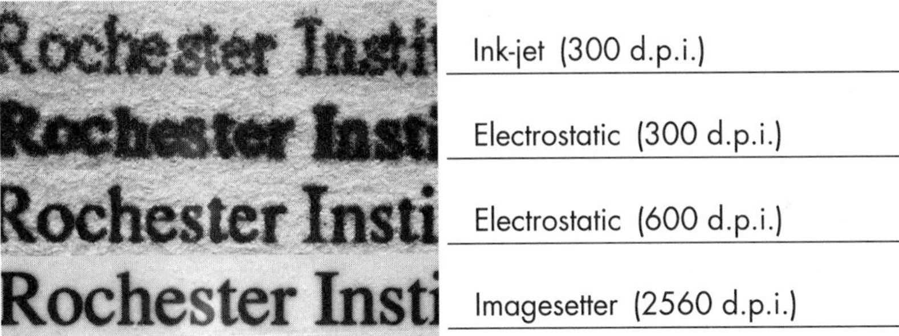

Figure 3-28 Output samples

process. Just because the film base appears clear does not mean all the light will pass through. If light does not pass through the nonimage areas sufficiently the stencil will not be hardened completely. If we measure the density of a 0.004" polyester film base, it has a density around 0.05. What does this value mean? In simple terms this means a clear base film with 0.05 density allows 89% transmittance of light. Or another way of explaining this is that polyester base blocks 11% of the light that it is subjected to. This is due to the composition of polyester. This film base density varies slightly between various manufacturers. Refer to Figure 3-27.

As mentioned earlier vellum can be used as a film base in conjunction with an electrostatic printer as a direct process to produce a film positive. Vellum has a base density of 0.19, much higher than polyester film base. This is obviously due to the difference in transparency between clear polyester and vellum. This increased base density must be compensated by an increase in exposure time to ensure complete hardening of the non-image areas of the stencil emulsion. Polyester blocks 11% of the light used to expose the stencil while vellum blocks 35% due to the differences in transparency and allows 65% of light to pass through.

Exposure must be increased by a factor of 1.5 to 2.5 to compensate for the loss of light depending on d-min. of vellum. So instead of a 2 minute exposure as with film, vellum may have to be exposed as much as 5 minutes. This increased exposure may cause burn-through of image areas since the d-max. is 2.8, lower than with film. This illustrates the critical role that exposure plays when using vellum film positives.

The smallest addressable spot determines the d.p.i. of a printer. d.p.i. = the number of these per inch.

The spacing of rows of halftone dots (indicated by the white arrow) determines the l.p.i. of the halftone.

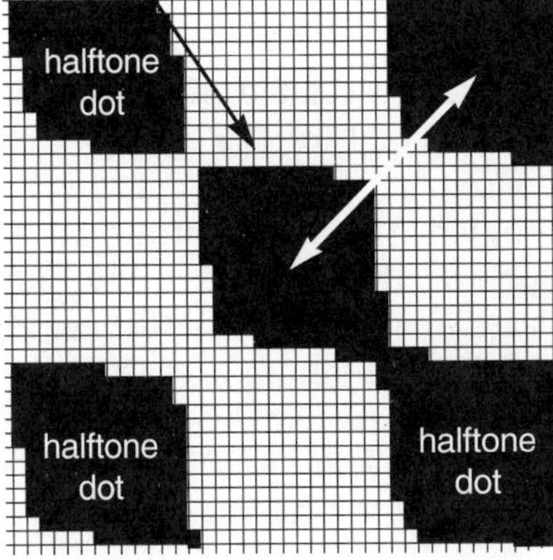

Figure 3-29 D.P.I. vs L.P.I. *(Frank Cost–R.I.T.)*

Image Resolution/ Edge Quality

A third aspect of the film is **image resolution.** This refers to the quality or sharpness of image edges of the film. This is usually referred to in a value of dots per inch (d.p.i.). Devices such as ink-jet printers have a relatively low resolution of 300 d.p.i. Electrostatic printers range from a low of 300 d.p.i. up to 1200 d.p.i. Sophisticated Postscript imagesetters can produce results up to 2560 d.p.i..See figure 3-28. At 300 d.p.i. this means that there are 300 by 300 dots or a total of 90,000 dots in one square inch. See Figure 3-29. This is a relatively large quantity of dots especially compared to a dot matrix printer of 72 d.p.i. producing a total of 5184 dots per square inch. When output is viewed under magnification this effect can be seen.

At a lower resolution of 300 d.p.i. a loss of image sharpness will occur which is eliminated at 2560 d.p.i. The imagesetter uses a laser to expose a film emulsion, with fine grain structure capable of high resolution. An electrostatic printer on the other hand uses toner particles quite large in size.

These individual particles when viewed at high magnification are quite visible at the edge of the image. This results in lower overall quality than the fine grain structure of the imagesetter film emulsion. See Figure 3-28.

The ink-jet printer produces image areas by spraying ink onto the film or paper. This spraying has an adverse affect on image edge sharpness, not that much different in appearance to the electrostatic printer. This is also due to some absorption of ink into the paper.

The next question is: Which resolution is needed to achieve proper results? The higher the resolution the higher cost incurred. There is no use paying for resolution that cannot be achieved. There are a number of factors to consider before this can be established. One factor is the substrate that will be printed. With textiles for instance the fabric weaving structure limits the printed result. In essence one is printing on threads, not on a flat surface. In this situation the highest resolution is beyond the substrates capacity to hold detail. In this case a low resolution of 300 d.p.i. may be adequate.

Generally speaking, when printing on smooth substrates the highest resolution of 2560 may be overkill for the screen printing process. Due to the effect the fibers of the screen mesh have on the process, one may not see significant difference between 2560 and 1200 d.p.i. Yet at 300 d.p.i. the final printed results will be noticeably crude with poor resolution and definition. For a majority of cases 600 to 1200 d.p.i. will produce satisfactory results. This is something that each shop must test out for themselves.

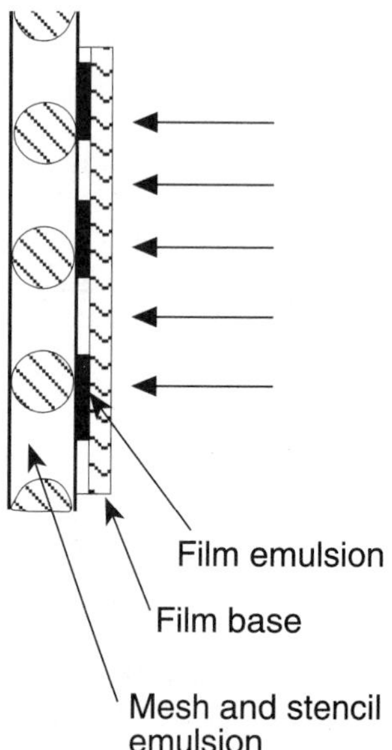

Figure 3-30 E to E: emulsion to emulsion orientation

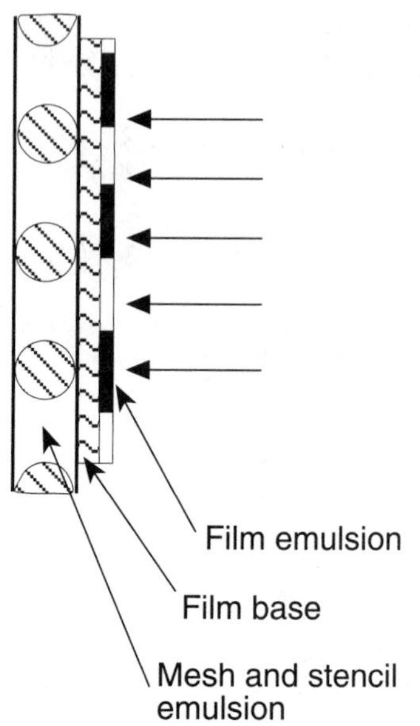

Figure 3-31 B to E: base to emulsion orientation

Film Emulsion Orientation

In order to print the finest details it is important for the emulsion of the film to come into contact with the stencil emulsion during exposure. See Figure 3-30. If the film base is in contact with the stencil emulsion it allows a space to be created between the two emulsions. See Figure 3-31. This permits light to undercut the image and eliminate small details or change the dot size of halftones.

When producing a contact positive it is important that it is right reading. That is, it should read correctly when the emulsion side is up. This is easy to accomplish during the film contacting process. A negative for lithographic use can be used. It is a wrong reading negative, reading backwards when the emulsion side is up. The emulsion of the contact film is in contact with the emulsion of the film negative. It is exposed and processed resulting in a right reading positive. When outputting on a computer, emulsion orientation can be controlled in the page setup menu between positive or negative, wrong or right reading.

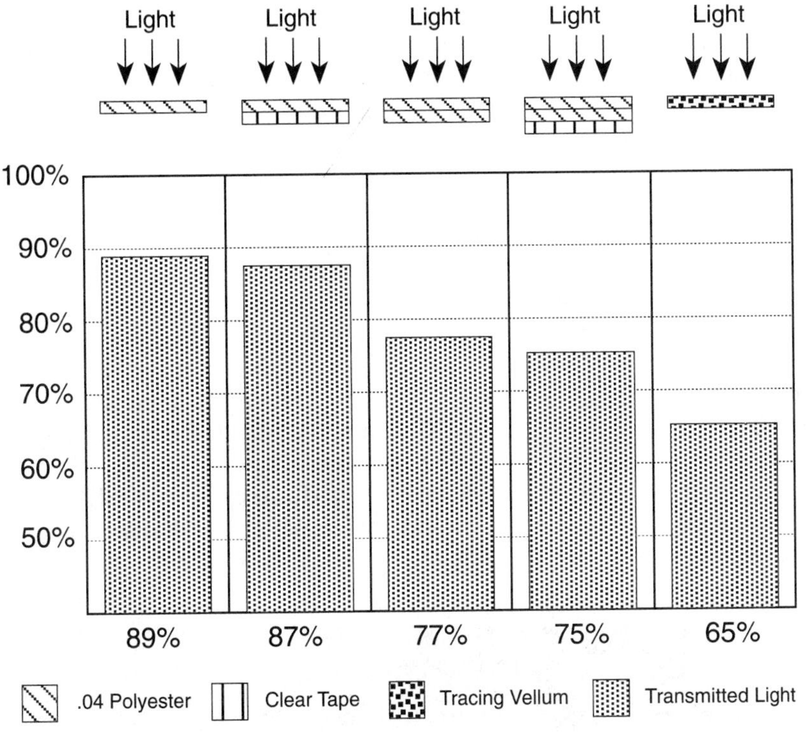

Figure 3-32 Light transmission of films

Film Layering

The practice of taping multiple film positives together is undesirable for a number of reasons. The first relates to the density of the film base. In placing layers of tape and film base together each individually blocks just a small amount of light, but collectively it adds up to block a significant amount of light. See Figure 3-32. For instance one layer of .004 polyester allows 89% transmission of light. When tape is added to the polyester the transmission value drops to 87% with clear tape, with frosted tape even less. When two film positives are exposed together the two layers of polyester allow 77% transmission of light in image areas.

In instances where tape is used to attach two positives together, this means that there are two layers of polyester in addition to tape. Using clear tape these three layers allow only 75% transmission of light. These multiple layers have an undesirable effect on light transmission. To compensate, exposure must be increased to achieve complete hardening of nonimage areas of the stencil.

Yet the multiple layers are not consistent throughout the film. In some places there may be only one layer of film base, in another area two layers of film base and other areas with two layers of film base and tape. This causes the stencil to receive differing amounts of light. Some areas will be hardened more than other areas. Many shops do not compensate for this difference at all. It may seem that light will have no difficulty in penetrating since it is easy to see through these clear areas of the film. Yet the areas of the film made up of multiple layers do not allow the stencil to become completely hardened. In fact if one looks at the stencil when back lit one can see these areas of underexposure. These areas of the stencil will be lighter in color than areas fully hardened. These underexposed areas may result in early stencil failure or low solvent resistance. Blockout may be applied to these areas to correct this situation, but this is time consuming and does not resolve the problem.

One recourse is to expose for the greatest number of layers. For example, two layers of polyester and clear tape which allows 75% light transmission. A 25% increase in exposure time is required, so a four minute exposure must be increased to five minutes. This may seem to be a simple solution to the problem. But this added time will cause a loss of detail due to additional light undercutting that occurs during the increased exposure time.

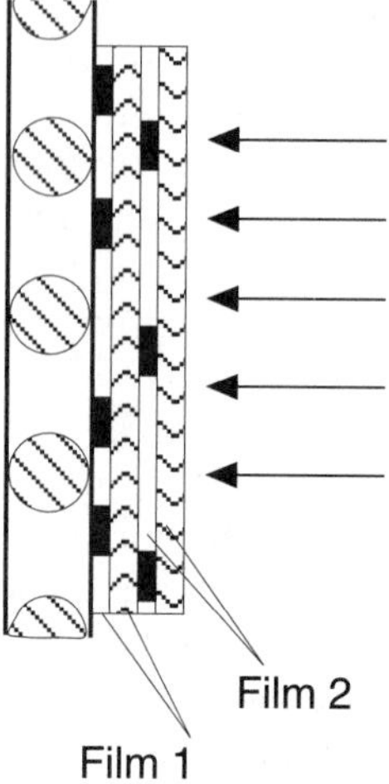

Figure 3-33 Film to film

A second problem using multiple layers of positives prevents emulsion to emulsion contact between the film and the screen, as shown in Figure 3-33. This also causes light undercutting to occur which causes a loss of detail from the film image. The film emulsion must contact the stencil emulsion (see Figure 3-30), to minimize loss of detail. With the film base touching the stencil emulsion a space occurs between the two emulsions during exposure, as shown in Figure 3-31. This causes a loss of detail with the light passing around the film image. When multiple films are sandwiched together, all of the film emulsions do not come in direct contact with the stencil emulsion resulting in light undercutting. Again, refer to Figure 3-33. One can see the number of problems that are introduced when films are combined in this manner.

A simple practical approach is to make intermediate films made up of multiple film negatives. These films can be combined in a film contacting operation to produce the final one piece film positive. In this way film images can be combined by film contacting rather than mechanically using clear tape.

There are a number of devices newly introduced for producing films for screen printing, such as thermal ink-jet, etc. Many of these devices have similar problems in producing the desired d-max or d-min, or both. These conditions require changes in the way screen exposures are made.

Film Inspection

Film inspection is an important quality control check performed before the screen is made. See Figure 3-34. The few minutes spent on this important operation may prevent problems from occurring during the printing operation. Some of these may be procedural problems that will be repeated on successive jobs until a new procedure is implemented.

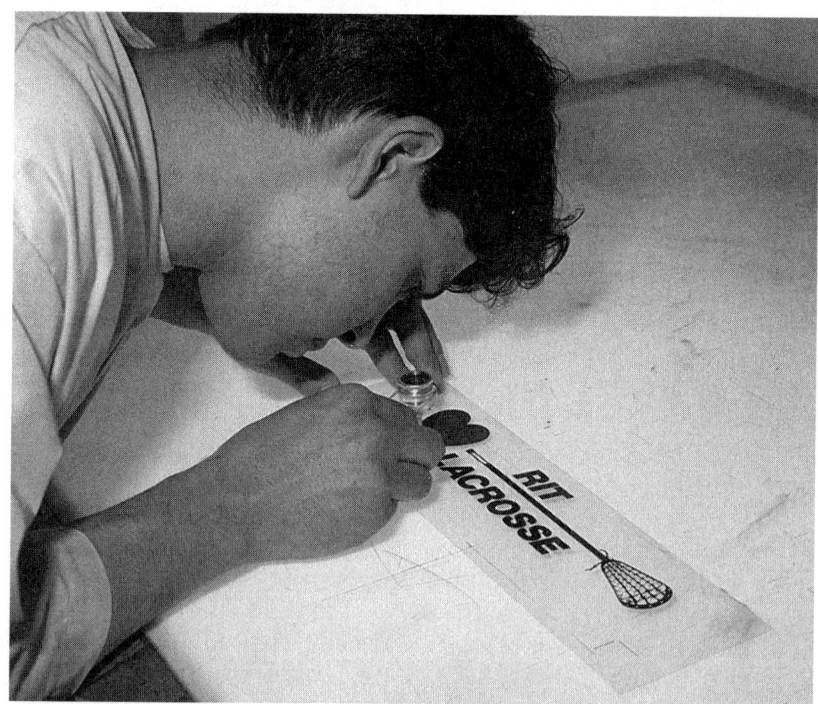

Figure 3-34 Film inspection

Other problems may be caused by equipment out of adjustment or calibration.

The first point is to compare films with the artist's layout to make sure they are consistent with the design. Other mechanical aspects need to be evaluated. Look at the films on a light table for evidence of pinholing. If pinholes are present it would be advisable to measure the image density of the film. Film density should be 4.0 for best results. With less density the film may have been underexposed or underdeveloped. Pinholes require time consuming application and drying of opaque. A second point is to check emulsion orientation to see if films are right reading with the emulsion up. Next, the films should be examined using a magnifier to check for image resolution and sharpness. Films should be inspected for cleanliness. Is there excessive dirt or scratches on the film? Measuring the base density of the film can be done to see the effect of excessive dirt. Polyester base should measure about 0.05 density or less or stencil exposure time may need to be adjusted. Next there should be one film for each color to be printed. Films should then be compared to each other to see if they are the same size. By carefully aligning the register marks of two films you can see if they line up. If the films don't line up visually they won't line up on press. These simple checks will help eliminate potential problems on press.

Getting the Most Out of Your Output Device

Low resolution output can be improved by reducing the output on the reproduction camera. For example, 300 d.p.i. output becomes 600 d.p.i. when photographed at 50%. Unfortunately this approach can only be used with small images. Output from a standard laser printer with an 8" x 10" image becomes 4" x 5" when photographed at 50%. Conversely, enlarging of low resolution output is not recommended. For example 300 d.p.i. output becomes 150 d.p.i. when photographed at 200% to enlarge an 8" x 10" image to 16" x 20".

Here are some guidelines for photographing ink-jet or electrostatic output. Paper quality has a significant effect on image quality. Absorbent or rough textured stock will cause detail to be lost. Special papers with coatings or improved surface are designed to produced optimum results on ink-jet or electrostatic printers. Low cost printers will not achieve consistent image densities as it lays down the toner or ink. A good quality printer will produce better results. Film development is critical in achieving consistent quality when photographing ink-jet or electrostatic copy. Overdevelopment will cause a loss of sharpness and details while underdevelopment will cause excessive pinholing with film negatives. Consistency is important in this stage of the process.

KEY TERMS

diffusion transfer
film base density
film contacting
film emulsion
film image density
film layering
flat
halftone
image resolution
layout
line art
litho film
pasteup copy
proof
ruby knife-cut film

REVIEW QUESTIONS

1. What advantages would computer assisted film cutting offer over a mechanical film positive or stencil?
2. What is the film image density of a high quality film?
3. What is the film base density of a high quality film?
4. In which cases are low resolution films such as 300 d.p.i. not suitable for screen printing use?
5. What is the correct film emulsion orientation to achieve best results?
6. Why is it not recommended to layer multiple films together for stencil exposure?

NOTES

1 "Too Hot To Handle," *Popular Photographic Magazine* 116 (August 1995): 172.

Screen Fabric

Screen fabric is the most important component in the screen printing process. Decisions made regarding fabric affect every other operation, thus stressing the importance in understanding this key component. It is one of three elements that make up what is referred to as the image carrier. The image carrier is made up of the screen frame, with fabric and stencil attached. See Figure 4-1.

Fabric performs three basic functions. The fabric supports the stencil which affects run durability and edge definition. The second function is controlling ink deposit, which influences ink deposit thickness, ink volume, color fidelity and ink drying. The third function is the regulating of elasticity which affects off-contact distance, registration and dimensional stability and printing speed. It is only one of three elements which affect ink deposit, yet it is the most important. Fabric has the largest effect on ink deposition, controlling fifty percent of the ink deposit.

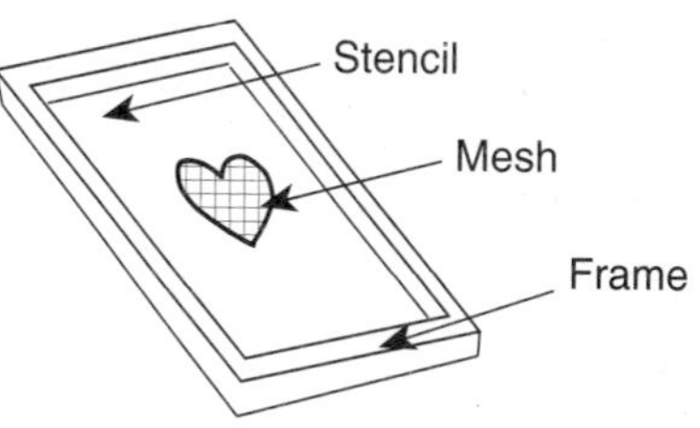

Figure 4-1 Image carrier

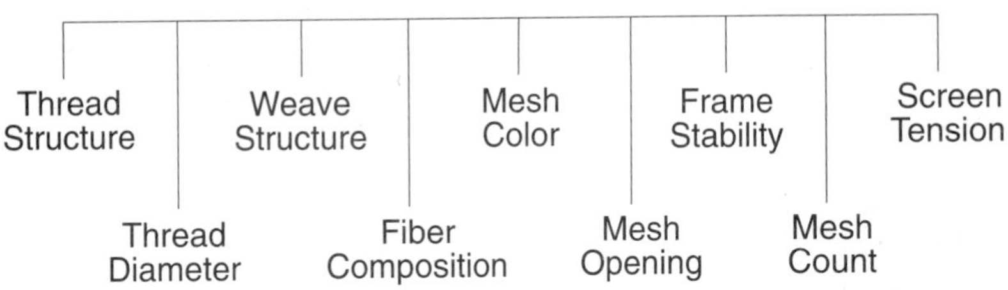

Figure 4-2 Fabric variables

There are nine variables related to the screen fabric that will affect final printed quality as shown in Figure 4-2. These variables are: fiber composition, thread structure, mesh count, thread diameter, mesh opening, weave structure, mesh color, screen tension and frame stability. These factors will be addressed in later chapters.

The Chinese used a simple stencil process back in the early beginnings of the screen printing process. Stencils with small details were supported by gluing strands of hair across to bridge the stencil. Some time later silk was introduced to provide support for the stencil. With silk supporting the stencil it would not be damaged by the squeegee forcing ink through image areas of the stencil.

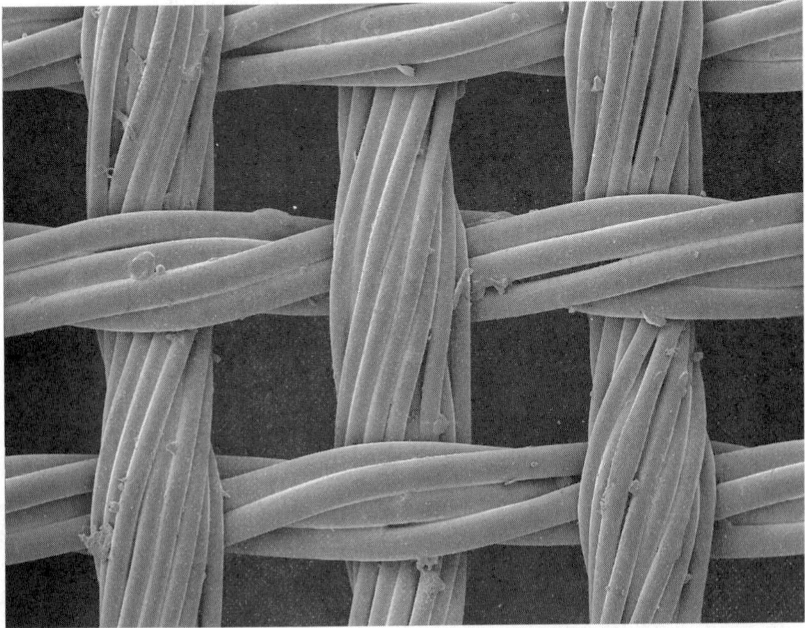

Figure 4-3 Silk is multifilament in structure

SILK

Silk is **multifilament** in structure as shown in Figure 4-3. This structure leaves cracks and crevasses where ink and stencil residues get trapped. It is very difficult to completely remove this haze from the mesh after printing. The multifilament structure also takes up more space with less open area through which ink may be passed.

Fabric stability is poor since fiber thickness and consistency varies due to the silk fibers. This makes it difficult to apply the tension necessary for high quality printed results. The increased surface structure that multifilament fabrics possess allows indirect stencils to adhere more completely to the fibers. The fibers produced by the silkworm have surface irregularities, which is why silk has been used in the past. Yet the disadvantages of silk outweigh the advantages. In addition the indirect stencil is declining in use by the industry. In essence you are paying more for silk and getting an inferior fabric. This explains the decrease in its use by the industry.

Multifilaments are rated by a system of two indicators, a number and the letter "x". A popular silk fabric used is 12xx. The number is a rating related to the number of threads per unit measure. Silk is available ranging from a low of 2xx, which is about 54 threads per inch (t.p.i.) up to 30xx, approximately 220 t.p.i. There is no mathematical formula to convert multifilament fabric ratings into threads per inch. To determine any given **mesh count** from the multifilament rating one can look it up in a chart such as the one in Figure 4-4. For example, a 10xx multifilament is the equivalent of a 110 monofilament.

The second rating "xx" is used to rate fabric durability. Fabric with an "xxx" rating is very thick and durable; a fabric with an "x" rating is the thinnest and least durable. An "xx" mesh is the most common, with other ratings seldom available.

The manufacturing process uses silk fibers produced by the silkworm. This makes this material very expensive. Another limitation is its limited range of mesh counts and fabric inconsistencies. In essence silk is more costly than synthetics and results in an inferior printed result. At lower mesh counts (6xx or 74 t.p.i.) silk costs four times as much as monofilament polyester. At higher mesh counts (30xx or 220 t.p.i.) its cost is seven times as much. Silk is no longer sold by fabric suppliers due to its high cost and poor printing performance. A Screenprinting and Graphic Imaging Association (S.G.I.A.) survey indicates its use by industry in 1995 as only 6.1 percent.[1]

MODERN SYNTHETIC FABRIC

There are a number of alternatives to the natural fiber of silk. These are manmade fibers. Each has its own characteristics which affect performance differently. Trends have changed over the years in fabric usage as shown in Figure 4-5. The chart shows the latest trends according to the latest S.G.I.A. survey of the screen printing industry. You will note monofilament polyester is the fabric most commonly used today.

Fabric Number	Mesh Count
6 XX	70
8 XX	78
10 XX	110
12 XX	128
14 XX	138
16 XX	148
20 XX	175
25 XX	195
30 XX	220

Figure 4-4 Mesh count chart

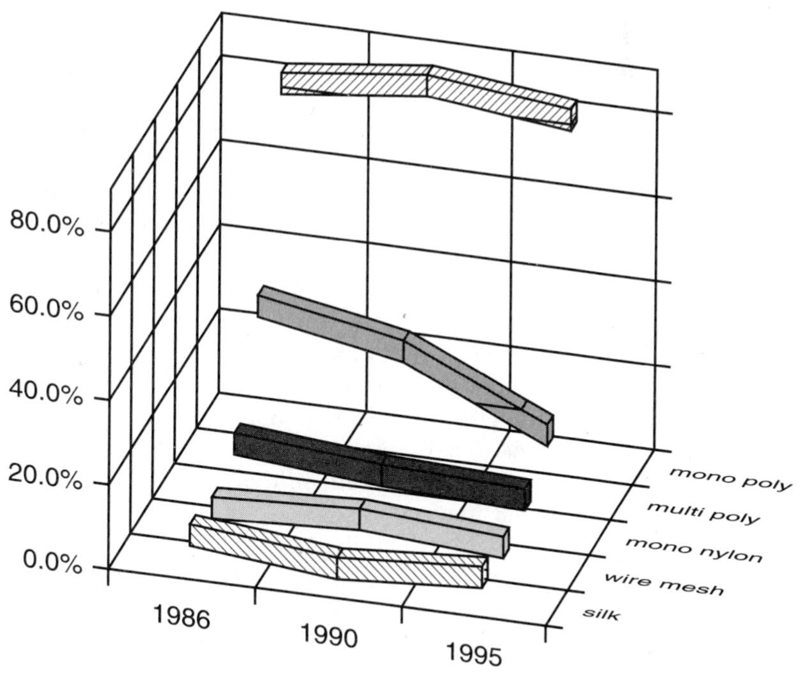

Figure 4-5 Fabric usage

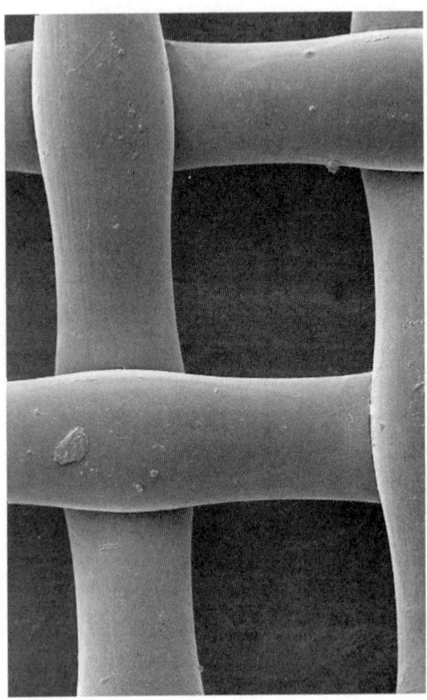

Figure 4-6 Multifilament 10xx vs monofilament 110T polyester

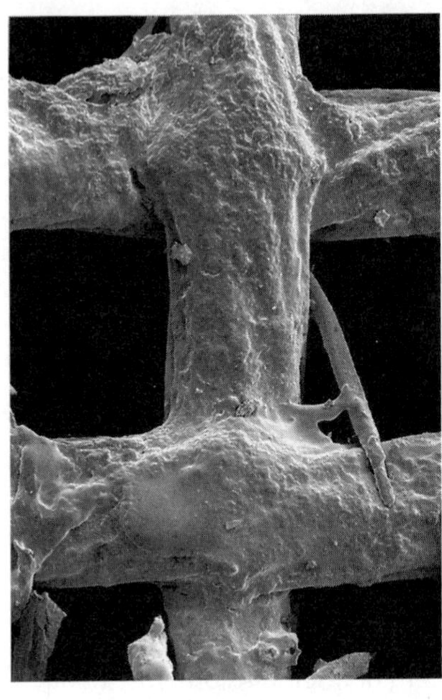

Figure 4-7 Ghost Haze 10xx polyester

Multifilament Polyester

Multifilament polyester is a lower cost alternative to silk. The thread structure is similar to silk, being made up of several small strands combined into threads, that are then woven into fabric as shown in Figure 4-6. The primary difference is the method of producing individual fibers. They are produced using an extrusion process where the consistency and composition of the individual fibers can be accurately controlled. This consistency makes it possible to tension this fabric to a level that will produce higher quality printed results than with silk. Polyester is formulated to provide superior results over silk. It provides elasticity, strength, resilience, and abrasion resistance, with low moisture absorption of 0.04 percent and resistance to most acids.

The multifilament structure allows stencils to adhere more easily. But this structure also makes it more difficult for ink to pass through and more difficult to reclaim at the end of the job. Multifilament polyester is much less expensive than silk. Multifilament polyester can produce higher quality results at a substantially lower cost than silk. This fabric has declined in use by industry from 36.4% in 1986 down to 14.7% in 1995.

Monofilament Polyester

Another fabric is composed of polyester, but uses a different thread structure. Each thread is a single individual strand that is woven into the fabric mesh. This **monofilament** structure, as shown in Figure 4-7, gives the fabric more stability which makes it desirable for high quality printing. This single thread structure is very stable without many of the disadvantages of multifilament composition. This structure has greater open area which makes it easier for ink to pass through to the substrate. Reuse of the fabric by reclaiming is easier with better results when using a monofilament structure. This fabric is used by 81% of the screen printing industry. (Refer to the charts on pages 77 and 104.)

Screen fabric varies in cost based on mesh count since it takes much longer to weave a high mesh count such as 355 over a coarse mesh count of 96. Yellow monofilament polyester ranges in cost from $11.65 (60T) up to $53.55 (470T) per yard in a 42" width bolt as shown in Figure 4-8. This equals $1.14 to $5.22 per square foot.

One disadvantage of monofilament structure is stencil adhesion. The smooth strands have less surface area, which may pose a problem in adhering capillary or indirect stencils. This can be overcome by abrading the surface of the fibers. This procedure will be discussed in Chapter 6.

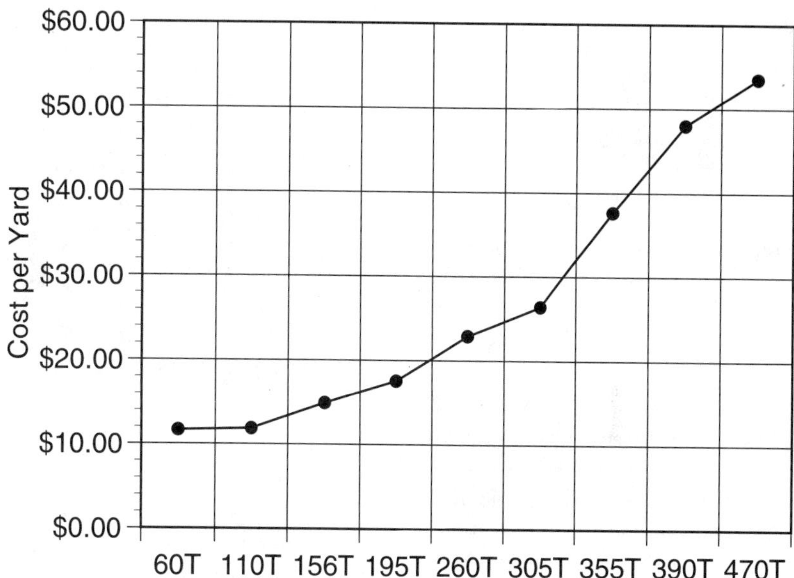

Figure 4-8 Monofilament polyester (yellow)

The rating for monofilaments is different than multifilaments, a system that is easier to use. A number is used which rates the number of threads per unit measure, in inches or centimeters. Monofilament polyester is available in a wide range of mesh counts from 16 to 500 in bolt widths from 42" to 82". The type of thread with monofilaments is often rated by a letter designation. (See also "Thread Types," page 74.) The three types are: "S" thread (the thinnest), "T" (medium thickness), and "HD" (heavy duty thread). A new ultra thin fabric, "SL," is now available in limited mesh counts.

Monofilament Nylon

Since its thread structure is identical to polyester it appears the same. Monofilament nylon is available in a similar range as polyester. The difference lies in the chemical composition of nylon. Since appearance cannot assist identification of the fabric the difference can be found by comparison of tensioning characteristics or by chemical analysis.

Nylon has greater elasticity than polyester which makes it ideal for printing on uneven surfaces or substrates. With increased flexibility it conforms more readily to various surfaces. But this increase in elasticity means it is less capable of maintaining a high degree of registration accuracy.

Another difference is nylon's lower resistance to moisture. Nylon can absorb up to four percent water, while polyester absorbs only one tenth that of nylon. This makes nylon less suited for inks with water in their composition. It has a higher resistance to abrasion and alkaline solutions than polyester. On the average it costs about seven percent more than white monofilament polyester. It is presently used by only 7.8 percent of the screen printing industry.

SPECIALIZED FABRICS

There are several fabrics designed for special purposes. These provide superior results when used in the proper situation.

Figure 4-9 Feathering *(Tetko® Inc)*

Carbonized Mesh

Another specialty fabric was developed to eliminate static problems when printing on plastics such as vinyls, acrylics, and plastic foils. Some of the evidences of static include: stock sticking to underside of screen instead of dropping immediately after printing; ink remaining in mesh openings, not entirely transferring to the printed substrate; and feathering around the outside of the printed image. See Figure 4-9.

Carbonized mesh is made up of a carbonized nylon thread placed between polyester threads in the weft direction (see "Warp and Weft," page 90). See Figure 4-10. This makes the mesh conductive in nature which "bleeds off" the static charge. It has very good ink passage and elasticity in addition to chemical resistance. Its registration accuracy and abrasion resistance are good. Carbonized mesh is available in four different mesh counts from 195 to 355 in bolt widths from 42" up to 102". It averages about two times the cost of white monofilament polyester.

Applications where this fabric may be beneficial are vinyls, decals, pressure sensitive sheets, reflective sheets, and POP displays.

Figure 4-10 Carbonized mesh *(Tetko® Inc)*

The aspects of tensioning and mounting of carbonized mesh will be addressed in Chapter 5.

Calendared Mesh

When printing with ultraviolet curing inks they will be difficult to cure if the ink deposit is too thick. A calendared mesh was developed to assist with this problem. During manufacture the fabric is flattened on one side with a heated

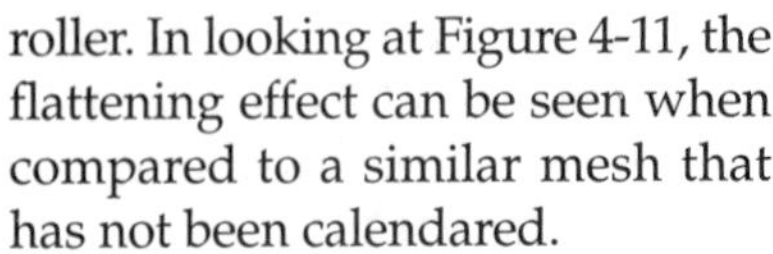

roller. In looking at Figure 4-11, the flattening effect can be seen when compared to a similar mesh that has not been calendared.

This creates two changes in the mesh geometry. It decreases both fabric thickness and mesh opening. To see how this affects the fabric and ink deposit refer to the chart in Figure 4-12. Refer to 355T and 355UV calendared mesh, both with the same 33µ thread diameter as shown in Figure 4-13. The calendaring process reduces mesh opening from 38µ down to 30µ and effectively decreases open area from 29% down to 18%. (Also, see the charts on pages 78 and 105.)

This in effect reduces ink deposit by about 25 percent. The calendared side is placed on the squeegee side for best results. This allows a coarse mesh to be used to obtain a thin ink deposit like a more costly fine mesh. Calendared mesh is available in mesh counts from 230 up to 470 in bolt widths from 42" to 80". It averages about thirteen percent higher cost than white monofilament polyester.

Figure 4-11 355 calendared vs. 355T monofilament polyester mesh

	Monofilament Polyester	Calendared Polyester
Mesh Count	355T	355UV
Thread Diameter	33 µ	33 µ
Mesh Opening	38 µ	30 µ
Open Area	29%	18%

Figure 4-12 Monofilament vs. calendared polyester

Monofilament Glass Mesh

In applications such as back lit displays or glass printing, defects visible by the eye are caused by mesh marks or smears. Very small deviations in mesh parameters can cause these defects resulting in changes in colored areas of the displays. Technical problems related to the weaving process can lead to these problems. Uniformity of the weave between the **warp** and weft directions or slight variations in the thread diameter can lead to these type of defects.

Monoglass is a specialized fabric that has been recently developed to eliminate these visual defects caused by fabric geometry. With this fabric the thread diameter and mesh openings are kept to a higher standard. This mesh is available in a range of mesh counts from 110T up to 355T in bolt widths from 42" up to 82". It costs about twenty-two percent more than white monofilament polyester.

Monoglass is guaranteed by the manufacturer to not cause mesh marks due to fabric geometry. It has established mesh parameters that are identical from one bolt of fabric to the next. This assists the printer in achieving consistency from one print run to the next.

Metal Composition Mesh

When fabric durability and stability are a concern, a fabric of metal composition is advantageous over other fabrics. Metal composition also is beneficial when static is a problem. There are three types of fabrics composed of metal.

Stainless Steel

Stainless steel fabric has been used for a number of years, commonly for printing electronic circuitry, membrane switches, glass printing and ceramic dinnerware or tiles. Nearly five percent of fabric used in the screen printing industry today is stainless steel. It can be tensioned to a high degree and will remain constant for long runs.

Stainless steel can also be used when printing with acids, caustic chemicals or specialized compounds or inks that are used in some screen printing operations. Nylon or polyester are not resistant to all types of chemicals, and this is where stainless steel plays a role. Stainless steel has the highest resistance to all chemicals used in the screen printing industry. The metal composition obviously gives it superior durability. It has excellent abrasion resistance and virtually no moisture absorption with very good ink passage. It is used by the ceramics industry with inks containing frit that abrades the mesh severely during printing.

Its composition gives it properties that help to eliminate static problems. This is the most durable fabric that is greater in cost and time but this can often be recovered over a long printing run. The

Figure 4-13 Stainless mesh

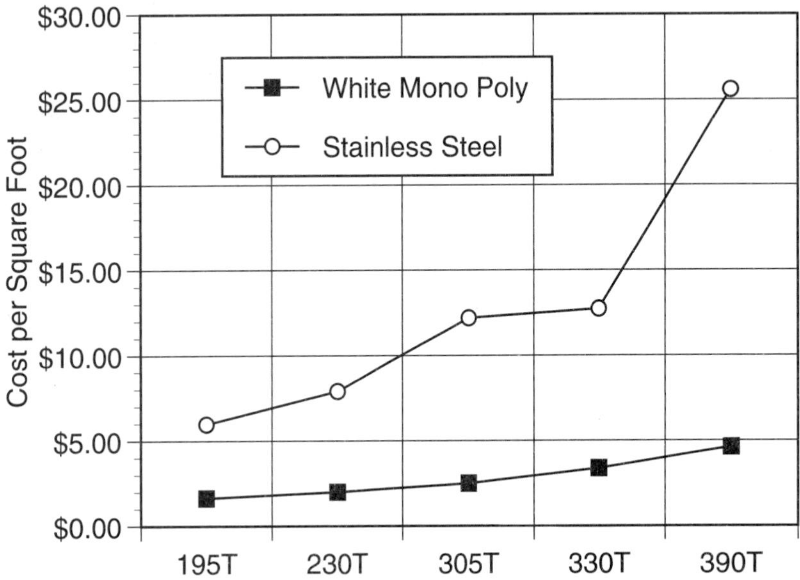

Figure 4-14 Stainless mesh cost comparison

main disadvantages are high cost and difficulty in tensioning the metal fabric properly. After a certain "break in period" the weave of the fabric flattens or compacts resulting in a slight drop in tension. This requires a second re-tensioning period. Its ability to conform to uneven substrates is poor due to its low elongation properties. It is subject to dents or kinks if it is not handled carefully.

Stainless steel mesh is available in a range of mesh counts from 80 up to 510 in 40" and 48" bolt widths. It is available in three grades (similar to monofilament synthetic fabrics) related to thread thicknesses: thin, medium and heavy. It differs in designation from monofilaments calling them ultra-thin, standard and heavy duty grades. Stainless steel is one of the most expensive fabrics. It ranges from $6.00 per square foot for a 200 mesh (0.0016") up to over $25.00 for a 400 mesh (0.0010"). See Figure 4-14 for a stainless mesh cost comparison.

Metalized Polyester

This fabric is a compromise between stainless steel and polyester with many of the features of both types. The core is a polyester fabric that has been coated through an electroplating process with nickel alloy as shown in Figure 4-15. This gives it increased abrasion resistance, durability and stability compared to conventional polyester. Its increased flexibility is easier to work with and more forgiving than stainless steel. It can be tensioned higher than polyester but less than stainless steel.

Applications for this fabric include ceramic printing with abrasive inks and thermo conductive inks. Its anti-static properties make it ideal for printing electronic circuitry. It is available in mesh counts from 123 up to 470 in 42" bolt widths. Metalized polyester is one of the most expensive screen fabrics costing three to four times the cost of white monofilament polyester. The nickel coating pro-

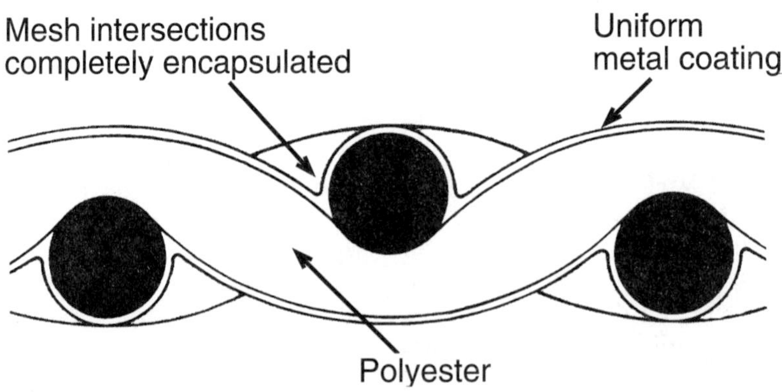

Figure 4-15 Metalized polyester *(Tetko® Inc)*

vides excellent adhesion for all types of stencils including indirect and capillary stencils. The unique coating seals the **knuckles** of the mesh which leaves no areas for ink and stencil residues to be trapped. This gives it excellent ink flow characteristics. Reclaiming is easy, with excellent results.

A word of caution in the use of this fabric: If undue stress is placed on the tensioned fabric, the screen may be damaged beyond use. The nickel coated polyester is somewhat brittle in nature and will not tolerate abuse. Its elasticity is 50 to 75 percent less than polyester. Since two different materials were used in the composition of this fabric, both have different coefficients of stretch. This makes it essential to follow the recommended tensioning procedures or the fabric will be damaged. (See the chart on page 105.) If too great of tension is applied to the fabric it will break at the knuckles. The aspects of tensioning and mounting of mesh will be addressed in Chapter 5. With tension low it will not deliver the proper printing results. Tension must be precise, with no more or less than prescribed.

The fabric specifications for metalized polyester (see page 78) are different than conventional polyester due to the nickel coating placed on top of the polyester. For example, look at a comparison of two fabric types in Figure 4-16. A 240T monofilament polyester has a 40µ thread, a fabric thickness of 65µ, mesh opening of 61µ and a 34% open area. A 240T metalized polyester has a 44µ thread diameter, a 72µ fabric thickness, with a mesh opening of 61µ and 37% open area.

	Monofilament Polyester	Metalized Polyester
Mesh Count	240T	240T
Thread Diameter	40 µ	44 µ
Fabric Thickness	65 µ	72 µ
Mesh Opening	61 µ	61 µ
Open Area	34%	37%
T.W.I.V.	22.1	26.6

Figure 4-16 Monofilament vs. metalized polyester

Low Elongation Mesh

The most recent fabric development promises to be one of major consequence. Fabrics used in the screen printing industry up to this time were developed for industrial filtering applications. There are problems to overcome using these fabrics for screen printing purposes. They will be discussed in Chapter 5. Recently it was realized that improvements in the mesh could initiate superior printing results. A mesh was developed known as **low elongation mesh.** It was produced using a new formulation of polyester exhibiting more stability. A new improved weaving process was also developed to improve the fabric's stability and consistency. It is available in mesh counts from 83 up to 460 in bolt widths from 42" up to 82".

This new fabric has resulted in a number of improvements. It achieves higher tensile strength allowing tension to increase up to fifty percent. Ink goes through the mesh more easily with quicker snap-off, with higher tension. This allows a significant reduction in off-contact. Lower off-contact reduces image elongation and distortion with higher quality fine line designs and halftones. It also improves registration accuracy and decreases squeegee pressure. Decreased squeegee pressure causes less squeegee edge wear, less resharpening of the squeegee, and reduced fabric wear. The fabric increases productivity with higher press speeds by as much as thirty percent with reduced make ready times.

However, this is not without

disadvantages. Increased fabric cost is not a factor since it is only six percent more than white monofilament polyester. But the frames currently used at lower tension levels may not possess the dimensional stability needed to achieve and support this substantial tension increase. This can require a significant investment for replacement with frames suited for this new mesh.

The same effect will trickle down to other stages of the screen printing operation that will need to be upgraded. Other defects hidden in the operation will surface. Press related defects such as press bed uniformity, registration devices, squeegee and flood bar inaccuracies, and ink inconsistencies can cause problems in production. They need to be resolved before the new mesh can be successfully used. Last, screens are more susceptible to damage at these elevated tension levels. Greater care and handling of screens must be exercised throughout the operation.

In summary, a number of hidden costs will arise when implementing low elongation fabric into a screen printing operation. Yet the substantial improvement that this advancement has to offer is the potential of elevating an operation to new levels of quality and performance previously thought impossible. Although this is only the first generation of a completely new screen fabric it has already had an impact on the industry. Further advancements will undoubtedly be made in this area in the future since technological change is just beginning on this important component of the process. The tensioning characteristics of this mesh will be discussed in Chapter 5.

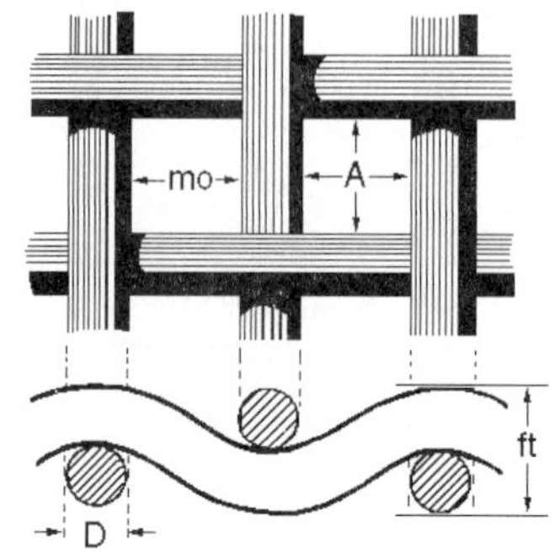

Figure 4-17 Fabric terminology

FABRIC TERMINOLOGY

It is important to have a thorough understanding of the terminology in regard to fabric geometry. Some fabric manufacturers mark mesh specifications along the selvage edge of the mesh. This includes mesh count (in inches or centimeters) thread diameter (in microns) and fabric type (polyester, nylon, and so on). Although a universal standard is not used here, the same basic fabric information is given.

Mesh Count

Mesh count identifies the number of threads per linear unit measure. For example a 390 mesh means 390 threads per inch. In metric countries mesh count is threads per centimeter, so the 390 mesh above is 150 threads per centimeter.

Thread Diameter

Nominal **thread diameter** (D) is indicated by either thousands of an inch or microns. It is far simpler to refer to a thread diameter of 33µ rather than 0.0013 inches.

Fabric Thickness

At the first look one might expect nominal **fabric thickness** (ft) to equal twice the fabric diameter since two threads overlap. This is not the case since the manufacturing process slightly compresses the fabric at the intersections. So a 390T monofilament polyester with a 33µ thread has a 65µ fabric thickness, not 66 microns as expected.

Mesh Opening

Nominal **mesh opening** (mo), as shown in Figure 4-17, is a linear measurement indicating the space between threads. This measurement is theoretically the same in both warp and weft directions. For instance a 390T monofilament polyester has a nominal mesh opening of 32µ.

Open Area

Open area (A), as shown in Figure 4-17, is not an actual measurement but it is determined by calculating the area the fibers occupy and subtracting it from the total area. This leaves the area not occupied by the mesh. This is less accurate than nominal mesh opening since it is a theoretical calculation, while mesh opening is a linear measurement that is more precise.

For example, compare two monofilament polyester fabrics, a 186T and a 215T which both have the same 30% open area. Since they both have the same open area it seems likely they will print similar deposits of ink. This is not necessarily the case. This issue will be explained when addressing ink deposit.

Theoretical Wet Ink Volume

Theoretical wet ink volume (T.W.I.V.) is the mathematical estimation of the amount of ink that is able to pass through a given mesh after the squeegee stroke is made. This number is given in mesh specification charts, which represents the number of cubic centimeters per square meter of the mesh (cm^3/m^2).

This measurement is defined by two mesh parameters. The two dimensions of mesh opening constitutes the base of the ink volume. The fabric thickness determines the column height. These three dimensions form a volume of ink that flows through the mesh as shown in Figure 4-18.

This value is theoretical since it is based on mesh specifications. In spite of rigid quality control standards there are some deviations in the mesh which will affect accuracy. But theoretical wet ink volume can be useful in making rough estimations of ink consumption or in comparing two different meshes for ink deposit.

Another consideration is the fact that this calculation is for ink in a wet state. This will not predict final dry ink film thickness. This is affected by various ink factors such as amounts of solvents, flow agents and additives in the ink.

The importance of these measurements will become apparent in the coming topic of fabric selection. It is also important to note that the fabrics specifications given by the manufacturer are based on samplings of readings taken during manufacture. Fabrics may vary slightly from these specifications due to slight variations in the manufacturing process.

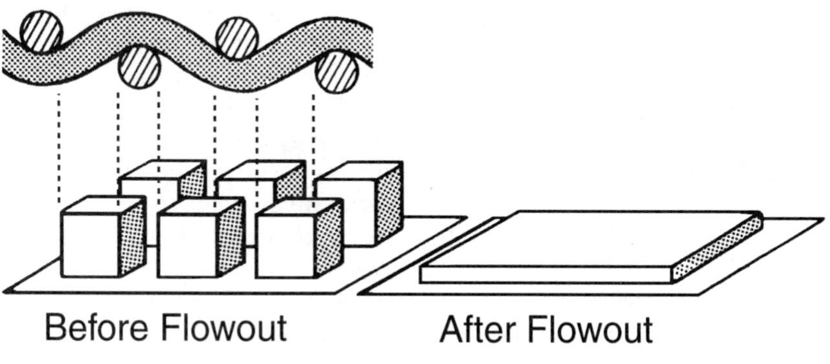

Figure 4-18 Theoretical wet ink volume *(Tetko® Inc)*

EFFECT OF TENSION ON FABRIC PARAMETERS

The Screen Printing Technical Foundation has conducted a study to find the effect that tension plays with regard to mesh parameters.[2] Both standard and low elongation mesh from a variety of manufacturers were used in the study. The following is a brief summary of the study:

Thread Diameter

There is no significant decrease in thread diameter from its initial state to final tension level.

Mesh Count

As tension is increased from its initial state to recommended tension level the mesh count decreases. For example, a 305 monofilament polyester (low elongation) with 40μ thread has an initial mesh count of 309.9. When tensioned to 25 N/cm (Newtons per centimeter), mesh count drops to 289.6.

Fabric Thickness

When tensioned to the recommended level the fabric thickness decreases. For example, a 305 monofilament polyester (low elongation) with 40µ thread has an initial fabric thickness of 66.1µ. When tensioned to 25 N/cm, fabric thickness decreases to 60.8µ.

Mesh Opening Area

As tension is applied to the fabric the mesh opening area increases. With a 305 monofilament polyester (low elongation) with 40µ thread, mesh opening was calculated as the number of square microns in 120 mesh openings. In a non-tensioned state the mesh had a total of 995 square microns mesh opening area. When tensioned to 25 N/cm, mesh opening area increases 33% to 1328 square microns.

Conclusion of the Study

Once the fabric is tensioned to the proper tension mesh count, fabric thickness and mesh opening decreases and thread diameter remains unchanged.

FABRIC SELECTION

When selecting fabric for a specific job there are a number of factors that should be considered. These are: resolution, ink deposit, weaving structure, mesh color, thread type, chemical properties, and substrate type.

Resolution

Although simple in concept there are several aspects to **resolution.**

Mesh Count	Type Size	Line Thickness
355	4 pt.	hairline
305	6 pt.	.5 pt. (.007″)
196	8 pt.	1 pt. (.014″)
156	10 pt.	1.5 pt. (.021″)
83	12 pt.	2 pt. (.028″)
60	14 pt.	2.5 pt. (.035″)
40	18 pt.	3 pt. (.042″)

Figure 4-19 Fabric selection for type

The definition of resolution is the process of making individual parts of an object distinguishable. Another way of saying it is the ability to produce fine details. In simplest terms the fabric must be fine enough to retain small details. With a coarse mesh details may fall through mesh openings and be lost. Common sense tells us that more than one thread is needed to support small details. Otherwise a halftone dot for instance will conform around the thread resulting in a distorted dot shape. With halftones it is recommended that three threads are needed to support each dot to retain its size and shape.

With this in mind the assumption is that the highest mesh count will deliver the finest details, which is not necessarily the case. Selecting a high mesh count to hold fine details in place on fibers does not assure that those details will be printed. The proper perspective requires a look at the stencil in addition to fabric in delivering the resolution desired. There is a relationship between these two elements that determines the final printed resolution. When the mesh opening becomes too small it is difficult to force ink through the openings onto the substrate. This becomes a problem when the mesh opening is smaller than the stencil thickness. The stencil thickness determines the height of the cube of ink sheared through the mesh opening. When the height exceeds the mesh opening it is difficult to shear the ink through the mesh opening. For example, a 40µ capillary film is applied to a 305 monofilament polyester. If a HD thread (40µ) is used the mesh opening is 37µ. This would not be recommended since the 40µ stencil thickness is greater than the mesh opening. The T thread (34µ) with a 43µ mesh opening or the S thread (31µ) with a 47µ mesh opening would produce better results.

The highest resolution is achieved by selecting a mesh count high enough to hold the details with the largest mesh opening to allow ink to flow through. This can best be accomplished by selecting the thinnest diameter thread resulting in the greatest mesh opening. At the highest mesh counts, threads are comparatively thick in relation to the large number of threads in a given dimension, resulting in a small mesh opening. In this instance a coarser mesh count may achieve higher resolution.

A general guideline is given in

Figure 4-19 showing what size of type or line width may be achieved using specified mesh counts. For example, when using a 40 mesh monofilament polyester the smallest type that may be printed is 18 point and 3 point rule (0.042"). Using a high mesh count of 355T, one can print 4 point type and hairline rule. Since these are only general guidelines each shop needs to test for itself what their own limits are.

Fabric is not the sole factor affecting resolution. There are a number of factors that may have some effect on resolution. They are film, stencil, ink, substrate, press and dryer. Ink has a major contributing effect on printing fine line detail. Much different results will occur when using U.V. curing inks than with solvent or water based inks. Due to the number of factors it helps to illustrate why screen printing companies may not all achieve identical results. Another factor that is changing the resolution issue is the advent of high tension fabric. In printing at these elevated tension levels new dynamics are taking place. Initial research indicates that present views on fabrics and their effect on resolution are not necessarily valid with this new fabric. Additional research needs to be conducted to clarify this new dynamic.

Ink Deposit

Another consideration in fabric selection is ink deposit. When a thick ink deposit is desired a coarse mesh is recommended and, conversely, a thin ink deposit requires a high mesh count. For example, a 60 to 80 mesh count is recommended when printing textiles using puff inks. When a thin ink is desired, such as with U.V. curing inks, a mesh count over 300 is required.

Mesh Count	186T	215T
Thread Diameter	55 μ	48 μ
Fabric Thickness	100 μ	85 μ
Mesh Opening	75 μ	64 μ
Open Area	30%	30%
T.W.I.V.	30.0	25.5

Figure 4-20

In screen printing there are two types of ink deposits. Just after ink is sheared onto the substrate a wet ink film is deposited. The wet ink film decreases because of flowout of the ink and evaporation of the vehicle from solvent and water based inks. This then becomes the dry ink film. Measurement of the dry ink film is simple to achieve, but wet film measurements are a bit more complex to conduct.

Now let us look at an example of the role that fabric selection plays with determining ink deposit. A job is printed with white ink on a dark substrate. After examining few prints during make-ready, the white ink appears like a washed out gray color. In spite of attempts to increase ink deposit through various squeegee techniques, improvement in the appearance was not achieved. Since changes in squeegee technique only affect 20 percent of the ink deposit something more drastic would need to be done. Fabric has the greatest potential for affecting ink deposit so this must be changed. It is obvious by now that the proper fabric was not selected. The question is how to determine how coarse of mesh is needed to get the desired ink coverage. Before that question can be answered one needs to look at the fabric structure and how it affects ink deposit. The amount of ink that is metered is largely dependent on the mesh opening which determines two dimensions of the ink volume. The fabric thickness determines the ink column height. Ink is forced through the mesh openings to produce a volume of ink. By evaluating the theoretical wet ink volume (T.W.I.V.) one can determine the optimum combination of mesh opening and fabric thickness to achieve an increase or decrease in ink deposit.

Let's look at two fabrics with the same open area (30%), the 186T and the 215T. See Figure 4-20. We find the nominal mesh opening of the 186T is 75μ and 64μ with the 215T. The 186T has a fabric thickness of 100μ while the 215T has only 85μ. It is clear to see why the theoretical wet ink volume is greater with the 186T. Both the mesh opening and fabric thickness of the 186T is larger so it will deliver more ink onto the substrate (30.0 cm^3/m^2) than the 215T (25.5 cm^3/m^2).

Figure 4-21 Monofilament polyester 355T twill weave

Figure 4-22 Twill weave footprint

Weaving Structure

Until recent advancements were made in weaving technology, fabrics over 280 threads per inch were woven in a twill weave. Now it is possible to produce higher mesh counts of up to 390 in the plain weave. In some mesh counts fabrics are available in either twill or plain weave. There are cases where each weave may be advantageous.

Twill Weave

There are two types of **twill weaves:** single and double twill. In the single twill each thread travels under one and over two threads in one direction. In double twill each thread travels under two and over two in both directions. See Figure 4-21. Due to the difference in weave uneven contact occurs at the point of contact between the screen and substrate with the twill weave. See Figure 4-22. This allows ink to seep out producing a "sawtooth" appearance as shown in Figure 4-25. Although similar in appearance this should not be confused with sawtoothing caused by applying too thin of a stencil coating.

Due to this effect of twill weave on fine line images and halftones there is some concern as to why this fabric is still produced. There are several cases for its production. It is a necessity at the highest mesh counts where it is difficult for the weaving process to get threads to travel between every thread. When the thread diameter is greater than the mesh opening it is classified as a dense weave. With a dense weave using the plain weave, mesh opening and fabric thickness are reduced. This creates a tighter binding as threads are forced into smaller mesh openings. This leads to fabric inconsistencies and excess elongation in the warp direction of the fabric during tensioning. A twill weave is often provided in mesh counts where plain weave is produced.

The twill weave will print a greater ink deposit than the same mesh in a plain weave. Compare the 390T plain weave to the 390T twill weave. Both are woven using the same 34μ thread. Yet with the twill weave fabric thickness is greater with the twill

Figure 4-23 Monofilament polyester 355S plain weave

Figure 4-24 Plain weave footprint

weave (60µ) than with the plain weave (54µ). The twill weave also produces a slightly greater mesh opening (26µ) than the plain weave (25µ). This results in a slightly greater ink column height which in addition to the mesh opening means the twill weave has a greater capacity for ink. Looking at the fabric specifications the theoretical wet ink volume for the twill weave is rated at 9.0 cm^3/m^2 while with the plain weave 7.0 cm^3/m^2.

Plain Weave

The fabric is woven by having every thread travel over one thread and under the next. This procedure is followed in both directions. See Figure 4-23. Superior print results can be achieved with **plain weave** fabric. The contact area of the mesh is more uniform. See Figure 4-24. This structure is less restrictive to ink flow during the printing process. The photo shows the difference in printed result between a twill and plain weave. See Figure 4-25.

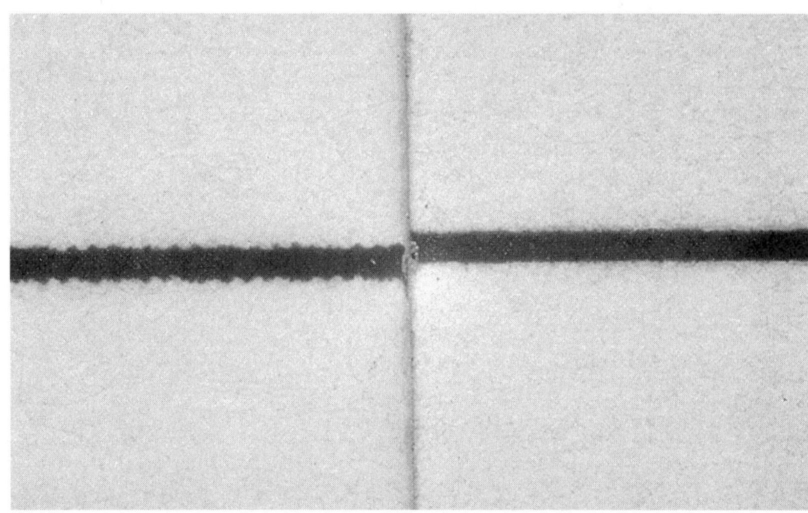

Figure 4-25 Twill vs. plain weave printed results

Mesh Color

In addition to white, fabric is manufactured in yellow, orange, pink and red. These colored fabrics will produce higher quality fine line designs over white fabric with direct emulsion and capillary film stencils as shown in Figure 4-26. With these stencils the fabric is embedded into the emulsion prior to being exposed. This causes light to scatter when the stencil is exposed causing loss of details with white fabrics. Colored fabrics have less light scatter resulting in higher resolution than with the white fabric. See Figure 4-27. Light scatter is absorbed by the colored mesh, requiring 50 to 100% longer stencil exposure times on colored mesh over white mesh.

There is no light scatter problems when using white fabrics with indirect films since the film is exposed before it is adhered to the screen fabric. The fabric does not interfere with exposure in any way. Since white fabric costs about 5% less than colored fabrics as a rule, it would result in some cost savings with indirect film without loss of quality.

Thread Types

When determining which thread type to use there are a number of factors to consider. Thread type affects open area of the mesh. An "HD" thread will give the least open area while the "S" thread offers the most open area. The "S" thread will deliver better quality

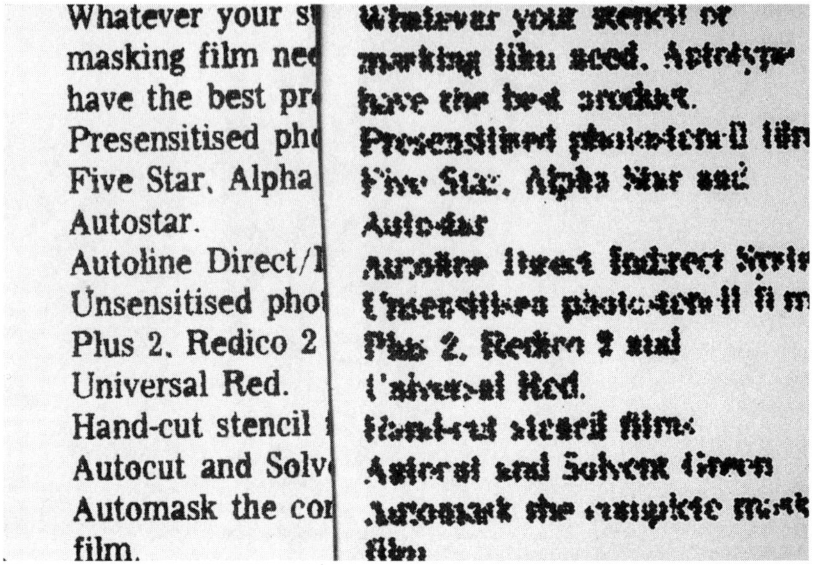

Whatever your s
masking film ne
have the best pr
Presensitised ph
Five Star, Alpha
Autostar.
Autoline Direct/I
Unsensitised pho
Plus 2, Redico 2
Universal Red.
Hand-cut stencil
Autocut and Solv
Automask the co
film.

Figure 4-26 Colored vs. white mesh: printed results

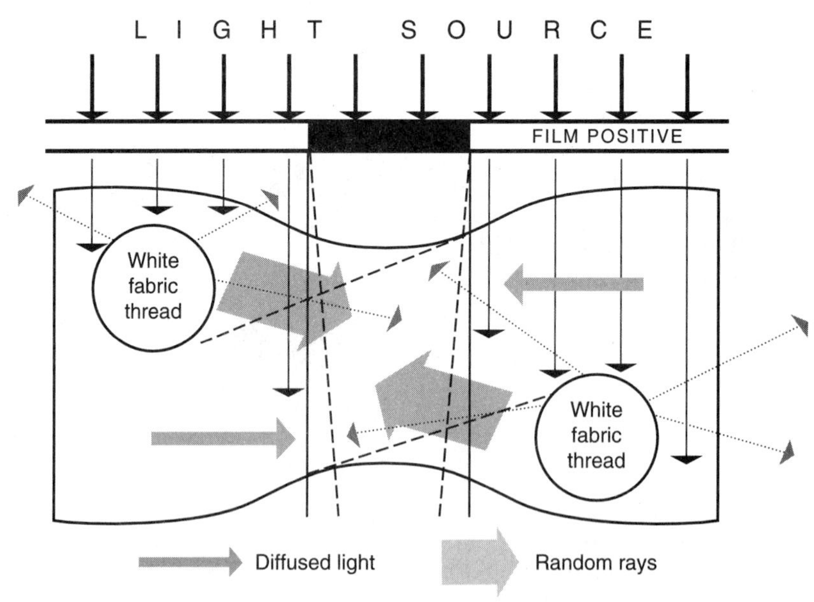

Figure 4-27 Light scatter

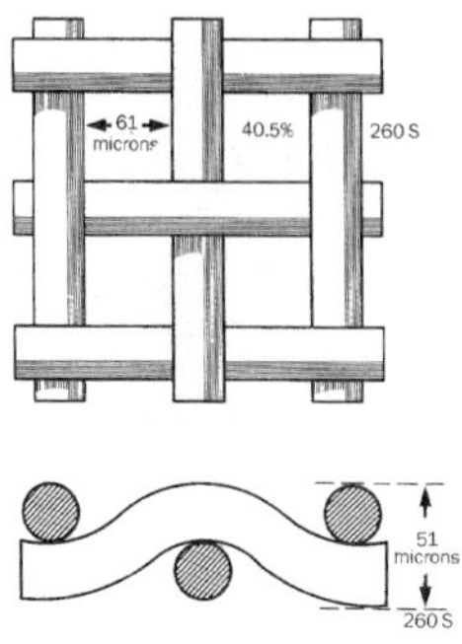

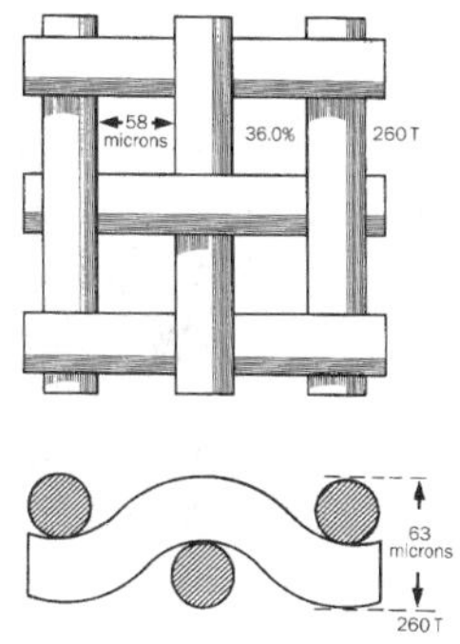

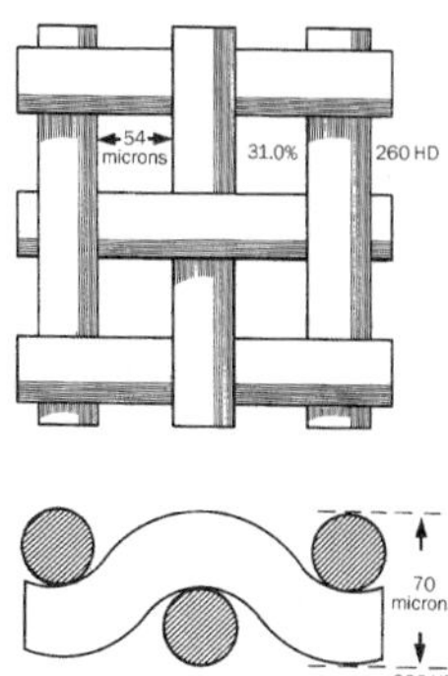

Figure 4-28 Thread types *(Autotype International Ltd.)*

than either the "T" or "HD" threads since there is less thread to interfere with ink transferring through the mesh. See Figure 4-28. Yet the trade off is in lower fabric durability. Each thread type may not be available with every mesh count. When selecting fabric it is important to determine which of the fiber types available is best suited for the job.

When looking at durability an "S" thread is the lowest while the "HD" thread is the highest. Certain inks used for screen printing have a detrimental effect on fabric life. For example, ceramic inks have abrasive particles in their composition. These abrasive particles can rapidly wear out the fabric during printing. The "HD" thread will offer increased durability over the "S" or "T" threads. This is the primary reason to select an "HD" thread. For greatest durability a metal fabric should be selected.

	420SL	420S
Thread Diameter	27 μ	31 μ
Fabric Thickness	43 μ	47 μ
Mesh Opening	30 μ	23 μ
Open Area	25%	14%
T.W.I.V.	10.8	6.6

Figure 4-29 Fabric comparison

A new ultra thin fabric, "SL," is now available in limited mesh counts. The advantages of a thinner thread diameter can be seen by comparing the specifications of a 420S to a 420SL monofilament polyester. In comparing these fabrics, the "SL" thread is 4μ (microns) less in diameter, as is done in Figure 4-29. This ultra thin thread results in a decrease in mesh opening and open area since there is less thread present. This results in more area available to allow ink to be held. This is evident by the theoretical wet ink volume of 10.8 cm^3/m^2 for the "SL" thread greater than the 6.6 cm^3/m^2 for the "S" thread. This results in greater ink deposition with the "SL" thread. Also the thinner thread is desirable when printing fine details.

Chemical Properties

Due to the versatile nature of the screen printing process, a wide range of inks and coatings may be used for these varied applications. These compounds have varied chemical compositions in some cases made up of acids, strong solvents, etc. When selecting fabrics one must be certain that they will be resistant to the chemicals they are to be exposed to. The fabric manufacturer provides information to assist in identifying the fabric suited for the chemicals in question, whether polyester, nylon, or one of the metal fabrics.

Polyester has low moisture absorption and resistance to most acids. Yet it has low resistance to alkaline solutions especially at high temperatures. Nylon has less resistance to moisture with high resistance to most alkaline solutions. It is sensitive to acids especially at high concentrations. Stainless steel is the ideal fabric for use with various chemicals since it is resistant to nearly all chemicals, acids and caustic chemicals.

Substrate Type

Screen printing is often called upon to print on a variety of textured substrates. In order to obtain the proper transfer of ink this requires the fabric and stencil to come in contact with the irregular surface. In these applications nylon is better able to conform to irregular surfaces due to its elastic nature. Polyester is more stable and is less able to conform to these irregular surfaces.

Using fabric with the greatest mesh opening will allow ink to flow into all image areas of the uneven substrate. Placing image orientation so the image is not parallel with threads of the mesh will also produce improved printed results on uneven substrates. Other factors affecting uneven substrates will be discussed in chapters on stencils, squeegee, and ink.

KEY TERMS

fabric thickness
knuckles
low elongation mesh
mesh count
mesh opening
micron
monofilament
multifilament
Newtons per centimeter (N/cm)
open area
plain weave
resolution
thread diameter
theoretical wet ink volume (T.W.I.V)
twill weave

REVIEW QUESTIONS

1. What advantages does low elongation mesh offer over conventional mesh?
2. What are the differences between multifilament and monofilament fabrics?
3. Under what circumstances should monofilament nylon be used?
4. Which fabric would be most suitable when printing fine line or halftone images?
5. Which type of fabric should be used when printing a heavy ink deposit?

NOTES

[1] Industry Profile Study (Fairfax: Screenprinting and Graphic Imaging Association International, 1990).

[2] Dawn M. Hohl and Dennis D. Hunt, *Physical Changes in Polyester Mesh During Tensioning* (Fairfax: Screen Printing Technical Foundation, 1992).

Tetko Monofilament Polyester Fabric Specifications

mesh count	thread diameter	mesh opening	fabric thickness	open area
16 T	350µ	1180µ	740µ	59%
25 S	275µ	750µ	520µ	53%
33 S	220µ	530µ	405µ	50%
40 S	200µ	425µ	355µ	46%
60 T	120µ	295µ	215µ	50%
60 HD	145µ	275µ	265µ	43%
76 T	120µ	212µ	210µ	41%
76 HD	145µ	177µ	290µ	31%
83 SL	70µ	240µ	120µ	60%
83 T	100µ	200µ	170µ	44%
92 T	100µ	180µ	175µ	41%
110 T	80µ	150µ	135µ	42%
123 HD	80µ	118µ	135µ	34%
137 T	64µ	115µ	110µ	41%
137 HD	70µ	108µ	122µ	35%
156 T	64µ	92µ	112µ	32%
175 T	55µ	90µ	90µ	38%
195 T	55µ	70µ	95µ	29%
230 T	48µ	55µ	84µ	25%
230 HD	55µ	52µ	100µ	21%
240 T	40µ	62µ	65µ	37%
260 T	40µ	58µ	65µ	34%
280 T	34µ	52µ	55µ	33%
280 HD	40µ	50µ	66µ	29%
305 T	34µ	44µ	57µ	28%
305 HD	40µ	38µ	66µ	20%
330 T	34µ	40µ	58µ	27%
355 S	31µ	38µ	52µ	28%
355 T	34µ	33µ	59µ	21%
390 SL	27µ	35µ	44µ	28%
390 S	31µ	32µ	52µ	23%
390 T	34µ	25µ	54µ	14%
420 T	34µ	22µ	66µ	13%
470 T	34µ	23µ	57µ	18%

Tetko Calendared Polyester Fabric Specifications

mesh count	thread diameter	mesh opening	fabric thickness	open area
305 T (pw)	41µ	42µ	50µ	25.6%
355 T (pw)	41µ	30µ	55µ	17.9%
355 T (tw)	41µ	30µ	55µ	17.9%
390 T (pw)	43µ	24µ	55µ	12.8%
390 T (tw)	43µ	24µ	60µ	12.8%
420 T (tw)	43µ	18µ	60µ	8.7%
470 T (tw)	40µ	15µ	60µ	7.4%

Tetko Metalized Polyester Fabric Specifications

mesh count	thread diameter	mesh opening	fabric thickness	open area
60 T	124µ	285µ	225µ	47%
137 T	72µ	110µ	118µ	35%
156 T	74µ	87µ	118µ	28%
195 T	64µ	61µ	107µ	24%
230 T	58µ	57µ	92µ	26.5%
240 T	46µ	56µ	72µ	30%
260 T	45µ	53µ	75µ	29%
280 T	40µ	49µ	64µ	30%
305 S	37µ	44µ	54µ	30%
305 T	42µ	39µ	64µ	23%
355 T	42µ	26µ	65µ	15%
470 T	43µ	20µ	74µ	10%

Fabric Tension and Frames

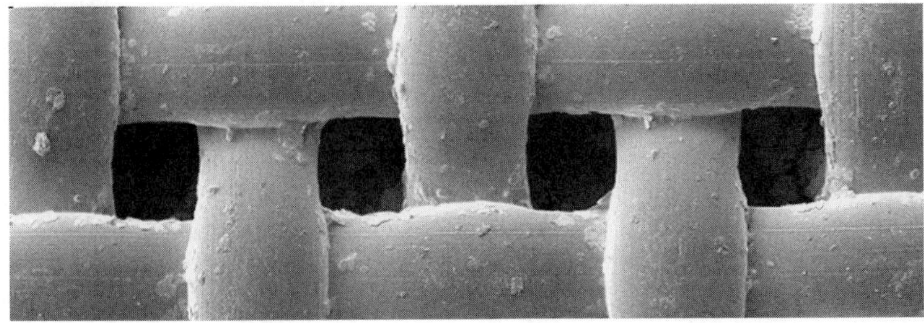

Fabric is the most important component in the screen printing process. It is an essential part of the process but should not be seen in the ink deposit. Yet to function properly it must be made stable through the tensioning process. The frame also assists in maintaining proper tension throughout the screen printing process. The importance of fabric tension cannot be overemphasized. It affects every stage of the process from stencil making to its use on press.

Yet the tensioning process is often overlooked or taken for granted. Control of the screen printing process is very difficult without monitoring of screen tension. This chapter explores various aspects of fabric tensioning and reveals methods to control this important aspect of the process.

CONSEQUENCES OF IMPROPER TENSION

There are three ways that fabric can be tensioned improperly. Tension can be excessive, inadequate or inconsistent within the tensioned area. Each creates problems in the screen printing operation.

Insufficient Tension

Fabric tensioned below its recommended level will cause two problems. There will be a reduction in the mesh opening and poor release or screen snap-off after printing occurs. There are a number of consequences to these problems.

Reduced Mesh Opening

- Poor passage of ink
- Visible mesh marks

Inadequate Screen Snap-off

- Poor edge definition and print detail
- Elongation of image size
- Slower press speed
- Inaccurate registration of multicolor images
- Inconsistent flood coat

The off-contact distance is increased instead of correcting screen tension to improve the screen snap-off. Unfortunately this results in further adverse consequences:

- Further registration problems
- Greater elongation of image size
- Reduced fabric and stencil durability
- Additional squeegee wear

Excessive Tension

When tension is applied beyond the limits of the screen fabric it becomes permanently damaged. The fabric is affected in several ways:

- Fabric stability is destroyed
- Fabric durability is significantly affected
- Image size changes during long press runs

Tension Inconsistency

When improper tensioning procedures are used the tension may not be consistent within areas of the tensioned screen. There are several potential consequences to this situation:

- Distortion of mesh geometry causing an uneven ink deposit across image
- Inaccurate registration of multicolor images
- Irregular flood coat on screen

FABRIC TENSION CHARACTERISTICS

The previous chapter dealt with the selection of the proper fabric for a given job. This chapter is concerned with the tensioning characteristics of each fabric type. Each has differences that affect their behavior with regard to tensioning as shown in Figure 5-1. Tensioning procedures also vary due to differences in composition and structure. For instance, tensioning is different for stainless steel mesh than with synthetics such as polyester. Tension specifications for each of the fabrics are listed at the rear of this chapter.

Silk

Silk was the first fabric used for the screen printing process. Yet due to its composition and structure it has a low tensile strength, is lacking in stability and can be tensioned to a minimal level of 7-9 N/cm. Due to this lack of stability there are problems with poor print quality and inconsistent registration.

Nylon

Nylon is now used as a replacement for silk. Yet nylon has greater moisture absorption and greater elongation. It can be tensioned to levels similar to polyester but is less stable. It is used primarily for printing on uneven surfaces. In the past nylon was dampened before tensioning to aid in the process, but is no longer recommended by fabric manufacturers as it is not deemed worth the effort.

Polyester

Polyester is an important improvement over nylon and silk due to its greater tensile strength and stability. Yet early synthetic fabrics were developed for high volume filtering uses and are less than ideal for use with screen printing. Once synthetic fabrics are stretched they do not remain at the same tension level over time. New mesh is the least stable when it is tensioned for the first time. When stretched the fabric reacts by settling to a lower tension level than initially set. This is referred to as **cold flow.** The tension loss is shown by the graph of a typical monofilament polyester fabric in Figure 5-1.

A 305T monofilament polyester is initially stretched to a recommended level of 13 N/cm. The greatest tension loss occurs within

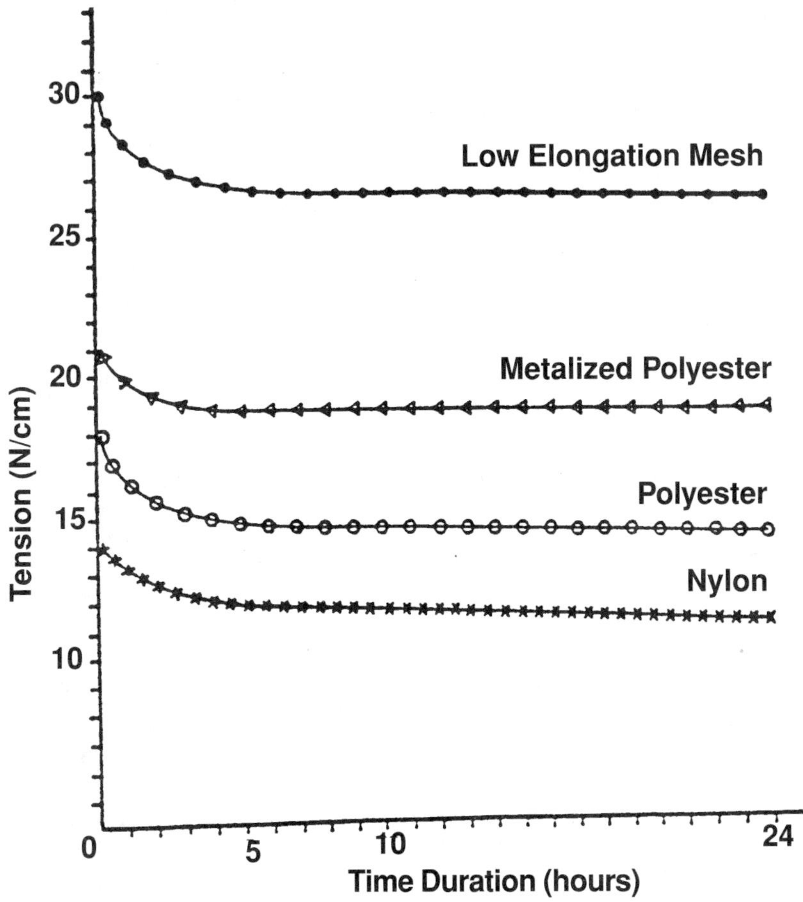

Figure 5-1 Fabric tension loss *(Tetko® Inc)*

the first 20 minutes after it is first tensioned where it drops 1.5 N/cm. After that point the decline in tension is much more gradual, down to 10 N/cm ten hours after initial tensioning.[1]

If greater force is applied to the fabric beyond the elastic limit of the fabric (or yield point) the fabric memory will be permanently damaged. This prevents initially over tensioning of the fabric allowing it to drop to the desired tension level. There are a number of different approaches dealing with cold flow. The issue of tension loss has led to the growth in popularity of self-tensioning frames. After each press run and screen reclaiming, it can be retensioned to the recommended tension level. The self-tensioning frame is used to compensate for the inability of the fabric to retain tension.

Yet self-tensioning frames and mechanical tensioning devices do not continue to apply force after the fabric slackens due to cold flow and tension loss. Tension should be applied in stages to effectively compensate for the loss. Pneumatic systems on the other hand continue to apply force during the tensioning process. The clamps maintain the same tension level and force as the fabric experiences cold flow. This device is one of the best ways to compensates for cold flow. The need to readjust the tension setting after initial tensioning is reduced. Maintaining this force for 30 to 60 minutes stabilized the fabric. The longer it is allowed to stabilize the less tension loss occurs.

Tension specifications for polyester are given at the end of the chapter. There are three tension levels given in the specifications. Standard level, high and maximum tension standards. These are based on the degree of tensioning equipment and skill that a screen department possesses. Not everyone can successfully tension fabric to the highest level. The best approach is to start at the standard level and work to higher standards over time.

Low Elongation Mesh

Cold flow has been a significant problem with monofilament polyester with screen printers for a number of years. A new mesh was developed specifically for screen printing to deal with the problems associated with cold flow. This is known as **low elongation mesh**. Every aspect of the new fabric was in response to screen printers needs.

A new polyester compound was developed with an increased molecular weight. Next, methods for extrusion of the fibers were changed to improve its characteristics and performance. Weaving techniques were also changed to equalize the stretch or elongation of the fabric in the warp and weft directions. And finally a finishing process was used to heat set the mesh to stabilize elongation. This provided a breakthrough in mesh providing a mesh specifically designed for screen printing use.

The advantages are primarily two-fold: greater fiber strength and stability. Fabric can be tensioned to higher tensions than ever before. A standard 110T monofilament polyester is tensioned 28 to 39 N/cm. A 110T low elongation mesh may be tensioned 32 to 51 N/cm. Less off-contact distance is needed with higher tension permitting faster press speeds with improved registration.

Lets look at a comparison of tension loss with low elongation mesh and standard mesh, using the same staged tensioning procedure. Standard mesh will lose typically between 10 and 20% of the tension after 24 hours while a low elongation will loose 6 to 12% tension over the same time.[1]

Low elongation mesh has greater stability since the elongation (stretch) is equalized in both warp and weft directions. Standard monofilament polyester requires different elongation in the warp and weft directions due to differences in the weaving process. This causes the fibers in the warp direction to be less stable than the weft fibers. The equalization of elongation in warp and weft directions gives greater stability of the final screen and improved printing uniformity over a print run.

Newman Roller Mesh

This fabric was developed specifically to meet the needs of screen printers. Over four years of research and engineering went into the development of this mesh, giving it superior strength and durability with lower elongation. Improved printing efficiency and print quality are achieved with both manual and automatic presses. This mesh has been printed with over one million impressions under actual industry testing to verify results.

This fabric is designed to be tensioned to very high tension. The coarsest mesh may be tensioned to levels up to 120 N/cm. The primary advantage of high tension is that lower off-contact is required. This results in less problems with registration on press, higher press speeds, and better quality transfer of ink.

TENSION MEASUREMENT

Due to the importance of fabric tensioning, an accurate method of measuring fabric tension is required. There are two primary methods of measuring fabric tension. One method is to measure the elongation or extension of the fabric; the second is to use a tension meter. There are two goals in measuring tension. The first is to determine the level of tension achieved through the stretching process. The second goal is to evaluate consistency of tension within various areas of the screen. Both are equally important in producing a properly tensioned screen.

Fabric Elongation or Extension Measurement

In order to tension the screen fabric it must be elongated or increased in size. One of the oldest ways to evaluate tension is to measure the degree of **fabric elongation** or extension. The principle of measuring the stretch of the fabric is simple. First, fabric is marked with four marks on the fabric before it is stretched. Two marks are placed 20 inches apart in the warp direction and two in the weft direction. If the mesh specifications require a 3% elongation of the screen fabric, the mesh is stretched until the marks measure 20.6″ apart in both directions. See Figure 5-2.

A ruler for measuring fabric elongation has been made by fabric manufacturers. The procedure for its use is simple. The ruler is placed on the fabric and two marks are made on two sides of the ruler before tension is applied. The ruler can be used to measure the stretch of the fabric as it is tensioned. There are graduated marks on the ruler to determine how much the fabric has been

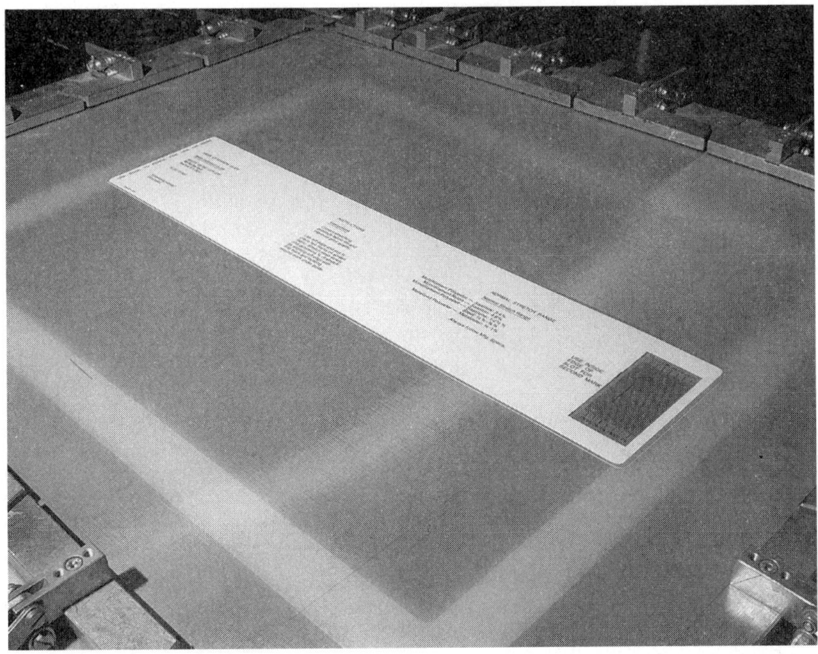

Figure 5-2 Fabric extension measurement

Figure 5-3 Mechanical tension meter

stretched, up to seven percent. Monofilament polyester should be stretched from 1 to 2.5%.

This method is not very precise, and cannot be used to measure uniformity of tension across the surface. It can only be used to evaluate tension as a whole in its two directions, warp and weft. With conventional polyester mesh the weave is different in the warp and weft directions. This requires slightly less tension in the weft direction, than the warp. Lastly this method is not practical to evaluate tension loss after screen has been used.

Tension Meter

A **tension meter** is a simple but accurate method of evaluating screen tension. It can be used as a tool to assist in the tensioning process and to continually evaluate screen tension over the life of a screen. There are two types of tension meter:, mechanical and electronic. Both function on the same basic principle and give a reading in newtons per centimeter (N/cm).

There are no international or federal standards for the measurement newtons per centimeter. Each manufacturer of meters has its own standard. Surprisingly, the standard varies only a few newtons between manufacturers. It is important to be careful not to use meters from different manufacturers indiscriminately as a lack of consistency of readings will occur. One way to eliminate this situation is to purchase all meters from the same manufacturer to maintain consistency.

Mechanical Tension Meter

A mechanical tension meter, as shown in Figure 5-3, works on a simple principle. The meter is a weighted device that causes the screen to move in relation to the weight. The meter will move more for a screen with low tension than one that is tensioned higher. The meter measures meter movement and translates it into a reading of N/cm. A reading of 7 N/cm would be a low reading by current standings, and a 50 N/cm reading is much higher.

The meter measures tension primarily in a linear direction. Two separate readings are required, one in each fabric direction (warp and weft). Until recently, meters that would read up to 25 N/cm were adequate. Now, with mesh capable of being tensioned to higher levels, mechanical meters are available that will measure up to 130 N/cm marked in 0.5 and 1 N/cm increments.

Mechanical tension meters are sturdy in construction but should be handled carefully for best results. They should be kept in the storage case when not being used to protect them from damage. The portion of the meter that contacts the screen should not be placed in contact with other surfaces or meter accuracy may be affected.

Electronic Tension Meter

This device is similar in concept to a mechanical device except accuracy is much greater. An electronic meter, as shown in Figure 5-4, measures tension to a tenth of a N/cm while a mechanical meter measures to only one-half of a N/cm. It offers a digital display for fast and accurate measurements. There are two units that make up an electronic tension meter: the measuring head and the digital meter. The head is heavily weighted using an electronic component that measures the force on the screen surface. This force is electronically measured and converted to a digital display. This greater accuracy is at a cost several times that of a mechanical meter. This greater accuracy is more than needed for most screen printers. Yet the electronic meter is useful as a control to assure accuracy of mechanical meters in use.

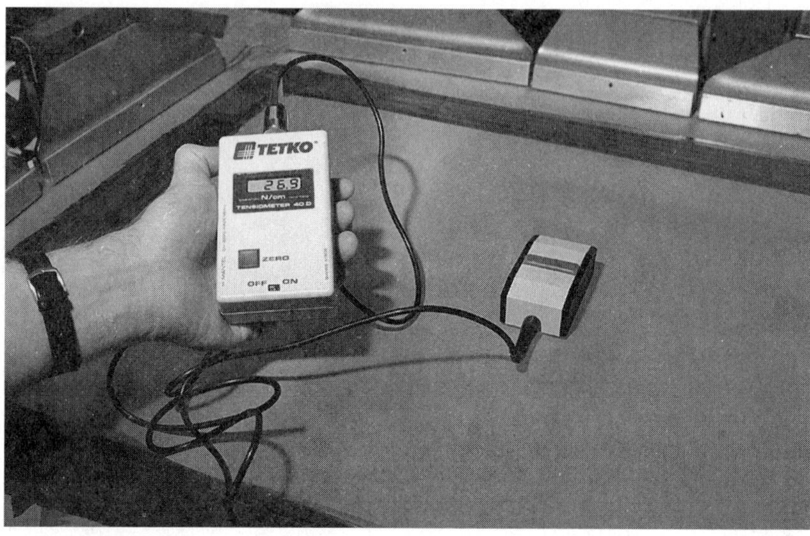

Figure 5-4 Electronic tension meter

Tension Readings

Another issue of importance with regard to tension measurement is the location of the measurements. Taking just one measurement at the screen center is acceptable during early stages of tensioning but is inadequate later in the process. Multiple tension readings should be taken. This assists in evaluating the accuracy of the screen mounting process and determines whether the corners of the mesh have been pre-softened adequately.

It is a wise practice to measure the corner tension of the frame during the tensioning process to watch for excess tension in the corners. After the screen has been tensioned to its recommended level the consistency should be checked across the screen. This is evaluated by taking measurements at a minimum of five locations on the screen. Take two measurements at each point, one in the warp and another in the weft direction.

The position of the five points is established by dividing the free mesh area of the screen into four equal quadrants. The center of the

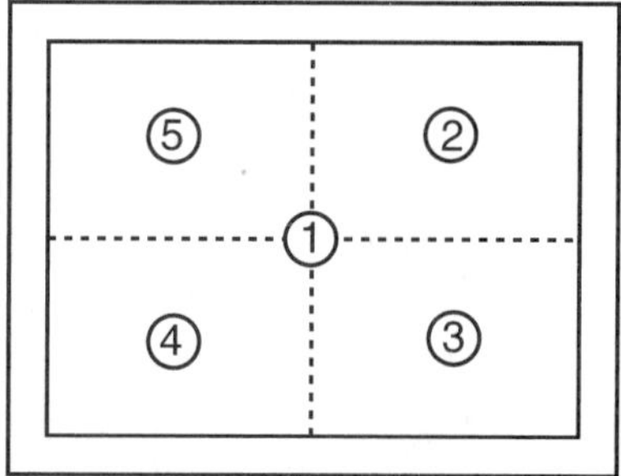

Figure 5-5 Five point tension

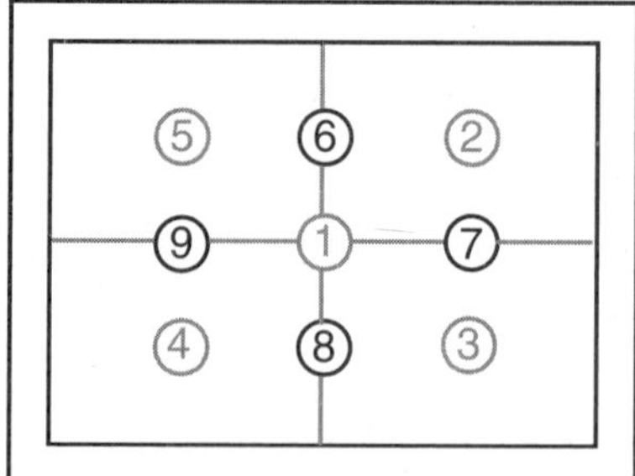

Figure 5-6 Nine point tension

Type of Accuracy Required	Allowable Variance in N/cm
High Quality Job	± 0.5 N/cm
Average Quality Job	± 1.0 N/cm
Minimum Quality	± 1.0 N/cm

Figure 5-7 Tension consistency within screen

Type of Accuracy Required	Allowable Variance in N/cm
Exact Register	1.0 N/cm
Average Register	1.5 N/cm
Poor Register	3.0 N/cm
Minimum Requirement	over 3.0 N/cm

Figure 5-8 Consistency between screens

four quadrants forms the first point, or the center of the screen. The center of each of the four quadrants becomes a point of measurement. See Figure 5-5. All points of measurement are clear of the frame sides, within the image area of the screen. This provides for accurate evaluation of the screen tension consistency to be determined. If for instance tension is lower in one corner than the other three, the low corner will not accurately register with an image printed using a consistently tensioned screen.

If a more comprehensive analysis of screen tension consistency is desired, measure nine points on the surface as shown in Figure 5-6. The additional four points are at the midpoints of the four outer points of measurement. Yet making additional measurements may not be better in actual practice since it increases the data to be collected, recorded and evaluated. The overwhelming volume of data collected may result in the information not being used effectively.

Once the tension data is collected it should be compared to in-house standards established to monitor screen tension performance. This can be used to determine the effective life of a screen over the course of time. The screen is only changed once it does not meet those tension standards.

Screen Tension Uniformity

Fabric tension consistency has two aspects. The first is consistency of tension within the screen itself. The lack of tension consistency within the screen will distort registration of the image. The amount of misregistration is directly proportional to the degree of variance in tension. See Figure 5-7.

"... the repeatability in screen tensioning remains an important contributor to register exactness in a large, overall sense."[2]

When the quality requirements for the job are high, the maximum variation in tension should not exceed ± 0.5 N/cm. The normal and minimum acceptable variation in tension is ± 1.0 N/cm. Any greater variation than ± 1.0 N/cm will lead to unacceptable variation in register.[3]

A second factor to consider is a difference in tension when more than one screen is used. If tension varies between screens printed for multicolor work registration will change accordingly. When a high degree of registration is required, such as with four color process, a variation of tension should not exceed 1.0 N/cm between screens used. Where accuracy is slightly less a variation of 1.5 N/cm is acceptable. Where registration accuracy is not as critical a variation of 3.0 N/cm is acceptable. If tension varies more than 3.0 N/cm, accuracy of registration will be at a minimal level.[4] See Figure 5-8.

TENSIONING DEVICES

Screen printing frames can be divided into two types: fixed and retensionable. Fixed or stationary frames require a separate mechanism to tension the screen mesh after which it is glued to the frame. Retensionable frames have a tensioning mechanism built into the frame itself. Refer to Figure 5-9.

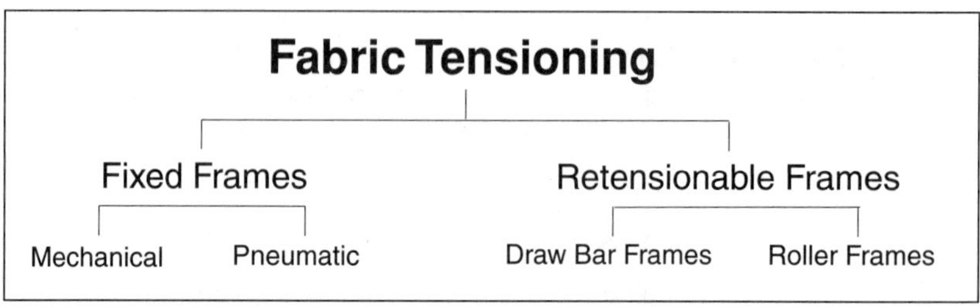

Figure 5-9 Fabric tensioning

Fixed Frame Systems

Fixed or stationary **frames** require a "stretch and glue" approach to the tensioning of fabric. After fabric is tensioned it is glued to the frame. There are a number of devices for tensioning screen mesh with fixed frames. Some of the less expensive tensioning devices at first appearance seem to have great merit. Yet after close examination they usually have difficulty in applying tension consistently to all areas of the fabric. It's a case where you get what you pay for. The only system that should be considered is one that consistently tensions the mesh. There are two types of tensioning devices for use with fixed frames: mechanical and pneumatic tensioning devices.

Mechanical Tensioning Devices

This type of stretcher applies mechanical force to screen fabric that is held in clamps. A **mechanical tensioning unit** is made up of movable sides or tracks that can be adjusted to accommodate a range of frame sizes from small to large. Each track has individual clamps (6 inches in width) that glide back and forth. The clamps are used to hold the fabric during the tensioning process. In some cases only two of the tracks are movable to apply force to the screen fabric in warp and weft directions. Tensioning is achieved with simple mechanical action. A wrench handle or wheel rotates a gear that causes the movable track to apply force to the screen fabric. The screen fabric expands as force is applied. Each individual clamp allows for expansion of the fabric, keeping the threads parallel and maintaining the proper mesh geometry. See Figure 5-10.

ADVANTAGES

- Mechanical tensioning devices may be used to produce a number of small frames at one time.
- Mechanical tensioning devices may be used to produce a screen where the mesh is biased or applied at an angle on the frame. Fabric is tensioned by applying force parallel to the threads and then the frame is glued to the mesh at the desired angle. The stretcher must be adjusted to a larger size to glue the frame at an angle, thus a larger piece of fabric is needed.

DISADVANTAGES

- The mechanical stretcher has a specific range of frame sizes that it can produce from small to large. If a larger frame is desired a larger tensioning device must be purchased.
- The tensioning device achieves a designated tension level after which the fabric is adhered to the frame. Once the fabric is cut free of the tension device the force of the tensioning is transferred to the frame and deflects inward slightly. This is referred to as a "cut off tension loss." This loss is in direct proportion to the structural integrity of the frame. Stronger frames suffer from less "cut off loss" than weak ones. Most mechanical stretching units do not prebow the frame and experience this tension loss.

Figure 5-10 Mechanical system

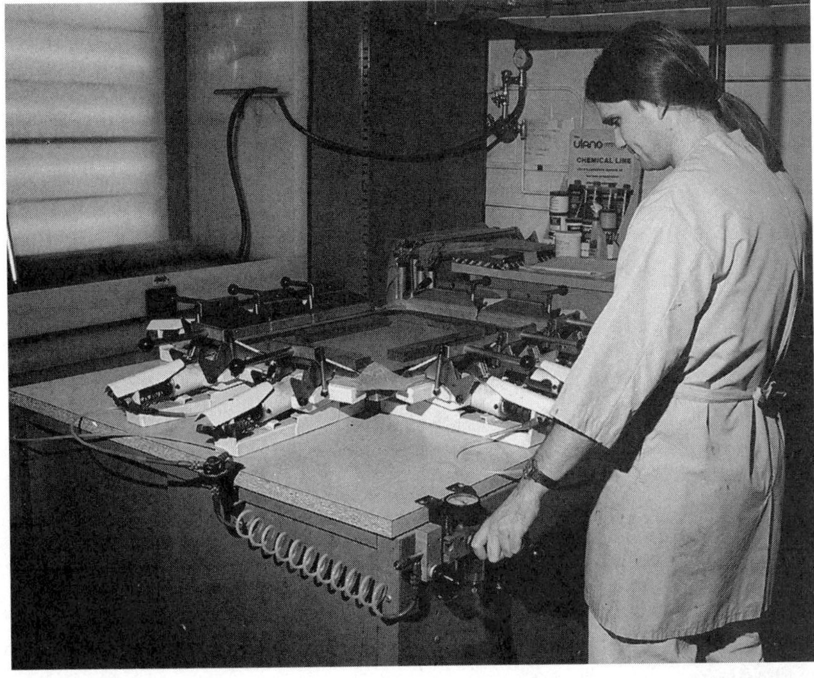

Figure 5-11 Pneumatic system

Pneumatic Tensioning Devices

Pneumatic tensioning devices use air pressure to exert force to tension screen fabric to its recommended level. A pneumatic system is made up of individual units that are arranged based on the size of the frame. A table 30 inches larger (in both dimensions) than the largest frame to be tensioned should be used to place individual clamping units. Each unit is made up of two jaws that are used to hold the screen mesh firmly in place while tension is applied. The jaws are connected to a piston that moves within a cylinder of each unit. As air is introduced into the cylinder, pressure is applied to the piston which in turn exerts force on the fabric, until the desired degree of tension is achieved. Each unit is easily interconnected by air lines to a regulator, which adjusts air pressure to the cylinders. As air pressure is increased the fabric tension is increased. Air pressure is supplied to the regulator from the air supply (air compressor). See Figure 5-11.

ADVANTAGES

- Pneumatic systems are easily expandable by adding units for increased frame size.
- Pneumatic systems achieve simultaneous four way stretch. Optimum tension is achieved in both warp and weft directions.

- Individual units allows the fabric to naturally expand as tension is applied. This keeps the threads parallel, achieving the optimum mesh geometry with uniform mesh openings.
- The adjustable nature of this system helps to minimize fabric waste.
- Pneumatic tensioning devices place a pre-bowing action on the frame to counteract the transfer of force to the frame after it is glued in place. This results in no significant loss of tension after the screen is removed from the tensioning device.

DISADVANTAGES

- Only one frame can be tensioned at a time with a pneumatic stretching device.
- Biasing the mesh on the frame is difficult to accomplish using a pneumatic device.

Retensionable Frame System

A **retensionable** or self-tensioning **frame,** as shown in Figure 5-12, has a mechanism built in for stretching the screen mesh. This makes it possible to re-tension the fabric each time the screen is reused. There are two retensionable frame types: **roller frames** and **draw bar frames**. Although there are a number of different designs of each produced by various manufacturers, the most popular types will be discussed.

ADVANTAGES

- Fabric can be adjusted to maintain optimum tension level each time the screen is reused.
- The life of the screen fabric is potentially increased.
- Less fabric is wasted over some stretching systems.
- No adhesives are needed to adhere screen to frame, eliminating odors and cost of adhesives.
- Greater throughput can be achieved since a number of screens can be stretched simultaneously instead of individually on a stretching device.

DISADVANTAGES

- Retensionable frames are usually heavier than fixed frames due to the built in tensioning mechanisms.
- Very large frames can be difficult to handle.
- Fabric must not be biased on retensionable frames since tension must be applied parallel to the fibers of the mesh to keep mesh openings perfectly square.
- Training of employees in proper use of retensionable frames is critical to achieve the greatest possible benefit.

Figure 5-12 Retensionable frame *(Stretch Devices Inc.)*

DRAW BAR FRAMES A draw bar frame is made up of an outer frame with bolts that extend to inner draw bars on each of the four sides. Fabric is held in each draw bar by a plastic rod that locks the fabric in place. As the bolts on each of the four sides are rotated force is applied to the

Figure 5-13 Draw bar frame

Figure 5-14 Roller frame

screen fabric to achieve the desired tension level. A draw bar frame is commonly used with stainless steel mesh. See Figure 5-13.

ROLLER FRAMES A roller frame is made up of rollers that act as the sides of the frame. Fabric is attached to each roller using a plastic strip or rod. Each roller is rotated to apply tension to fabric using a wrench. A lock bolt is then tightened to hold each roller in place. In some cases one frame side is rectangular in shape (and does not rotate) to facilitate mounting the frame in the press. See Figure 5-14.

TENSIONING PROCEDURES

The procedure for tensioning the fabric can be used to compensate to reduce the effects of cold flow. The tension procedure used is critical in reaching the most stable tension results. There are several approaches based on the tensioning device and type of fabric used.

Fabric Loading

It is important to inspect the frame for any nicks or burrs on contact areas of the frame that can cause the fabric to break during the tensioning process. The positioning of the screen fabric into the tensioning mechanism is important regardless of the tensioning devices used. This is also true with self-tensioning frames. It is important that tension is applied parallel to the threads in both the warp and weft directions. When tension is applied at an angle to the threads, uniform tension is not reached and the threads are no longer completely parallel. This causes the square mesh openings to become distorted and thus interferes with the printed result. It can also lead to fabric breakage. The fabric should be aligned using a selvage or other edge that is perfectly straight. This edge should be aligned with the clamp before it is locked into place.

Corner Adjustments

Tensioning devices and self-tensioning frames are prone to developing greater tension in the corners than in the center. Excess corner tension will lead to premature screen breakage and tension loss. Excess tension buildup must be prevented by slackening or softening the corners of the fabric in the tensioning clamps.

Corner adjustments, as shown in Figure 5-15, must be made prior to tensioning of the mesh with stretch and glue systems and may not be changed after the fabric is fully tensioned. A small amount of slack is introduced in the corners. If properly done the tension in the corners will not exceed that in the center once the final tension has been reached. If the corners have been pre-softened too much, tension in the corners will be lower than in the center. The proper technique can be mastered after some trial and error. With self-tensioning frames it can be done before or after fabric has been tensioned. Post-softening must be done each time the fabric is retensioned to prevent excess tension buildup in the corners with self-tensioning frames.

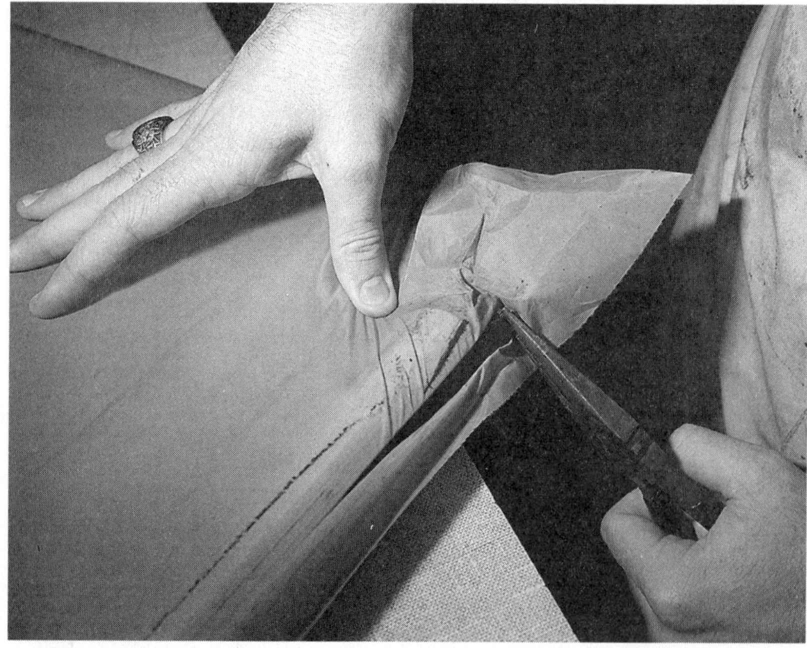

Figure 5-15 Corner adjustment

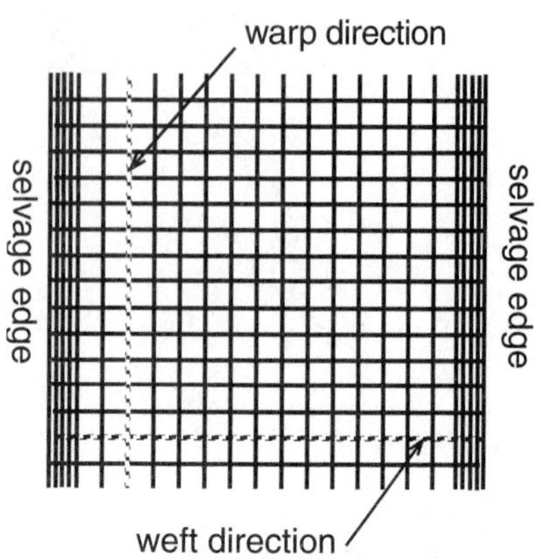

Figure 5-16 Warp vs. weft

Warp and Weft

There are two thread directions in a bolt of fabric: the **"warp"** and the **"weft."** The threads that run the entire length of the bolt are the warp threads. The weft threads are shorter, as they run only the width of the bolt. See Figure 5-16. The warp threads of standard monofilament polyester have greater elongation since they are not as straight as the weft threads due to the weaving process. This requires greater stretch in the warp direction to achieve the same tension as in the weft direction. Low elongation mesh does not have this problem since the elongation is nearly equal in both warp and weft directions.

Mechanical Tensioning Procedures

1. The mechanical stretcher is adjusted to match frame size.
2. Frame is placed in the stretcher below the level of the fabric.

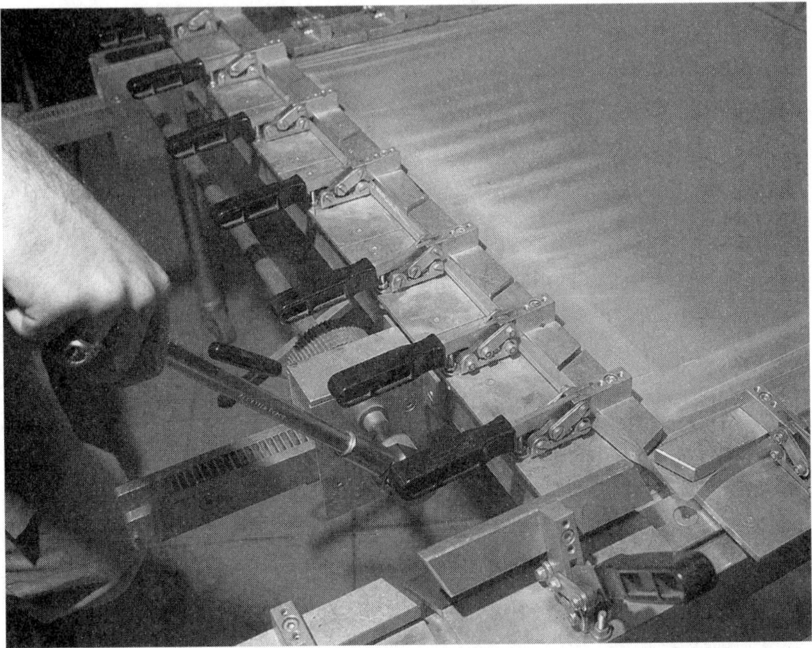

Figure 5-17 Mechanical tensioning

Figure 5-18 Pneumatic tensioning

3. Fabric is carefully aligned and locked into clamps so that tension is applied precisely parallel to the threads.
4. Corner tension is reduced by pre-softening the corners.
5. Tension is applied to each movable side until the desired tension level is achieved.
6. Frame is raised until it contacts the screen fabric.
7. Adhesive is used to glue screen fabric to the frame.
8. After adhesive is set, frame is removed from tensioning device and excess fabric can be trimmed from the frame. See Figure 5-17.

Pneumatic Tensioning Procedures

1. Tensioning units are arranged per frame size. For example a 20″ x 30″ frame requires three 10″ clamps for the 30″ side and two 10″ clamps for the 20″ dimension.
2. Clamps air hoses are interconnected with the air regulator.
3. Clamps are adjusted in height based on frame profile.
4. Corner tension is reduced by pre-softening the corners.
5. Fabric is aligned so tension is applied parallel to the fibers and jaws are locked in place.
6. Tension is applied to the mesh until the desired tension level is achieved.
7. Adhesive is applied to secure the screen fabric to the frame.
8. After adhesive is set, frame is removed from the tension device and excess fabric is trimmed from the frame. See Figure 5-18.

Roller Frame Tensioning Procedures

1. Fabric should be marked with lines to assist in accurate alignment of the fabric on the frame.
2. Mesh near the corners of the frame must be pre-softened to prevent excessive tension buildup.
3. One side of the roller frame is rotated with a wrench to initially tension the screen fabric.
4. The opposite side is rotated until half the desired tension level is achieved and then locked into place.
5. A third side of the frame is rotated until tensioned to three quarters the recommended tension and then locked.
6. The fourth side is rotated until tension is brought up to desired tension level and locked into place.
7. Tension level is checked at several points in the screen to evaluate tension consistency.
8. If tension is excessive in the corners they must be post-softened to eliminate tension buildup. See Figure 5-19

Figure 5-19 Roller frame

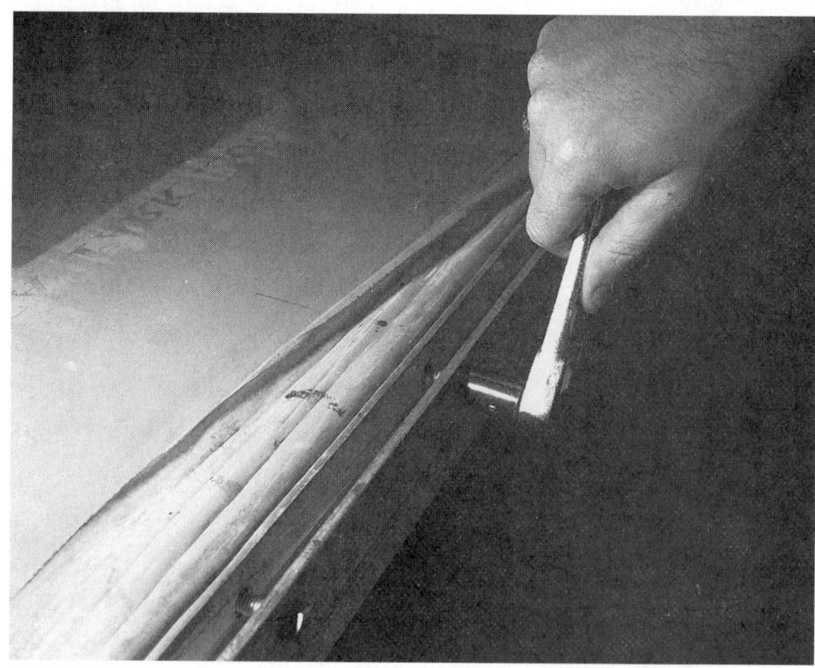

Figure 5-20 Draw bar frame

Draw Bar Frame Tensioning Procedures

1. The fabric is marked with lines to assist in accurate alignment of the mesh in the draw bar.
2. Fabric is aligned and locked into the draw bars for each of the four frame sides.
3. Mesh near the corners of the frame must be pre-softened to prevent excessive tension buildup.

4. Bolts are tightened beginning with the longest frame side, starting with the center bolt, then working outward. It is important to rotate each bolt in only 180° turns. By turning each bolt the same amount consistent tensioning can be assured.

5. After the first side has been tensioned the opposing side should be tightened following the same procedure.

6. One of the short sides should be tensioned as with the other two.

7. The final short side should be tensioned.

8. Tension reading should be taken at several points of the screen to evaluate tension level and consistency.

9. Either short or long side should be re-tensioned to achieve the desired tension level.

10. If tension is excessive in the corners they must be post-softened to eliminate tension buildup. See Figure 5-20.

Staged Tensioning For Stretch and Glue Frames

Initial tension should be applied a little at a time starting with the warp direction and then the weft direction until half the recommended tension has been reached in both directions. The fabric should be left for one minute to relax after initial tension has been reached. Tension should be increased 2-4 N/cm in both dimensions and left to relax for a one minute period. This procedure should be repeated until the recommended tension level has been reached. At the time the fabric should be allowed to stabilize for 10 to 15 minutes. The tension should be brought back to its recommended level and allowed to stabilize an additional 10-15 minutes. This procedure should be done a minimum of one time and even better three times if possible. This procedure counteracts the drop in tension caused by cold flow. Once the tension/stabilization process is complete, the screen fabric may be glued to the frame.

Work Hardening

The instability of standard monofilament polyester due to cold flow has been a problem for screen printers for many years. Self-tensioning frames have been in existence since the 1950s as an alternative to stretch and glue frames. They were first used with stainless steel mesh. Self-tensioning frames later came into use with monofilament polyester.

The self-tensioning frame gave the screen printer the opportunity to re-tension the screen after it was reclaimed at the end of the print run. This allowed the screen maker to compensate for cold flow after the screen was reclaimed for reuse. But many screen makers noted that the fabric did not behave consistently over time. The screen did not lose the same amount of tension each time it was retensioned; tension loss decreased until, at a certain point, the loss was minimal.

It was obvious that something was happening to change the behavior of the mesh, making it more stable. Yet a precise explanation of exactly what was happening was not so obvious. Key points that initiate the change are initial fabric tensioning, squeegee action placing force on the fabric, followed by re-tensioning of the mesh. This is often referred to as **work hardening,** where the fabric is hardened or stabilized by squeegee action of the press.

There is a cautionary note with regard to work hardening. Each time the fabric is retensioned fabric elongation is increased, causing open area to increase and mesh count to decrease. This results in a change in the printing characteristics of the screen.

Rapid Tensioning

The Screen Printing Technical Foundation has conducted a recent study on different tensioning techniques. Three **rapid tensioning** techniques were compared to the staged tensioning procedure, described earlier in the chapter. The staged tensioning procedure applies tension in two to four N/cm increments after which it is allowed to stabilize for sixty second intervals. This procedure is repeated until final tension is reached.

Rapid tensioning is a process of bringing the fabric directly to its recommended tension level in one stage. Rapid tensioning involves two aspects. The first relates to the time interval that tension is applied. The second aspect relates to the time interval that the fabric is stabilized before it is attached to the frame.

The study found that tension could be applied at rates from 0.5 Newtons per second up to 5 Newtons per second with acceptable results. A 36-second time interval to reach full tension was used for this study. It also tested the effect of three different stabilization periods: five minutes, thirty minutes and eight hours. Fabric from three different manufacturers was tested. Monofilament polyester was tested in mesh counts ranging from 230 (48μ thread) up to 508 (30μ thread). Both standard and low elongation mesh were tested. A pneumatic tensioning system was used with this study.

Tension was measured at various stages from initial readings to after the press run. Measurements were made in both warp and weft directions. Over two years of laboratory press runs, and field testing with runs over 200,000 impressions were made. Field tests used this method effectively with mesh as coarse as 28 threads per inch. The primary advantage of rapid tensioning is to decrease the time required to tension a screen, allowing more screens to be produced in a day. Time savings can be from 30 to 60 minutes per screen by using rapid tensioning. The primary concern is whether rapid tensioning adversely affects the screen tension at various stages of the screens life.

It was found that the rapid tensioning procedure using the longest stabilization period (8 hours) lost the least tension of all methods tested including staged tensioning. Unfortunately this practice is not feasible for production since only one screen can be produced per 8 hour period. All of the rapid tensioning methods did not vary more than 2.0 N/cm over staged tensioning. In some cases tension loss was less than with staged tensioning.

This method may be used with any mesh count from coarse to fine in addition to standard or low elongation meshes using fabric manufacturers' tension recommendations. Initially screen breakage during tensioning may increase slightly since applying the full force to the mesh quickly is prone to such problems as burrs, and so on. Extra caution may be needed to prevent this problem from occurring. Field testing found no adverse effects on screen life or tension using rapid tensioning compared to staged tensioning. This technique is currently in use by a number of companies with excellent success.

Figure 5-21 Calendared mesh

Tensioning Calendared Mesh

Calendared mesh, as shown in Figure 5-21, is produced from monofilament polyester that has been modified to decrease the fabric thickness and mesh opening. This changes the shape of the fibers from a completely round thread to one that has a flattened side. For best results the manufacturers' tension specifications for calendared mesh should be followed (see charts at the back of the chapter). It can be tensioned using a wide range of tensioning devices following the same procedures for monofilament polyester fabrics. The squeegee side of the mesh is indicated on the selvage edge for proper mounting of the mesh on the screen frame.

Tensioning Anti-Static Mesh

Anti-static or carbonized mesh is composed of two types of fibers. One is monofilament polyester and the second is nylon in composition with a coating of carbon on the thread surface. It may be tensioned using a number of tensioning devices using the same tensioning procedure as with conventional polyester. Yet due to its unique composition tensioning specifications for this fabric must be strictly adhered to or excess tension will damage the fabric. The recommended tension specifications are included at the rear of the chapter.

Tensioning Metalized Mesh

Since this fabric has a core of monofilament polyester with a nickel coating, it is a compromise between polyester and stainless steel fabrics in performance. It has greater stability than polyester but increased elasticity over stainless steel. Yet since its elasticity is lower than polyester it has less tolerance for excess tension, and the recommended tension specification must never be exceeded. The mesh can be damaged at the knuckles when too much tension is applied. The recommended tension specifications are included at the end of the chapter.

The nickel coating makes the fabric somewhat brittle and less forgiving after it is tensioned. The screen will break if mishandled or subjected to abuse. Its brittle nature makes it more fragile if it is bent at a sharp angle. This may pose a problem when it is placed in some types of clamps with different tensioning systems.

Tensioning Stainless Mesh

Stainless steel fabric is very strong and stable due to its composition. It has the lowest elongation (or stretch) and supports high tension levels compared to synthetic fabrics. Tensioning alone does not stretch fabric to its final elongation due to the nature of the mesh. After the screen is placed on the press for printing, the squeegee exerts pressure on the mesh. This pressure causes the mesh to flatten slightly resulting in further elongation of the mesh causing registration problems.

After the screen is reclaimed the mesh can be retensioned to remove this slack and bring the mesh up to its recommended tension level. This effect is somewhat like cold flow except it is not the composition of the mesh that causes the tension loss but rather the weave of the wire mesh. The need to re-tension stainless steel mesh after printing eliminates a stretch and glue approach. Stretch and glue may be used only with small frame sizes. Self-tensioning frames have long been preferred for use with stainless steel mesh.

Tensioning Newman Roller Mesh

This mesh is designed for use on Newman roller frames. Due to the mechanical nature of the self-tensioning frame, fabric tension must be applied in stages to compensate for cold flow of the mesh. (Refer to the chart on page 104.) The procedure to tension Newman Roller Mesh N300 (300 threads per inch) is as follows.

- Fabric is initially tensioned from 38 to 50 N/cm on a Newman roller frame.
- The screen is allowed to relax for about 30 minutes.
- Fabric is re-tensioned by rotating one roller to achieve 42 to 60 N/cm.
- A third re-tensioning is optional.
- The screen is now ready to image and printed on press for the first time. Tension will be lost during the first press run.
- After the first press run is complete the screen can be reclaimed and re-tensioned (45 to 65 N/cm).
- The screen can be imaged and used for a second press run.
- After a second press run the screen is reclaimed and can be re-tensioned (49 to 70 N/cm).
- After fabric has been printed, reclaimed, and re-tensioned for two press runs, it becomes more stable through work hardening and will experience less tension drop between press runs.

Figure 5-22 Stair-stepping effect

Figure 5-23 Biasing closeup

Biasing Mesh on Frame

In situations where parallel straight lines are printed nearly parallel with the threads of the screen fabric, an undesirable "stair-stepping" printed results will occur. See Figure 5-22. Another undesirable result occurs where thread interference with halftone dots results in a moiré effect. These undesirable results may be prevented by simply angling the image on the screen by placing the threads at an angle usually greater than 20°. The angles most commonly used are 22.5°, 30°, and 45°.

Angling the image on the screen is not an approach that can be used when printing on an automatic or textile press since the substrate cannot be placed at an angle during printing. Angling or **biasing** the fabric on the frame is an alternative that can be used under these conditions. Biasing means using an oblique or diagonal line of direction across a woven fabric. See Figure 5-23.

There are two primary approaches in biasing mesh on the frame. One approach is to stretch the mesh directly at the desired angle. This is not recommended especially at angles greater than 15°. Stretching the mesh an an angle causes the mesh openings to be deformed since they are no longer square in shape with perfectly parallel threads. This results in poor quality printed results and increases the chances of fabric breakage. This is why biasing the mesh on self-tensioning frames is not recommended.

A better approach is to stretch the fabric straight and then glue it to the frame at the desired angle. This prevents the fabric from being distorted from stretching at an angle. This is most easily accomplished using a mechanical stretching device, as shown in Figure 5-24, where the frame angle can be easily set before it is glued onto the frame. More fabric is needed to accommodate biasing the mesh over applying it with the threads parallel to the frame sides. The greater the angle the more fabric is needed. When biasing the mesh at a 45° angle up to four

Figure 5-24 Biasing on mechanical tension system

times the mesh is needed using some stretchers over placing the threads parallel. This increases the expense of the screen.

It is possible to bias mesh using a pneumatic tensioning device although it is more difficult. Since most pneumatic systems pre-bow the frame during tensioning, the frame cannot be placed at an angle by itself. The fabric can be tensioned by using a larger master frame or support board to line up with the clamps. The frame can be placed at the desired angle once the final tension is achieved and the mesh glued into place. Unfortunately this method circumvents pre-bowing of the frame so there will be a tension loss once the tensioned screen is removed from the tensioning device. This loss of tension should be compensated by an increase in the tension before gluing.

Figure 5-25 Frame profile *(Majestech Corporation)*

IMPORTANCE OF FRAMES

Since screen tension is critical to the screen printing process the frame is of obvious concern to sustain the tension achieved. The ideal would be to tension the fabric to the desired level, attach it to a frame and the screen would stay at that desired tension. Yet unfortunately it is not that simple. Frame selection assists the fabric in achieving the desired end result.

Rigid Frame Types

The selection of a frame is based on several factors. Each contributes to the strength or structural stability of the frame. These factors are material, profile, frame wall thickness, and frame side length. **Frame profile** and wall thickness are regulated by frame size, as shown in Figure 5-25. Small size frames may use thinner wall thicknesses and smaller profiles. Larger frames require greater wall thicknesses and profiles to maintain tension over longer frame lengths. Frame material used will govern wall thickness and profile. Materials with greater tensile strength such as steel require thinner wall thicknesses with smaller frame profiles than lower tensile strength materials like aluminum. Due to the strength and stability of metal frames they retain tension levels with less bowing of frame sides and are capable of higher tension levels. They are also unaffected by water and most chemicals used in screen printing. Self-tensioning frames are often constructed of aluminum to provide the needed strength and light weight.

Wood Frames

The primary reason wood frames are used by screen printers is for their low initial cost. Wood frames are primarily suitable for screen printing jobs where precision is not essential. Wood frames have a number of disadvantages over the long term. Structurally they are weaker than metal frames and also absorb solvents, ink and water unless they are sealed or coated. Frame warpage is difficult to avoid which makes it difficult to use on press.

The two prime disadvantages are their need to be replaced over time and their inability to maintain screen tension level. Wood frames are not a viable option if looking to increase fabric tension. Rigid metal frames cost anywhere from two to four times the cost of wood frames initially but since they have a long life (when used properly) they are more cost effective since they do not require continual replacement.

Due to wood frames' lack of consistency in maintaining tension they add an additional variable to the screen printing process which cannot be easily compensated. Another important factor is the environmental impact of wood frame use. Use of wood for frames is continually using a natural resource which later ends up becoming a waste disposal issue, often filling landfills.

Many screen printers have their screens prepared by commercial screen makers who stretch and adhere the fabric to the wood frame for the screen printer. This may be more cost effective than making them in house, especially with smaller screen printing companies. After the screens are no longer usable they are discarded and new frames are purchased.

Yet this leaves one of the most critical issue of the screen process (fabric tensioning) out of the reach of screen printer's control. Tension may be lost during storage or transport before it is received by the screen printer. If screens are purchased in this fashion it is important that the screen printer take tension readings of screens for both tension level as well as uniformity. If screens are low in tension or lack tension uniformity they should be returned to the supplier.

A similar but slightly different approach is a supplier that prepares tensioned frames using a plastic frame made of recycled plastic. The plastic is resistant to solvents, thinners and inks used with screen printing and will withstand heat and humidity levels common to the screen printing environment. The frame can support tension levels 25-30 N/cm and higher. This process uses a proprietary tape to permanently attach the fabric to the frame. Once the screen is no longer usable it is returned to the manufacturer for reuse and a deposit is returned to the screen printer. This recycling of frames is an action to encourage environmentally responsible actions on the part of the screen printer.

Aluminum Frames

Aluminum is the most common metal frame used due to its light weight. It is produced from a high tensile strength alloy that is extruded in profiles 1.5″ square or larger. Frame corners are welded and must be flat and not warped. As the frame size is increased the profile should be increased proportionately. Selection of a small frame profile to save money will result in a frame that is unable to maintain tension consistency.

To assist the fabric in adhering to the surface of the aluminum, one side must be roughened by sandblasting to increase the surface area of the aluminum and improve adhesion. Aluminum should not be exposed to alkalis or acids.

Steel Frames

One of the most significant characteristics of a steel frame is its high tensile strength, but the disadvantage is its greater weight. Yet its higher tensile strength allows wall thickness of steel frames to be thinner than aluminum, which cuts down on weight to some degree. In larger sizes aluminum frames cannot provide the necessary strength to prevent bowing of the frame sides. In these instances the increased strength of steel is needed to maintain the needed tension levels.

Steel frames must be coated with a protective layer to prevent exposure to water or moisture causing rusting. The steel surface can be galvanized with a zinc coating or sprayed with a protective paint such as epoxy that will resist chemicals and solvents used in screen printing.

Magnesium Alloy Frames

Magnesium is desirable for screen printing frames since it is two thirds the weight of aluminum and also very strong. It is available in different profiles for different size frames. Corners are joined together by welding as with other metal frames. Their light weight makes it easier to handle than other metal frames. Unfortunately they are higher in cost than other metal frames.

Frame Profile

Tensioned fabric places considerable force on the frames once it is glued in place causing deflection of the frame, and resulting in tension loss. Tension loss leads to undesirable results in screen making and during the press run. It is important that the frame resists deflection under the force that tensioned fabric exerts on the frame. This requires the frame to possess the proper profile to resist this force. Screen deflection will occur if the frame profile lacks in structural integrity.

Structural integrity is dependent on the profile of the frame. It is determined by wall thickness, size and shape as shown in Figure 5-26. Research has found that greater structural integrity can be achieved using profiles where one or more sides are convex or concave instead of square or rectangular in shape.

Another approach in achieving greater strength is use of a profile that places an additional member within the frames interior. This forms a kind of figure eight cross section. This is done in an aluminum extrusion process. It results in an increase in strength for the frames, reducing deflection as much as 50% with a weight increase of only 25% to 30%. This is used with high tension mesh.

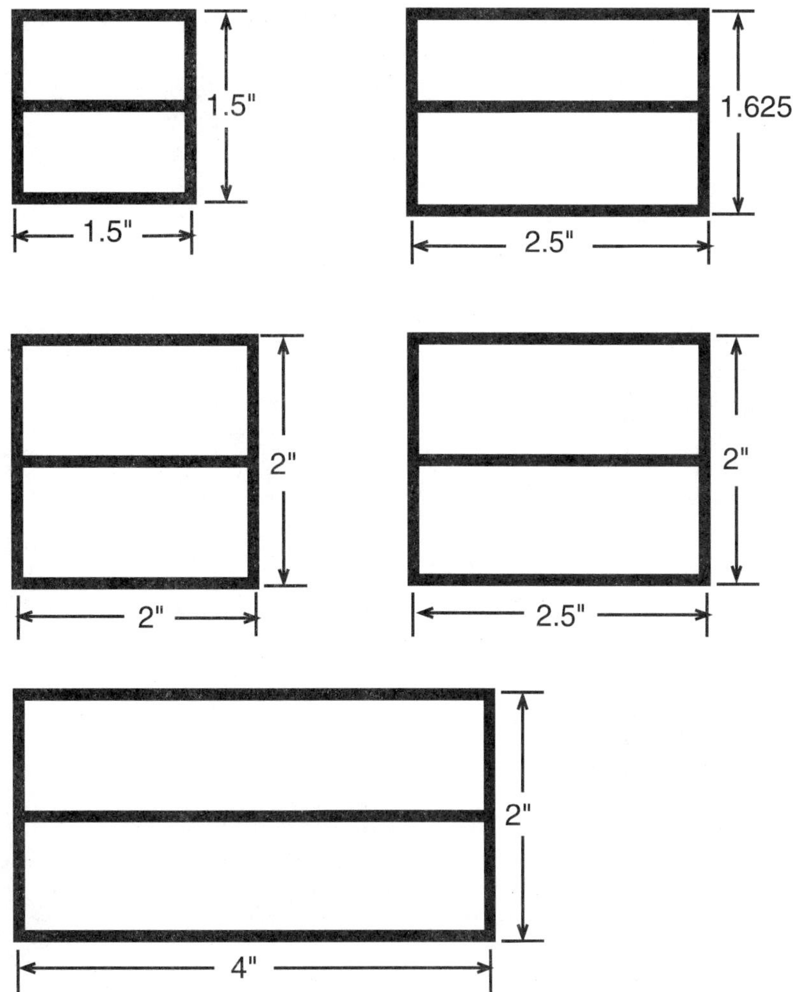

Figure 5-26 Double hollow frames

STRETCH AND GLUE FRAME ADHESIVES

The frame surface must be receptive to adhesives before the mesh can be adhered. There are several conditions that interfere with adhesion to the frame. New aluminum frames must be sandblasted to roughen the surface to assure adhesion. Frames that have been previously used may allow the mesh to be glued on top of old adhesives. This may pose a problem if the surface becomes too irregular to maintain proper contact of the mesh with the frame. If solvents or ink combine with the surface of the adhesive the new layer of adhesive cannot bond properly. This requires the old adhesive to be removed mechanically by using a motorized abrasive disk or using a chemical stripping agent.

The surface must be free of solvents, oil, grease or dirt before application of adhesive. The frame may require application of a degreasing agent to remove oily residues from the frame. In difficult cases a thin layer of glue may be initially applied to the frame surface and allowed to dry. After tensioning, a second application of adhesive will completely secure the mesh to the frame. Placing heavy weights on the screen near the frame, as shown in Figure 5-27, insures complete contact of the fabric with the mesh prior to gluing. A close inspection should be made to make sure the fabric contacts the frame at all points.

Figure 5-27 Weight placement

There are two types of adhesives commonly used with stretch and glue systems. They are both two-part adhesives. The two types vary primarily in the way the catalyst is added to the glue. Two component reactive adhesives are most often used since a change in composition occurs once cured that makes it resistant to a wide range of solvents and inks used for screen printing. These adhesives may be used with either wood or metal frames. See Figure 5-28.

Figure 5-28 Adhesive application

The most frequent adhesive used requires a measured amount of catalyst to be added to the adhesive before it is applied to the tensioned frame. It reaches a cured state in anywhere from twenty minutes up to two hours, with much longer pot life. The mixed adhesive is applied on top of the mesh. A plastic applicator is used to force adhesive through the mesh into contact with the screen frame. Bubbles showing through the mesh indicates poor contact of the mesh to the frame. As soon as

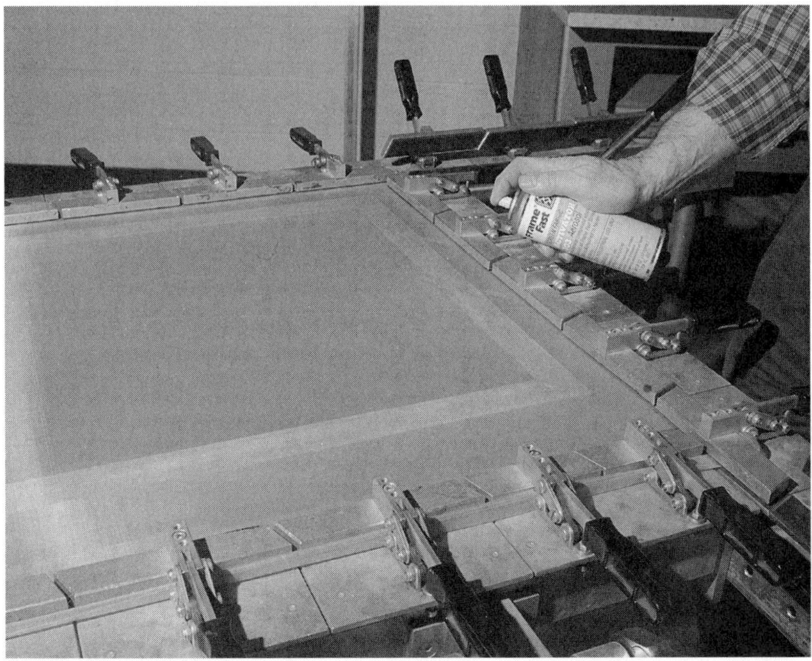

Figure 5-29 Spray adhesive

the adhesive sets up, the frame may be removed from the tensioning unit. It's recommended to not use the frame immediately since the adhesive does not reach its greatest resistance to solvents and water for 24 hours. A protective coating may be applied on top of the adhesive to make it more resistant to aggressive solvents or adverse reclaiming procedures.

A second adhesive type, a cyanoacrylate adhesive, does not require mixing. A thin layer or bead of adhesive is applied on top of the mesh around the frame perimeter. The entire surface of the frame does not need to be covered to be effective. Even application produces the best results. The catalyst is lightly sprayed on the surface of the adhesive and the adhesive sets up in less than 30 seconds. After the adhesive is set up, the frame may be removed from the tensioning device. Two different viscosities are available for use on coarse mesh and fine mesh counts. In cases where the adhesive is accidentally bonded on hands or other areas, a debonding solvent may be used. See Figure 5-29.

FRAME SIZE CONSIDERATIONS

Determination of frame size for a given image size is an important decision. Yet the proper relationship between image and frame size is often overlooked in the interests in getting the job done quickly. But once the press operator starts to print the screen with an image that barely fits, he soon experiences difficulties. The press operator has to use far greater squeegee pressure to get it to print properly.

Since the screen printing process places the screen slightly above the surface of the substrate the squeegee must bring the screen into momentary contact during the print stroke. After contact the screen quickly separates from the substrate. When the image is too close to the sides of the frame much greater squeegee pressure is required to bring the screen into contact with the substrate. This greater pressure near the frame sides causes the ends of the squeegee to distort and cause uneven ink deposits and poor print quality. The excessive pressure will also result in greater fabric and stencil wear in the areas of greater stress. See Figure 5-30.

To prevent this problem the proper space must be maintained between the frame sides and the image. The proper relationship of free mesh to image size is based

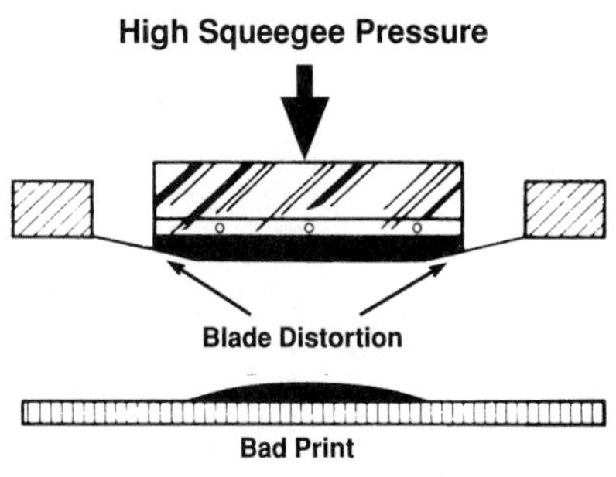

Figure 5-30 Screen size *(Tetko® Inc)*

frame size	frame vs. image
up to 10″	1.5: 1.0
10″ to 30″	1.4: 1.0
over 30″	1.35: 1.0

Figure 5-31 Frame/image ratio

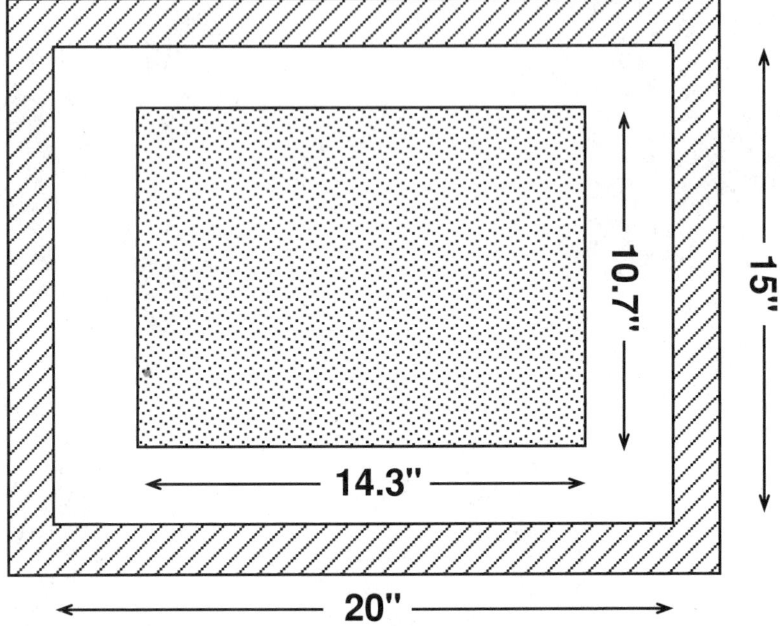

Figure 5-32 Frame vs. image size

on frame size, as shown in Figure 5-31. For small frames under 10″ sides the ratio should be frame size 1.5 times the image size. For frame sides from 10″ to 30″ the ratio should be frame size 1.4 times the image size. Frames larger than 30″ sides should be 1.35 times the image size.[5]

To find the maximum image size for a 10″ x 10″ frame, the 10″ dimension is divided by 1.5 for a result of 6.7″. This means the maximum image size for a 10″ x 10″ frame is a 6.7″ square image. An example of a medium size frame 15″ x 20″ in size, each dimension is divided by 1.4. The maximum image size for a 15″ x 20″ frame is 10.7″ x 14.3″. A large frame 30″ x 40″ in size must have both dimensions divided by 1.35. This results in the maximum image size of 22.5″ x 29.6″.

Another approach in achieving proper space between the image size and frame is to compare the free mesh area to the image area as shown in Figure 5-32. A 10″ x 10″ frame has a total of 100 square inches free mesh area. The maximum image size for this frame is 6.7″ x 6.7″, a total of 45 square inches. The maximum image size for a frame 10″ x 10″ should be 45% or less of the free mesh area.

A frame 15″ x 20″ in size has 300 square inches free mesh area. The maximum image size of 10.7″ x 14.3″ has a total of 153 square inches. The maximum image size for a 15″ x 20″ frame should be 51% or less of the free mesh area. A large frame 30″ x 40″ in size has 1200 square inches free mesh area. The maximum image size of 22.5″ x 29.6″ has a total of 666 square inches. The maximum image size for a frame 30″ x 40″ in size should be 55% or less of the free mesh area. You can see that each of the three frame size ratio recommendations are that the image size should be nearly 50% of the free mesh area.

Frame size	Free mesh area	Image area	Image area
10″ x 10″	100 sq. inches	45 sq. inches	45%
15″ x 20″	300 sq. inches	153 sq. inches	51%
30″ x 40″	1200 sq. inches	666 sq. inches	55%

Figure 5-33 Frame vs. image size

This leads to a simple approach based on the above relationship. With screens very small in size (up to 10″ frame sides), the image area should be no greater than 45% of the free mesh area. For medium size screens (10″ to 30″ frame sides), the image area should be no greater than 50% of the free mesh area. And with large screens (over 30″ frame sides), the image area should be no greater than 55% the free mesh area. To prevent the screenmaker from using too small a frame for a given image size, a chart listing various screen sizes and the maximum image for each screen should be posted in the screen making room. See Figure 5-33.

KEY TERMS

biasing
cold flow
draw bar frame
fabric elongation
fixed frames
frame profile
low elongation mesh
mechanical tensioning unit
pneumatic tensioning devices
rapid tensioning
retensionable frame
roller frame
tension meter
warp
weft
work hardening

REVIEW QUESTIONS

1. What are the consequences of tension that is too low?
2. What are the consequences of tension that is too high?
3. What are the consequences of inconsistent tension?
4. How can tension be most accurately measured?
5. Under what conditions should a mechanical tensioning device be used?
6. Under what conditions should a pneumatic tensioning device be used?
7. What advantages do retensionable frames offer over fixed frames?
8. What is cold flow? What can be done about it?
9. What method can be used to check consistency of tension within a screen?
10. What is biasing mesh and when should it be done?
11. What is work hardening?
12. What are the reasons for using low elongation over standard mesh?
13. How is image quality affected when frame size is too small?

NOTES

[1] James Schall, "High-Tension, Low-Elongation Mesh," *Screen Printing Magazine* November 1989: 129-133.

[2] Dr. Elmar Messerschmitt, *The Measuring of Screen Tension* (Fairfax: Technical Guidebook of the Screen Printing Industry, Screenprinting and Graphic Imaging Association International, June 1987).

[3] Messerschmitt:

[4] Messerschmitt:

[5] The Screen Printers Notebook, Tetko Technical Topics.

Fabric Tensioning Specifications

Tetko Monofilament Polyester			
mesh count	thread diameter	tension-standard	tension-LEM
60 T	120µ	20-35 N/cm	—
110 T	80µ	18-46 N/cm	32-51 N/cm
137 T	64µ	24-38 N/cm	26-42 N/cm
156 T	60µ	27-43 N/cm	30-48 N/cm
195 T	55µ	22-35 N/cm	27-43 N/cm
230 T	48µ	23-36 N/cm	24-40 N/cm
260 T	40µ	18-28 N/cm	20-32 N/cm
280 T	34µ	14-22 N/cm	16-26 N/cm
305 T	34µ	14-24 N/cm	17-27 N/cm
355 T	34µ	16-26 N/cm	18-29 N/cm
420 T	34µ	20-32 N/cm	—
420 S	31µ	—	19-31 N/cm

Tetko Monofilament Nylon		
mesh count	thread diameter	tension
54T	151µ	35 N/cm
110T	83µ	23 N/cm
137T	62µ	17 N/cm
156T	64µ	19 N/cm
195T	52µ	16 N/cm
230T	47µ	15 N/cm
260T	42µ	12 N/cm
280T	40µ	12 N/cm
305T	39µ	12 N/cm
355S	33µ	11 N/cm
420S	33µ	13 N/cm
420T	40µ	17 N/cm

Newman Roller Mesh		
mesh count	thread diameter	tension
70	140µ	70-120 N/cm
88	104µ	70-110 N/cm
115	83µ	62-90 N/cm
138	75µ	56-80 N/cm
166	68µ	58-85 N/cm
205	55µ	50-74 N/cm
228	55µ	57-82 N/cm
272	42µ	46-65 N/cm
300	42µ	49-70 N/cm
380	36µ	42-60 N/cm

Silk	
mesh count	tension
2xx-30xx	7-9 N/cm

Multifilament Polyester	
mesh count	tension
6xx-25xx	15-18 N/cm

Fabric Tensioning Specifications

Metalized Polyester

mesh count	thread diameter	tension
60	124μ	35 N/cm
137	72μ	22 N/cm
156	74μ	25 N/cm
195	64μ	23 N/cm
230	58μ	21 N/cm
240	48μ	15 N/cm
260	45μ	16 N/cm
280	40μ	13 N/cm
305	42μ	14 N/cm
355	42μ	16 N/cm
420	43μ	19 N/cm

Tetko Carbonized Polyester

mesh count	thread diameter	tension
195	55/52μ	14-16 N/cm
260	40/52μ	12-14 N/cm
305	31/31μ	10-12 N/cm
355	31/31μ	9-11 N/cm

BOPP-SD Stainless Steel

mesh count	wire diameter	tension
80	97μ	63-65 N/cm
135	60μ	42-44 N/cm
200	41μ	25-27 N/cm
230	36μ	22-24 N/cm
280	32μ	21-23 N/cm
300	30μ	22-24 N/cm
400	25μ	20-22 N/cm

Calendared Mesh

mesh count	fabric diameter	tension
305T	41μ	14 N/cm
355T	41μ	16 N/cm
390T	43μ	17 N/cm
420T	43μ	19 N/cm
470T	40μ	22 N/cm

6 Stencil Systems

The stencil is one of three components that make up the image carrier. It is made up of a screen frame upon which the fabric is supported so that the stencil can be applied. See Figure 6-1.

The stencil is the component that forms nonimage areas. It is responsible for setting quality standards and durability for the image carrier. It also assists in the metering of ink deposit. The stencil has the least effect on ink deposition, affecting only twenty percent of the ink deposit. Industry professionals feel that production problems related to the stencil are the foremost issues to be addressed in the 90s.

There are nine variables related to the stencil that must be controlled to achieve optimum results. See Figure 6-2. We will explore each of the following variables in this chapter: mesh preparation, stencil characteristics (**resolution, definition, bridging** and **sensitivity**), stencil durability, stencil thickness, stencil moisture content, exposure intensity, exposure distance, exposure time and stencil processing.

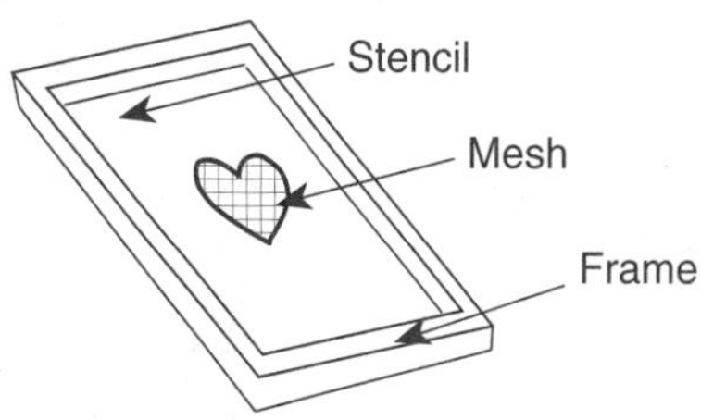

Figure 6-1 Image carrier

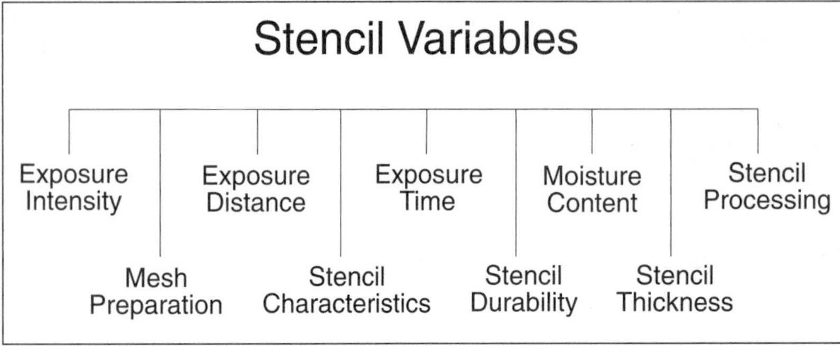

Figure 6-2 Stencil variables

FABRIC PREPARATION

Improper mesh preparation may lead to production problems such as **pinholes,** fish-eyes or poor stencil durability. The fabric must be prepared for stencil application by abrading and degreasing. If not done properly, both affect stencil adhesion resulting in premature stencil breakdown (unable to deliver the maximum number of prints).

Abrading

The smooth strands of monofilament polyester make it difficult for the stencil to bond. See Figure 6-3. This is more of a problem with capillary, and especially, indirect films. Abrasion is unnecessary when using liquid direct emulsion stencils. Fabric **abrading** or roughening is a process that increases the surface area of the threads, making stencils adhere more readily to the monofilament polyester strands.

Figure 6-3 New vs. abraded mesh

Screen fabric can be treated by mechanical or chemical methods. Chemical methods etch into the composition of the fibers or coat the surface to produce a roughened surface. This approach uses a chemical treatment to make the screen fabric more receptive to stencils. One type of chemical treatment, Autobond X, produces a hydrophilic layer on the surface of the fibers. This does not affect or damage the fibers of the mesh. The solution is applied by sponge to dry mesh and allowed to dry in a drying cabinet. Drying occurs quickly since it is a solvent based solution. After treatment the stencil may be applied to the mesh. This treatment must be repeated each time a stencil is applied.

The mechanical method is a simple process which is commonly used. An abrasive material such as silicon carbide or aluminum oxide powder is used. It is produced by grinding to a small particle size that will easily pass through fabric as fine as 500 t.p.i. This compound is physically applied to roughen the mesh surface. Roughening the surface of the fibers produces surface irregularities that assist the stencil in bonding. The objective is to slightly abrade the mesh without excessive damage or weakening of the fibers.

The paste or gel, which is a combination of abrading powder and degreaser, is applied in one step. Paste or gel is often preferred over powder since powdered abraders are easily airborne and very abrasive. These powders can scratch anything they come in contact with, including eyeglasses, contact lenses, and so on. Pow-

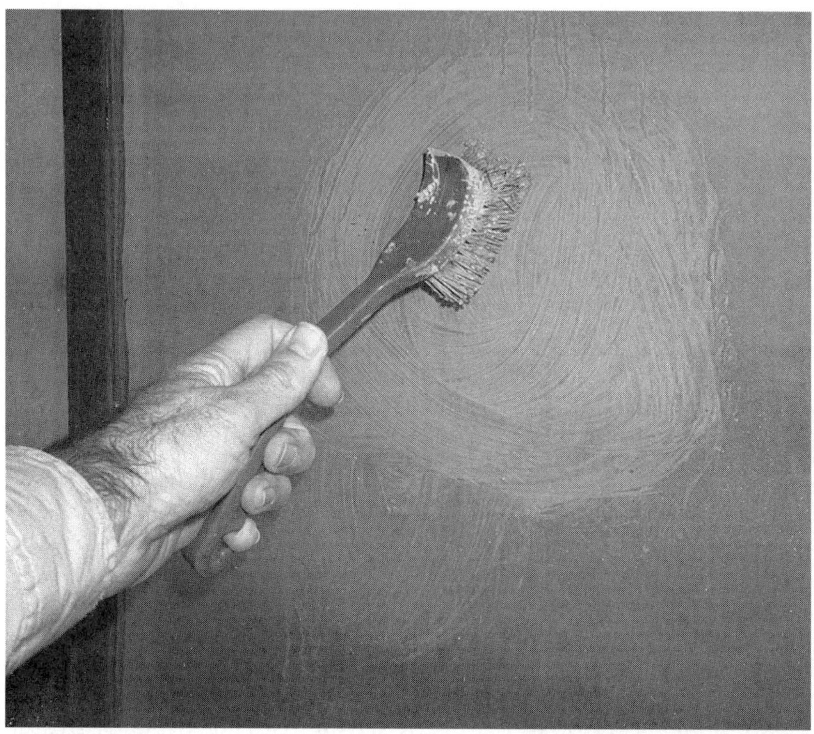

Figure 6-4 Fabric abrading

Figure 6-5 Improper abrading

ders are more difficult to control and may be inhaled by accident.

The first step in fabric abrading is to wet the screen with water. A small amount of powder, abrading gel or paste is applied to the wet screen using small circular motions such as used when waxing an automobile. See Figure 6-4. A high density polyester or nylon bristled brush should be used for best results. A large coarse brush may lead to poor abrading action. The entire screen area should be abraded. There will be a difference in ink deposit between abraded and nonabraded areas. The screen should then be rinsed with a pressure washer or garden hose.

The purpose is to lightly abrade the mesh and not damage or weaken the fibers with excessive force. Mesh should be abraded no more than fifteen seconds to prevent excessive abrasive action which reduces fabric life. Only the print side of the mesh should be abraded. Abrasion of both sides would cause excessive action on the mesh and reduce fabric life. Roughening the mesh again at a later time is unnecessary especially if haze remover is used during reclaiming of the screen. It need not be abraded every time a new stencil is applied. This would unnecessarily weaken the fabric over time reducing its effective life and also cause additional time to be spent in the stencil making process.

Undesirable results will occur if the mesh is abraded using improper products. Household cleanser (such as AJAX) has large abrasive particles which will excessively damage the fibers and can get trapped in the mesh as shown in Figure 6-5.

Degreasing

After fabric has been abraded properly there is another condition that may interfere with stencil adhesion. Oily residue present on the surface of the fibers will not allow the stencil to bond securely. New fabric may have oil present from the weaving machinery. Fabric that has been reclaimed after printing may have an oily residue if solvents have been used to remove solvent based inks.

A **degreasing** solution is needed to properly clean the mesh prior to application. A degreasing solution will remove undesirable residues of dust, solvents, and oil. It is incapable of removing dried inks or stencils. These must be removed with the appropriate stencil reclaimers or ink wash up solutions.

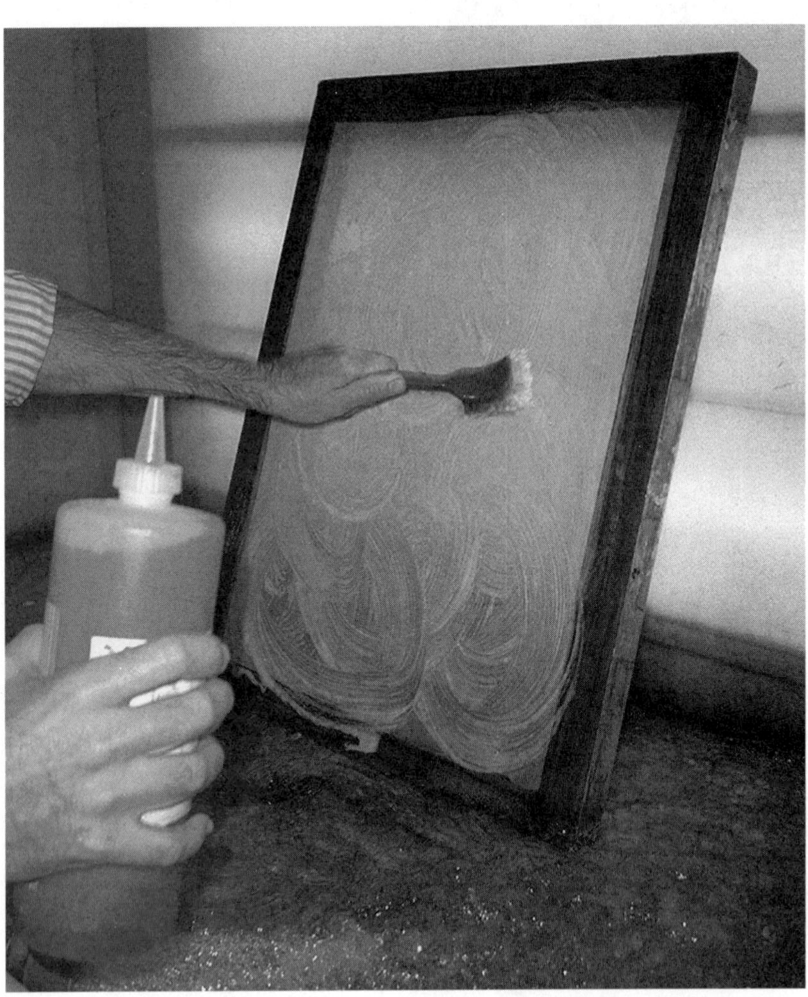

Figure 6-6 Fabric degreasing

There are a number of industrial solutions that may be used to degrease fabric. For best results it is recommended to use products made specifically for screen printing use. Under no circumstances should household cleaners be used. They contain chemicals or fragrances that may interfere with or dissolve the stencil, decreasing screen durability.

Degreaser is available in liquid form as a gel or solution. It should be applied to both sides of the screen with a brush to break down solvents and oils on the screen. See Figure 6-6. Degreaser may be easier to apply in gel form as it is easier to control on the screen. Liquid solutions may flow through the screen and down the sink. After the degreaser is applied the screen should be thoroughly washed to remove the degreaser. A low pressure washout hose provides the best results.

Water will flow freely over its entire surface if the screen has been properly degreased. If water is repelled from areas of the screen it indicates that an oily residue is present and degreasing is not complete. Details pertaining to degreasing with each stencil type will be discussed later in the chapter.

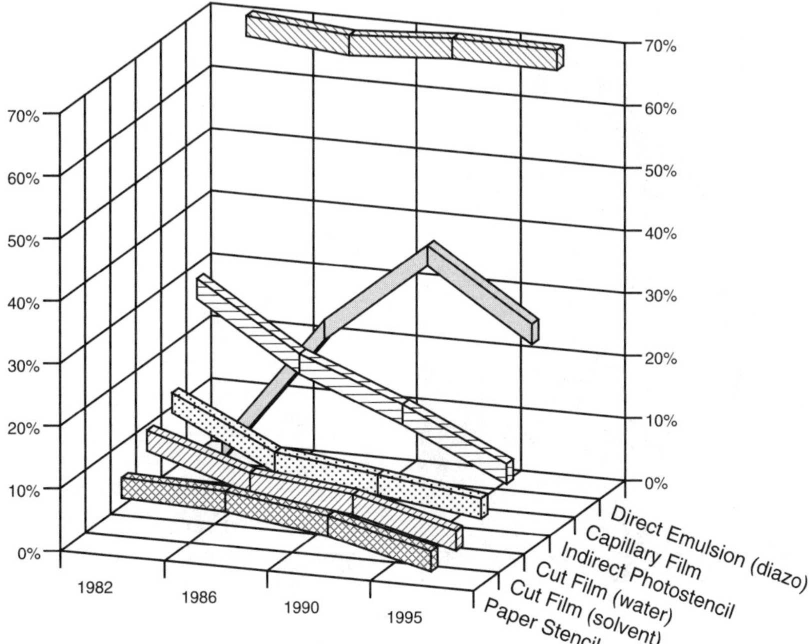

Figure 6-7 Stencil usage

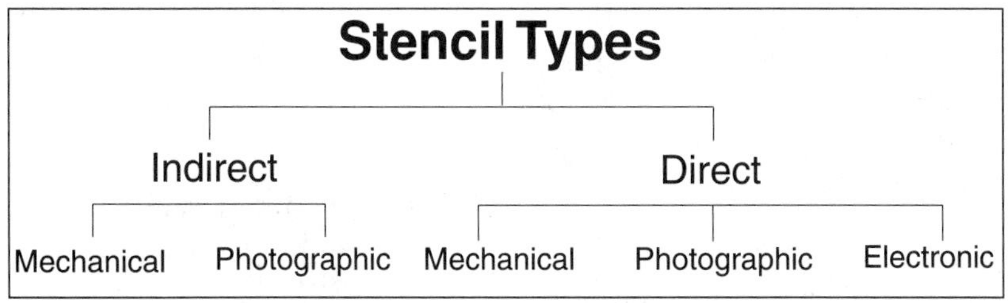

Figure 6-8 Stencil types

STENCIL TYPES

There are a wide range of stencils that may be used in the screen printing process. Each will be explained under its stencil name. Trends in stencil usage, as surveyed by the S.G.I.A., are shown in Figure 6-7. Liquid direct emulsion is the most common stencil used, followed by capillary film. All other stencils are declining in use.[1]

There are two categories that stencils fall into based on the way they are produced: indirect and direct. With direct stencils imaging is done directly on the screen fabric itself. There are three forms: mechanical, photographic and electronic imaging. See Figure 6-8. Direct stencils will be discussed later in the chapter.

Indirect Stencils

An **indirect stencil** is one that is prepared separately or indirectly from the screen mesh and then applied. For example, a knife-cut stencil is cut and then adhered to the fabric. Indirect stencils can be broken down in two types: mechanical and photographic.

Mechanical Stencils

Mechanical stencils are mechanically produced by cutting with a knife. The two types are paper stencil and knife-cut film stencils. With mechanical stencils cutting skill is an important factor in producing high quality stencils.

PAPER STENCILS Paper stencils are one of the simplest, as they can be cut and applied to the screen quickly. This is a less complex stencil requiring fewer production steps. It is limited to very simple designs or images. Paper stencils are the least durable stencil capable of a dozen or so prints. They can be used to print large areas such as a background that is to be overprinted with darker colors. They are also commonly used in the imprinted garment

Figure 6-9 Numbered jerseys are printed using paper stencils

industry for numbered jerseys where only one print is needed. See Figure 6-9.

When cutting paper stencils with a design that has the letter "O," two circles must be cut out. See Figure 6-10. Since both are free they will both fall out and only a round area will print, with the center of the "O" omitted. The way to remedy the situation is to place small bridges across to hold the center of the "O" in place, as shown in Figure 6-11.

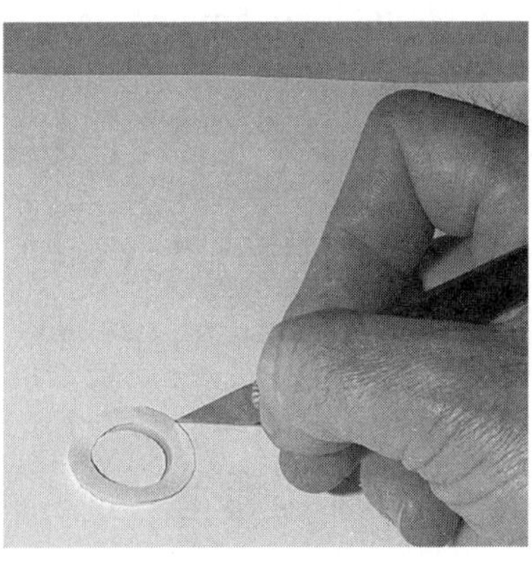

Figure 6-10 Cutting an "O"

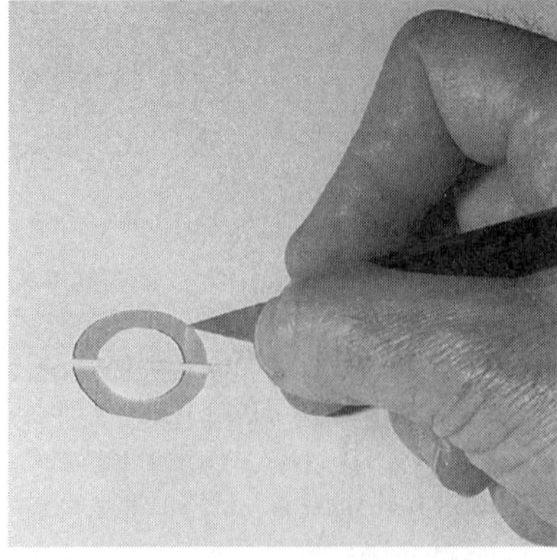

Figure 6-11 Use of bridges

KNIFE-CUT FILM STENCILS The most common type of mechanical stencil is cut film. Instead of cutting paper, a film designed for knife cutting can be used. It is made of two layers, the stencil emulsion and a supporting backing sheet. See Figure 6-12. There are two types that may be used: solvent resistant and water resistant knife-cut films.

When a cut film is used, two circles can be cut for the "O" and both will be held in place by the backing sheet. The image areas of the cut film can then be peeled away from the backing sheet leaving all nonprinting areas to remain behind. See Figure 6-13. This allows greater detail to be produced. Adhering liquid is then used to bond the stencil to the mesh. After adhering to the mesh the backing sheet can be removed leaving only nonimage remaining on the screen. When squeegee action is applied ink is transferred through cut areas of the stencil.

Photographic Stencils

Stencils can be produced using a photo mechanical process. This makes it possible to print fine details such as type or halftones which would be impossible to cut

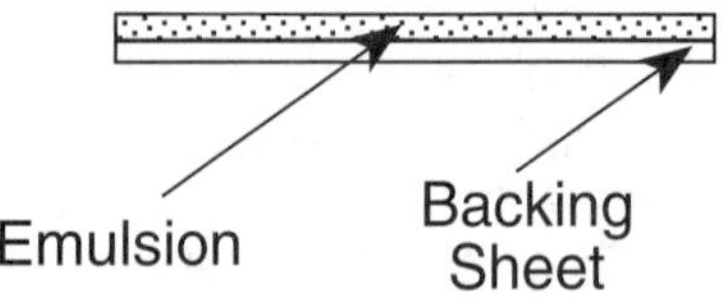

Figure 6-12 Knife-cut film

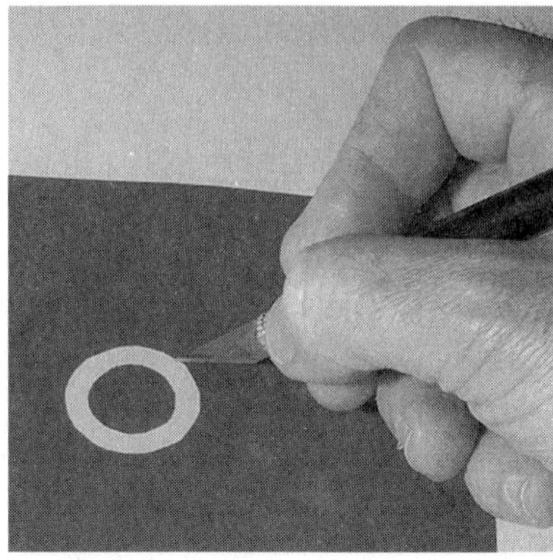

Figure 6-13 Knife cut film

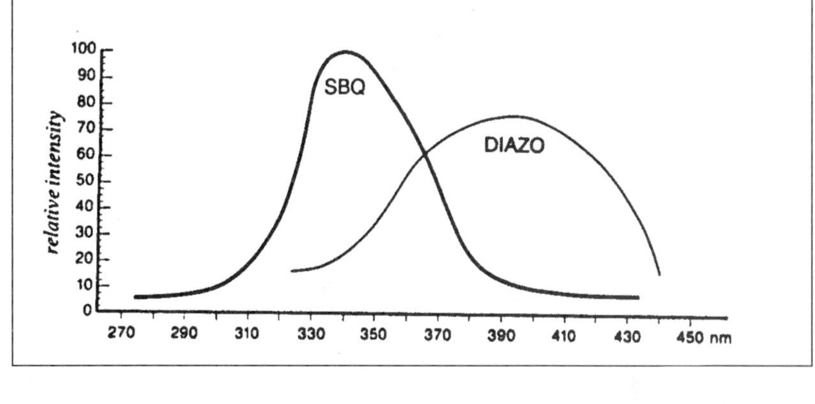

Figure 6-14 Diazo vs. SBQ sensitizer spectural distribution *(Dr. Dieter Reichel)*

mechanically. It uses a light sensitive emulsion that is used in conjunction with a film positive. Areas exposed to a light source harden to form nonimage areas. Image areas remain soft and wash out with warm water. Warm water can remove irregular image shapes which are too difficult to cut by hand. Photographic stencils can be produced directly on the mesh or indirectly and then transferred after processing.

STENCIL CHARACTERISTICS There are four characteristics of a photographic stencil emulsion that are established by the formulation of the emulsion: sensitivity, definition, resolution and bridge meshing. These variables establish the best use for a particular emulsion. An emulsion formulated with high resolution characteristics would be suited for printing halftones or fine line details. The screen maker cannot change the characteristics of the mesh so he or she must select the emulsion best suited to a job's needs.

SENSITIVITY Stencil sensitivity relates to the speed of the stencil emulsion whether fast or slow. A stencil with high sensitivity will require less time to expose. This relates to the frequency at which an emulsion has the greatest sensitivity.

The sensitivity of the emulsion is controlled by the type of sensitizer used in the emulsion. Diazo sensitizers have been in existence a number of years, but are relatively low in sensitivity. The sensitivity of pure polymer emulsion on the other hand is high due to the sensitizer Strylpyridinium Groups Compound (SBQ). Dual cure emulsions combine both diazo and SBQ sensitizers providing excellent results for water and solvent resistant properties. (See also pages 118-119.)

Diazo sensitizers have a spectral distribution between 360 and 420 nanometers. Its peak sensitivity is about 400 nanometers. Spectral distribution of SBQ sensitizers is between 320 and 360 nanometers with peak sensitivity at about 340 nanometers[2]. See Figure 6-14.

The differences in these aspects of sensitivity have a major affect on stencil exposure. For example a diazo sensitized emulsion may require a two minute exposure time while a pure polymer needs only twelve seconds. Dual cure emulsion would need 1½ minutes exposure time.

Photographic stencil emulsions are not sensitive to light in the yellow part of the visible light spectrum (550 nanometers). By using yellow safelights in the screen making area, sensitized screen can be left out for extended periods of time with no fear of exposure. Conventional fluorescent lights emit a small amount of light in the 400 to 500 nanometer range. If the screen is left out for an extended period of time in fluorescent light it will cumulatively expose the screen.

DEFINITION Definition is the quality of the edge, or the stencil's ability to produce a clean, sharp result. This can be affected by production problems such as improper ink flow out during printing resulting in a loss of sharpness or definition.

RESOLUTION Resolution is the ability of the emulsion to produce fine details. Some stencils provide higher resolution than others. It is best to consult the manufacturer's representative for the proper stencil to meet your needs.

BRIDGING Bridging relates to the stencil's ability to faithfully reproduce the image without being affected by the fibers of the mesh. This is more difficult to achieve with a coarse mesh than with a fine one. Also, some stencil products have better bridging characteristics than others.

EMULSION LIFE Various stencil types have differing life spans based on the type of sensitizer used. Sensitizers for pure polymers have a long life span while other sensitizers have a relatively short life span. To maximize the life span of liquid direct emulsions, the diazo sensitizer is kept separate from the emulsion until needed. Once the sensitizer is added the life span is limited. Unsensitized liquid emulsion has a shelf life of 36 months. Once the sensitizer is added the emulsion has an effective life as long as three months which varies by product and manufacturer. If refrigerated the pot life can be increased significantly. Pure polymer emulsion has a shelf life of over one year.

Once coated the screen is at its maximum sensitivity for 1½ to 3 months based on the emulsion composition. Screens should not be coated too far in advance or they will decease in sensitivity. Presensitized films such as capillary and indirect are sensitized by the manufacturer. Once it is sensitized its shelf life is limited. The life of diazo capillary films is from 12 to 18 months before sensitivity of the film diminishes. Once past its expiration it will be increasingly difficult to wash out image areas of the stencil.

Gelatin type indirect films have a shelf life of 18 to 24 months and polymer type indirect film has a shelf life of 36 months. Some manufacturers have a coding system to identify when the film was sensitized to keep track of its shelf life.

Photographic Indirect Stencils

The stencil is exposed and processed indirect from the screen fabric with this method. Once processing is complete the stencil is adhered to the screen fabric. Since the stencil is exposed without the fabric present high definition results can be achieved. With other **photographic stencils** the screen is embedded into the emulsion. Light scatter occurs during exposure which causes light undercutting and a loss of definition.

Since the indirect stencil is applied to the screen after processing it is merely hanging on to the bottom of the screen fabric. It lacks the durability of stencil systems such as direct emulsion. Generally run lengths up to 5,000 can be expected. Indirect stencils can only be used with solvent based inks, and are incompatible with water based inks. The indirect stencil is declining in use according to recent surveys due to its lack of durability and versatility. Refer back to Figure 6-8.

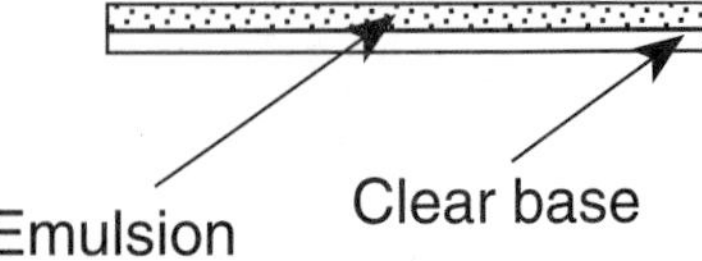

Figure 6-15 Photographic indirect film

STENCIL COMPOSITION Indirect stencils consist of a clear polyester or vinyl base (0.02", 0.03" or 0.05") that has been coated with pigmented gelatin or polymer emulsion as shown in Figure 6-15. The film has been pre-sensitized during coating by adding ferric salt. A colored dye (red, blue and green) is added to differentiate between different stencils made by a manufacturer. This enables personnel to readily establish the product used.

STENCIL PROCESSING There are several steps in producing an indirect stencil as shown in Figure 6-16. The stencil is exposed and processed. After processing is complete the stencil is adhered to the screen fabric. Processing of gelatin or polymer types vary slightly. Polymer type indirect stencils do not need the hardening stage used with gelatin stencils. Processing steps for gelatin type indirect stencils are: degreasing, exposure, hardening, washout, adhering, and drying.

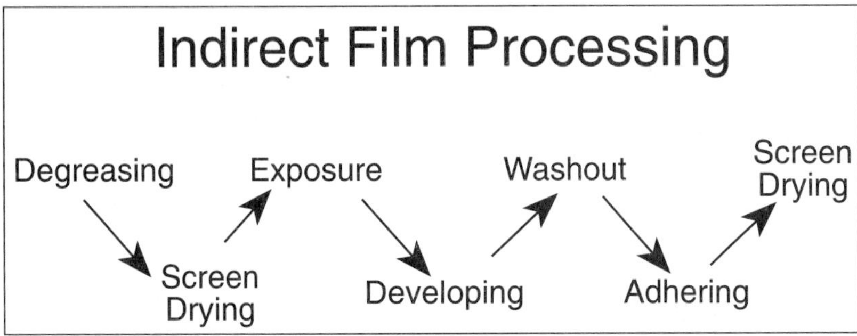

Figure 6-16 Indirect film processing

DEGREASING The importance of abrading and degreasing of the fabric has been stressed earlier in the chapter. Fabric abrasion is particularly important with indirect stencil to insure there is adequate surface areas for the stencil to attach. The indirect stencil has more trouble adhering to the monofilament fibers than other stencil types. Once degreased the screen must be placed in a drying cabinet since indirect stencils are applied to clean dry fabric. In some cases the stencil is adhered to the mesh while it is slightly wet.

EXPOSURE Indirect film should be cut one inch larger than the image size in each dimension. Indirect film can be exposed in a conventional exposure unit with a hard blanket, commonly used for platemaking in commercial printing facilities.

Indirect film is placed in the vacuum frame base side up (toward the light source). The film positive is then placed on top of the indirect film so the image is wrong reading. See Figure 6-17. The film is exposed backward so when adhered to the screen it will be right reading (toward the light source).

Procedures for establishing the correct exposure time will be addressed later in the chapter. In simple terms insufficient exposure causes the stencil to lack durability. On the other hand if exposure is too long details will be lost. Correct exposure is very important in achieving high quality results.

Film Positive

Indirect Film

Vacuum Base

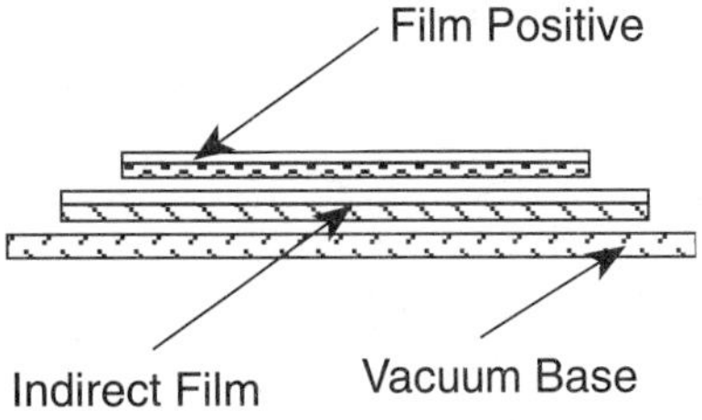

Figure 6-17 Film orientation for indirect stencil exposure

HARDENING Polymer type indirect stencils become hardened through the exposure process alone. Gelatin stencils require a second stage or development to complete hardening. This is accomplished by immersion in a hydrogen peroxide solution as shown in Figure 6-18. This developer (or activator) as it is sometimes called is available in powdered form from the manufacturer. Using developer provided by the manufacturer provides

Figure 6-18 Stencil hardening

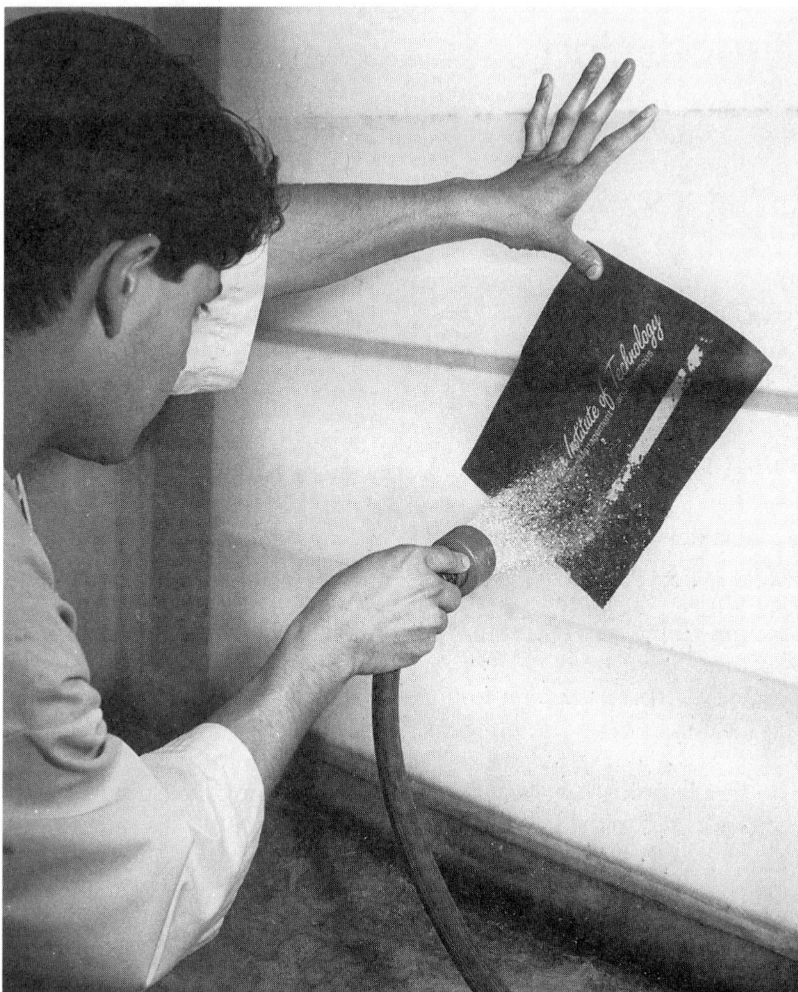

Figure 6-19 Indirect stencil washout

the best results with the proper dilution. If commercial solutions are used they must be diluted to the proper strength of 1.2%. Commercial solutions are often at 3% concentration and can be diluted with an equal volume of water to achieve a 1.5% solution.

Gelatin films must be completely immersed emulsion side up in developer at 66 to 70°F , from one minute to 90 seconds according to the manufacturer's recommendations. Developer may be used more than once and will change in color. It should be discarded when it becomes dark in color and should not be stored once used.

WASHOUT Image areas of the stencil should be washed out using a spray nozzle, and with a medium force to remove image areas from the stencil. See Figure 6-19. The stencil can be held on a vertical board emulsion side up for washout. The recommended washout temperature varies between products. Gelatin films require washout temperatures between 95 to 115°F. Polymer films may be washed out by using cold water although warm water speeds washout and produces the best results.

As image areas of the stencil are washed out they appear clear. The last stage of washout is critical. While image areas may appear to be clear this does not mean that all of the emulsion is entirely removed. In the final stage of washout a thin layer of gelatin remains in a clear state. This is known as scumming. This thin film blocks the flow of ink.

There are several ways to minimize problems with scumming. The stencil must be thoroughly washed out, including nonimage areas. Soft gelatin from nonimage areas left unwashed may flow into image areas. The stencil should be chilled in cold water (60-68°F) for 10 to 30 seconds after washout to partially harden the gelatin stencil. Dampening the mesh prior to application of the stencil may also minimize scumming problems.

ADHERING Adhesion is especially critical with indirect stencils. The stencil is applied to the bottom of the screen after washout. There are a number of factors that may interfere with adhesion. Mesh preparation, both abrasion and degreasing, are essential with an indirect stencil. Proper contact is also important between the film emulsion and screen fabric. This is best accomplished using a buildup board. This board must be smaller than the frame to function properly. The proper contact is essential in forcing the emulsion to bond onto the fibers of the screen fabric. See Figure 6-20.

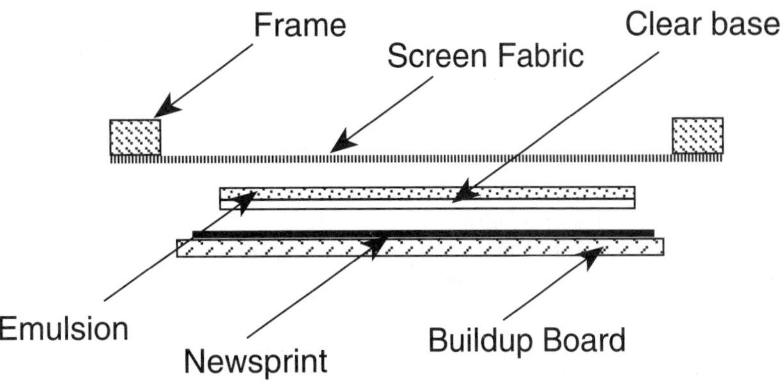

Figure 6-20 Adhering indirect stencils

Newsprint should be placed on top of the buildup board to prevent the indirect film from sticking to the buildup board. The stencil may be placed on top of the paper in place on the buildup. The degreased screen can then be lowered to establish contact between the stencil emulsion and the screen fabric. It is important to not allow air pockets to form between the stencil emulsion and fabric. Another approach is to place the screen frame on a table print side up and carefully place the stencil emulsion onto the screen. After placement the frame is inverted and placed on the buildup board.

Excess moisture should be removed by blotting with several sheets of newsprint. A painting roller may be used to apply light, even pressure to assist in removal of water from the emulsion. Excess pressure will cause damage to the fragile gelatin stencil, reducing its durability.

DRYING The frame should remain in place on the buildup for ten minutes to allow the emulsion to harden and bond onto the fibers of the fabric. If removed from the buildup prematurely adhesion problems may occur. Once removed from the buildup a water based liquid blockout may be applied so the stencil and blockout will both dry at the same time. The screen should then be placed in a drying cabinet to speed drying. For best results the drying cabinet should not exceed 100°F. High drying temperatures can cause stencil brittleness or curl of the stencil edges.

A minimum of 30 minutes drying time may be needed for the stencil to dry completely. All moisture must be removed from the stencil before the plastic base is removed. Once dry the base will easily separate from the emulsion. If removed by force detail areas may not adhere to the fabric but remain on the plastic base when removed. The stencil will not achieve maximum durability unless completely dry. After removal of the base, final touch-up with blockout may be done to eliminate unwanted pinholes or defects prior to printing.

Direct Stencils

Direct stencils produce image areas on the screen itself. There are a number of methods to produce a direct stencil as shown in Figure 6-21. Artists make stencils using a tusche and glue technique.

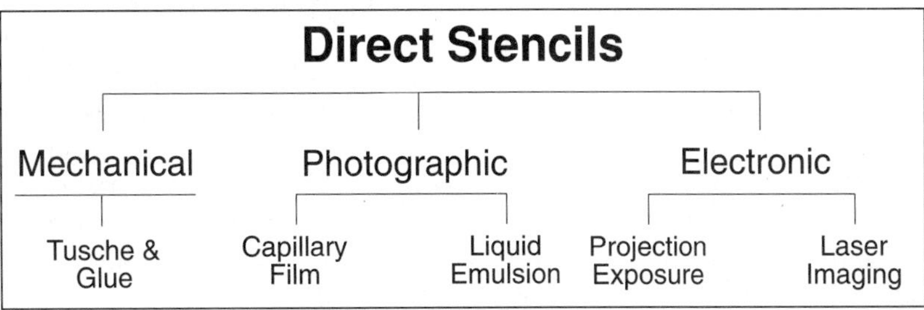

Figure 6-21 Direct stencils

It is a mechanical method that requires skill. The artist paints directly on the screen to create an image.

Other direct methods are photomechanical using a film to replace the mechanical skill required in cutting. With a film that is prepared properly the same screen can be produced every time. There are two direct photographic stencils in use today: liquid emulsion and capillary film. Modern electronic methods can be used to produce a direct stencil. One method is to project an image at an enlarged size directly on the sensitized emulsion on the screen. The latest method uses a laser to image directly on the screen eliminating the need for film.

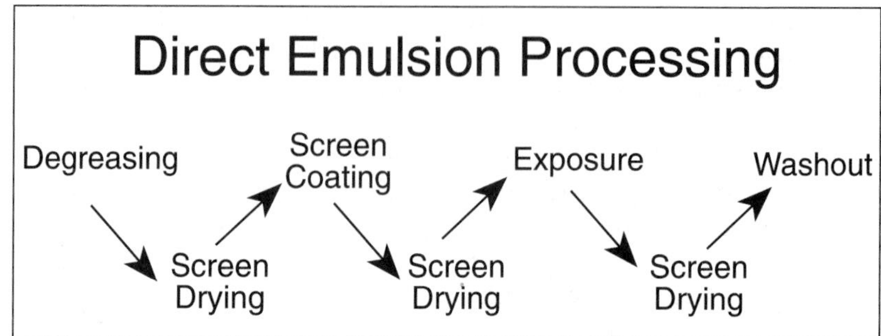

Figure 6-22 Direct emulsion processing

Liquid Direct Emulsion

With this method a light sensitive liquid emulsion is coated on the screen fabric and allowed to dry. Once dry the stencil is exposed and washed out with water. It is ready to print once the stencil is dry. Direct emulsions are compatible with both solvent and water based inks. It is the most durable of stencil types with run lengths of over 200,000. This is the most common of all stencil types used in the screen printing industry to date.

STENCIL COMPOSITION Stencil products are composed of various polymers, resins and other compounds to give them their various properties. Using different combinations of these basic compounds makes them suited for different applications. Each formulation has advantages and disadvantages. The three common formulations of liquid direct photo emulsions are diazo sensitized, pure polymer and dual cure.

DIAZO SENSITIZED EMULSION Three components make up this type of emulsion: polyvinyl alcohol (PVOH), polyvinyl acetate (PVA) and diazo sensitizer. The amount of PVOH controls the degree of solvent resistance. The amount of PVA gives it its water resistance. Both water and solvent resistance cannot be achieved with this emulsion. The stencil manufacturer formulates the emulsion based on its use. If it is to be used with water based inks, a high PVA content would achieve the water resistance needed. An emulsion for use with solvent based inks would be formulated with a high PVOH content. Fillers and other additives are used to regulate flow and viscosity of the emulsion.

Diazo sensitizer must be added to make the emulsion light sensitive. Diazo is biodegradable and sensitive to light between 360 to 420 nanometers. Diazo sensitizer comes in a small bottle and must be added by the screen maker prior to application. It is either in powdered or syrup form. This gives the emulsion a longer shelf life by not adding the sensitizer during manufacture.

The diazo sensitizer initiates a photo chemical reaction which causes the molecules on the emulsion to form bonds and crosslink after exposure to light. The sensitizer will not achieve its greatest sensitivity unless completely dry. Any water remaining in the emulsion will decrease the effectiveness of the diazo sensitizer. (See also Figure 6-14, page 113.)

PURE POLYMER This emulsion uses light sensitive resins which eliminates the need for a separate sensitizer to be added before use. These light sensitive resins are produced by using PVOH and adding Strylpyridinium Groups Compound (SBQ). The SBQ becomes linked to the PVOH during manufacture. Due to the molecular structure of the emulsion it has low water resistance and it not recommended for use with water based inks. SBQ has its highest sensitivity in the range of 320 to 360 nanometers.

DUAL CURE This emulsion is made up of a mixture of PVA, PVOH, and diazo sensitizer. Light sensitive resins (containing SBQ) are added instead of fillers. This gives the formulation properties of both emulsion types. It offers higher solids content, higher water resistance, higher resolution, and fast exposure times. This makes it possible for a stencil to offer both water and solvent resistance with the same formulation.

Stencil Processing

There are several steps in producing a liquid direct emulsion stencil as shown in Figure 6-22. The screen fabric must be coated with a light sensitive emulsion and allowed to dry. Once dry the screen is exposed and processed to create the image areas of the stencil. The processing steps are degreasing, coating, drying, exposure, washout and drying.

EMULSION MIXING Diazo sensitized and dual cure emulsions require sensitizer to be added by the screen maker. Pure polymer formulations do not require the addition of sensitizer as they are ready to use.

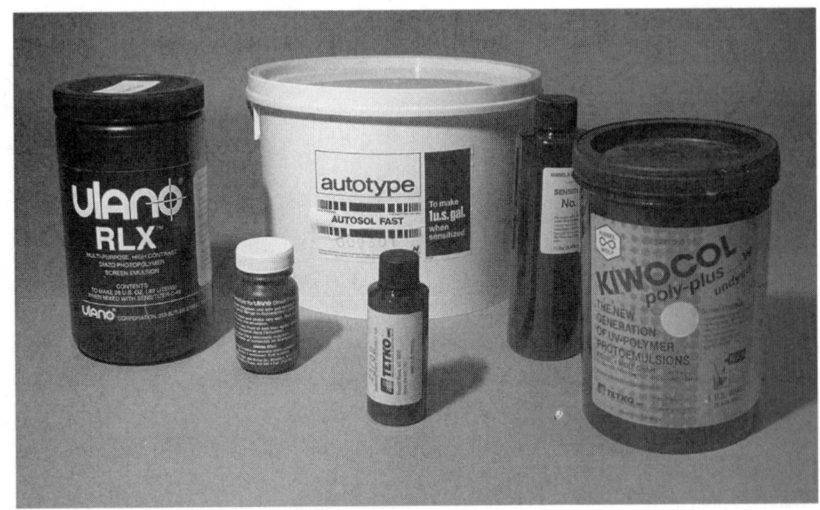

Figure 6-23 Emulsion and sensitizer

It is essential that the sensitizer is added to the emulsion correctly to achieve the proper emulsion performance. Diazo sensitizer is supplied in a small bottle to which water is added as shown in Figure 6-23. It is important that the diazo is thoroughly dissolved. Lukewarm water may help in dissolving the powder or syrup more easily. Distilled water is often recommended to prevent problems with impurities in the water affecting the emulsion.

Sensitizer must not remain in the bottle after addition to the emulsion. All of the sensitizer must be added for the emulsion to achieve the performance it was designed for. One method to achieve this is to fill the bottle part way with water the first time. After adding to the emulsion the bottle is rinsed a second time to remove the remaining sensitizer from the bottle. Excess water should not be added to the emulsion or the viscosity and coating characteristics may be affected.

In some cases a colored dye is provided in a separate container to be added to the emulsion. This allows the screen maker to choose between dyed and undyed emulsion. Most emulsion comes with the dye already added. The dye can be helpful in color coding various emulsion types, keeping them from being confused. Using undyed emulsion is not without consequence. White fabric allows light scatter to occur during exposure of the direct stencil. That is the reason that fabrics are dyed yellow, orange or red to absorb light and minimize this scattering effect. Emulsion is dyed for the same reason.

Undyed emulsion will allow light scatter resulting in a loss of resolution and definition. How much will be lost can vary depending on the job. The best approach would be to make a test with two identical screens, one using undyed emulsion and the second with dyed emulsion exposing both with a film positive of the finest type or detail you need to reproduce. Both screens should then be printed and results carefully analyzed. It it critical that everything is the same in the test (except the emulsions) with both screens such as tension, mesh count, ink, and so on or else this test will not be valid.

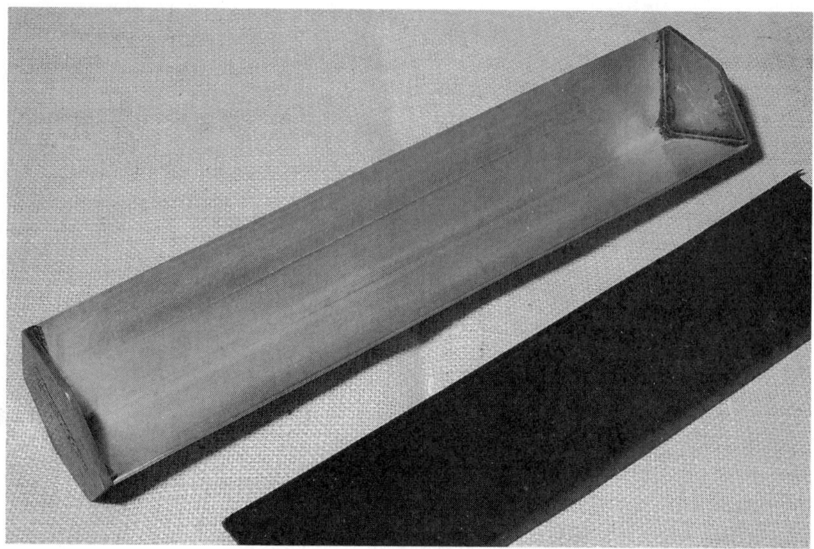

Figure 6-24 Coating trough

The reason why undyed emulsion is used is that it allows faster setup on press. It is easier for the pressman to see through the emulsion to line up the job. On the other hand dyed emulsion produces superior resolution and definition. Each situation must determine which is the most important for their circumstance. If a printer did not desire to print fine details there may not be significant differences in the printed results, and undyed emulsion could be used without consequence.

After being added to the emulsion the sensitizer must be thoroughly combined into the emulsion. The emulsion should be viewed briefly under white light to insure complete mixing has occurred. The mixing process allows air to be trapped within the emulsion. If the emulsion is used to coat a screen too soon after mixing it will be difficult to achieve optimum coating results. For best results allow the emulsion to sit for several hours or overnight for the air to work itself out. Ultrasonic devices are available that will speed the removal of air bubbles from the emulsion so it can be used directly after being mixed. Another method uses a vacuum device to draw air bubbles out.

DEGREASING The importance of abrading and degreasing of the fabric has been stressed earlier in the chapter. Direct emulsion stencils must be applied to a clean dry screen. The screen should be placed in a drying cabinet once degreased until completely dry. This will help to keep it free from dust.

EMULSION APPLICATION The stencil is created by applying a liquid emulsion directly to the mesh. Once dry the light sensitive stencil is exposed with a film positive to create image and nonimage areas. Coating of the liquid emulsion is critical to the process. It can be a difficult task to achieve a coating that is consistent throughout the screen area. Liquid emulsions are composed of up to 50% water in some cases. When the water evaporates from the emulsion it can result in inconsistency as the emulsion dries around the fibers of the mesh. This is most extreme with a thin coating (such as a 1 x 1) on a coarse mesh. By increasing the number of coats the wet emulsion thickness is increased. A thick coating will achieve greater uniformity than a thin coating. For this reason multiple coats such as a 2 x 2 or greater is commonly used.

Each side of the screen is coated

Figure 6-25 Coater edge profile

to achieve uniformity. Initially, the print side is coated first with the squeegee side coated last. This forces the emulsion to the print side of the screen. The screen is placed in the drying rack print side down to keep the emulsion build-up on the print side of the screen. This is essential to achieve proper ink flow out during printing.

COATING TROUGH The coating trough is an important tool in achieving the best results. It can be purchased in different sizes based on screen sizes. See Figure 6-24. The coating trough should be at least 2 inches smaller than the inside frame dimension for best results. A modern coating trough is designed to eliminate many of the variables of the coating process. The variables of coating are: coating edge profile, coating angle, coating pressure and coating speed.

COATING EDGE PROFILE Coating troughs are available in two distinct edge profiles: rounded and sharp edge. A rounded edge deposits more emulsion and delivers faster buildup to achieve the desired emulsion thickness. A sharp edge is used for achieving a thin emulsion buildup such as wet on dry coating technique. By selecting between the two, the thickness of the emulsion can be regulated. A rounded edge is used under most circumstances with wet on wet coating procedures. Coaters are available that incorporate both profiles into one trough with a rounded edge on one side and a sharp edge on the second side. See Figure 6-25.

COATING ANGLE Changing the angle of the trough will change the emulsion deposit. Increasing the angle increases the deposit. It is most important for the angle to be consistent during the coating process otherwise the screen will not be coated consistently. A modern trough is designed to place the coater at the best coating angle. This is achieved with plastic end caps that act as a guide to set the proper angle.

During the coating process the edge of the coater is brought into contact with the screen near the bottom. The trough is then rolled to bring the end caps into contact with the screen. This forms a reservoir of emulsion that is in contact with the screen. The trough is then pulled in an upward direction to apply an even coating of emulsion.

COATING PRESSURE Often an inexperienced screen maker may not exert enough pressure to coat the screen. Insufficient pressure will cause uneven or improper emulsion thickness. On the other hand too much pressure could cause the mesh to be ripped. Most important of all, consistent pressure must be maintained throughout the entire coating process otherwise the thickness will vary.

COATING SPEED Coating speed may need to be changed with the viscosity of the emulsion. With high solids emulsions viscosity is higher and will require a slower coating speed. If coating speed is

Figure 6-26 Coating rack

too fast air bubbles may become trapped in the emulsion.

COATING RACK A coating rack is essential in achieving high quality coating of liquid direct emulsion stencils. It should be adjustable to work with a variety of sizes of frames. See Figure 6-26. The rack should allow adjustment of the angle that the frame is held. The best coating results can be achieved if the screen is tilted slightly from a direct vertical position.

The rack should hold the frame securely so that the operator can use both hands to manipulate the trough easily and consistently. The rack should allow the screen to be placed in a reasonable working position so the operator does not have to strain to do the coating. This will assist in achieving the most consistent results.

AUTOMATIC COATER An automated coating machine can be used to control the coating process. See Figure 6-27. The device is programmed to coat a screen the same each time with a specific coating procedure. This device will produce the ultimate in coating consistency. Although this is the ideal solution to coating consistency, the price of this device is often beyond the financial resources of the average screen printer.

COATING TECHNIQUE The mesh count of the fabric sets the standard for stencil thickness regardless of the stencil type. A coarse mesh requires a thick stencil coating while a fine mesh requires a thin coating. Changing stencil thickness with direct emulsion is more complex than with capillary films. Various techniques must be employed to create the desired thickness needed.

During the coating process the edge of the coater is brought into contact with the screen near the bottom. The trough is then rolled to bring the end caps into contact with the screen. The trough is then pulled in an upward direction to apply an even coating of emulsion.

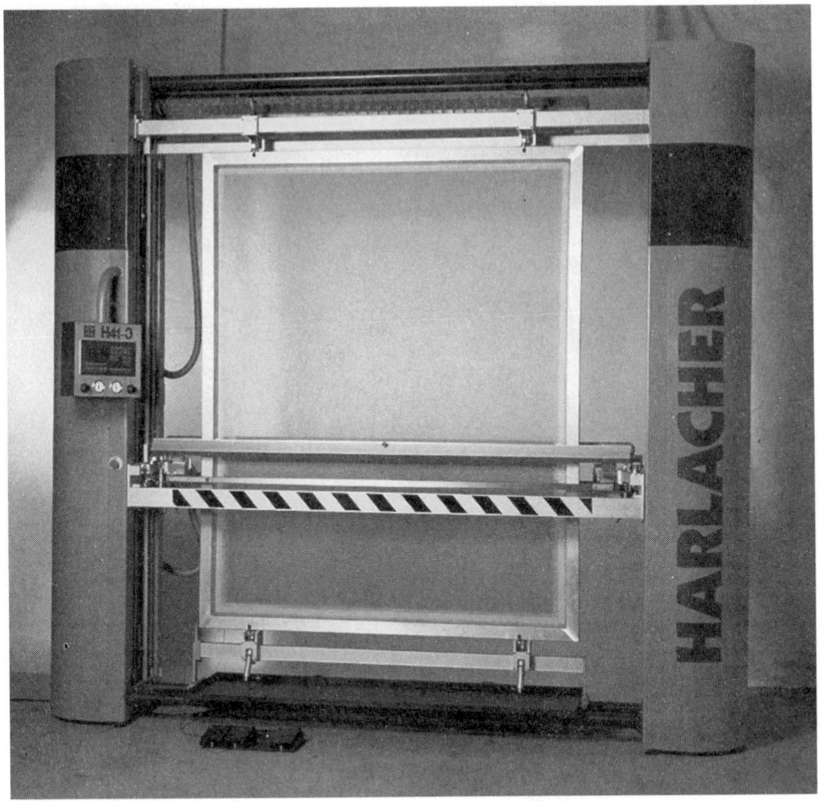

Figure 6-27 Automatic coater *(Majestech Corp.)*

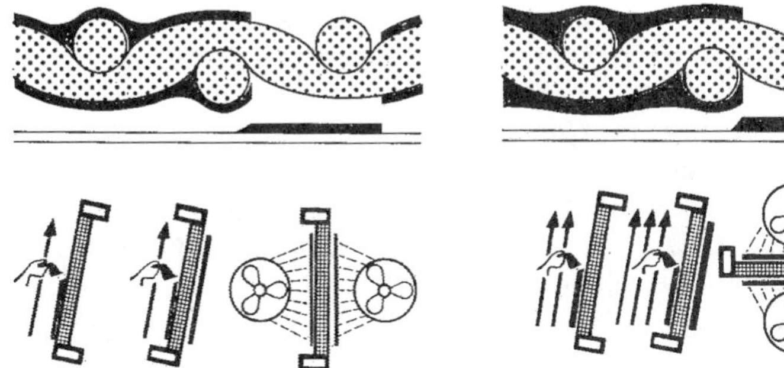

Figure 6-28 Wet-on-wet (1 x 1) *(Ulano Corp.)*

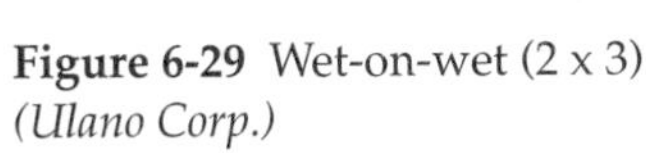

Figure 6-29 Wet-on-wet (2 x 3) *(Ulano Corp.)*

Near the end of the stroke the trough is then rocked to draw the emulsion back into the trough away from the screen. The edge is then removed from contact with the screen. This is repeated until the desired number of coats are made. It is important to keep an adequate supply of emulsion in the coating trough. A small quantity of emulsion in the trough will produce a different emulsion buildup than if the trough is full. The trough includes a cover to protect the edge from nicks or dents.

WET-ON-WET COATING Liquid emulsion is applied to both sides of the screen. Due to the high proportion of water in the emulsion, coating each side of the mesh with emulsion (such as 1 x 1 coating) will result in an inconsistent surface as it dries around the fibers. See Figure 6-28. Additional coats must be applied wet-on-wet to compensate for the loss of water to achieve a uniform surface coating which can increase the ink deposit. Increasing the number of coats applied to the screen increases the stencil thickness. This places two or more coats on both the printing and squeegee side of the mesh. The minimum coating normally used is a 2 x 2 or 2 x 3 wet-on-wet technique. See Figure 6-29.

EMULSION THICKNESS CONTROL Another production problem is the difficulty in maintaining emulsion thickness consistency with direct emulsion stencils. This often results in significant printed color shifts between press runs. Obviously the nature of the manual coating process contributes to this problem. Proper coating tools and techniques are crucial in achieving consistent results.

Coating procedure must be varied between a low and high mesh count for best results. A coarse mesh has greater open area than a high mesh count. For example, if a 255 monofilament polyester mesh (40μ thread) is coated with a 2 x 2 wet-on-wet technique, typically the emulsion coating will be 8μ when dried. Coating a 355 monofilament polyester mesh (37μ thread) with the same 2 x 2 technique produces an emulsion buildup of only 4μ. To create a buildup similar to the 255 mesh a 2 x 4 wet-on-wet coating gives a 355 mesh a 10μ coating.[3]

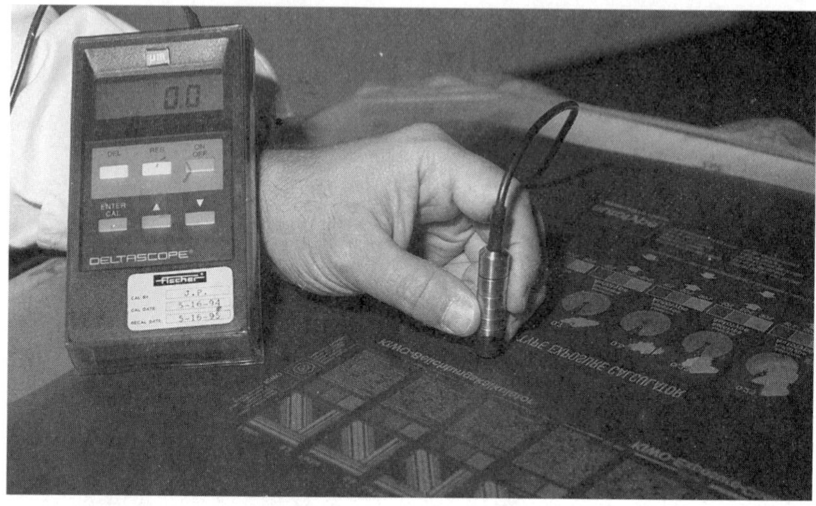

Figure 6-30 Emulsion thickness measuring

This illustrates the relationship between mesh and coating technique. Tests should be conducted under your own conditions to determine the proper coating procedure to use for each mesh in your inventory. Once a procedure is determined for maintaining a consistent coating thickness the question of emulsion thickness must be answered. As can be seen, changing the number of coats of emulsion applied increases or decreases the thickness. First let us look at the extremes. If too few coats are made the emulsion will result in an uneven surface as it dries around the fibers. When the print side of the screen has an uneven surface it will allow ink to flow into nonimage areas causing a poor quality print which gives it a **sawtoothed** edge. By increasing the number of coatings the surface consistency will improve when dry. But there are consequences of using too many coats. With each additional coat more emulsion is deposited on the screen resulting in an increase in emulsion thickness. For example, when coating a 305 monofilament polyester (37μ thread) with a 2 x 2 coating it results in a 5μ emulsion buildup. With a 2 x 3 coating it increases to a 10μ buildup, and with a 2 x 4, a 15μ buildup. Each coat increases emulsion thickness and the resulting ink film thickness to a certain extent. At a certain point when the emulsion buildup is too thick it will be difficult to force ink through the image areas and the ink may remain in the mesh after the print stroke.

There is another reason for the importance of emulsion thickness. It relates to the ability of ink to flow out during the printing process. The emulsion thickness must be sufficient to allow the ink to flow under the threads of image areas. If the emulsion is too thin, ink will have difficulty in flowing under the threads resulting in visible mesh marks or sawtoothing effects.

To eliminate emulsion thickness inconsistencies, a quality control check should be made to monitor the emulsion thickness. The emulsion thickness can be measured using a test instrument as shown in Figure 6-30. This device measures the mesh and stencil thicknesses and gives a measurement known as percent emulsion over mesh (E/M %R). The emulsion thickness of the stencil can be compared to recommended values to determine effectiveness of the coating process. For fine line halftones it is recommended to have 8–15% E/M %R, while with textiles from 20–25% E/M %R.

Emulsion measurements must be taken prior to exposure. This assures the proper thickness consistency between screens as well as within the screen itself. This allows the emulsion thickness to be

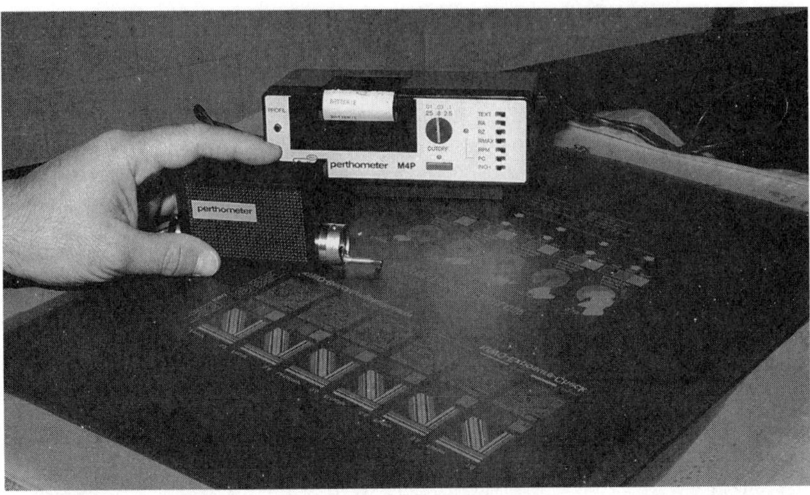

Figure 6-31 Perthometer

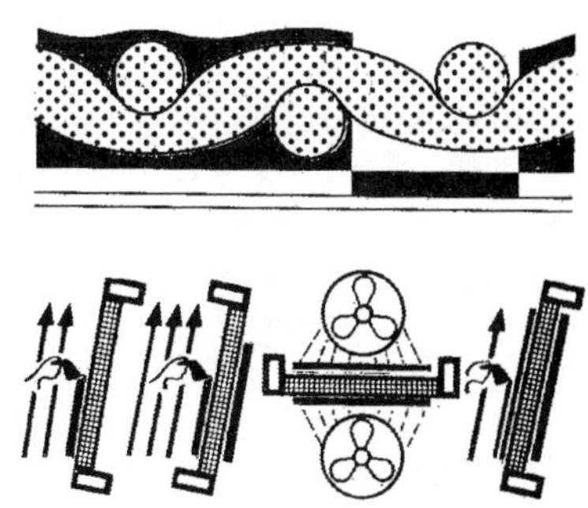

Figure 6-32 Wet-on-dry (2 x 3 x 1) *(Ulano Corp.)*

monitored from day to day to evaluate consistency of procedures.

In addition to bench marking the emulsion thickness it would be useful to measure the surface consistency. This can be evaluated using a device known as a perthometer that moves a probe over the surface of the coated screen. See Figure 6-31. It assigns a numerical value to the reading that helps predict the screen potential for printing a high quality image. A smooth emulsion coating is indicated by a low value which would achieve a high quality printed result.

A high value indicates an uneven surface. For instance glass has a reading of 0.09μ and bond paper a value of 12.36μ. For best results it is recommended that stencils have a reading of 3 to 7μ.

WET-ON-DRY COATING Another technique which improves surface quality of the emulsion without drastically affecting ink deposit is known as wet-on-dry. A screen is coated wet-on-wet (2 x 3 for example) and the emulsion is allowed to dry. Then an additional face or fill coat is applied to the underside (print side) of the screen. See Figure 6-32. This fills in the uneven areas of the stencil and improves the evenness of the coating. It does not increase the overall stencil thickness significantly. Yet this operation requires an additional coating and drying step.

EMULSION DRYING A drying cabinet as shown in Figure 6-33 is needed to achieve the drying consistency required. A drying cabinet of the proper design provides consistent airflow at a controlled temperature and humidity. It also filters the air, preventing dust

Figure 6-33 Drying cabinet

from attaching to the wet emulsion, thus averting problems with pinholes and minimizing touch-ups before printing. It can also be used to dry the screen after degreasing, keeping it dust free. Ideally the dryer should be set at 104°F with 40% humidity or less.

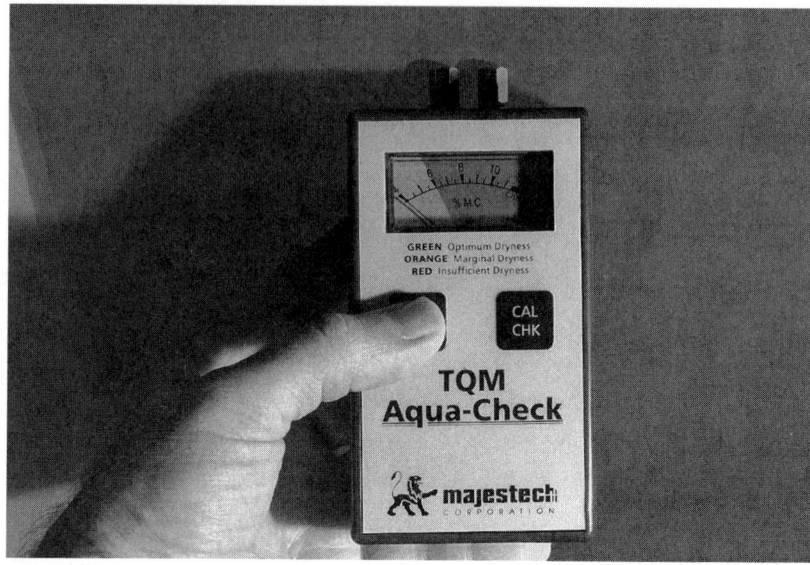

Figure 6-34 Aqua-Check device

EMULSION MOISTURE CONTENT Direct emulsion is composed of up to 50% water and is applied in liquid form to the screen mesh. As the emulsion dries, water content decreases and sensitivity increases. In order to reach maximum sensitivity the emulsion must be completely dry. Any moisture in the emulsion will decrease its sensitivity resulting in underexposure. Under exposed stencils will have decreased durability and lower solvent resistance.

If direct emulsion is not dried consistently each time it will vary in moisture content and sensitivity, and accurate exposure will be impossible to predict. With varying degrees of moisture present all screens will not be exposed consistently, even though they have been exposed the same time. The solution is to dry the emulsion consistently every time. Then after an exposure test has been made it will be consistent with each screen produced.

Here is an example of a case which illustrates the problem of moisture in the stencil and its effects on exposure and durability. One shop produced 15,000 prints using water based ink where the stencil was dried properly in an approved drying cabinet. Another printer used the same water based ink and stencil without drying the screen properly and experienced stencil breakdown after only 150 prints. Moisture in the stencil prior to exposure caused its sensitivity to be diminished resulting in an underexposed stencil with reduced durability and resistance to water based inks.

Since elimination of moisture from the emulsion is so important, how can this be monitored? A simple approach is to dry the coated screen in the drying cabinet for an extended time or overnight. This would assure complete drying. But due to the production needs of the typical screen printing company this is not practical. A better approach would be to establish a procedure to dry each coated screen for the same length of time.

It would be better if there was some moisture present, with the same content from screen to screen than if the moisture content varies. When an exposure calibration test is made the moisture content can be compensated by a increase in exposure time. The most important point is consistency. The same moisture content in each screen when exposed the same will result in the same exposure result. To achieve this each screen should be dried a set time based on productivity needs.

With the proper drying cabinet at the proper temperature and humidity, a 305T monofilament polyester with a 2 x 3 coating requires about 10 minutes for complete drying. A coarse mesh such as a 110T with a 2 x 2 coating requires about 20 minutes drying time. The time should be as long as possible yet maintaining a flow of screens for productivity.

A device called TQM Aqua-

Check by Majestech measures stencil moisture content. See Figure 6-34. This device measures from 4 to 14% moisture content. It also rates moisture content, indicating green when drying is sufficient, yellow when caution is recommended and red when additional drying is required.

This can be helpful in evaluating moisture content of emulsion. For example, with a high mesh count the emulsion thickness is considerably less than a coarse mesh count. A thick emulsion coating (coarse mesh) will require more time to dry than a thin coating (with a high mesh count). This device gives you the ability to monitor and dry varying thickness of stencil emulsions consistently.

Capillary Film

Capillary film is an improved version of direct/indirect stencils. It combines properties of indirect and liquid direct photographic emulsions. Liquid emulsion is precoated on a plastic base, as shown in Figure 6-35. The thickness can be controlled consistently by the stencil manufacturer. It is available in a range of different thicknesses from 15μ up to 80μ. Capillary films have greater durability than indirect stencils but less than liquid direct emulsions. They are capable of run lengths up to 40,000.

Stencil Composition

Composition of the emulsion is the same between liquid emulsion and capillary films. Capillary films are available in the same three formulations as with the liquid emulsion type: diazo sensitized, pure polymer and dual cure. Capillary films consist of a clear polyester base that has been coated with liquid emulsion. See Figure 6-35. This allows a simplified application technique over liquid direct emulsion.

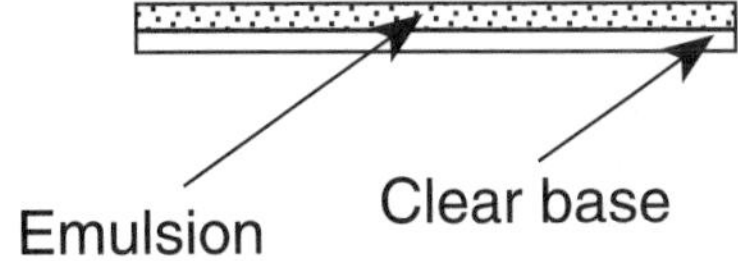

Figure 6-35 Capillary film

Stencil Processing

There are several steps in producing a liquid direct emulsion stencil, as shown in Figure 6-36. First, capillary film is applied to the mesh using water. Capillary action draws the emulsion up onto the mesh. After the film is applied to the mesh and allowed to dry the plastic base can be removed. It is exposed and processed the same as with a liquid direct emulsion. Processing steps are: degreasing, film application, stencil drying, exposure, washout and drying.

Degreasing/Wetting Agent

The screen must be degreased prior to film application. There are two ways to apply the capillary film to the screen. One method requires the screen to be dry prior to application; the second requires the screen to be wet. If the fabric has been properly degreased water will flow freely over its entire surface. If water is repelled from areas of the screen it indicates an oily residue is present and degreasing is not entirely successful.

Film Application

Capillary film is applied to the screen fabric prior to stencil exposure. There are two ways to apply capillary films: the wet screen method and the dry screen method. There are advantages and disadvantages to each method.

WET SCREEN APPLICATION METHOD This is the most common method used to apply capillary film. Once degreasing is completed the film is immediately applied. This eliminates a drying stage prior to film application. This

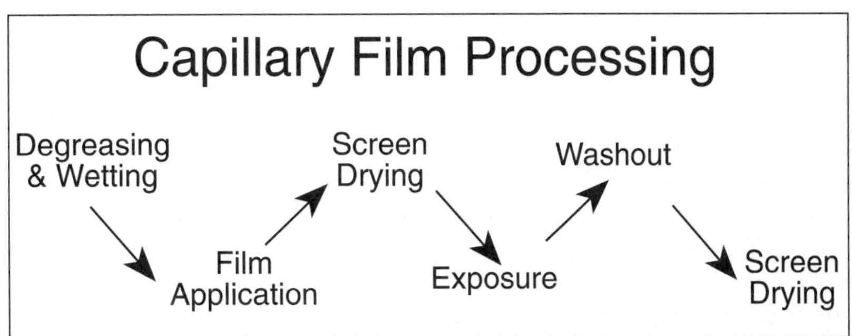

Figure 6-36 Capillary film processing

Figure 6-37 Capillary film roll down

minimizes opportunities for dust to be deposited onto the screen. This method can be used with large screens although may require some practice with very large sizes. It is essential that a uniform film of water is achieved on the screen for proper film application.

The screen should be placed in the degreasing sink in a vertical position with the print side facing the screen maker. Once the screen has been degreased a uniform film of water must remain on the screen for proper film application. A wetting agent assists water in forming uniformly on the screen. This can be done as a separate step after degreasing, or a degreasing agent containing a wetting agent can be used. This allows degreasing and wetting to be accomplished in one step. After a uniform flow of water has been achieved on the screen, capillary film should be applied.

Capillary film should be cut to size, several inches larger than the desired image size in each dimension. Film should be rolled on a narrow diameter plastic tube with the emulsion side out to simplify application. An anti-static may be used to remove dust particles from the film. A small amount of film should extend from the tube. The film is brought into contact starting with the top of the screen. The tube can be used to roll the film down to bring it into contact with the wet screen. See Figure 6-37. It is important that capillary film is applied immediately after degreasing to insure there is adequate water on the screen for capillary action to occur completely. If allowed to set even for a short time there will be inadequate water on the screen for proper application.

Once application is complete the screen can be turned around to remove moisture using a window squeegee. Firm steady pressure should be used to remove moisture. See Figure 6-38. The pressure used must be controlled and consistent due to its effect on final stencil thickness. Capillary action draws the emulsion into the mesh, not the squeegee stroke. The squeegee is used merely to remove the moisture once it has done its job and speed drying of the emulsion. Moisture should be wiped from outside areas of the screen to keep water from flowing back onto the stencil. This will cause thin areas on the stencil.

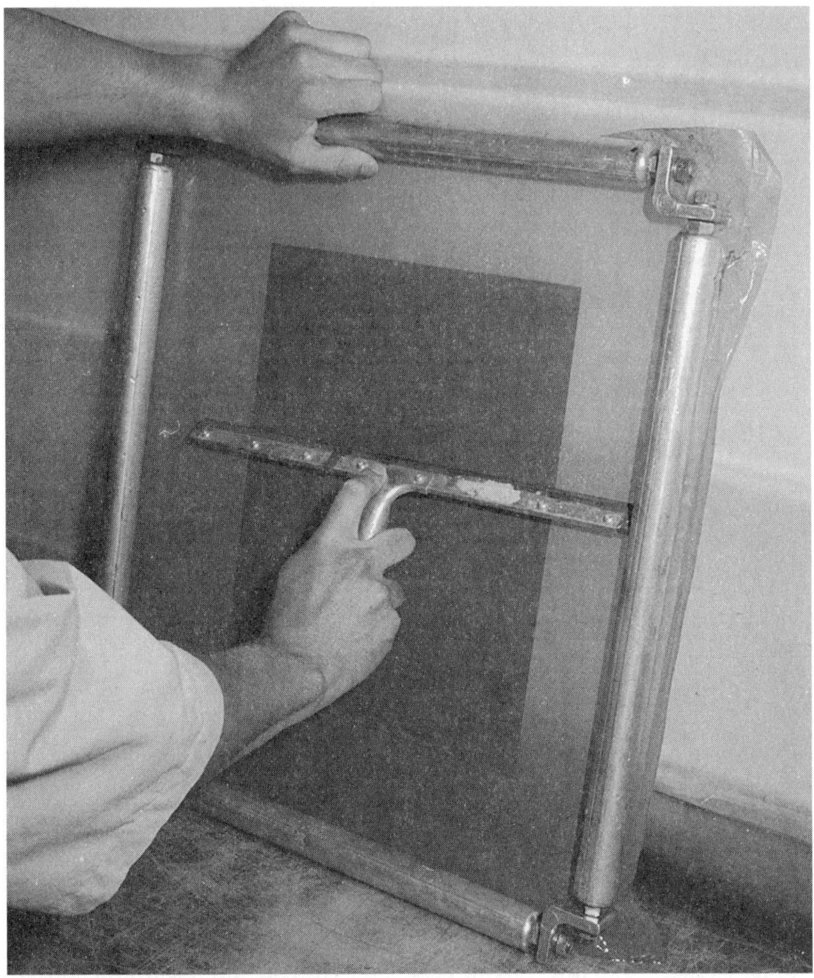

Figure 6-38 Squeegee action

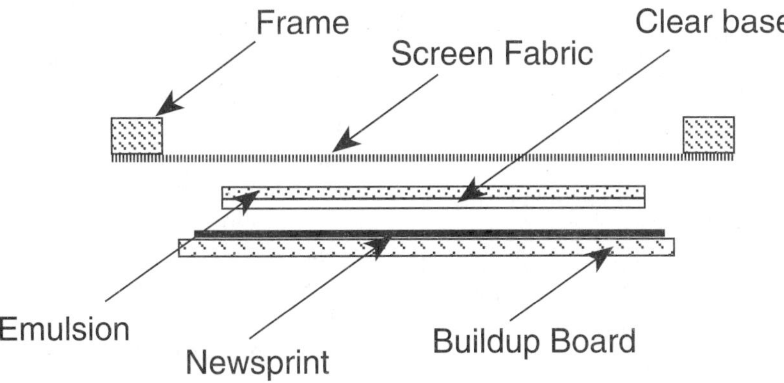

Figure 6-39 Dry screen application method

DRY SCREEN APPLICATION METHOD This method is used primarily with small screens and is not practical on a large scale. Application of water can be easier to control using this method. But there may be more problems with dust and dirt being trapped between the emulsion and fabric. Dust will have a greater opportunity to come into contact with the screen during the drying of the screen.

This method uses a screen that has been degreased and dried prior to film application. Contact between the capillary film and the screen fabric is important with this method. This can best be accomplished using a buildup board. The board should be smaller than the inside dimension of the frame. Several sheets of newsprint should be placed atop the buildup board to prevent the capillary film from sticking to the board after application.

Capillary film should be cut to size and placed on the newsprint with the emulsion side, dull side up. See Figure 6-39. The prepared screen should be then placed in contact with the film emulsion of the buildup board. This contact will cause the emulsion to bond onto the screen mesh once water is applied.

A spray bottle can be used to apply water to the screen in a controlled fashion. Water should be applied starting on one side working to the opposite side. Only enough water should be applied to cause capillary action to draw the emulsion into the mesh. As water is applied the emulsion will darken in color. Light areas indicate that additional water needs to be applied. An excessive amount of water creates undesirable consequences such as a loss of durability.

Once water is applied it should be removed by wiping clear using a window squeegee. Film steady pressure must be used to remove moisture. The pressure used must be controlled and kept consistent as it has a distinct effect of final stencil thickness. Capillary action draws the emulsion into the mesh, not the squeegee stroke. The squeegee is used merely to remove the moisture once it has done its job, speeding drying of the emulsion. Moisture should be wiped from outside areas of the screen to keep water from flowing back onto the stencil. This will cause thin areas on the stencil.

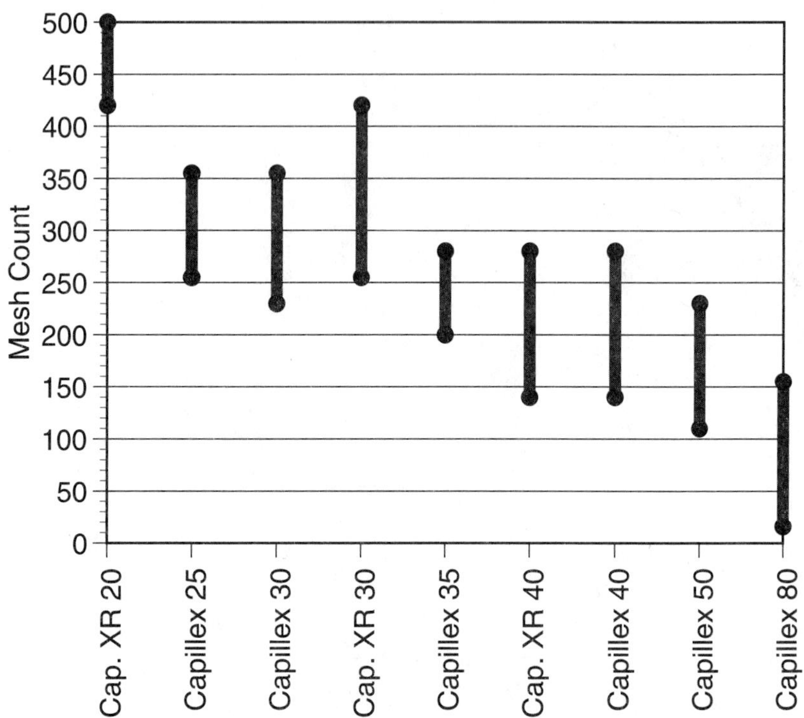

Figure 6-40 Capillary thickness chart

Stencil Drying

Once the stencil has been applied it should be placed in a drying cabinet to speed drying. It is best to place it in a horizontal position to prevent water from flowing back onto the stencil. For best results maximum temperature during drying should not exceed 104°F. As with liquid direct emulsion maximum sensitivity of the stencil will not be reached unless it is entirely dry. It is important to achieve complete drying of the stencil prior to exposure. Once dry the plastic backing sheet will easily separate from the emulsion. Any residual moisture present in the emulsion will make it difficult for the backing sheet to be removed. After removal of the backing sheet the film should be allowed to dry a few more minutes for best results.

Emulsion Thickness Control

Stencil thickness is a function of the screen fabric. A thick ink deposit requires a coarse mesh and a thick stencil coating should be applied. The converse holds true for a thin ink deposit. For a thick ink deposit a coarse mesh is selected which requires a thick capillary film. A chart can be consulted to determine the capillary to use for various mesh counts used. See Figure 6-40. For example, when using mesh in the range of 16–155 threads per inch mesh, an 80µ capillary film is recommended.

In a recent study by the Screen Printing Technical Foundation it was found that several factors related to stencil application can influence the final emulsion thickness of a capillary film.[3] Using various techniques during film application with 30µ capillary film, results in the final emulsion thickness varying from 10µ up to 17.2µ. There are over thirty factors that contribute to these variations. The two most significant factors are pressure exerted to remove excess water after film application and mesh count. It is imperative to maintain a consistent procedure each time a stencil is produced to minimize variations in the stencil thickness.

Capillex Laminator

This device is designed to quickly and easily produce capillary films up to 300μ thick. This is advantageous for specialized applications requiring thick ink deposits. Since 80μ film is the thickest film available this makes it possible to create greater thicknesses by combining them. The device is made up of two rubber rollers that apply uniform pressure so two thicknesses of capillary film can be laminated together creating a thicker film. See Figure 6-41. By laminating together two layers of 50μ film a 100μ film can be produced.

The laminating process is simple. Two sheets of capillary film are inserted into the laminator. Water is applied as the rollers bring the two layers of emulsion to contact with each other. The rollers are rotated to continue the process. After complete and allowed to dry, the plastic base can be removed from one side and the capillary film can be applied to the screen using normal application procedure.

Figure 6-41 Capillex laminator *(Autotype Int.)*

Backing Up Capillary Films

Due to the difference in application technique between liquid emulsion and capillary film, stencil durability varies significantly. With liquid direct emulsion the mesh is entirely encapsulated from both sides with emulsion. This is what makes liquid direct emulsion the most durable stencil. Capillary film migrates up into the mesh through capillary action from the print side of the screen.

Capillary films can be made more durable by backing up with a liquid emulsion. First capillary film is applied to the mesh. The screen should then be placed on a buildup board covered with newsprint. A small amount of backing emulsion should be placed on the screen, much the same as ink is applied. A slightly rounded squeegee can be used to draw the emulsion across the top surface of the screen. Excess emulsion should be removed from the screen before drying.

This extra coating will increase the stencil durability and run length of the capillary film. It is important to use the proper backing emulsion, one that is compatible with the composition of the capillary film used. The stencil manufacturer should be consulted for recommendation. Products from different manufacturers are not interchangeable for this procedure.

Direct Stencil Processing

After a stencil has been exposed it requires processing. The stencil must be washed out, as shown in Figure 6-42, and dried. Processing of both liquid emulsion and capillary film is nearly the same with only a few minor differences.

WASHOUT Image areas of the stencil are washed out with warm water after exposure. The higher

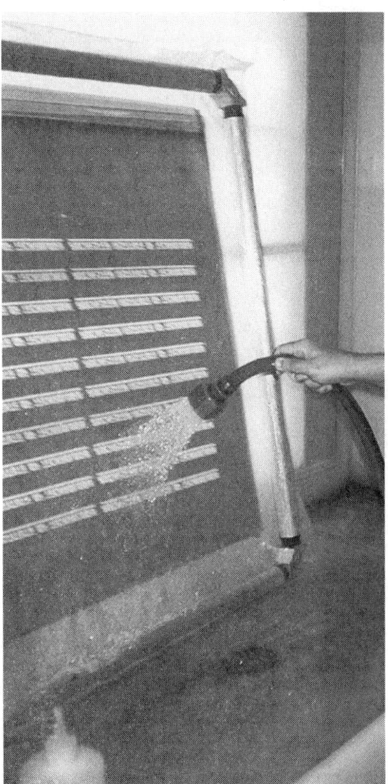

Figure 6-42 Stencil washout

the pressure or temperature of the water the faster it will wash out. But excessive water pressure or temperature can influence stencil quality or durability. The force of water applied to the stencil during washout can affect the quality of the stencil. It is best to use a nozzle that will produce a spray effect to reduce the force of the water. The use of a directional nozzle to direct a stream of water onto the stencil may exert excessive force that could adversely affect stencil quality and durability especially if placed in close proximity to the stencil during washout. Both sides of the screen should be initially dampened.

Washout of direct emulsion using high washout temperatures is not recommended. It causes water to be absorbed into the pores of the emulsion. It will take longer for the stencil to dry before ready for press. The best washout temperature would be somewhere between room temperature and body temperature (about 90°F). Capillary films are less affected by washout temperatures. They may be washed out anywhere from 64° to 104°F, although low washout temperatures require additional time to washout detailed areas of the stencil.

Capillary film should be washed out from the squeegee side until image areas wash clear. Most of the washing of liquid direct emulsions should be done from the squeegee side. The print side becomes fully hardened since it is exposed from that side. Nonhardened emulsion may remain in nonimage areas of the squeegee side and must be removed during washout. The stencil should be washed out long enough to wash all image and nonimage areas. If washout is incomplete detailed areas will not print. A final rinse should be done on both sides of the screen after washout is complete to insure any softened emulsion or scum is removed from the screen.

STENCIL DRYING After washout excess moisture should be removed from the screen. This can be done by blotting with newsprint or using a wet/dry vacuum. It should then be placed in a drying cabinet to reach a dry state. The screen must be completely dry prior to going on press or it will not achieve its greatest durability. Moisture in the stencil will cause it to break down prematurely.

Stencil Exposure

The purpose of exposure is to harden nonimage areas of the stencil. Image areas remain in a nonhardened state which allows them to be washed out with warm water. Specifics of establishing the optimum exposure will be discussed at a later point. Simply stated, exposure affects two vital aspects of stencil performance: durability and resolution. It affects how long the stencil will last as well as how fine of details can be reproduced. Exposure is the most important factor in achieving durability and resolution.

Light Sources

There are a number of light sources that may be used to expose photographic stencils for screen printing. See Figure 6-43. There are advantages and disadvantages for each. The most important point in achieving both efficiency and quality is for the spectral distribution of light to match the sensitivity of the stencil.

CARBON ARC The carbon arc has been used in the printing industry for a number of years. See Figure 6-44. It is a high intensity point source of light that reaches its full intensity rapidly. Its spectral distribution from 340 to 440 nanometers makes it ideally suited for exposure of screen printing stencils. It uses two carbon electrodes. When electricity is introduced to the electrodes an electrical arc is generated producing light. Spectral output changes due to changes in voltage or spacing between electrodes.

Unfortunately there are undesirable side effects produced as a result of this process. During the reaction heat, dust, and dirt is generated as the electrodes are subjected to electricity. Research has found the airborne residues produced in the process to be a health hazard. Ventilation is essential to

Figure 6-43 Stencil exposure

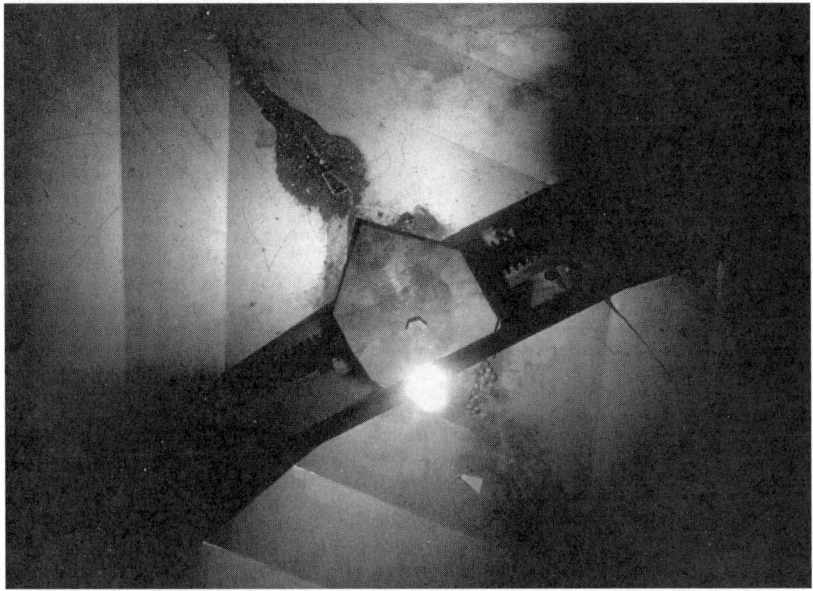

Figure 6-44 Carbon arc

exhaust these hazardous emissions. Due to these health concerns the carbon arc is declining in use.

HIGH PRESSURE MERCURY VAPOR This is an electrical discharge lamp. It is a glass tube or bulb containing mercury vapor. When current passes through the bulb the mercury starts to vaporize and ionize. It takes several minutes for the bulb to come up to full intensity. After exposure the mercury must condense before it can revaporize. This cool down cycle prevents instant start and stop operation.

This bulb has relatively low output with a life of about 1000 to 1500 hours before UV output drops off significantly. Heat is also generated which requires constant ventilation. It is less vulnerable to voltage changes.

METAL HALIDE This is an enhancement on a mercury vapor lamp. It is widely used in the screen printing industry and the most efficient light source used today. It is high in output with a spectral distribution mainly in the 365- to 420-nanometer range. A short warmup time is required for operation. A shutter mechanism is often used to minimize this start up delay. The bulb is operated at reduced power until the shutter opens for more efficient operation.

A quartz bulb containing mercury is used as with the mercury vapor lamp. Metal halides, mercury and gallium iodides are added to the bulb to adjust spectral distribution to modify it for screen printing use. It is not a true point light source due to the design of the bulb. Lamp life is about 1000 hours. It provides good consistent spectral distribution and output. Due to the nature of the bulb no dust or gasses are produced, eliminating health hazards.

PULSED XENON This device provides high intensity with instant start and stop operation. It is clean to use, being less sensitive to voltage changes. The lamp life is from 300 to 1000 hours and it is not a true point source of light. The pulse xenon was developed from the electronic flash. It is a quartz tube filled with low pressure xenon. When a voltage is introduced into the tube light is produced. The spectral distribution for this device is high at the infrared portion of the spectrum. These radiations cause heat to be produced requiring constant cooling and ventilation.

FLUORESCENT TUBES Low pressure mercury vapor and inert gas are enclosed in a glass tube with two electrodes. The inside of the glass tube is coated with phosphor. When electricity is introduced to the electrodes the mercury vapor produces ultraviolet energy that bombards the phosphor coating causing it to emit light. By changing the type of phosphor coating this will affect the frequency of light produced. For instance a number of colors from warm to cold can be selected for home or office use. Another type is designed for growing plants indoors. For this reason care must be taken in selecting a fluorescent exposure device whose light output is in the correct range for the stencil material used. It is also important when replacing bulbs that the type is used that is designed for the exposure unit.

The lamp starts up instantly and produces no heat. It is low in output and requires a number of bulbs placed close to the material to be exposed. It provides a consistent output of light. However, due to the shape and number of bulbs it is difficult to design a reflector with this light source.

LIGHT INTEGRATOR One of the problems with light sources is the aging process that occurs over the lifetime of the device. The output diminishes over time more with some types than others. The stencil exposure process requires a quantitative amount of light to expose the stencil properly. For example, an exposure test is conducted for a mercury vapor light source and finds that a one minute exposure is the optimum exposure. As the light source ages the output decreases. As this occurs the one minute exposure will no longer adequately expose the stencil.

A light integrator, as shown in Figure 6-45, will assist with this situation. A light integrator is made up of a photocell connected to a timer control. It is placed as close to the screen as possible. The amount of light that comes in contact with the device is measured and compensates with longer exposure times as output decreases.

Figure 6-45 Light integrator

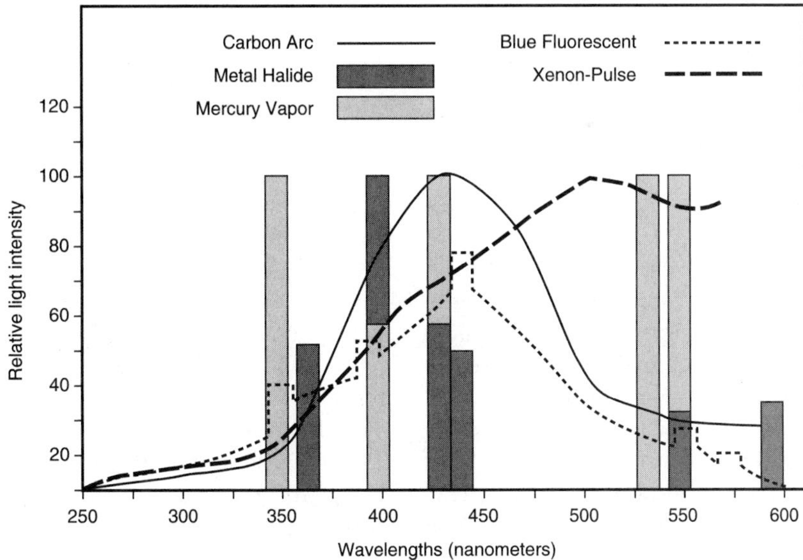

Figure 6-46 Light output frequency

Exposure Intensity

There are different types of light sources used to expose stencils. Each has different output frequency and power. These two factors affect the efficiency of stencil exposure. The higher the output power of the lamp the shorter the exposure time needed. A 4,000 watt lamp provides twice the output power of a 2,000 watt lamp and exposure time of the 4,000 watt lamp will be half that of the 2,000 watt lamp.

When the frequency of the lamp matches that of the emulsion it will also require less exposure time than one that does not match. To achieve the highest efficiency with the shortest exposure time the lamp frequency should match that of the sensitivity of the emulsion and have maximum output. An exposure device with low output or poor frequency match requires a longer exposure. Yet these devices are capable of providing the exposure to fully harden the stencil. The problem is that the long exposures will allow light to scatter more, which results in a loss of fine details. A short, high intensity exposure will cause less light undercutting and produce finer details.

A low cost, poor quality exposure device can cause inadequate exposure. Ineffective design can lead to poor resolution or under exposure. Only a high quality device can deliver consistent quality results.

Light Frequency—Source vs. Emulsion

The differences between the sensitivity of each stencil type has been explained. In addition, the spectral distribution of various light sources has been discussed. To achieve the best results the sensitivity of the emulsion should be matched by the light source used.

For example, diazo sensitized emulsions have the greatest sensitivity at about 400 nanometers. The best match would be to use a carbon arc or metal halide light source which also produces the highest output at 400 nanometers. A very poor match would be the use of an incandescent light with a peak intensity in the infrared portion of the spectrum around 700 nanometers. This light has low power at the desired frequency of 400 nanometers, less than one quarter of the output of metal halide. This would require the stencil to be exposed four times as long to get a similar amount of light. As exposure times increase the ability to achieve fine details decrease significantly. Long exposures allow light to scatter and fill in detailed areas. For this reason long exposure times are undesirable. See Figure 6-46.

Lamp Distance

If the exposure lamp is placed too close to the vacuum frame the result will be a hot spot in the center and fallout around the edges. This uneven exposure will cause the stencil to be hardened more in the center than outside edges.

Increasing the distance of the lamp from the vacuum frame will improve the evenness of light across the surface. Yet the greater the distance the longer the exposure time. The optimum distance

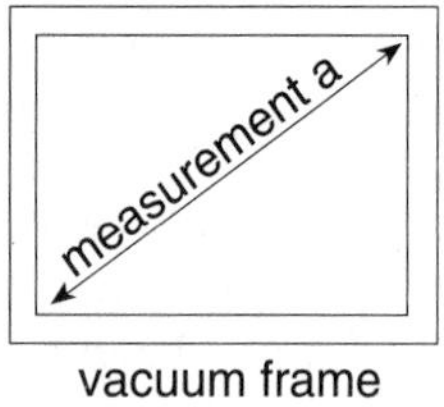

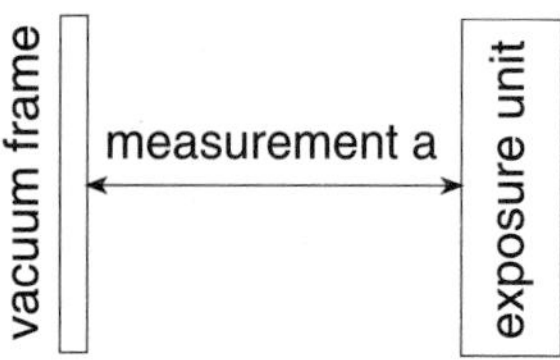

Figure 6-47 Lamp distance

that will produce evenness of light can be achieved by placing the light source at a distance equal to the diagonal distance measurement from corner to corner of the vacuum frame. See Figure 6-47.

Exposure Time

The purpose of exposure is to harden nonimage areas of the stencil. Insufficient exposure duration will not allow the stencil to harden completely resulting in premature stencil breakdown, low run durability and poor reclaimability. Overexposure will result in a loss of resolution since there is more time to allow light undercutting to occur. The optimum exposure is a balance between the two extremes of underexposure and overexposure.

This importance of exposure is so obvious one might think that underexposure would rarely be the case, that nearly everyone places the needed exactness on the correct exposure to ensure complete hardening. In actuality this is not the case. In fact a majority of screen printers are using underexposed stencils more often than not without realizing it. Why compromise durability? There are a number of reasons for this action.

One reason is to speed up productivity, especially when making very large screens where long exposures are required. For example, during an eight hour shift only sixteen screens may be produced if each screen were exposed 30 minutes. Another common reason for underexposure is to produce finer detail and resolution. By underexposing intentionally there is less loss of detail since there is less time for light to scatter. The trade off with this approach is a loss of stencil durability.

In some instances exposure time has been established where only low run lengths are needed. At a later time a higher run length is attempted and failed. On first impulse the quality of the stencil is questioned. In fact the stencil product is not at fault but was originally underexposed since it was never subjected to a normal run length. The stencil may be underexposed at times, but durability will always be compromised.

Solvent based inks are less reactive with the stencil allowing underexposure to be tolerated. Yet the new breed of multipurpose water based inks have a harmful effect on an underexposed stencil. The stencil will become softened and eventually break down.

DIRECT PHOTOGRAPHIC EMULSION Direct photographic emulsion includes both liquid emulsion and capillary films. An exposure test is essential in setting standards for exposure time required to achieve optimum durability and resolution. The best way to determine optimum exposure is by conducting an exposure test using a device known as an exposure calculator. There are a number of exposure calculators made by various stencil manufacturers. The Autotype Exposure Calculator is made up of a resolution target of varying thickness lines and also includes 65 line screen ruling halftone dots in 10%, 50% and 90% values. It has a square dot shape placed at a 22° angle. This can be used to assist in finding how fine a line can be successfully screen printed. See Figure 6-48.

There are a series of five test areas on the calculator, each with an incremental neutral gray filter. This will produce five different exposure times with one exposure. For example, if the test screen is exposed 100 seconds, incremental exposures of 100, 70, 50, 33 and 25 seconds will be produced. The purpose is to position the best exposure time in the middle of the test range so both underexposure and overexposure can be seen.

Once a diazo sensitized emulsion is completely hardened a color change occurs. The exposure test creates a range of test exposures on one screen with one exposure. By evaluating the color changes of the emulsion, the lowest exposure time that causes complete stencil hardening can be established. This determines the optimum balance between durability and resolution.

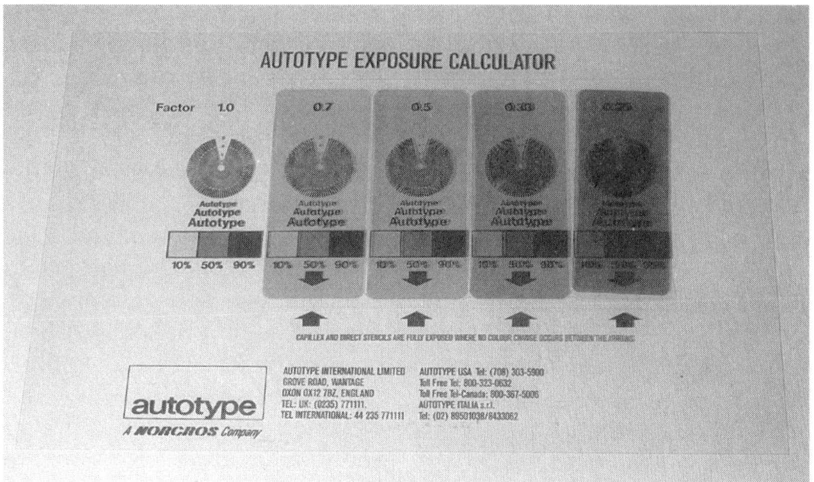

Figure 6-48 Exposure calculator

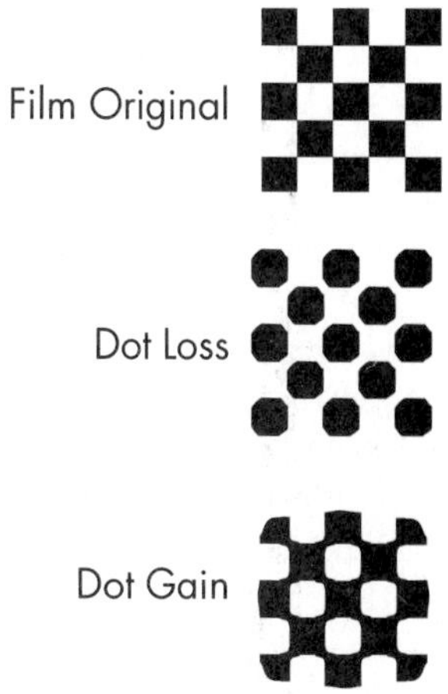

Film Original

Dot Loss

Dot Gain

Figure 6-49

The resolution target is made up of lines ranging from 0.015 (375µ) down to 0.002 (50µ). After the test screen is printed, the finest line that may be printed using a particular fabric, stencil, ink, and so on can be established.

Pure polymer films require an alternate approach to establish exposure time, since no color change occurs at the point of polymerization. An evaluation of resolution and definition can assist in determining the proper exposure time using these emulsions. The halftone portion of the Autotype Exposure Calculator may be used to establish the optimum time with pure polymer emulsions. The three areas of the halftone portions have 10%, 50% and 90% dots. The 50% dot area under magnification looks just like a checker board due to the square dot shape. The corners of the dots just meet at one point. This can be used to evaluated various problems that cause "dot gain" or "dot loss." For best results printed results of the screen test should be evaluated. It is less important what the screen looks like than what the printed results will be.

If the corners of the dots do not meet it indicates a dot loss has occurred. There are several conditions that may cause this condition. Light undercutting due to overexposure, or improper light geometry may cause dot loss. Use of a low resolution stencil or ink drying into the stencil may also cause dot loss. When the point of contact between dots increases or thickens, dot gain is indicated. This could be caused by a stencil with poor edge definition or with ink that is thinned excessively. See Figure 6-49.

The question of the importance of an exposure test can be illustrated by the following case. In one company they were unknowingly underexposing their stencils. It resulted in low durability which affected run length and resistance to solvents. They constantly experienced screen breakdown on press. In another shop screens were given long exposure times to prevent premature stencil breakdown. This resulted in a loss of resolution; small details disappeared from their screens.

From these two examples it is obvious that neither solution is practical since both durability and resolution are a requirement for most every job in the shop. What is needed is to determine the optimum exposure that will give the needed degree of durability yet not seriously affect resolution.

INDIRECT PHOTOGRAPHIC EMULSION Exposure determination of indirect film is different than with direct emulsion. The emulsion thickness is determined in direct relation to the length of the exposure. A short exposure will produce a thin stencil and a long exposure a thick stencil. With the proper exposure three layers of emulsion are created. A hardened layer is produced next to the clear base. A second layer above the hardened layer is called the soft top. This is the part of the stencil that embeds into the mesh during the adhering process. The third layer receives the least light and is completely removed during washout. Overexposure will cause a thick hardened stencil with insufficient soft top to achieve the proper stencil adhesion. There will also be a loss of details.

To determine the optimum exposure time an exposure test should be conducted using an exposure calculator. The stencil should be exposed at twice the recommended exposure time with the test film. This will achieve both under- and overexposure in one test. It should be processed as recommended but not mounted on the screen. After being allowed to dry it can be visually analyzed. By viewing the resolution target the amount of detail that can be produced at different exposure times can be determined. The most accurate method of determining the optimum exposure is to measure the thickness of the stencil produced (excluding the base) using a micrometer. The exposure that results in a stencil thickness of eight to ten microns is the ideal exposure time.

Stencil Preparation

Once a stencil has been produced there are several steps that must be done to prepare the screen for press operation. These steps should not be cut short to rush the screen to press or problems could surface during the press run that may not be repaired on press. The steps to prepare a screen for press are inspection, blockout and touchup.

Screen Inspection

After washout the screen should be inspected to evaluate stencil quality as shown in Figure 6-50. This is important to predict success on press or to correct problems created during screen making. For instance if problems of under- or overexposure are evident screen making procedures should be reevaluated and corrected.

A magnifier of at least 30X is essential when inspecting screens for image quality of fine line designs. Devices are available that magnify up to 100 times. The screen should be inspected for evidence of pinholing, image undercutting, and sawtoothing. The final evaluation of screen quality is by printing. Visual examination alone cannot predict the final printed results.

Problems with pinholing are corrected by hand. Sawtoothing and undercutting problems are more serious requiring corrective measures to be performed during screen making.

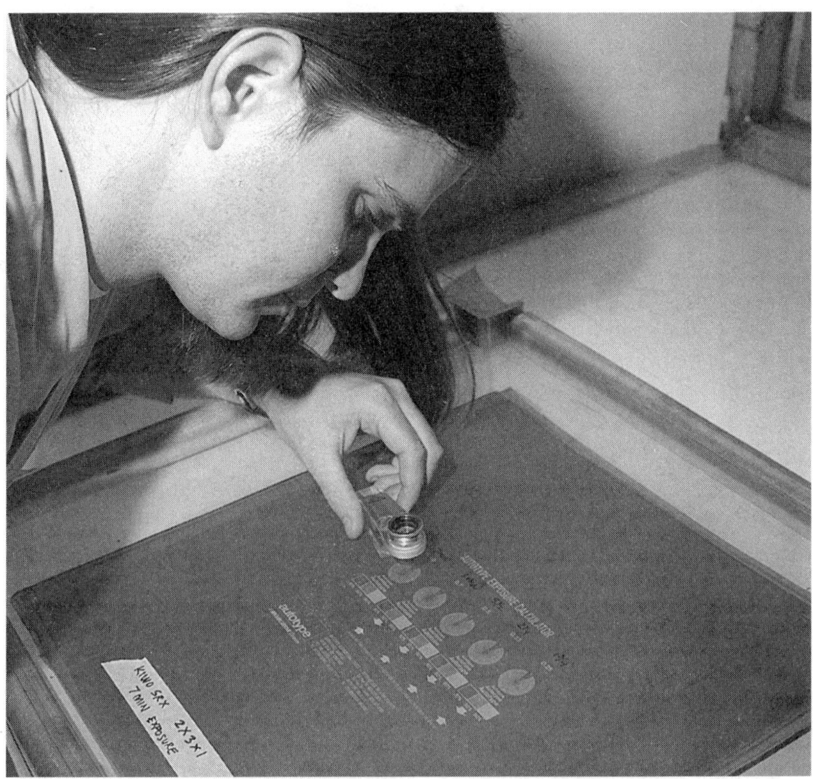

Figure 6-50 Screen inspection

Screen Blockout and Touchup

There are several types of blockout or fillers that may be used for screen printing. **Blockouts** are used primarily with indirect and capillary films. They are not needed with liquid direct emulsion as the entire screen is covered with the coating process. Most blockouts are water based and may be used only with solvent based products. An effective blockout that is completely water resistant and reclaimable has not been found in spite of various attempts by manufacturers. There are three basic types: a regular type for most circumstances, a heavy filler for when using a coarse mesh, and a fast dry blockout.

Once dry, blockout can be applied to open areas of the mesh. For ease of application the blockout can be stored in plastic bottles. A small amount can be squeezed onto the mesh. This speeds application and minimizes waste. A small card or plastic squeegee can be used to spread the blockout to fill open areas of the mesh. See Figure 6-51. Effort should be made for uniform application to all areas for best results. A thick coat is undesirable since it will take greater time to dry.

With indirect stencils the blockout may be applied before the plastic base is removed. By applying blockout from the print side the plastic base will prevent damage to image areas of the stencil. Once dry, the plastic base can be removed for printing.

Touchup can be done using a small brush. It should be done to the print side of the screen. Touchups are commonly done to correct pinholes caused by dust or defects in the stencil. The screen should be placed in a drying cabinet at 68°–86°F until blockout and stencil are completely dry.

Stencil Selection

Selecting the stencil best suited to meet job requirements is not a random matter. It is a process of finding the stencil that matches the needs of the job. The closer the match the better overall results will be achieved. There are a number of factors that should be evaluated. The factors are: run length, image resolution, mesh count, ink compatibility, substrate type, speed and convenience of production, and cost.

Run Length

Due to the nature of the screen printing process, run lengths are often relatively low compared to other printing processes. But that is not necessarily the case, as long printing runs may be screen print-

Figure 6-51 Stencil blockout

ed. Imprinted garments are often screen printing in large quantities. We define low quantities as under 3,000, medium quantities as under 30,000 and large quantities as over 50,000.

The three photographic stencil types fall into these quantities. An indirect gelatin stencil is one of the most fragile and is viable only with a low quantity run length. Direct emulsion on the other hand is the most durable and can deliver large quantities. Capillary films can produce medium quantities under 30,000.

In looking at the job requirements the quantity may eliminate a given stencil from being used. If a customer desires a quantity over 50,000 only liquid direct emulsion will achieve this quantity. However, if only a few thousand are needed any of the three photographic stencil types can be used.

Image Resolution

When image resolution requirements are moderate, any of the photographic stencils can be used. When pushing screen printing to its upper limits with extremely fine line designs or halftones (over 100 lines) there are fewer choices. The stencil emulsion must be formulated to achieve the highest resolution. Stencil manufacturers recommend stencils best suited to high resolution needs as either the indirect gelatin stencil or capillary film. It is important to consult stencil manufacturers for their recommendations. It is equally important to conduct your own in-house tests to determine which stencil is best suited to meet your needs.

Mesh Count

Mesh count is important in establishing resolution or ink deposit requirements for a job. Some jobs require a low mesh count, while others need a high mesh count. Not all stencils are compatible with the range of mesh counts available. Garment printing often requires coarse mesh counts to achieve special effects or ink deposits. However, indirect gelatin stencils are not recommended to use with mesh counts below 155. Capillary or liquid emulsions will function successfully with mesh counts as low as 100 and up to 500.

Ink Compatibility

A majority of screen printing inks can be classified as either solvent based or water based. Most inks have been solvent based up to recent years. With increased concerns with environmental problems related to solvent based products, water based inks are growing in popularity.

Not all stencils may be used with both water based and solvent based inks. Gelatin based indirect stencils are not water resistant, and may be used only with solvent based products. Other stencils may be used with water based inks for a short time before breaking down. Stencils must be formulated to function with water or solvent based inks for best results.

Speed and Convenience of Production

The answer to the question of speed and convenience is how to meet the needs of the customer in the most effective manner. In some cases a mechanical stencil can be cut and applied more quickly than it takes to produce a film and photostencil. It is a judgement call based on past experiences.

Stencil Cost

Stencil cost is complex to determine as well. The cost of a stencil is based on two factors: material and labor cost. Other costs such as equipment, facilities and utilities are less significant. The material cost is low with liquid emulsion but the labor cost is higher. With capillary films the material cost is greater but the labor cost is lower. All in all they nearly balance each other out. The most important point is which stencil will achieve the desired results most easily. Stencil cost is a very small portion of the overall cost of a screen printed job. This is not a good place to cut costs as quality may be affected.

Substrate Type

Due to the versatile nature of the screen printing process it is often used for printing on unusual surfaces or substrates. Since it is required for the screen to contact the substrate in the printing process the surface texture will affect final printed results. For that reason it is important for optimum contact to be achieved between the two. To achieve this contact, it is recommended that the stencil have the greatest flexibility so it can conform to the uneven surface. Some stencils are quite brittle and do not have the ability to conform to uneven surfaces.

Screen Reclaiming Procedures

Once a job is printed the screen must be cleaned so it can be reused. If the stencil is to be stored for printing at a later time only the ink needs to be removed, otherwise the screen must be reclaimed of ink, stencil and any other residue. The purpose of screen **reclaiming** is to reuse the screen as many times as possible before the fabric has to be replaced, reducing screen making costs. The stages of reclaiming are ink removal, stencil removal and ghost haze removal.

Figure 6-52 Ink removal

Ink Removal

Ink is most easily removed if it is done as soon as printing is complete. Inks become increasingly difficult to remove the longer they dry. The appropriate solvent should be used for ink removal. A solvent washup is used to clean solvent and UV curing inks, while water based inks require different washup solution based on composition.

The first stage of cleanup is to card out excess ink using a small piece of cardboard as a squeegee. See Figure 6-52. It would also be helpful to apply a spray and wipe product or solvent to the screen and wipe off ink from the image areas before they dry in. Once this has been done the screen may be removed to the screen reclaiming area. A quick onpress cleanup can speed the reclaiming process by preventing ink from drying into the screen. Once ink removal is complete the stencil can be removed. When solvents are used for ink removal an oily residue may remain on the screen which may act as a barrier in preventing the reclaiming product from reacting on the stencil. Use of a degreasing agent can remove this residue for more effective stencil reclaiming.

Stencil Removal

The reclaiming product must be selected based on the stencil used. The two stencil compositions are gelatin and polymer. Gelatin films require an enzyme-type product. It is available in a powder or gel. The gel can be brushed on both sides of the stencil and allowed to react for three to five minutes. It should be removed using a high pressure washout unit.

Capillary and liquid emulsion

stencils are polymer based and require a different reclaiming product. Sodium meta periodate is commonly used in reclaiming products. This is an oxidizer that breaks down the molecules of the crosslinked emulsion so they can be removed. Reclaiming products are available in liquid solution, paste or gel form. Liquid solutions can be applied using a spray bottle. Gel or paste can be applied by brush. Although liquid can be applied quickly by spray bottle, gel or paste can be applied for more stubborn stencil removal. The reclaiming product should be applied to both sides of the stencil and allowed to react for three to five minutes. The reclaimer must not be allowed to dry completely or the stencil will harden and become permanent. Once softened the emulsion can be removed using a high pressure washout unit. See Figure 6-53.

Figure 6-53 Stencil removal

Ghost Haze Removal

This is evidenced by a slight image that is visible in the mesh after reclaiming. There are several situations that may cause a **ghost haze**. This haze may be due to the incomplete removal of ink or stencil from the mesh. This may cause a faint image to appear in the print in image areas of the print where ink is prevented from flowing through mesh openings. This is most noticeable when printing transparent or certain colors such as light green. It is also apparent in back lit signs or displays. See Figure 6-54.

One of the most common causes is ink residue due to incomplete removal during reclaiming. It will show up during the beginning of the print run. If the same ink type is used solvents in the ink will start to dissolve the dried ink residue. After a number of print strokes, squeegee action begins to work out the ink residue until it is completely removed after about fifty prints have been made.

Other causes of ghost haze are conditions that affect the surface of the fibers. Inks that have an abrasive effect cause image areas of the fibers to be roughened. In some cases a chemical reaction may occur between the emulsion and the screen fabric. This reaction may cause the mesh to become roughened. In other cases stencil reclaiming may not entirely remove the dye of the emulsion from the mesh, leaving a residue. A stain remover is available that may be used to remove diazo stains on undyed nylon or polyester fabric. The staining is more of a problem with white mesh than colored. Once the white mesh is stained that area reacts differently than unstained areas during the exposure process, after being recoated with emulsion. This affects the final printed results. This effect is less severe with colored mesh.

A haze remover may be used to remove residues of ink or stencil that remain in the screen fabric. A haze remover is a strong caustic solution that requires careful use. The haze remover should be applied to both sides of the mesh using a brush. The compound should be worked into the stained

Figure 6-54 Ghost haze

Figure 6-55 Haze removal

area of the mesh. See Figure 6-55. It should be left to work on the haze for the recommended time, usually 5 minutes, to completely soften residues in the mesh. A gentle spray of flowing water should be used to wash away the haze remover. Once the haze remover is completely removed a high pressure sprayer can be used to remove the remaining residues from the fibers of the mesh. This product can be used to remove residues with good success from monofilament fabrics. If multifilament fabrics are used the residues that become trapped in the fiber structure cannot be removed with haze remover.

Caution must be exercised in the use of this product. If it remains on the mesh longer than the prescribed time the mesh can be permanently damaged. It will attack the composition of the mesh with too much exposure. Due to the caustic nature of the product protective wear must be used. Gloves, apron, and a face shield should be used at all times to protect the body and clothes from damage. The haze remover should not be removed using a high pressure washout unit. This would cause caustic chemicals from the product to become atomized into the air with the water vapor that is produced from the washout unit. This would be hazardous to one's health if inhaled. It is important that there is adequate ventilation in the reclaiming area to prevent inhalation of harmful fumes.

KEY TERMS

abrading
blockout
bridging
capillary film
definition
degreasing
direct stencil
ghost haze
indirect stencil
photographic stencil
pinholes
reclaiming
resolution
sensitivity

REVIEW QUESTIONS

1. How does abrading differ from degreasing?
2. What are the differences between diazo, pure polymer and dual cure sensitized emulsions?
3. What are the differences between wet-on-wet and wet-on-dry coating techniques?
4. How can emulsion thickness be changed with liquid direct photographic emulsions?
5. How is emulsion thickness changed using capillary films?
6. What aspects of the screen printing process does stencil exposure affect?

NOTES

[1] Industry Profile Study (Fairfax: Screenprinting and Graphic Imaging Association International, 1990).

[2] Dr. Dieter Reichel, "The Metamorphosis of Stencils," *Screen Process Magazine*, August 1988: 73-79.

[3] Wolfgang Pfirrmann, "The Influence of Processing Variables on Direct Emulsion Stencils," *Screen Printing Magazine* August 1990: 118-123.

[4] Dawn M. Hohl and Dennis D. Hunt, *Capillary Film Application Variables* (Fairfax: Screen Printing Technical Foundation, 1994).

7 Squeegees

The squeegee has four functions. First, it brings the screen in contact with the substrate (except with on-contact printing). Next it assists in metering the amount of ink deposited on the substrate. In simple terms this means that the squeegee is capable of transferring ink onto the substrate in either thick or thin deposits. It also wipes the surface of the screen clear of ink. Lastly it assists the screen in coming into complete contact with irregular surfaces or objects. See Figure 7-1.

Thirty percent of the ink deposit is controlled by the squeegee versus the fabric which controls 50% and the stencil a mere 20%. Due to this relationship the press operator can either reduce or increase the ink deposit to get the desired result by changing squeegee techniques. For example, when printing white ink on a dark substrate after a few initial prints the results may appear grayish in color due to insufficient ink deposit. The press operator may be able to compensate for the low ink deposit if the proper fabric and stencil were selected. It should be noted that best results can be accomplished

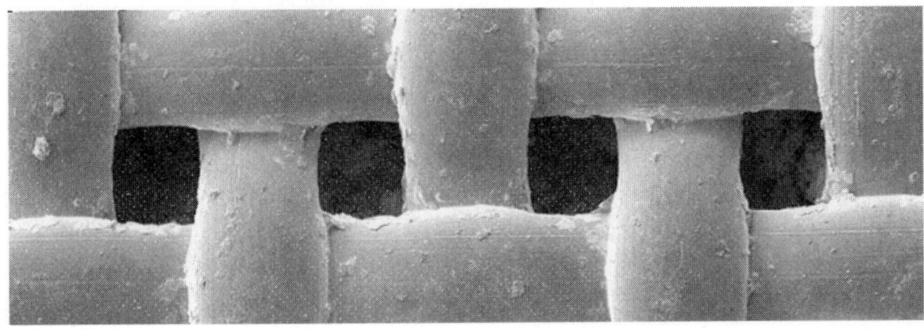

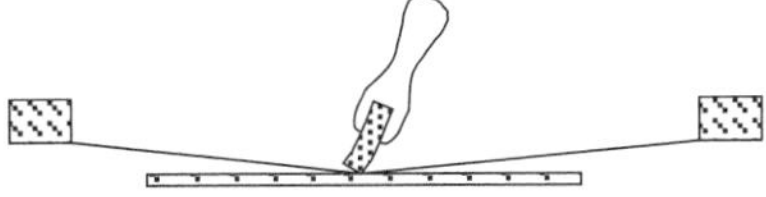

Figure 7-1

by proper selection of fabric, stencil and squeegee technique.

SQUEEGEE COMPONENTS

The two components making up the squeegee are the handle and blade.

Handles

There are a variety of handle shapes and materials based on individual applications. For instance, manual squeegees are generally made of wood and shaped to be held in the hand. New ergonomics shapes have been recently introduced to lessen operator fatigue. (See also page 157.) With automated presses the handle is often metal, such as aluminum, and shaped to fit on the press.

With manual wood handles wear is not a major factor but cleanup can be somewhat difficult since the ink tends to soak into the wood. After a period of time the handle can become heavily coated with inks. Aluminum handles offer a solution to this situation since ink can easily be wiped from the metal surface. In addition with minimal cleanup these handles need never be replaced. See Figure 7-2.

Blades

The blade forces ink through openings in the stencil onto the substrate. As with handles there are various materials and shapes depending on their use. See Figure 7-3. Rubber was one of the

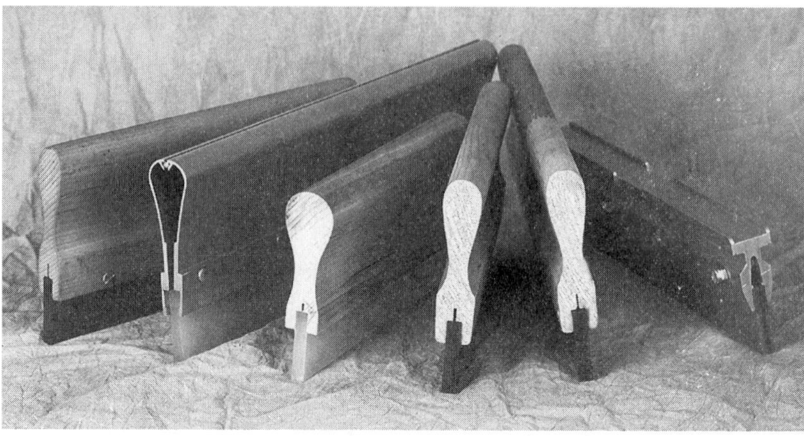

Figure 7-2 Handle shapes *(Pleiger Plastics Company)*

Figure 7-3 Blade materials *(Pleiger Plastics Company)*

Figure 7-4 Blade sizes *(Pleiger Plastics Company)*

first materials used. The problem with this material is its poor resistance to chemicals and wear. Neoprene, a synthetic rubber, was developed as an early replacement for rubber. Neoprene can be identified by its tan color while rubber is generally black.

Polyurethane was more recently introduced and found to be superior to both rubber and neoprene. Although it is considerably higher in cost its performance over both rubber and neoprene more than justifies the cost differential. Polyurethane offers resistance to a wide variety of solvents and chemicals. It also offers increased durability resulting in lower squeegee replacement costs.

Squeegee blade material comes in several thicknesses and widths. The blade thickness is kept thin (3⁄16″ or 1⁄4″) when printing small parts. When printing average or large areas 3⁄8″ is most common although 1⁄2″ is available. A variety of widths are available ranging from 7⁄8″ up to 5,″ with 2″ width most common. See Figure 7-4.

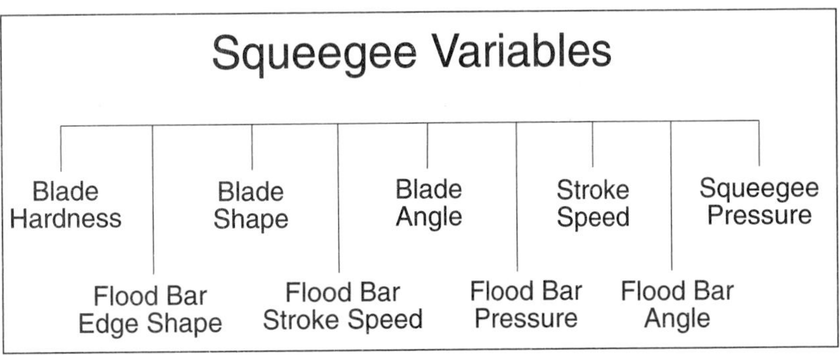

Figure 7-5 Squeegee variables

Figure 7-6 Durometer gauge

METHODS OF VARYING INK DEPOSIT

There are five variables related to the squeegee that affect the ink deposit. They are: blade hardness, blade profile, blade angle, squeegee speed, and squeegee pressure. Each is different yet the same in one aspect. Each affects the amount of downward force of the squeegee forcing ink onto the substrate. See Figure 7-5.

Blade Hardness

When ordering blade material, whether it be rubber, neoprene or polyurethane, you must specify which hardness is desired. Blade hardness is measured in a value known as "shore." The range of values range from 40 to 90 shore hardness. Number 40 is a soft blade while a 90 is a hard blade.

Blade hardness is measured by using a **durometer gauge** as shown in Figure 7-6. This gauge is used to measure a variety of materials used in the printing industry such as rubber rollers, blankets, and so on. This device functions in a simple manner. It has a sharp point built into the device which penetrates the material tested. This determines the resistance of the material related to its hardness. This is an important measurement for a number of reasons. Even with good quality squeegee blade material that is new its hardness may not be exactly what it is rated. Also, blade material may change in hardness over time or after it has been exposed to solvents or other chemicals.

With a soft blade such as 40 a number of conditions will occur. A soft blade will bend more which means more pressure will be directly transferred to the ink forcing a heavier deposit of ink. See Figure 7-7. This thick deposit may be advantageous when printing on an absorbent substrate such as cotton fabric or for a durable outdoor application. A soft squeegee may be desirable when printing on rough surface substrates. It conforms more readily to uneven surfaces which means improved printing action on the press. It is somewhat like equipping a car with the proper shock absorbers to smooth the ride on a rough road.

This will require longer drying time, however, which slows the printing process down. A thick ink deposit can be undesirable on large ink coverage T-shirt jobs since it may result in a shirt that is uncomfortable to wear in hot weather since it may not allow sweat to evaporate. A rule of thumb is that it is undesirable to print a thicker ink deposit than needed as it will increase drying time, ink cost and may result in undesirable end results. Since more downward force is exerted on the ink with a soft squeegee, more ink will be pushed through the stencil openings. This will prevent a clear sharp image from being produced.

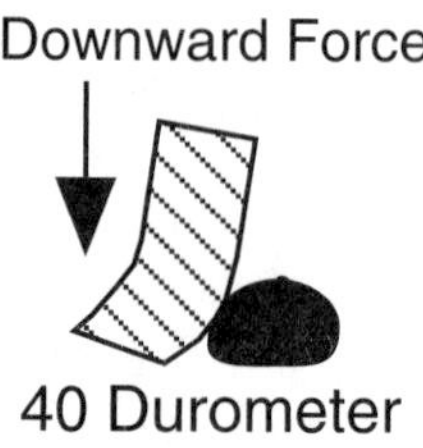

Figure 7-7 Low durometer blade

Figure 7-8 High durometer blade

A hard squeegee produces results which are the opposite of a soft squeegee. When force is exerted on a hard blade there is less bending of the squeegee material. With less bend of the blade, less force is directed down on the ink as demonstrated in Figure 7-8. This results in a thin ink deposit. A thin deposit is desirable with applications such as UV curing inks. A UV ink deposit that is too thick may be impossible to cure.

With a thin ink deposit less time is required for drying with solvent or water based inks, resulting in increased production time. A hard durometer blade also produces better results when printing halftones or fine line designs. This blade is best suited for printing on smooth surfaces and is inappropriate to use with rough surfaces.

Blade Profiles

There are several different profiles for squeegee blades as shown in Figure 7-9. Some are shaped for printing on specific substrates or

Figure 7-9 Blade profiles

applications. Other profiles primarily regulate the amount of ink deposited.

Square Blade

A sharp, square shaped blade will deposit the least amount of ink and give a clean wiping action during the print stroke. This will give the sharpest quality results making it suitable for printing halftones or fine line designs.

Square Blade (slightly rounded)

A slightly rounded blade will produce less of a wiping action, applying slightly more downward force on the ink. This in effect will increase ink deposit and produce a slight decrease in sharpness.

Round Blade

Compared to the slightly rounded square blade, this shape will increase ink deposit to a greater extent due to the increase in downward force on ink. With this increased force it will produce a decrease in sharpness. As such it should not be used with fine line designs or halftones as it will drastically affect edge sharpness. This blade profile is normally used when printing a heavy ink deposit on fabric where edge sharpness is less important.

Double Sided Bevel

This profile is used when surface irregularities of the substrate require the squeegee to conform more easily. It is often used to print on cylindrical shapes, for use with container printers, as shown in Figure 7-10. Double bevel blades are placed perpendicular to the cylindrical shape. They do not have to be angled on the press as they are already at the correct angle. Fully automatic machines sometimes use another approach by using diamond edged blades. These provide a 45° angle to the substrate by placing it in the squeegee holder at 90°.

Single Sided Bevel

This profile is designed to print on flat substrates such as plastic or glass. This sharp edge improves its sharpness on the flat smooth surfaces above.

Flat Point Double Bevel

This profile is designed for printing on ceramic materials requiring a heavy ink deposit.

Blade Angle

By changing the angle of the blade the amount of downward force on the ink is altered. This can be used to increase or decrease ink deposit. The angle can be given with reference to the horizontal although it is most often given with reference to the vertical direction. From vertical the angle is 20°, while from horizontal it is 70°. See Figure 7-11. Sometimes presses have the angle indicated on the squeegee support mechanism, although often it must be measured manually using a protractor.

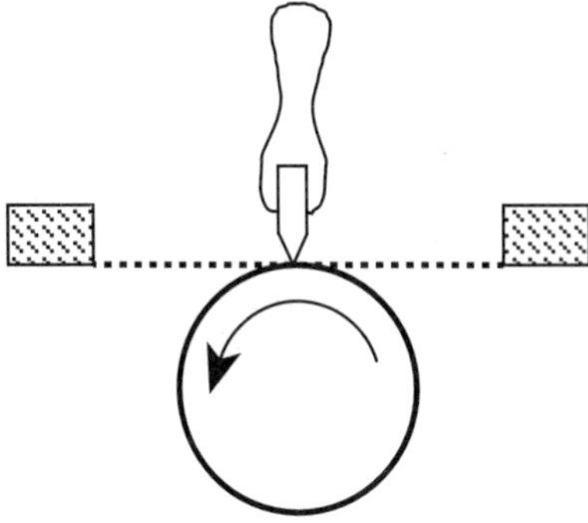

Figure 7-10 Container press

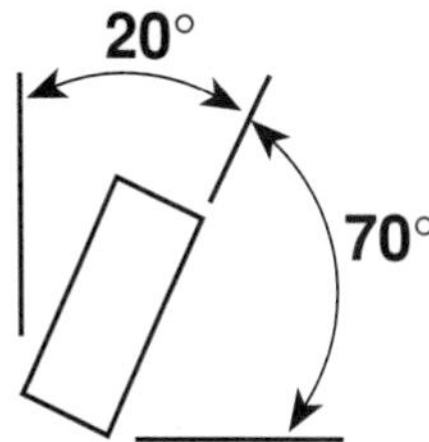

Figure 7-11 Blade angle

Once the squeegee is placed at a specific angle this does not necessarily mean that the same angle will be achieved where the squeegee blade comes in contact with the mesh. If the blade were entirely rigid (90 durometer) this same angle would be maintained. Yet with soft durometer blades this angle will change from the angle set. This is known as the angle of attack or actual print angle. This angle will change based on blade hardness, profile shape, squeegee pressure and stroke speed.

When the squeegee is near a vertical position, at 20°, this gives less downward force resulting in a

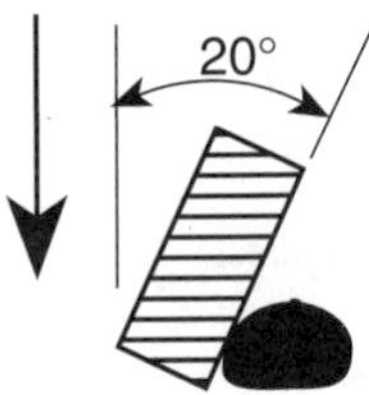

Figure 7-12 High angle

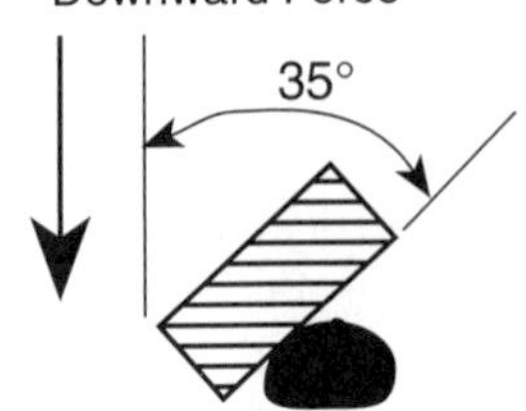

Figure 7-13 Low angle

lower ink deposit. See Figure 7-12. With the squeegee at a 35° angle, more downward force is exerted on the ink resulting in an increase in ink deposit. See Figure 7-13.

Not all presses have the ability to change the angle of the squeegee. This angle is often fixed in position with low priced presses. Bevel or double bevel blades are mounted perpendicular at 90° to the substrate. In this way the angle is built into the blade and may not be changed on the press.

Squeegee Speed

A fast squeegee speed may result in a different amount of ink deposited than a slow speed. As a rule a slow squeegee speed allows more ink to flow onto the substrate than a fast squeegee speed. The difference is dependent on the rheology, or flow characteristics, of the ink. When the viscosity is low (ink thin) the speed can make a considerable difference. But with a high viscosity (ink thick) the difference in speed results in little change in ink deposit. Some presses do not allow the squeegee speed to be changed.

Squeegee Pressure

One method of increasing ink deposit is to increase squeegee pressure by forcing more ink on the substrate. See Figure 7-14. Using excess squeegee pressure results in several undesirable results. Excess pressure distorts image quality and size. In addition, excess pressure results in decreased fabric and stencil durability, tension loss and excessive squeegee wear.

The method of setting the correct amount of squeegee pressure is to start with the pressure backed off, where the image is not printing onto the substrate. Squeegee pressure should be increased incrementally until the image is printing cleanly onto the substrate. Once this is achieved no additional squeegee pressure is needed.

The goal is to use the lowest squeegee pressure possible to **shear** the ink through the mesh onto the substrate. This will achieve the best results with the least consequences. One must resist the impulse to use "just a little more pressure." As squeegee pressure is varied so it will affect the ink deposit. With this in mind, the importance of maintaining the same squeegee pressure when a

Figure 7-14 Squeegee pressure

job is run at a later time to get the same printed results and colors seems evident. However, this is not easy to establish and repeat.

Mechanical Pressure Control

Pressure is increased or decreased by mechanically raising or lowering squeegee position. With some presses it is a simple control yet with more sophisticated presses it is a precise micrometer control device, as shown in Figure 7-15. Mechanical systems exert pressure on the ends of the squeegee where the adjustments are made. This arrangement allows different pressure to be used on each side of the squeegee unless it is carefully monitored and controlled.

Although the setting on the micrometer controls can be recorded, this information is not effective for use in statistical process control. If these same settings are used again at a later time it will not necessarily give the same squeegee pressure or printed results due to wear of the squeegee. This requires another approach.

Figure 7-15 Micrometer control

Squeegee Pressure Equalizer Systems

Many presses today are equipped with pneumatic or electromechanical pressure to control squeegee pressure. These systems equalize pressure across the length of the squeegee. One of the latest of these systems is the Theime High-Tech Squeegee Unit. This utilizes a single metal beam carrier mounted with two or more pneumatically controlled pressure cylinders. The pneumatic cylinders may be moved along the carrier beam with the ability to regulate and apply optimum pressure to the squeegee. This makes it possible for the press operator to accurately control overall ink density across the press sheet by changing the position of the pressure cylinders. This is especially advantageous for printing full coverage transparent inks, four color process and other critical jobs.

Making a change in the squeegee angle during printing can create additional problems. In addition to changing the angle the relationship of the squeegee to the screen and substrate is affected. This is due to the fact that the squeegee is pivoted near the top of the holder requiring the print end of the blade to move. See Figure 7-16. This requires changes to be made in squeegee pressure once the angle has been changed.

The Theime High-Tech Squeegee Unit uses a different approach to change squeegee angle. The angle adjustment is made around a center of rotation which causes the squeegee to touch the screen at the same point of contact each time regardless of angle. This is accomplished by rotating the top of the squeegee handle to create the change in angle while maintaining the same point of contact for the blade tip. This assures less set up time as positioning of the squeegee height and parallelism of the squeegee to bed is determined by the system. See Figure 7-17.

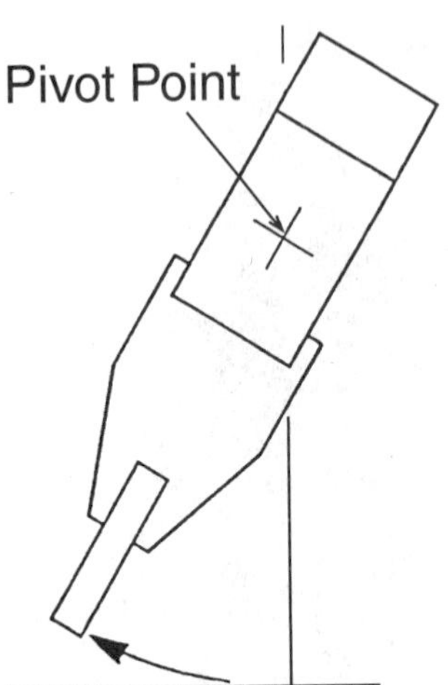

Figure 7-16 Standard squeegee unit

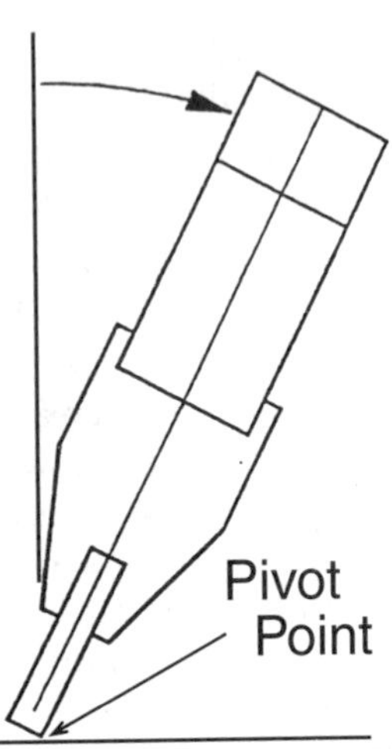

Figure 7-17 Theime squeegee unit

Figure 7-18 Dynamometer

Squeegee Pressure Measurement

One approach is to measure the friction that occurs as a result of the pressure exerted between the squeegee and the substrate. This can be measured using a gauge known as a dynamometer as shown in Figure 7-18. A simple device, it consists of a strip of plastic material which is inserted on top of the substrate that is in position on the press bed. The screen is lowered and the squeegee stroke is started and allowed to rest on top of the plastic strip. The strip extends beyond the press bed so it can be connected to the gauge. Pressure is exerted upon the gauge until the strip moves slightly. The gauge can be read to indicate the force needed to move the strip in either pounds or newtons. This reading should be made on at least two positions on the press to get accurate reading of the squeegee pressure.

Figure 7-19 Squeegee/flood bar

FLOOD BAR

The squeegee and **flood bar** work together to control the ink during the screen printing process as shown in Figure 7-19. The flood bar fills the openings in the mesh so the squeegee may then force ink onto the substrate. It also keeps ink from drying in the mesh openings of the stencil with solvent based inks.

The importance of the flood bar is often overlooked in the screen printing process. It can be instrumental in improving print quality without adverse effects to registration.

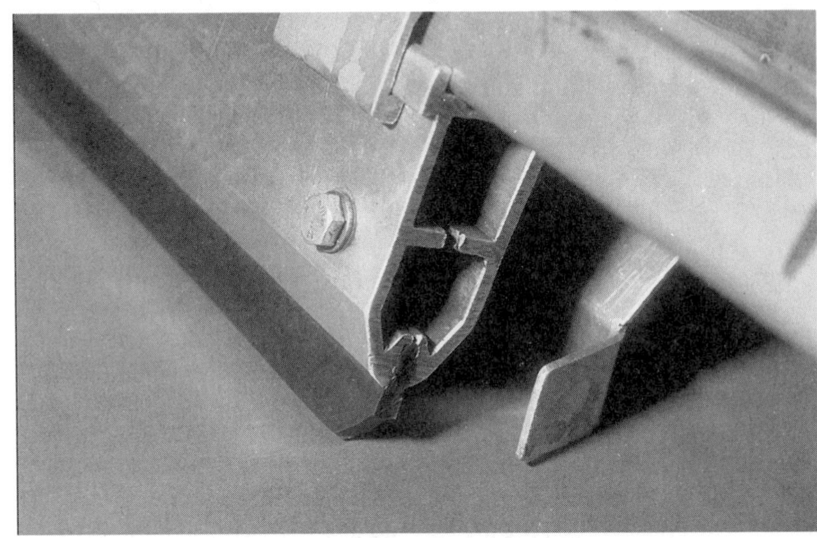

Figure 7-20 Flood bar angle

Flood Bar Angle

This relates to the angle of the flood bar in contact with the screen. See Figure 7-20. By placing the flood bar at a 90-degree angle to the mesh, more ink will be left on the screen. This is often beneficial when printing reverses, heavy coverage jobs or a heavy ink deposit. Angling the flood bar at a 15- to 45-degree angle to the mesh causes the thinnest flood coat to remain on the screen. This is recommended for fine line work or halftones. Less ink is forced into the mesh openings with less chance for ink to flow onto the bottom of the screen by angling the flood bar.[1]

Flood bars are available that are made with a slight angle or a 90-degree angle. By changing the type of flood bar the angle can be changed if it cannot be adjusted on press. Many of the higher quality presses allow the flood bar angle to be adjusted. This allows any angle to be set as needed.

Flood Bar Pressure

The flood bar can be used to control how much ink fills the mesh openings and the ink film remaining on top of the screen. By applying a thin flood coat less ink will be produced than with a heavy flood. When flood bar pressure is set low, a heavier ink film will remain on the screen; with higher pressure, a thin film will be left on the screen.

When excess pressure is applied to the squeegee, registration will be affected. Yet flood bar pressure will not affect registration regardless of its setting since it occurs while the screen is off-contact. However, flood bar pressure should not be adjusted indiscriminately since too much pressure will push ink through screen openings allowing it to seep onto the screen bottom. This will cause ink to print in nonprint areas and result in dot gain with halftones.

Flood Bar Speed

Flood bar speed has a similar effect to squeegee speed. Less ink is deposited with a fast speed and a slow speed which allows more ink to be deposited (depending on the ink viscosity). If the viscosity is high (thick ink) speed will not have a major effect on ink deposit. Yet with a viscosity that is low, as with some water based inks, the effect will be more significant.

Flood Bar Edge Shape

Flood bars are often of aluminum construction approximately ⅛" in thickness. The edges are rounded off to prevent damage to the screen and stencil during printing. A rounded flood bar acts much the same as a rounded squeegee. It forces ink through image areas and leaves a heavy coat of ink on the screen. This can be advantageous in printing certain types of jobs or using various ink types. But the amount of ink that is deposited in the image areas may lead to problems such as dot gain when printing halftones.[2]

A thin, sharp-edged flood bar is better suited for printing fine line images or halftones. It fills the image area during the flood coat without overdoing it, leaving less ink behind. It is important that there are no irregularities in the edge especially with this type flood bar. The edge should be carefully inspected using a fingernail. Any imperfections must be corrected using fine sandpaper or another abrasive approach.[3]

SPECIAL SQUEEGEE TECHNIQUES

There are circumstances where special techniques must be used to achieve the desired printed result. Following are two such conditions.

Camber

For the majority of screen printing it is important to use a squeegee that is straight and sharp. This emphasizes the importance of a squeegee sharpener. An interaction occurs on press between the squeegee and the screen. There is less resistance of the squeegee near the center than at the ends, especially when the squeegee length is too long for a frame size. Due to this difference in pressure the squeegee becomes **cambered** or tapered in shape after used on press. See Figure 7-21. This camber may be small but exists nonetheless.

This effect can be minimized by rounding the two ends of the blade. This reduces the pressure placed on the squeegee ends. This is also caused when low screen tension and excess off-contact is used. By keeping screen at recommended tension level and low off-contact, camber can be kept to a minimum.

Skewing

Under normal circumstances the squeegee is held perpendicular to the direction it is moved during

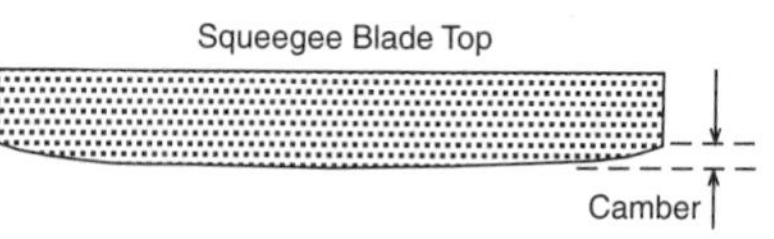

Figure 7-21 Camber

the print stroke. As the squeegee moves along the fabric it travels parallel to the threads. This will produce undesirable results under certain circumstances. As it moves along this direction a vibration is produced. This may result in ink smearing or sawtoothing. This is a problem when printing an image with parallel lines when the image, fabric and squeegee are all parallel to one another.

One approach is to bias (or angle) the mesh on the screen. This cannot be done on all tensioning systems and is more time consuming and costly. Another approach is to **skew** or angle the squeegee during the print stroke, as shown in Figure 7-22. By slanting the squeegee 3° to 10°, one end of the squeegee travels ahead of the other much like a snowplow. This may reduce the problem if skewing is kept to a minimum or it could cause problems with registration. It may cause the ink to move to one side of the screen. Skewing cannot be done on all presses.

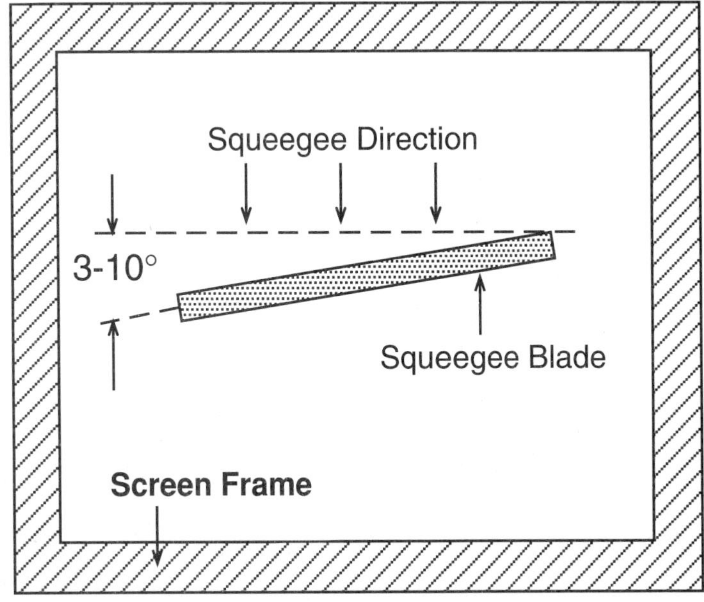

Figure 7-22 Skewing

Squeegee Blade Stiffener

A simple technique which supports the squeegee blade and prevents it from bending excessively is to support the back side of the squeegee blade with a thin steel shim (0.015"–0.030"). This inexpensive approach will minimize blade flex with soft blades. See Figure 7-23.

Figure 7-23 Blade stiffener

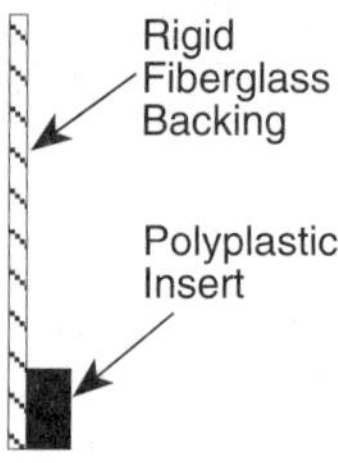

Figure 7-24 RKS blade

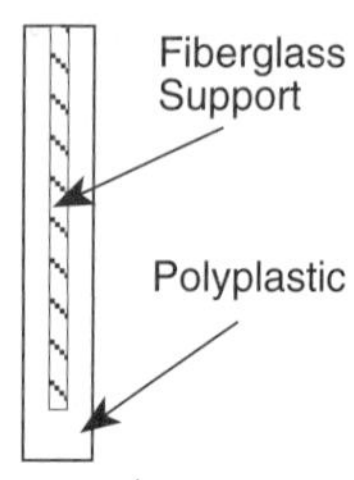

Figure 7-25

RECENT DEVELOPMENTS IN SQUEEGEES

Due to screen mesh that is capable of much higher tension greater demands are placed on the squeegee. This makes it difficult to achieve high quality. New blade types have been developed to work under these circumstances. This can result in increased life of the squeegee, stencil and fabric. It can also lead to reduction in squeegee pressure, off-contact required, and reduced registration errors.

Composite Blades

A **composite blade** is a blade made up of more than one material to produce more stability. There are several designs that have been developed over recent years. One such blade is known by the name of the manufacturer, RKS. It is made up of two parts, a fiberglass backing and a polyplastic insert as shown in Figure 7-24. The polyurethane portion is available in various durometers. The fiberglass backing provides consistency even over long press runs. Conventional squeegees may change in durometer due to the friction that occurs resulting in heat that can change its characteristics especially during a long press run. This blade has greater stability with less image distortion and superior ink control. Less swelling of blade material occurs since less blade is exposed to solvent. Other advantages include easy resharpening of the blade with the proper sharpener.

Another type of composite blade is made of fiberglass and polyurethane, like the RKS, but is different in construction. It appears much like a conventional squeegee because the fiberglass backing is embedded into the squeegee material. See Figure 7-25. This enables it to be resharpened and used much like a conventional blade, but with greater stability.

Multidurometer Blades

Multidurometer blades are made up of more than one durometer blades which are bonded together to act as one squeegee. This gives it additional stability which makes it more suitable for fine line and high quality results. The first type of multidurometer blade (see Figure 7-26) was produced by bonding a soft durometer tip (60 or 70 durometer) onto a harder durometer blade (90 durometer). This produces better stability of the blade. However, after sharpening a number of times the soft tip will be removed and the squeegee can no longer be used.

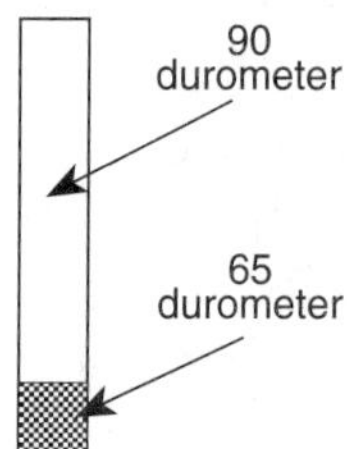

Figure 7-26 Multidurometer blade

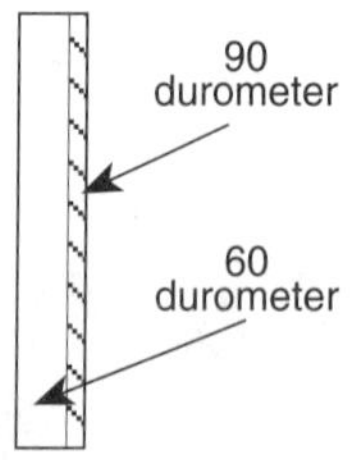

Figure 7-27 Dual durometer blade

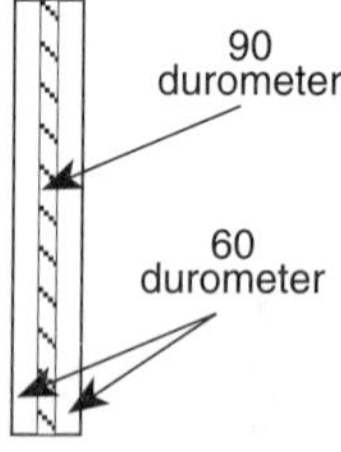

Figure 7-28 Tridurometer blade

Another type of multidurometer blade bonds two different durometer blades together laterally. See Figure 7-27. It is known as a dual durometer blade. This gives it the needed stability and allows it to be resharpened for the entire life of the blade. Since it can only be used in one position it can develop a curved shape after it has been used a number of times. This makes it less effective in maintaining control of the same blade angle.

A third type is a modification of the earlier type, with three layers laminated together. It is known as a tridurometer blade. See Figure 7-28. Two layers of soft durometer material are on the outside placing the harder durometer on the inside. This further increases the life of the blade as after one side becomes dull, the squeegee can be turned around and the other side can be used. Since both sides off the frame are used it is less prone to develop a curved shape as with the dual durometer blade type.

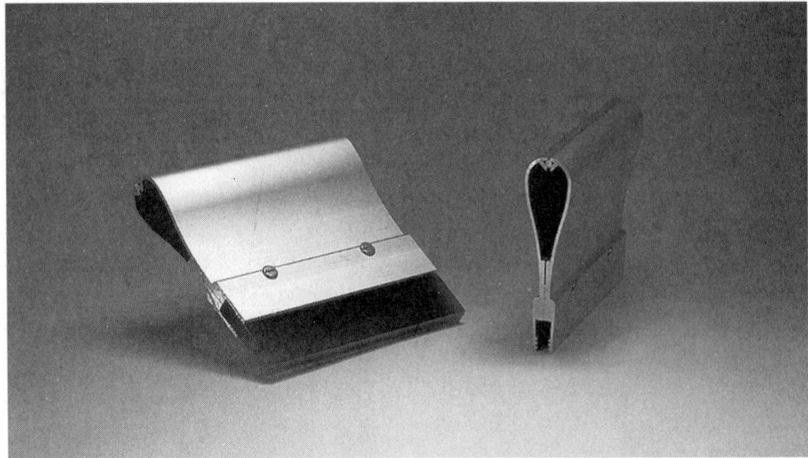

Figure 7-29 Ergonomic handle *(Majestech Corporation)*

Figure 7-30 One-man squeegee

Ergonomic Handle Shapes

It has recently been found that various conditions in the workplace can lead to health related problems. For instance, printing manually, due to the repetitive action used to operate the squeegee, can lead to carpal tunnel syndrome. Only full automation can completely eliminate this problem, but this is not practical due to the short run nature of our business which makes manual operations economically most feasible.

There are other less drastic measures that can be taken to reduce operator fatigue. An ergonomically shaped squeegee handle has been developed that fits more easily into the operator's hand. See Figure 7-29. Another approach is to partially automate the squeegee operation. One way to accomplish this is a type of one man squeegee device that simplifies operation so that the squeegee can be operated with one hand instead of two. See Figure 7-30.

BLADE SHARPENING

As stated earlier, the squeegee shape has a direct impact on the ink deposit. A new square edge blade becomes rounded with wear as it is used, as shown in Figure 7-31. As this occurs over a period of time it results in an increase in ink deposit. With UV curing inks this can result in undesirable consequences where excess ink deposit may not entirely cure. This illustrates the importance of blade sharpness in maintaining a uniform thin deposit.

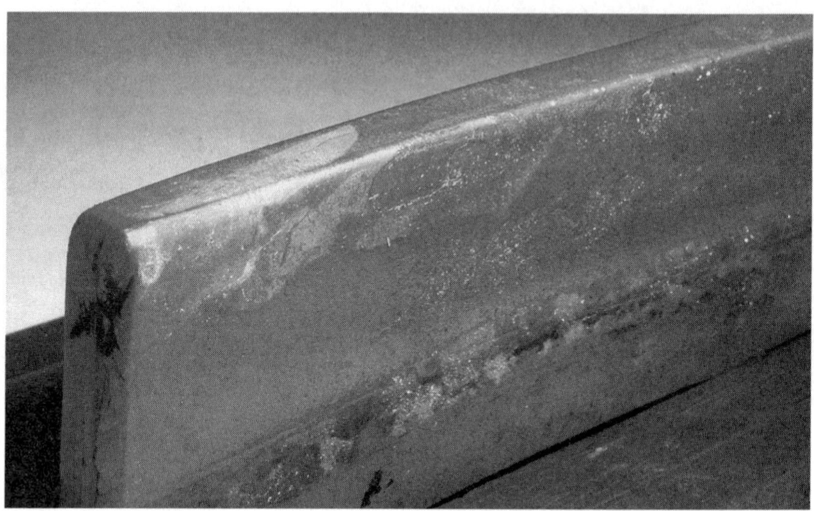

Figure 7-31 Dull blade

Once it is determined that the blade is worn, one approach would be to replace the blade with a new one. This is obviously an expensive solution. A better solution would be to sharpen the squeegee blade. When properly done, sharpening removes just enough squeegee material to produce a sharp clean edge.

There are several designs of squeegee sharpeners. Two of these designs have been in use for a number of years. One design uses a small belt that rotates during the grinding process. Another uses a wheel that rotates in a circular fashion during the grinding process, as shown in Figure 7-32. Both of these devices use abrasive material that is replaceable. The belts or wheels are available in various grits. There are also sharpeners available made up of industrial diamond grinding stones.

When properly done the grinding process removes a small, uniform amount of squeegee material over the entire surface. A course grit will remove more material quickly but produces a rough finish. A smooth grit will produce a smooth finish but takes longer. For best results a two stage process is recommended, starting with a coarse grit and finishing with a fine grit. When sharpening rubber and neoprene material, satisfactory results can be easily accomplished. Sharpening may pose a problem with some polyplastic blades. Heat is often generated due to the abrasive action that takes place, which may cause the blade to melt. It is best to test the blade material to make certain satisfactory results can be obtained.

A new approach is a sharpener that uses a knife blade as shown in Figure 7-33. This slices away a thin layer of the surface of the blade in a mechanical action producing a clean new surface. This device offers fast and effective results over sanding or grinding units as shown in Figure 7-34. The primary difficulty occurs when the sharpener blade dulls. As this occurs the uniformity of the cut is affected. This is primarily a problem with soft durometer blades. It is recommended that more material be removed from soft durometer materials to maintain better control of the cut.

SQUEEGEE SELECTION

There a number of aspects regarding selecting the best squeegee for a particular job. Each aspect must be carefully considered when preparing to print a job.

Blade Composition

Polyurethane is by far the preferred squeegee material due to its superior performance. It has improved durability and solvent resistance over other materials.

Figure 7-32 Blade sharpener

Figure 7-33 Knife type sharpener *(Pleiger Plastics Company)*

Blade Thickness and Width

Blades with a 3/8" or 1/2" thickness are superior over blades 3/16" in width. Due to the effect of solvents and the pressure exerted, thin blades will bend excessively. Blade heights of 2" to 3" are recommended as permitted by the press used.

Blade Hardness

Hardness of the blade is only one of many ways to regulate ink deposit. If a heavy ink deposit is

Figure 7-34 Sharpened blades *(Pleiger Plastics Company)*

desired a soft blade may be used. A hard blade on the other hand will deliver a thin ink deposit. Changes in hardness will alter the ink deposit. It is important to remember that the primary mode of altering ink deposit is by changing fabric. This will have a far greater impact on ink deposit than changing the squeegee.

Blade Profile

The square edged blade is the most common profile used for screen printing. It produces the best image quality over other types, especially with fine line designs or halftones. Under special circumstances other profiles may be beneficial.

Squeegee Length

The larger the squeegee blade in relation to the frame size the more squeegee pressure is required to shear the ink through image areas onto the substrate. More force is required for the screen to come in contact with the substrate. This requires more force to deflect the screen closer to the sides of the frame than in the center. Using a squeegee which is too large for the frame will distort the blade resulting in an inconsistent ink deposit.

Thus, it is important to select a frame that is the proper size in relation to the image area to be printed. Also, the squeegee should not be 1" to 2" larger than the image areas. Violating this guideline has numerous consequences. It requires greater off-contact to be used to achieve proper release of the screen from the substrate. This slows the rate that the press can be run, and requires greater squeegee pressure with greater wear on the squeegee, stencil and fabric. This also creates greater force at the ends of the squeegee which increases the chance of breaking the screen. Also, it creates greater distortion of the screen image resulting in registration problems. It is important to select a squeegee that does not exceed the optimum size for a given screen size. This is also discussed in Chapter 5: Fabric Tension and Frames.

New Blade Types

Many of the new composite and multi durometer blades are growing in popularity. With the advent of higher screen tensions, control of the squeegee grows in importance. With the significant higher tensions these new blade types are capable of producing better quality than traditional blades. Testing is the only way to determine which blade type will achieve the best results in any given circumstance.

SQUEEGEE MAINTENANCE AND STORAGE

Rubber absorbs solvent because of its composition. Even the most solvent-resistant polyurethane will absorb solvent over time. There are several recommendations that will minimize this effect. The squeegee should be cleaned using a cloth dampened with the proper solvent. The blade should not be immersed in solvent to soften and remove ink as this will cause solvent to be absorbed into the blade.

After cleaning, the squeegee should be allowed to dry for 24 hours to allow the squeegee to restore before it is resharpened. After a period of time this solvent will cause the blade material to harden making it unsuited for further use. Squeegees should be stored at room temperature in low humidity. High temperature and humidity will adversely affect the blade. The blade should be stored with pressure off the blade so it is not distorted in any way.

KEY TERMS

camber
composite blade
durometer
durometer gauge
flood bar
multidurometer blade
shear
skewing

REVIEW QUESTIONS

1. How can changes in durometer be used to regulate ink deposit?
2. Which blade profile is most commonly used?
3. How does the blade angle affect ink deposit?
4. What is camber?
5. In which situation should skewing the squeegee be considered?
6. What is the purpose of the flood bar?
7. What should be done differently with the flood bar when printing halftones?
8. What do some of the new blade types offer over the traditional blade?
9. Why is it important to keep the blade sharpened?

NOTES

[1] Mike Young, *The Register Guide, 2nd ed.* (Stockholm: Up to Date Publishing, 1993).

[2] Michel Caza, *Screen Printing of Fine Line Halftones* (Fairfax: Technical Guidebook of the Screen Printing Industry, Screenprinting and Graphic Imaging Association International, June 1983).

[3] Mark Coudray, "Screen Printing Halftones", *Screen Printing Magazine* February 1990: 106-111; pt 4 of a series, Production Planning.

Screen Printing Inks

Inks have been an integral part of each of the printing processes since the beginning of printing. The earliest known use of printing inks dates back to about 1100 B.C. in China and Egypt although records are limited. Early ink formulations were made of lampblack mixed with gum. Technical advancements have improved ink formulations over the centuries. An early achievement used linseed oil as a vehicle with lampblack. Synthetic oils were developed because of the limitations of the linseed oil base and led to faster drying inks. The development of synthetic resins produced ink with greater versatility and durability. Developments in pigments led to colored inks.

Early screen printing inks were very similar to paints, to which they are sometimes incorrectly referred. Today their formulations classify them as inks. Screen printing is ideally suited for printing fluorescent or other inks that are adversely affected by exposure to light since it applies a thick ink deposit (compared to other printing processes). Screen printing differs in the way ink transfer occurs. Most printing processes accomplish ink transfer by a roll-to-roll process. With roll-to-roll transfer the image carrier is a cylindrical form that comes into contact with the paper (either directly or indirectly) through another cylindrical roller. This arrangement makes ink transfer very efficient without compromising print quality. With ink transferring from one roll to another ink must be formulated to be "long." When the ink is touched with the finger and pulled away a string will form with an ink that is long. If a long ink were used for screen printing strings would form once the screen separates from the substrate in the printing process. This effect does occur under certain adverse situations producing what is known as a "cob webbing" effect. For this reason screen printing inks are formulated to be short and buttery. This allows the ink to flow through the image areas of the screen onto the substrate.

Figure 8-1 Ink manufacturing laboratory

Another difference with screen inks is the variety of substrates that may be printed. It is rare if anything other than paper is printed by lithography (although metal and plastic are printed on occasion). Far fewer ink formulations are needed with lithography than with screen printing due to this fact. In addition to printing on different materials, screen printing can be used to print on different surfaces. This creates a dilemma for ink formulation. Ink formulated to print on textiles for instance will not adhere to a substrate such as glass due to the differences in surface structure and composition. A different binder is needed to adhere the pigments to different substrates. There is a trend toward ink manufacturers to produce multipurpose inks, formulated to function on more than one substrate. This eliminates the printer from stocking a number of lines of inks to print on different substrate types. However, in some circumstances multipurpose inks do not work as well as an ink that is formulated for one specific substrate, since they are a compromise. It is very important to test ink compatibility before printing a job.

Ink must meet the needs of the customer and the printer. The customer's requirements are in the areas of appearance and performance:

1. To match a desired color and finish on a specific substrate or surface.
2. Achieve performance standards for outdoor or indoor use,
3. Achieve durability and resistance to chemical, abrasion or weather.

The printer has slightly different concerns:

1. Achieve fast drying without drying in the screen during the printing process
2. Be compatible with finishing operations as required by the customer (cutting, folding, die cutting, and so on).
3. Achieve desired standards for intercoat adhesion, scratch resistance and so on.
4. The ink must also be available at an affordable price.

This clearly illustrates the challenges present in formulating and producing ink for the screen printer.

INK INGREDIENTS

There are a number of ingredients required for producing screen printing inks. In recent years the number of ingredients available to the ink manufacturer has continued to increase due to a number of new raw materials. Demands placed on the ink manufacturer by environmental regulations and the customer's need to print on a wide range of substrates under differing conditions have also initiated demands for new ink ingredients. Over the years, new pigments and synthetic resins have been developed producing materials better suited to ink manufacture. The primary ingredients to formulate an ink are pigments, resins and solvents. These give the ink its most important properties. However, once these ingredients are mixed they may not meet the necessary standards due to slight variations in the ingredients or the manufacturing procedure. Modifiers are added to adjust the ink to the desired standards.

Some of the characteristics of a desirable ink are viscosity, flow and drying rate. Modifiers can also be added by the printer to further fine tune the ink for a particular situation. A formulation may function right out of the can in one location yet problems may be experienced on press and require modifiers to be added due to adverse climatic conditions in another part of the country. Even though the manufacturer attempts to formulate an ink that will function under a broad range of situations there are always unique situations requiring some modification to be made. By consulting the manufacturer's data sheets or calling the company for their recommendation the required modification can be made to the ink.

Colorant

Colorant is used for the manufacture of paints, plastics, textiles, cosmetics and printing inks as an agent to provide color. Since materials come from a variety of sources they differ in many ways. They have different particle size, specific gravity, wettability, opacity or transparency. Inks must be formulated taking these different characteristics into account. Inks of different color within the same ink line cannot be formulated using the same formula.

There are two different ingredients to provide color for inks: **dyes** and **pigments.** Dyes are soluble in a solvent or vehicle while pigments are insoluble. Pigments are commonly used as a colorant for inks. Pigments are organic or inorganic. The term organic means that the pigments are produced from living organisms. Organic pigments such as lampblack are derived from petroleum, oil or gas burned to produce a black colorant. Other organic pigments are produced using coal, animal or vegetable fats or oils, and wood. Inorganic pigments are produced in several ways. They may be produced by mixing dry reactants and applying heat to create a synthesized compound. In some cases a mineral is collected by mining and is processed and purified. Other cases use chemical reactions or mixing of aqueous solutions to produce the desired pigments.

Screen printing inks can be opaque or transparent. Opaque inks are made using opaque pigments. Transparent pigments are used for process color inks. There have been regulations to encourage the elimination of heavy metal-from paints and inks. With heavy metal free or non-lead inks the pigments are not made up of lead or heavy metals. Many inks are free of heavy metals but its advisable to check the ink technical sheet or call the manufacturer. Pigments are sometimes treated with resin during pigment manufacture. This makes the pigments more disbursable resulting in improved wetting by the vehicle.

Vehicle

A **vehicle** is a means by which something is carried. With inks the vehicle is a fluid in which pigments are suspended for printing use. Once the vehicle has transferred ink onto the desired material it then leaves by means of evaporation of solvent (with evaporative inks).

Binder

A **binder** is needed to hold the pigments together once the vehicle has transferred ink onto the substrate to which it is printed. The binder combines with the pigment to form the ink film. A binder is a substance that acts like glue or cement to adhere pigments onto the substrate. The selection of binder is made based on the substrate printed. For instance the binder for an absorbent paper will not adhere pigments to a smooth surface such as glass. The binder affects the drying time of the ink since it controls the solvent retention of the ink.

Figure 8-2 Resin

Resin

Screen printing inks are formulated using **resins** whether traditional solvent-based, water-based or UV curing. A resin is a solid or semi-solid material that can be dissolved into a liquid, and suspended in a vehicle to make an ink, which when dry becomes the solid part of the dry ink film. The types of resins used are acrylic, alkyd, epoxy, polyester, urethane and vinyl. The vehicle and binder are formulated by dissolving resin in a dry powdered state with a solvent. These resins are selected based on the substrate and ink characteristics desired. Resins are formulated into a liquid state with the proper viscosity and flow characteristics suitable for the screen printing process. These formulations vary considerably for each ink type to change from its liquid state into a dry ink film.

There are a number of different resins and solvents that determine the ink's characteristics. A resin is a solid or semi-solid material of relatively high molecular weight. Organic resins are obtained from vegetable matter, or in a fossilized form or the secretion of an insect (shellac). Synthetic resins are produced by condensation or polymerization reactions where chemical molecules are simple in structure and much less complex than the molecular structure of most natural resins. This results in a chemical composition that can be controlled with greater accuracy. This allows the physical and chemical properties of synthetic resins to be tailored to the specific application. By selecting the proper resin and solvent, the properties of the ink can be modified, to produce properties such as gloss, hardness, adhesion, flexibility, flow, and viscosity. See Figure 8-2.

Solvents

A **solvent** is a liquid that is capable of dissolving one or more substances. Solvents are used in ink manufacture to dissolve resins, oils, or dyes into a solution to which pigments can be added. After the ink has been printed solvent is no longer needed and escapes by evaporation or absorption. Inks contain solvents and

Figure 8-3 Solvents

thinners to give the desired characteristics of flow, viscosity and ink density.

"The final film properties are influenced by the molecular arrangement or structure that is formed as the solvents evaporate. That is why it is so important to use the correct solvent(s) when manufacturing the original ink and also when adjusting it for press."[1]

The amount of solvents used in inks varies based on ink type. Solvent-based inks have the highest solvent content with as much as 70% in some cases. Water-based inks are made up of a large proportion of water but also have a small amount of volatile solvents to assist in achieving the desired characteristics. In cases with some plastics the solvent reacts with the surface causing ink to adhere. In cases where two or more solvents are mixed it forms what is called a co-solvent. A co-solvent used with many solvent-based ink formulations is a mixture of ethylene glycol monoethyl ester and mineral spirits (aliphic hydrocarbon). This mixture gives the solvent-based ink its fast drying properties.

Some of the solvents used for screen printing ink formulations include methyl glycol acetate, cyclohexanone, xylene, ethylene glycol, ethylene glycol monobutyl esther acetate, butanol, isophorone, benzyl alcohol, ethyl glycol, high boiling point aromatic solvents and water. Solvents can be explosive and toxic in some cases and cause skin irritation or injury. See Figure 8-3.

Additives or Modifiers

A modifier is something that is added to change or affect the characteristics of the ink in differing conditions. The ink may need to be modified prior to printing a job to achieve the best printing results. Additives are used to change viscosity, drying, flow out or other characteristics of the ink. For instance ink must be modified differently to print on a hot humid day than on one that is cold and dry.

Thinner

A **thinner** is a liquid such as paint, varnish or other chemical solution, used to dilute a solution to a desired consistency. Thinners are an essential ingredient used in making the ink perform most effectively in differing conditions. A thinner may or may not be volatile, such as water used in dilution of water-based inks. Addition of thinner to an ink causes a number of changes. It lowers the ink's viscosity resulting in increased ink flow characteristics. It decreases the dry ink film thickness due to its decreased solids content.

There are three types of thinners: fast, slow or regular. A **fast drying thinner** speeds the drying process of the ink. A **slow thinner** is a solvent blend that helps to keep the ink open and wet in the screen and evaporates more slowly than a regular thinner. Yet a slow thinner has less effect than a retarder. Water-based inks can be thinned using water although specific thinners are also formulated.

The addition of thinner to ink should not exceed the manufacturer's recommendations. The amount of thinner that may be added is based on its formulation. Too much thinner, regardless of the ink type, will adversely affect the printability, intensity, opacity or adhesion of the ink. For best results the recommendations of the manufacturer should be followed and the ink should be tested before printing it on press.

As a rule of thumb, many inks will allow the addition of 10% thinner with some as low as 5% and others as high as 20%. The amount of thinner also varies with the age of the ink. Over time, solvent evaporates from the can as the ink is used. As the last of the ink is used (over a period of time) the ink thickens and requires addition of thinner to return it to the consistency of the ink when it was fresh.

Retarder

One of the challenges of the screen printing process is to get the ink to dry as rapidly as possible on the substrate after printing without drying the printing screen. **Retarder** can be helpful in achieving this action. A solvent or thinner makes the ink evaporate or dry more slowly. A retarder is particularly useful for printing fine line details or halftones under adverse environmental conditions and high temperatures.

It is important to use the retarder recommended by the manufacturer. It must thoroughly dissolve with the solvents and vehicle in the ink. In addition to slowing the drying time of the ink a retarder also lowers its viscosity. If retarder is inappropriately used it may cause the ink to penetrate into the substrate due to increased ink flow resulting in solvent retention. This may lead to problems with adhesion of the ink to the substrate. It is important to not add retarder over the prescribed amount.

Use of retarder resulting in an increase in ink flow can create problems with dot gain or loss when printing halftone images. A retarder paste or gel may be used when printing halftones. It is made up of solvents in a nonfluid state, which slows the evaporation rate of the ink without affecting its viscosity. Using a gel or paste retarder with a jet dryer allows ink to stay wet in the screen without seriously affecting the printing speed of the press. Retarder pastes or gels are not available with every line of ink but are offered with process ink colors.

Flow Agent

Ink is forced through image areas of the screen in the screen printing process. As ink flows around the fibers of mesh it must continue to flow out to form a flat uniform ink film. If the ink is not formulated properly an orange peel effect or mesh marks may be present. Other effects such as fisheyes or bubbles may form. When the above conditions are present they may be remedied by adding a small quantity of flow promoter (as specified by the ink manufacturer). This changes the surface tension of the ink and increases flow out of the ink.

Flattening Agent

Some lines of inks offer both flat and gloss finishes. In some cases , however, only gloss finish is available. By adding a **flattening** paste or powder the gloss level of an ink may be reduced to achieve a satin or flat finish.

Bases

There are several different types of bases that may be added to modify inks. Two characteristics of these bases are the same. Bases do not have any colorant. Since they are in a gelled state and not a liquid state they do not decrease ink's viscosity as a thinner or solvent. Different types of bases are **extender base, transparent base, halftone base** and a **clear base**. These types of bases are not available in all lines of ink. In some cases there is only one base that is used for more than one purpose.

EXTENDER BASE Extender base is a pastelike compound, whitish yellow in color. It is used to increase ink volume without affecting viscosity. Extender base is less expensive than ink and can be added to ink that is heavily pigmented to make a lower cost ink. This should be done when printing on white or light colored substrates since extender will have some effect on ink opacity and color intensity based on the amount added, yet less than a transparent base. In addition to lowering ink cost it also improves the printability of the ink. Extender base is also useful in color matching.

TRANSPARENT BASE A transparent base is used to make the ink more transparent and to significantly reduce the color intensity of the ink. It makes the ink softer or less intense in appearance. Attempting to add excessive amounts of thinner or solvent to an ink will affect it to the point where it becomes difficult to print due to the change in viscosity. A significant amount of transparent base may be added without affecting its printability. A transparent base is also useful in color matching of inks.

HALFTONE BASE Halftone base is clear in color although over time it may darken and lead to problems with color matching. There are two purposes for halftone base. Many of the process inks are available in concentrated form. The inks are more intense in color than desired and must be reduced by adding halftone base. When printing halftones it is important for the ink to be deposited on the surface of the substrate and not to flow or change in dot structure. If the ink spreads on the surface it will result in dot gain or may penetrate into the surface of the substrate excessively. A second purpose of halftone base is to increase its viscosity or thixotrophic nature. Addition of the proper amount of halftone base will prevent this from occurring.

CLEAR BASE A clear base has several uses. It may be used as a mixing varnish for metallic inks. For example, to mix a gold metallic ink, 1½ pounds of gold bronze powder are added to a gallon of clear base. For best results, mixing should be done by adding a small amount of the base to the metallic powder to form a heavy paste. It should be completely mixed until it is smooth and free of lumps. The remainder of base should then be added and mixed until it is uniform in consistency. If stored over time the metallic pigments settle to the bottom of the container, requiring extensive remixing of the ink before it can be used again. It is best to mix only the amount of metallic ink needed for the job.

It is important that the clear base selected is compatible with the substrate to be printed. Adhesion will be affected if too much metallic powder is added to the base. Metallic powders are available in different particle sizes from fine to coarse to produce different effects. It is important that the mesh opening of the fabric is large enough to allow the metallic pigments to pass. For instance, with the smallest particle size a monofilament polyester with a 330 mesh or less can be used. Coarse particle sizes create more brilliant effects but require a a 140 mesh or less for best results. Metallic powders are available in various shades of gold, aluminum, and copper colored pigments.

A second use for clear base is as a varnish. By overprinting a varnish it improves durability, rub resistance and maximizes the print for exterior use. It can also be to make an area appear glossy in appearance by applying the clear base in desired areas.

INK MANUFACTURE

There are three steps in the manufacture of inks. These steps are mixing of raw ingredients, milling on a three-roll mill and the final remixing stage. The purpose of these steps is to get the ink processed into its final state. Ink making is more complex than merely combining ingredients following an ink formula. The way they are mixed affects its final quality as much as the quality of the ingredients used. It's similar to giving a recipe to a cook and expecting it to turn out the same as if a chef were preparing the dish. Due to the differences in the raw ingredients used for different ink formulations each must be prepared slightly differently.

Mixing

Powdered resins are initially combined with solvents to form the vehicle and binder for the ink. Solvents dissolve the resins to form a liquid solution. The resins selected determine its flow characteristics and viscosity, although they can both be adjusted later to some degree in the final remixing stage. There are two or three grades of resins available that will determine its viscosity. The resins and solvents are weighed and added into a mixing container in the correct proportions. Initial mixing of ingredients is done using a large mixer, similar to one used by cooks but on a larger scale using up to a 75 horsepower motor as shown in Figure 8-4. Two basic designs in blades are used, one for inks of high viscosity and another for low viscosity inks. See Figure 8-5.

Figure 8-4 Mixer

Pigments are weighed and added in a dry state to the liquid solution of resins and solvent. The most critical stage of ink manufacture is disbursing the dry pigment evenly throughout the liquid solvent/resin solution. Pigment dispersal is accomplished in two stages. The initial premix is done on a mixer. Initially the pigment when added to a liquid solution forms clumps or clusters in a lumpy consistency somewhat like oatmeal. At this time pigment are not separated into individual particles immersed in the liquid solution. The pigments cannot entirely be dispersed by mixing to achieve the desired pigment dispersal. Some pigments disperse more easily and require less mixing than others.

There are several ways of evaluating the process of pigment dispersal. One way is by sensing the change in temperature that occurs as the ink is mixed. An increase in temperature can be felt on the sides of the container as the ink begins to mix. With this change in

Figure 8-5 Mixing blade

Figure 8-6 Initial mixing

temperature comes a change in ink viscosity, and pigment dispersal becomes more complete. After a given temperature is reached the mixing operation has achieved its maximum result and is ready for milling.

Another method of evaluating pigment dispersal is by the change in visual appearance of the ink from a grainy to more uniform consistency texture. A third method of evaluation is the visual shape of the ink surface during the mixing process. Initially during the first stage of mixing the surface is flat with the mixing blade fully hidden in the ink and only the shaft visible as shown in Figure 8-6. At the final stage of the mixing operation a vortex is formed where a portion of the blade becomes visible in spite of the fact that it is placed at a considerable depth in the mixing container. See Figure 8-7. This is due to the change in viscosity and pigment **dispersal** that occurs when mixing is nearly complete. This emphasizes the skill in knowing how to combine and mix the ingredients and when they have been prepared properly. The next stage of the dispersal process is milling the ink.

Figure 8-7 Mixing complete

Milling

This operation is sometimes referred to as **grinding** the ink on a mill. It is not actually a grinding operation since the particle size of the pigments do not necessarily change in size. **Milling** is primarily used to complete the dispersion of pigments and removes air from the ink. Dispersion is accomplished using a three-roll mill which combines a shearing stress action with pressure.

A three-roll mill is the most common type mill used in ink manufacture although there are also four- and five-roll mills. See Figure 8-8. As the name indicates this mill is made up of three iron rolls which are water cooled. The three-roll mill is normally used with high viscosity inks made of pigments and pastelike vehicles. The rollers are mounted in a sturdy cast frame that is secured on a strong concrete foundation. The rolls rotate in opposite directions at different speeds. The rear roll is the slowest with each roll increasing in speed to the front. Ink is introduced between the back two rolls and travels from one roll to the next until it emerges at the front roll to flow to a storage container. By driving the rolls at different speeds, a rubbing action creates both shear and crushing stress that results in improved dispersion of the pigment particles.

Figure 8-8 Three roll mill

The operation of the three-roll mill is a highly skilled task. If the pressure between rolls is insufficient complete pigment dispersal will not be achieved although processing time will be reduced. With too much pressure, processing time will be excessive and the mill will run too hot. Perfect pigment dispersal is not desirable as it would require greater processing time. The milling operation is a slow costly process at best and requires a highly skilled operator. Pigment dispersal needs not to be overdone, only enough to achieve satisfactory results. Ink that is milled a short time may cost less but printed results will be adversely affected. Poor pigment dispersal will not print well on the press.

Measurement of Pigment Dispersal

It is important to evaluate the degree of **pigment dispersal** during

Figure 8-9 Mill operation

Figure 8-10 Hegman gauge

the milling process. In some cases one pass through the mill is not enough to achieve the desired pigment dispersal and a second pass is needed. Although there are four methods of evaluating an ink for pigment dispersal, the method most commonly used is the Hegman gauge, a device used in the paint industry (ASTM D-1316). It is also known as a fineness-of-grind gauge. It is a piece of hardened steel about 8 inches in length with a surface machined to a smooth finish with several wide grooves or channels recessed into the surface. See Figure 8-10. The grooves gradually increase in depth from zero at one end to 100 microns (μ) at the other end. A scale is engraved in the steel indicating the particle size or degree of pigment dispersal. A reading of 7 on the gauge indicates a particle size of 12μ while a reading of 1 at the other end indicates a particle size of 100μ. This device can only be used to measure large particle sizes ranging from 12μ up to 100μ which makes it suited to screen printing inks. This device is easy to use but the results are more challenging to interpret.

A small sample of ink is placed in the deep end of the channel. A steel doctor blade is used to scrape the ink and draw it down the length of the groove making sure the recessed area is filled along the full length of the device. The results are then viewed looking for scratches in the ink film and the distance

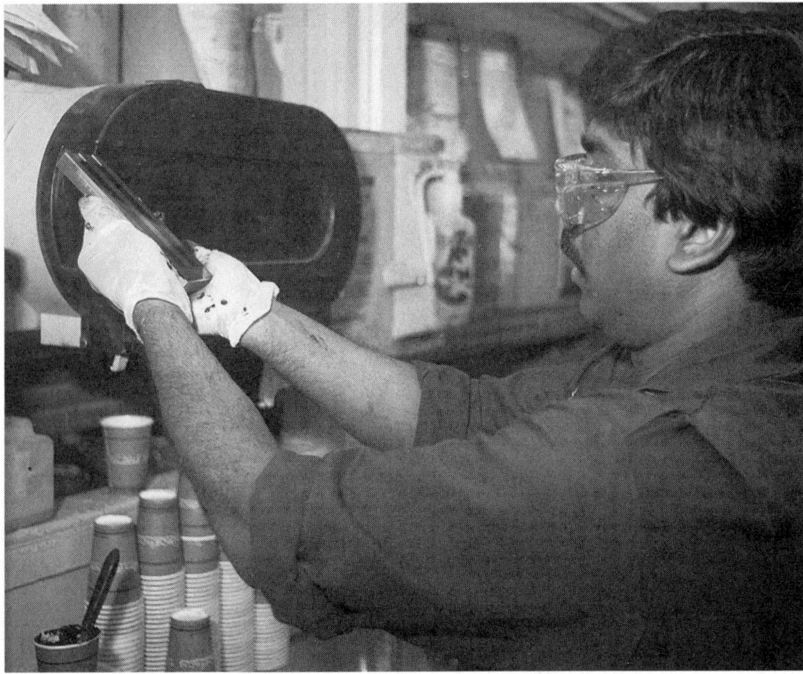

Figure 8-11 Viewing gauge

where they occur along the gauge. See Figure 8-11. A number along the edge is located to determine the point at which ink dispersal has occurred. Each ink has a pigment dispersal that will deliver the best printed results.

Remixing of Ink

Once the ink has been processed by the milling operation and the proper pigment dispersal has been attained, the ink is remixed. Solvents, thinners and other modifiers are added to the ink to achieve its final characteristics (viscosity, flow characteristics, and so on). If all ingredients were added at the initial stage of ink manufacture the greater volume would require substantially more time to process through the three-roll mill. Instead the desired pigment dispersal can be achieved in a concentrated state adding modifiers to achieve its desired volume in the final mixing stage. The procedure is similar to mixing a cup of hot cocoa; it is more effective to start with a small amount of hot water in the cup to get all the lumps out, and then add water to achieve the desired dilution.

INK CLASSIFICATION

Inks must be in liquid form to be printed by the screen printing process. After ink has been applied to the substrate by squeegee action it goes through a conversion process where it changes into a solid film. This conversion from liquid to solid form occurs in different ways based on the composition of the ink. Conversion can be classified into two types: temporary and permanent conversion.

Temporary Conversion Inks

Conversion takes place on a temporary basis, as changes from a liquid to a solid are achieved through solvent evaporation. It can change back into a liquid again by immersing the dry ink film into a solvent. The dry ink film is not permanent. The temporary conversion is one that is reversible, to go from liquid to solid and back to liquid any number of times. A solvent-based ink is an example of a temporary conversion ink.

Evaporative Inks

The earliest inks used for screen printing dried by evaporation of solvents. There are two basic types: solvent evaporative and water evaporative inks.

SOLVENT-BASED INKS Solvent-based inks are converted into a dry ink film by evaporation of solvent from the wet ink film. In some cases solvent-based inks dry by absorption of ink into the substrate (although solvent evaporation has a greater effect on drying). If significant absorption of ink has occurred stacking may be a problem. Once drying has occurred pigments are adhered to the substrate by the binder of the resin system. The drying rate of the ink is primarily governed by the amount and type of solvent used and its volatility. Other ingredients in the ink formulation also regulate the degree to which solvent is released from the ink. The drying process can be accelerated by application of heat. High efficiency dryers produce the best drying results and will be discussed in Chapter 9. Excess heat can cause adverse affects with registration due to stock shrinkage. The drying temperature must be carefully regulated for best results. Poster inks, for instance, air dry in 20-30 minutes but jet dry in seconds.

No chemical agents are required for drying, but heat will accelerate the rate. The solvent used governs how much heat is needed but the substrate limits how much is too much heat. When heat must be kept low the ink formulation must be regulated to balance between getting the ink to dry rapidly on the substrate without drying in the screen. Examples of solvent-based inks include poster inks, lacquers, and acrylics.

Poster Inks are formulated to print posters on paper or cardboard. They dry by solvent evaporation and can be thinned with mineral spirits. These inks are available in flat or gloss finish and are relatively inexpensive and easy to use. They are available in both opaque and transparent colors. Poster inks air dry in thirty minutes or less and jet dry in 10-15 seconds at 115°F.

Lacquer Inks are similar to high quality enamel inks. They can be used with a wide range of substrates such as paper, cardboard, wood, acrylics, cellulose acetate, and some polyester. They have outstanding opacity with high gloss and mar resistance. They can be used in industrial applications where resistance to abrasion, mild acids and gasoline are needed. They are made up of a transparent or clear resin solution that dries by solvent evaporation. Lacquer inks air dry in 40 minutes or less and jet dry in 20-30 seconds at 200°F.

Vinyl Inks are formulated to fuse into the surface of vinyl. They may be used with both flexible and rigid vinyl, some vinyl coating, and on vacuum-formed vinyls. They can be used with applications such as shower curtains, pressure sensitive decals, inflatable toys, tablecloths, and PVC bottles. Lucite™, Lexan®, Plexiglas and top coated polyester may also be printed using vinyl inks. When dry they are as flexible as the vinyl surface itself. They have good printability with excellent opacity and fast drying qualities. Most vinyl inks air dry in 40 minutes or less and force dry at 160°F for 45 seconds.

WATER-BASED INKS The vehicle and binder for a water-based ink is water soluble or dispersible in water. This requires a water soluble resin. Acrylic resins are used with water-based inks. Water-based inks are evaporative in nature and dry by evaporation of water. This is environmentally cleaner than with solvent-based inks but the evaporative process with water is slower than solvents. Many of the water-based inks are made up of 80% or more water. Yet a water reducible ink may have as little as 10 percent. A water reducible ink is one that may be thinned using water.

In addition to water, the ink's formulation includes pigments, resins and various additives. Water-based inks have a 65% to 75% solids content compared to solvent-based inks with 40%, and UV curing inks with 100% solids. Additives include flow promoters, anti-fungal agents, adhesion promoters, and other chemicals as needed. A small amount of solvent is added to enhance its printability, drying and adhesion qualities. When two or more solvents are used this is referred as co-solvents.

Water-based inks have been sought as a solution to the environmental dilemma that solvent-based inks and other petrol chemicals have created. However, substituting water for solvent is not a simple matter when dealing with inks. Using water as a major component in an evaporative ink leaves the formulation compromised. There will be difficulty getting ink to adhere to various substrates such as plastic. Printability and drying are also seriously affected. Addition of a small amount of the proper solvent can make the ink function more successfully.

Yet using co-solvents in the ink formulation creates a problem in screen making. Diazo sensitized emulsions (commonly used for a number of years in the screen printing industry) are available in formulations that are either water resistive or solvent resistive. You must choose between the two. If you use a solvent resistive formulation, the water in the water-based ink is absorbed into the emulsion and it becomes increasingly tacky. As you print, the substrate begins to stick to the bottom of the screen due to the tacky emulsion until the point where each print must be manually pulled off. On the other hand, if a water resistant stencil is used, the solvent from the water-based ink eventually is absorbed into the emulsion in the same fashion. This is one of the reasons why water-based inks have been rejected after use by many companies in the past.

One of the newest emulsions are pure polymer (SBQ) sensitized emulsions. Unfortunately, this emulsion has poor resistance to water-based inks and should only be used with solvent-based inks. The stencil system that is best suited to the needs of a water-based ink containing co-solvents is known as a dual cure emulsion. This emulsion has the characteristics of both diazo and pure polymer (SBQ) sensitizers. This gives it the ability to be both solvent and water resistant.

For stencils (especially dual cure) to achieve their greatest state of resistance to solvents and water, however, complete exposure must be achieved. If incompletely exposed, the emulsion will soften during the press run as described earlier. The best way to achieve proper exposure of a stencil is by making an exposure calculation test. Stencil exposure is not as critical using solvent-based inks. An underexposed diazo sensitized emulsion is less prone to breakdown in printing solvent-based inks than a dual cured emulsion using water-based inks.

In addition to the changes in stencil making required, water-based inks perform differently on press. The viscosity is often lower with many of the water-based inks than solvent-based inks. This requires some changes in press procedures. Drying is slower with water-based inks since the evaporation rate is slower. To minimize this factor it is important to keep the ink deposit thin, and use a jet dryer using air flow and heat to remove water from the ink film.

Water soaks into stock causing it to pucker or distort when printing on lightweight paper (70 or 80 lb.). Water-based inks also have difficulty in adhering to some plastics and may pose problems with finishing operations such as diecutting or embossing. However, the advantages of removing solvent fumes from a screen printing operation and improving the environment are significant reasons to convert to water-based inks. This also reduces the use of solvents in a shop for additives and screen washup since many water-based inks can be thinned with water.

Permanent Conversion Inks

A permanent conversion ink experiences a chemical change during the drying/curing process which alters its original composition and is not reversible. This chemical change is known as polymerization. There are several different conversion methods: oxidation, catalyst, thermal setting and ultraviolet radiation. This physical change is the result of an action that initiates a polymerization reaction that is initiated by an agent either by catalyst action or some form of energy. After the process in initiated heat may speed up the process. Once the physical change has taken place the ink film will have enhanced chemical and mechanical properties.

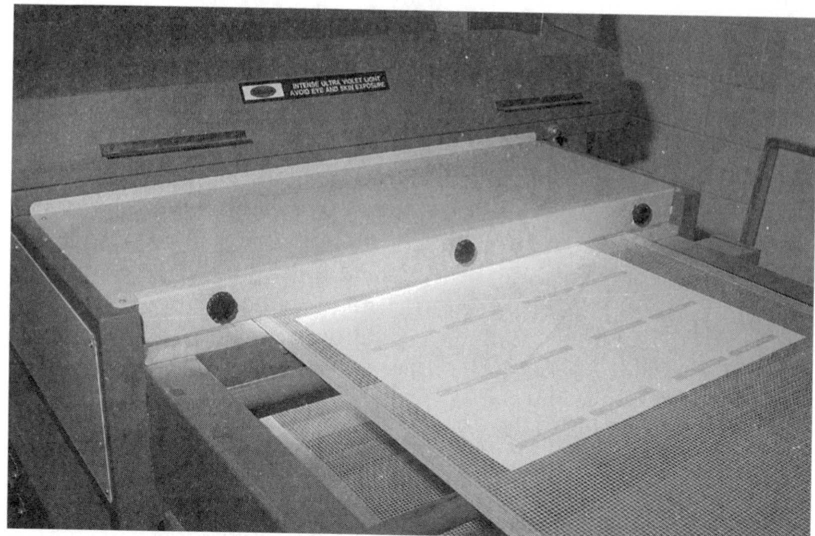

Figure 8-12 UV reactor

Oxidation

Enamel inks are one of the earliest screen printing inks, and cure or dry by **oxidation.** These inks are formulated using drying oils such as linseed oil, chinawood oil or soya bean oil. Drying/curing takes place in two stages after ink is deposited on the substrate. In the first stage solvent evaporation occurs. Although it may appear to be dry it has not developed its final properties since its complete conversion has not taken place. Air drying can take up to six hours but when heated to 180°F it becomes dry to the touch in 30 minutes.

In its final stage, oxygen in the air combines with the drying oil in the ink to cause the polymerization process to begin. Polymerization is a process where individual molecules join or crosslink into molecular chains. This process starts on the surface but continues downward through the ink layer until the entire ink film is converted into a solid ink film with chemical and mechanical resistive properties. It is a slow process requiring 24 to 48 hours to reach maximum resistance to abrasion and chemicals.

Enamel inks have a glossy finish and provide excellent adhesion to a wide range of substrates such as metal, wood, glass and cardboard. It has good outdoor durability and is used for outdoor signs and displays, decals and packaging containers.

Ultraviolet Curing

UV curing inks are unique in their composition and in the way they cure or dry. The components that make up a UV ink are oligomers, monomers, colorants, photoinitiator and additives. Oligomers are the resins that form the base of the ink. They establish adhesion qualities, wetting ability and the body of the ink. Monomers are like solvents used to thin the ink. They establish gloss, hardness and flexibility of the ink. It is also the portion of the ink that gives its toxicity. Colorant is used to establish the ink's color. Additives or modifiers are used to adjust the ink to achieve its final desired flow, consistency and so on. The photoinitiator is the catalyst that initiates a chain reaction that causes curing to take place once exposed to UV light.

Once UV light comes in contact with the ink, polymerization occurs instantaneously, unlike polymerization with oxidation inks which take several hours to cure. The photoinitiator reacts to UV light and transfers the energy to the oligomers and monomers causing a chain reaction of polymerization where a solid ink film is formed. If UV light does not completely penetrate into the ink film, a partial cure takes place. This can occur due to excessive ink deposits or with pigment types that are more difficult for light to penetrate (black, for one). It is important to print a thin ink film to insure complete cuing with UV inks.

There are a number of advantages of using UV inks over other types. High speed printing and drying can be achieved over other ink types due to the instantaneous cure rate. UV curing reactors use lower energy than when heat is used to dry evaporative inks. The space required for a UV reactor system is substantially less than with other dryers. Since UV inks do not dry prematurely in the screen during printing there is increased productivity since few mid-run screen washups are needed. Environmentally UV ink is better than solvent-based inks that evaporate into the air.

UV inks are not without their disadvantages. Screen making is more critical with UV inks. The screen must be made to print a thin ink deposit to achieve proper curing. The choice of screen mesh and emulsion are important in achieving the desired deposit. Screen touch up is important since the smallest pinhole will stay open during printing. The thin ink deposit achieved is more vulnerable to fading or wear in adverse or outdoor use. Since UV inks do not evaporate or dry when spilled they will spread throughout the facility if not cleaned up promptly. They can easily be picked up by contact (shoes, hands, and so on) and transferred several days after they have been spilled. Greater attention must be paid to proper ink handling to prevent these problems from occurring. UV inks in addition to all inks (including solvent-based inks) are potential skin sensitizers and the skin should be protected from direct contact. The UV reactor must be shielded to prevent eye damage from the lamp and it must be vented to protect from exposure to ozone fumes. Yet in spite of its limitations UV inks offer the screen printer great productivity due to its fast cure rate.

UV inks are 100% solids since there are no volatile chemicals to evaporate during the curing process. The ink deposit remains the same thickness when it is cured as it was when wet. The ink film thickness once cured remains thick even when using a high mesh count (up to 470) due to its high solids content. With lower solids content inks the ink film thickness decreases with the loss of solvents. So for instance with an ink that is 40% solids it achieves only 40% of its wet ink film thickness when it is dry. This poses a problem when printing four color process using UV curing inks. When the dots for the process colors overprint it becomes increasingly difficult to print each color on top of the previous ink film deposits. By the time the fourth color is printed it can be a considerable problem.

With this in mind a water reducible UV curing ink was developed. A resin system was developed to include water in its formulation. Water contained in the ink evaporates during the curing process. This retains the printing benefits of a UV ink without the high ink film buildup. There are several manufacturers that have developed an ink of this type.

Thermal Setting

These are inks that are composed of resin systems that require heat for the ink film to achieve a complete cure. Once the ink deposit has been subjected to heat at a given temperature and time an insoluble polymer is formed. Some thermal setting inks dry by solvent evaporation or oxidation but require heat to cure. For example an ink of this type requires exposure to heat at 275°F for 15 minutes to cure. Once cured the ink film possesses resistance to many solvents, chemicals, humidity and abrasion.

Catalyst Inks

Epoxy inks are **catalyst inks** and are available in either one- or two-part systems. Each is capable of excellent adhesion to hard surfaces such as metal or glass. They may also be used with phenolics, polyester, melamine, silicone, ceramic and textiles. Epoxy inks form a tough film layer that is resistant to chemicals and mechanical abrasion. One-part epoxy inks do not air dry and require heat to initiate curing. Two-part epoxies initiate polymerization by use of an acid catalyst. Polymerization is the process where individual molecules crosslink to form a hardened material that is unaffected by chemical or mechanical forces. Once polymerization is initiated with two-part epoxies it will continue to react at room temperature but can be accelerated by applying heat. Since two-part systems have a pot life of only 5 to 6 hours it is recommended that the ink is mixed just prior to use.

One-part epoxies cure when heated for 3 minutes at 400°F or 7 minutes at 350°F. Two-part epoxies air dry in 2 to 3 hours, but at 180°F ink will cure in 30 minutes. They require 7 to 10 days for this ink to achieve maximum adhesion and chemical resistance.

Specialty Inks

There are screen printing inks that are specific to the needs of various specific applications such as with electronic circuitry of various sorts, ceramics, and textiles. Each must meet certain basic criterion to achieve the desired end result. Every type of specialty ink will not be looked at due to the large number. Only a few of the most significant inks will be introduced.

Electronic Inks

Various inks are used to produce various electronic components through screen printing. In past years screen printing was used to print a resistive ink on copper clad boards as a stage of the circuit board manufacture. With recent technological advancements in the electronics industry the complexity of circuitry has increased to the point where it is no longer possible to produce the circuit boards using the screen printing etch resist method. Circuit boards are now produced using a different process.

Yet other electronics components have been developed that are produced by the screen printing process. Some of the components include membrane switches, force-sensing resistors, and different types of flexible circuitry. The two inks that are most important with these types of printing are conductive and dielectric inks.

CONDUCTIVE INKS Polymeric **conductive inks** are made up of three basic components: conductive metal powder, polymer and solvents, and other additives. Silver is the most common conductive powder used due to its consistent conductivity over time. When other metals such as copper or nickel are used problems of oxidation of exposed surfaces occur.

The polymer has three basic functions. It binds the conductive metal to the substrate, it holds the metal particles together and it protects the conductive ink from being damaged. The types of polymers used include acrylics, polyesters, polyurethane, vinyl acetates and epoxies. In its wet state a conductive ink is non-conductive. Conductive inks require evaporation of all of the solvents in the ink formulation for the ink to reach a state of complete conductivity. The ink is cured in an oven to achieve a complete bond to the substrate and to achieve the desired abrasion resistance. Conductivity can be achieved with incomplete curing but abrasion resistance will be poor.[1]

DIELECTRIC INKS A **dielectric** is a material that does not allow electric energy to flow or pass through. It is a formulation that can be screen printed and when dry achieves its insulative properties. It is used for different functions. It is used as an insulation between layers of conductive circuitry paths. It is also used to protect exposed conductive circuitry from damage caused by oxidation or corrosion. There are three types of dielectric inks: those that are air dried, UV curable and epoxy-based.[2]

Ceramic Inks

There are two different types of inks used for decoration of ceramic materials. The differences relate to the application to the surface, whether before or after the firing process. If the decoration is applied after the firing process, an epoxy type ink is used to achieve resistance to abrasion and chemicals.

The second type of ink is printed before the glaze is applied and fired. This results in a surface that is highly resistant to various chemicals, rigorous dish washing over an extended period of time and meets the F.D.A. standards for lead content. Ceramic inks are made up of pigments made from fine particles or frit that are essentially small glass particles suspended in a vehicle. After the ink has been printed on the ceramic material and dried a glazing material is applied. It is then fired at temperatures of 1500°F or greater, depending on the materials used. The vehicle in the ink is entirely burned away during the firing process resulting in a glazed surface of ceramic material.

Special Effects Inks

There are a wide range of inks that may be screen printed to produce a range of special effects.

FLUORESCENT INKS A fluorescent ink contains pigments that add brilliance to the light reflected from the printed substrate. It changes the wave length of part of the visible light spectrum to create this effect. Fluorescent pigments are transparent in nature and fade over time especially in outdoor applications. For best results, a heavy ink deposit should be printed using a coarse (approximately 230 mesh) monofilament polyester. Since these inks are not opaque they should be printed on white or light colored substrate. They may be mixed with other transparent colored inks to achieve more vibrant effects. To enhance the ink's impact a fluorescent ink can be surrounded with a dark color ink. Cleanliness of the squeegee and screen are essential in achieving the best results with fluorescent inks.

PHOSPHORESCENT INKS This ink produces a glow-in-the-dark effect referred to as phosphorescence or luminescence. The ink appears as light green when viewed under daylight conditions, with a green glow when viewed in the dark after exposure to light. The degree of brilliance and duration of the glow is directly a function of the intensity and duration of the exposure to light.

Phosphorescent pigment is available in powdered form which can be added to a clear metallic base for use. As a rule, 8 to 10 pounds of pigment should be added to each gallon of base. A coarse (30-60 mesh for textile printing) monofilament polyester can be used to achieve the desired ink deposition. Phosphorescent pigments should be printed on white or light colored substrates due to their transparency. In some instances a small amount of fluorescent colored ink may be added to enhance the effect.

Textile Inks

There are a number of different types of screen printing inks that may be used to print on textiles. These are but a few of the inks used for textile printing.

PLASTISOL INKS Plastisol is one of the textile inks most commonly used in the United States. **Plastisol inks** are polyvinyl chloride resins finely dispersed in a solution of organic solvents (known as plasticizers) that are combined to form a pastelike substance. Plastisol inks are thermosetting and do not air dry. They require the application of heat to cause the ink to form into a solid, flexible material. Once plastisol ink is heated the resin particles and plasticizers react and begin to gel. The degree of hardening is in relation to the duration and intensity of heat applied. In general, curing is done at 325°F for 1 to 2 minutes. When curing is complete it results in a durable but flexible film with the ability to withstand countless washings.

After the plastisol ink film is cured it does not decrease in height due to the loss of solvents. It is therefore classified as an ink that is 100% solids. The organic solvents (plasticizers) are retained in the ink since they have much higher boiling points than the curing temperature. Due to this fact the volatile organic compound (V.O.C.) level of plastisol inks is very low. Adhesion of the plastisol ink is the result of a mechanical bond that is formed with the garment fibers. The squeegee forces ink into the weave of the fabric so it completely surrounds individual fibers. Once heat is applied and curing is complete the bond becomes permanent. There are various tests that may be used to determine if the ink is fully cured.

WATER-BASED INKS Water-based textile inks have a significant proportion of water in their formulation but also contain evaporative solvents. After it is printed the ink is cured using infrared heat to set the ink. This allows the ink to be dry cleaned or ironed. This type of ink has a soft hand, meaning the ink will not significantly change the feel of the fabric to touch. Water-based inks are commonly used for printing textile yardage goods.

PUFF INKS A **puff ink** produces a dimensional effect simulating an embroidered garment as shown in Figure 8-13. Once the ink is printed on the garment it is heated to a specific temperature (usually 325 to 350°F) for about 30 seconds during which the ink expands. A relatively heavy ink deposit is required to achieve the most dramatic results. A coarse (30-60 mesh) monofilament polyester is recommended with a soft durometer squeegee blade on a soft printing pallet printing off-contact. When printing multicolor designs it is important that the puff ink is printed last in the sequence

Figure 8-13 Puff ink

to achieve the best results. Puff inks may be purchased in a ready-to-use form or separate for addition to plastisol or water-based textile inks.

GLITTER INKS Glitter is a special effect used with textiles. It is made of small decorative flakes suspended in a glossy plastisol base which produces a sparkle-like appearance. It is similar to metallic inks except particle size is greater and particle composition is different. Due to the large particle size of the flakes a coarse (30 mesh) monofilament polyester is required to allow the particles to pass the mesh openings. Another approach is to screen print a clear plastisol base and dust the glitter upon the surface making sure the particles become anchored into the base. This produces greater brilliance than printing the glitter in the base itself.

HEAT TRANSFER INKS There are two methods of screen printing on an intermediate carrier sheet and transferring the image by heat to textiles: sublimation dye transfer and plastisol melt. There are economic advantages that transfer offer over direct printing. It is much easier, less expensive and faster to print on paper than directly on textiles. Inventory is less costly than with direct printing. Yet transfers do not give the same results or durability as direct printing.

PLASTISOL MELT TRANSFER
A **plastisol melt transfer** (or hot split) is a plastisol ink that is screen printed on a release paper. Ink for transfers is slightly different than plastisol that is used for direct garment printing. Its formulation allows it to more effectively transfer from the release paper after printing. Any number of colors can be printed on the release paper one at a time in the reverse sequence after drying each color. After it is printed it is partially cured (at 220°F) just enough to allow stacking. Application of the plastisol melt transfer is accomplished using heat and pressure. Heat (at 375°F) resoftens the partially cured plastisol ink and pressure (approximately 25 p.s.i.) is used to force the ink to adhere around the fibers of the garment. After the ink cools, the plastisol ink is completely crosslinked and fully hardened. The release paper can be removed. When curing is properly done the ink and garment will withstand numerous washings and retain its color and flexibility. If insufficiently cured it will lack the durability to withstand repeated washings. Transfers are less durable than garments printed with plastisol inks due to their better penetration and bonding to the textile fibers.

SUBLIMATION DYE TRANSFER
Sublimation is a process where dyes are changed from a solid state into a gas (or vapor) upon heating. Sublimation ink is made up of dye capsules that are suspended within the ink vehicle. The sublimation ink is screen printed on glassine paper or a good quality book paper. A porous stock will not be effective since the ink will soak into the paper and not transfer properly. The ink prints and dries like an evaporative ink. It can be air dried or jet dried.

Image transfer is different than with plastisol melt transfers that are mechanically fused into the garment by heat. Once heated to 350°F or greater sublimation ink releases a vapor from the dye capsules from the surface of the transfer. The dye penetrates as a vapor into the fabric and impregnates the surface of individual fibers. When heat is removed the dye is permanently set on the fabric. Unfortunately this chemical dying action will only be effective with synthetic fabrics. It will not produce satisfactory results on natural textiles such as cotton. Synthetic and natural blends may be used if there is less than 30% natural fibers. Ink colors are less intense when using blends of natural and synthetic fibers than pure synthetic fabrics. Yet this ink is not commonly used since cotton fabrics are more comfortable to wear and thus preferred.

DISCHARGE INKS Discharge printing is a unique approach for printing on dark textiles. Once the ink is screen printed on a textile a chemical removes the dye of the original fabric and it is replaced with the desired color ink. When printing on dark textiles it is sometimes necessary to print a white ink first so the desired ink will show its true color. Yet this approach makes the garment uncomfortable to wear due to the heavy film of ink. Discharge ink eliminates the need for this procedure with dark textiles. Yet there are certain disadvantages with using discharge inks. They are only effective with selected fabrics and dyes and cannot be used universally. They are not effective when printing fine details and the ink is not readily visible until it is cured. This makes inspection and spot curing impractical. Discharge inks also may cause skin irritation so they must be carefully controlled so their best application is on automatic presses. Yet in spite of their limitations they are growing in use due to their unique advantages.

Scratch-Off Inks

Scratch-off inks are used with lottery tickets, instant winner games, direct mail coupons, and sweepstakes. The ink forms a tough film covering portions of a ticket yet is easily removed using a coin or fingernail, as shown in Figure 8-14. It has excellent opacity with a matte finish. For best results the ink should be applied to cardstock after it has been sealed with an overprint varnish by one of the printing processes. Scratch-off inks air dry by solvent evaporation in 10 to 20 minutes or can be jet dried in seconds at 150°F. Heat must be carefully controlled since excessive temperatures make the ink more permanent preventing them from being scratched off. To achieve the proper opacity the proper ink deposit is important. A monofilament polyester with a coarse mesh count of 200 or less is recommended. Scratch-off ink is available in gold, silver, gray and black.

Figure 8-14 Scratch-off ink

STAGES OF INK DRYING

Screen printing inks are printed in liquid form and change into a solid film during the drying or curing process. Each ink type goes through a different process to achieve this change. As a general rule ink is considered dry when it doesn't stick or transfer when placed in contact with another substrate. Yet this does not necessarily mean that the ink film is entirely dry. The ink goes through five different phases during the process of drying. These phases are wet, tacky, set-to-touch, print free and dry.[3]

Wet Stage

In its initial phase the ink is in a liquid state. It must be carefully handled since it can be easily smeared. In solvent-based inks, there is a strong solvent odor present in this stage.[4]

Tacky Stage

In the initial drying stage of evaporative or oxidation inks, as the solvents begin to evaporate the ink film becomes gummy and is still vulnerable to touch. Solvent-based inks have a strong solvent odor.[5]

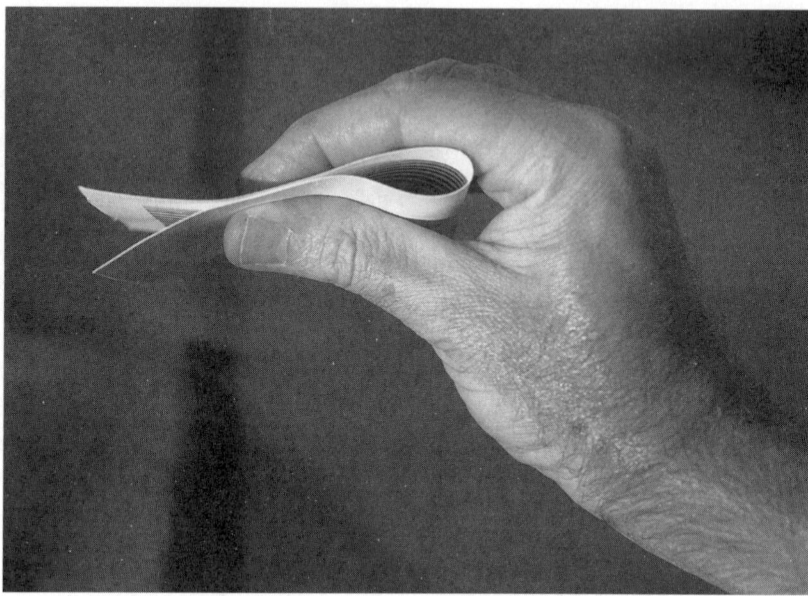

Figure 8-15 Face-to-face test

Set-To-Touch Stage

At this stage the ink film may be touched without smearing the ink. Set-to-touch means that only the surface is dry with inks that dry by evaporation or oxidation. There is still a small amount of solvent below the surface and a solvent odor can be detected. If the ink film is scratched at the surface a less hardened layer is exposed. If thumb pressure is applied to the ink film a surface impression may be observed.[6]

Print Free Stage

In this phase it will be difficult to scratch the ink film with a fingernail although it may leave a slight impression. There will be a slight solvent odor and adhesion of the ink is not at its full potential.[7]

Dry Stage

In this phase the ink may not be scratched or damaged. There are no solvent odors present and it may be stacked and handled without any difficulties.[8]

INK TROUBLESHOOTING

There are a range of problems related to the application of ink with the screen printing process. Most of these problems can be traced to two basic causes: a drying/curing problem or an adhesion problem. The problem and its source can be determined by conducting one or more of a number of standard tests. Once the results of the tests are evaluated the problem can usually be isolated. In some cases they may be inter related. For instance, in order for an ink to adhere it must be fully dry or cured, since in a partially hardened state it may not adhere completely. In some cases there can be both curing and adhering problems.

Curing Problems

Temporary conversion inks dry while permanent conversion inks cure. Due to these differences there are slightly different procedures for evaluating their state of drying or curing. The main point in this case is whether the ink film is fully dry or cured. There are three ways to evaluate the degree of curing or hardening that an ink film has attained. These methods are the blocking test, the face-to-face test and the solvent rub test.

Blocking Test

Blocking is undesirable adhesion between layers of printed material when they are stacked or placed under moderate pressure. A blocking test is used to simulate the effect of stacking printed sheets. A weight is applied to a stack of several printed sheets. The weight should simulate that of the stack height to be used. After about 15 minutes the weight can be removed and the printed sheets separated. If any sticking is noted this is an indication that blocking may occur during the stacking process and drying may not be complete.

Face-to-Face Test

The face-to-face test evaluates solvent retention of the ink film. A printed piece to be tested is folded inward placing the ink in contact with itself. The two inked surfaces are held together applying pressure between two fingers or placing a weight for about five seconds. See Figure 8-15. Allow the inked surfaces to separate. If the two inked surfaces stick and produce a slight sound as they separate it indicates the ink is still tacky due to solvent still present in the ink film. Additional drying time is needed to achieve complete drying of the ink film. This is an effective test placing the ink film in contact with itself since the results are more apparent than with substrate to ink film contact.

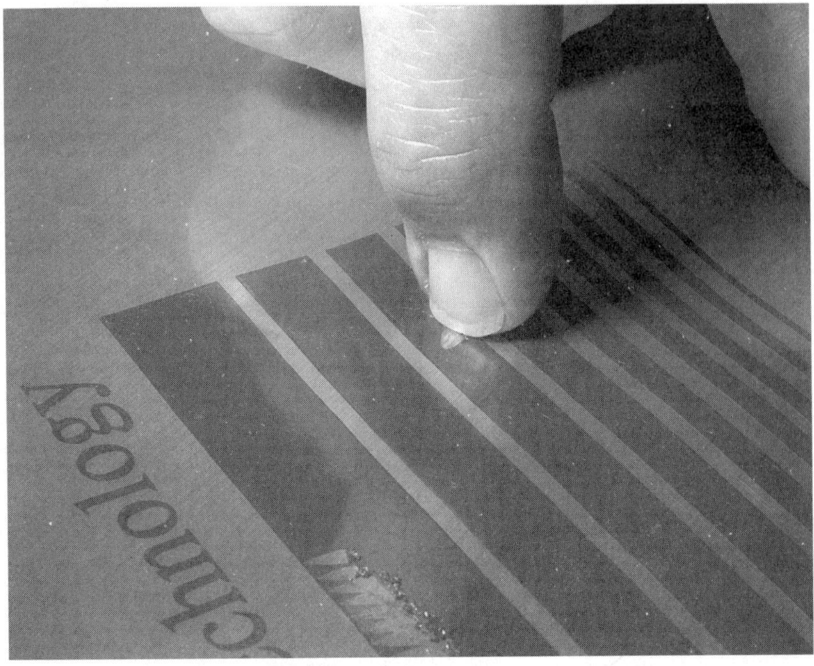

Figure 8-16 Simple scratch test

Solvent Rub Test

This method evaluates cure of an ink using a strong volatile chemical such as MEK. By applying the volatile chemical using a rubbing action across the ink film surface, the ink film will break down after a certain point. This determines an ink's rub resistance. By rating the number of strokes for a given ink a standard can be set to rate other printed jobs using the same ink substrate combination. This can be effectively used to evaluate the degree of curing attained.

Adhesion Problems

A second critical problem with screen printing inks is their ability to adhere or stick to the desired substrate or surface. The first question to ask early in the job planning process is what ink is formulated to adhere properly to a given stock or surface. Using an ink not formulated to adhere to a substrate will obviously be a difficult if not impossible task. This can easily be determined by reading the ink technical data sheet or contacting the ink manufacturer. For best results the ink should be pretested on the desired substrate and subjected to adhesion testing to be certain that the best ink has been selected to meet the specific job requirements, before printing the entire job.

An important premise for adhesion testing is that the ink film tested is completely dry or in a cured state. An ink film that is incompletely cured has not necessarily achieved it maximum adhesion to the substrate. There are a number of tests that are effective in evaluating adhesion of an ink to a given substrate. These tests range from simple to more comprehensive. There are also other tests that are more rigorous to simulate the inks performance under the most demanding conditions. The tests used to rate adhesion are the scratch or tape test with the cross-hatch tape test.

Simple Scratch Test

This is the simplest of tests to administer and evaluate. After the ink has dried a fingernail is used to scratch the film layer. Ink that is adhered will not be easily removed by scratching. See Figure 8-16.

Simple Tape Test

A more comprehensive adhesion test that is simple to conduct is the tape test. Adhesive tape is applied to the ink film surface placing the tape in contact with both ink and substrate. After the tape is applied it should be rubbed down securely and allowed to set for about one minute to bond properly before removing the tape. For best results use adhesive tape approved for this procedure (Scotch 810). When the tape is removed it exerts pressure on the ink film testing for partial adhesion. It is best to use a rapid jerking action to exert the desired force on the ink film layer. If the ink film is not adhered to the substrate securely it will peel off the substrate and remain attached to the adhesive tape.

Figure 8-17 Cross-hatch blade

Cross-Hatch Tape Test

The cross-hatch tape test is an even more demanding test for adhesion than the previous two tests. The cross-hatch tape test procedure is a standard industry practice for evaluating adhesion of paints and other coatings as specified by ASTM test method D-3359. The purpose of the cross-hatch test is to cut the ink film into tiny squares using a blade to produce a "cross-hatch" pattern. This can be done by hand cutting a series of lines in two directions (at 90° angles) using a single sharp blade. A special cutter is available made of multiple blades that simplifies the task. See Figure 8-17. Pressure must

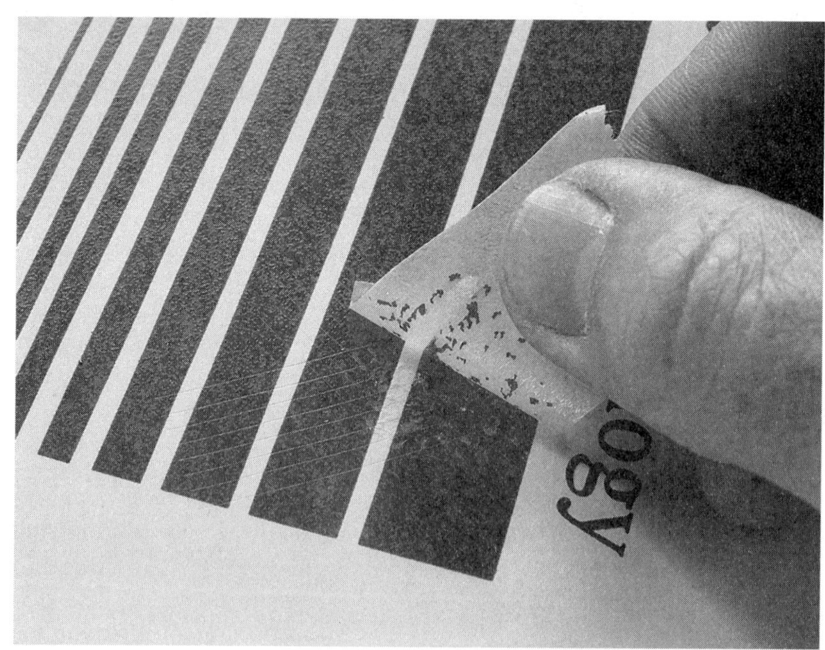

Figure 8-18 Cross-hatch tape test

not be excessive since only the ink film need be penetrated. This is particularly critical with pressure sensitive or thin materials. The pressure sensitive layer may be pulled away from the liner and void the test. Tape (Scotch 810) is applied to the cross-hatch area, rubbed down and removed as in the previous test. The number of squares that are removed from the cross-hatch areas tested determines the degree of adhesion attained as demonstrated in Figure 8-18.

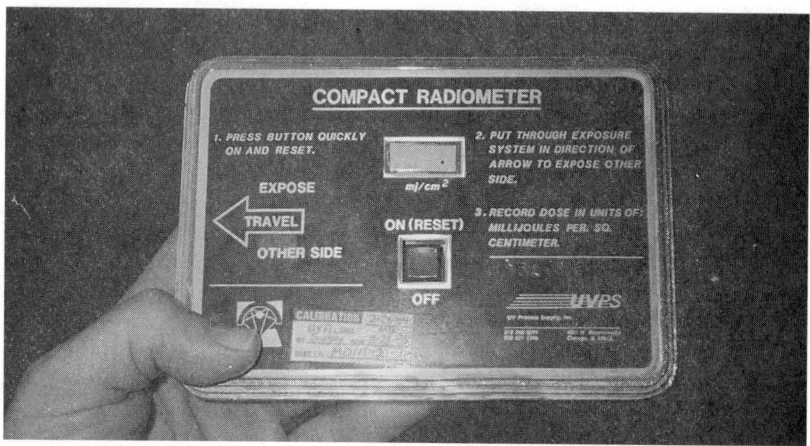

Figure 8-19 Compact radiometer

Ultraviolet Curing Ink Problems

Due to the differences of UV curing inks, curing and adhesion problems are interrelated and may be difficult to sort out. There are three basic problems related to UV curing inks: ink that does not cure, surface curing and adhesion problems.

Ink Does Not Cure

Under this situation the ink does not pass a simple scratch test. When sent through the reactor a second time there is still little change. The proper chemical reactions do not occur within the ink formulation after exposure to the UV reactor. There are two areas to check. First check the age of the ink. If the ink is beyond its recommended shelf life (usually one year) it will not react properly. If it is a special color match (with over five colors used) it may be more difficult to cure. The ink manufacturer should be contacted with the batch number to see if there are problems with curing.

Next the UV reactor should be examined for its light output. How old are the bulbs? If the bulbs have been used for more than 1000 hours they need to be replaced since their output is decreased to the point of being ineffective. The lamp reflectors should also be inspected and cleaned regularly, usually once a month to keep the surface at its most reflective state. As cleanliness declines the output of the reactor will decrease. It is important for the reactor to operate at its maximum output level. It should be operated at the highest intensity, with the belt operating at the lowest speed to achieve the greatest amount of light energy.

An effective method of evaluating bulb condition is a device known as a radiation dose meter. It measures the amount of radiation emitted from a UV reactor in a unit of measurement known as joules per square centimeter. There are a number of different types available. One of these devices, a compact radiometer, is shown in Figure 8-19. After the device is activated it is placed on the conveyor of the UV reactor to record the amount of energy emitted. This is done several times to assure an accurate reading.

If the reactor has been ruled out as the problem there is a procedure to determine if the ink is the cause. A clear or halftone base is added to the ink and printed. If the modified ink cures then it proves the ink formulation to be defective. If using another UV ink to print the same job results in successful curing it proves the old ink formulation to be the problem.

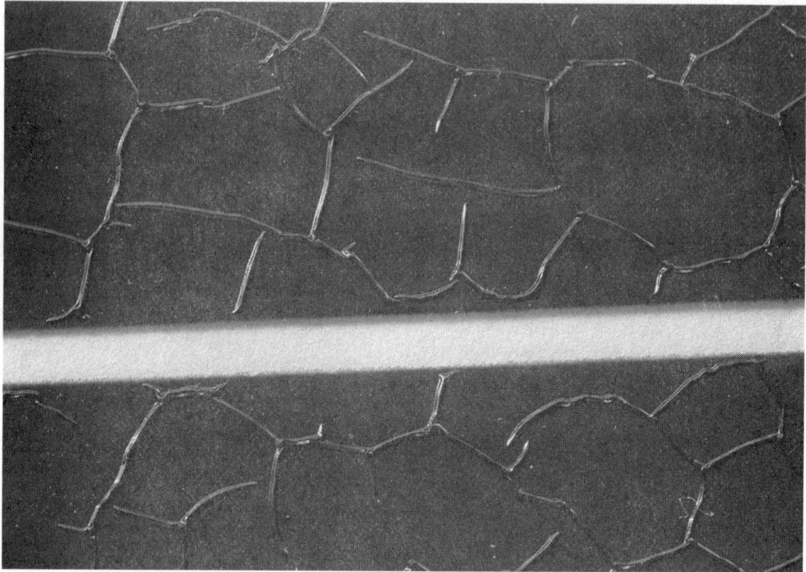

Figure 8-20 Surface cured ink

Surface Curing

Surface curing is a common problem. The top surface is cured and the ink below the surface is wet. In some cases the top surface shrinks and creates a wrinkled or "alligator skin" effect, as shown in Figure 8-20. A surface cure is easy to diagnose. By using a twisting force of the thumb, the ink film can effectively be tested for a surface cure. If the ink smears on the stock, leaving the thumb clean, it indicates a surface cure. Another technique to evaluate the ink film involves carefully removing the surface of the ink film to reveal wet ink remaining. This is further evidence of a surface cure.

A surface cure is the result of light not passing through the entire ink film. The ink film not reached by the light remains in an uncured state. The source of the problem could be the reactor. It is important that the reactor is set to produce its greatest light energy output. If the reactor is ruled out as a source of surface curing the cause is usually a heavy ink film thickness that prevents full passage of light. Production procedures must be modified to print a thinner ink film. The most significant factor contributing to the ink film thickness is the screen fabric. A coarse mesh count will deposit too great an ink thickness and it will be impossible to cure. For effective printing of UV inks a fine mesh count (over 305 t.p.i.) is recommended.

Another approach to regulate ink film thickness is squeegee technique. Changing blade hardness, angle, profile and pressure allows the ink deposit to be regulated. A hard blade with a sharp edge set at a near vertical angle using as little pressure as needed will achieve a thin ink deposit, assuming the proper fabric has been used.

Adhesion Problems

Adhesion of the ink to the substrate is a critical issue with screen printing. However, determining the problem causing adhesion is difficult, especially with UV cuing inks. If the UV ink is not cured completely adhesion will be poor. In this case adhesion is a curing related problem. A pure adhesion problem occurs when the ink film is completely cured but does not adhere to the substrate.

There is a simple procedure to differentiate between the two. After curing is complete a small area of cured ink is removed from the substrate using a blade or sharp object. The areas of the substrate where the ink has been removed should be examined. If the ink film comes off cleanly leaving no residue or stain this indicates an adhesion problem. When evidence of a stain is present an incomplete cure is the source of the problem. Solutions to achieving a complete cure have already been discussed.

Adhesion problems can be

due to surface related problems such as a residue on the surface that prevents proper adhesion. Surface treatment with the appropriate cleaner or solvent will remedy the problem. If this is not the cause the question is to the suitability of the ink for the substrate. The ink manufacturer should be consulted to determine the ink best suited to print on the substrate in question. The best results are obtained by supplying the ink manufacturer with a sample of the material to run a draw down test using various inks to find the best solution.

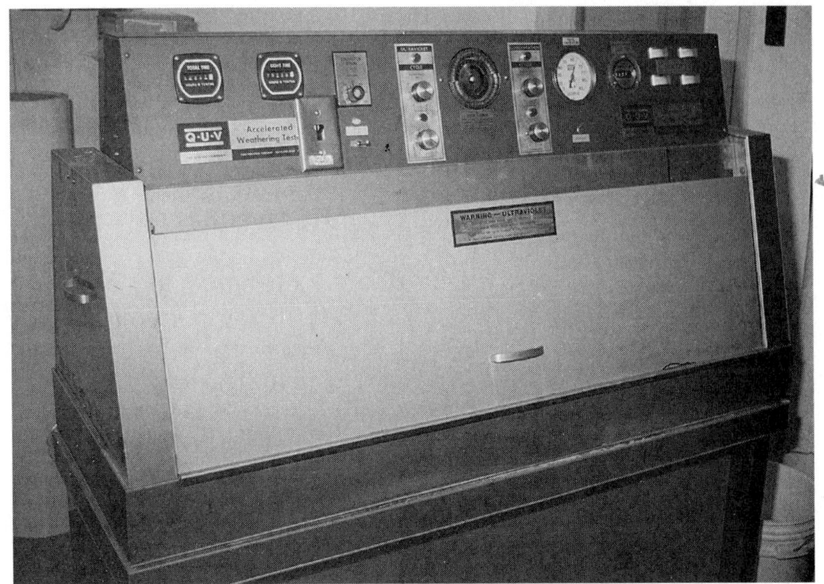

Figure 8-21 Accelerated weathering instrument

Advanced Testing

There are tests that can be conducted to test inks to meet higher standards. These tests are more demanding than the tests that are normally used. These tests are in two areas: abrasion and weathering testing. These tests are used to more accurately assess an ink's performance.

Abrasion Tests

A gravelometer is used to test an ink for its ability to withstand abrasion. This device directs a stream of gravel onto the surface of the ink film. This will eventually wear away the ink film. Another device called the Taber Abrasion test also tests an ink film's resistance to abrasion. This device is a machine that uses rotating wheels to apply friction to the ink film. It simulates a cumulative effect of wear on the ink film. A third approach has two steps. In the first step the printed substrate is immersed in a heated solvent bath. After a designated time interval the ink film is subjected to abrasion testing.

Accelerated Weather Testing

This is an instrument that can be programmed to simulate the results of weathering. It accelerates the effect to produce the equivalent of months or years of exposure in a matter of hours or days. This allows ink performance to be tested without waiting for several years under natural conditions. See Figure 8-21.

Surface Treatments/ Adhesion Promotion

Adhesion of the ink to a substrate is very important in achieving a final printed result. As mentioned earlier in the chapter, selection of the proper ink is essential in achieving a final solution. Yet there are certain situations where there is no ink ideally suited to a particular substrate. Another approach is to treat the surface of the substrate to be compatible with the ink used. There are several methods used to treat the surface of the substrate.

There are two forms of adhesion of ink with the screen printing process. The simplest form of adhesion is where the ink adheres to surface irregularities as points to affix through a mechanical process. A second type of adhesion is based on chemical adhesion, by changing the surface tension of the substrate to make it receptive to ink. Surface tension is referred to as dyne level. Although dyne level is complex in nature it can be measured simply by using a dyne level kit. It is made up of a number of solutions that can be applied to determine the dyne level (or surface tension) of a substrate. Dyne level is especially important with plastics such as polyethylene and polypropylene. For best results surface treatment should be done just before a surface is to be printed. Surface treatment drops off in effectiveness over time and ink adhesion degrades.

Surface treatment is accomplished by surface oxidation where it is polarized or oxidized to change its surface tension to be more receptive to ink. There are several methods used to achieve the desired surface treatment. The two most commonly used methods are flame treatment and corona discharge.

Flame Treatment

Flame treatment is the most common method used, oxidizing the surface through contact with a flame to make it receptive to ink. The flame is placed close to the material to be treated. The surface must be free of contamination such as dust, oil or other chemicals prior to flame treatment. The substrate must not be touched in any way between the time it is treated and printed. Flame treatment is often done as an inline operations of the printing process to provide the most effective results.

Corona Discharge

Corona discharge is ionization of the atmosphere or corona. It is achieved using a spark generator that produces a high voltage, low amperage that is directed to the anode (treater bar) and ground. This method is commonly used to treat polyethylene.

Topcoating

Another approach to ink adhesion problems is the practice of **topcoating**. Some manufacturers apply a top coat to the surface of a material that has difficulty with ink adhesion. This eliminates the need for the screen printer to treat the material to prepare it for printing.

HEALTH AND SAFETY ISSUES

During our everyday lives we are constantly exposed to various chemicals. It is impossible to eliminate all contact with chemicals unless we place ourselves in an isolation environment. Yet this extreme approach is not necessary to protect ourselves. Most chemicals that we come in contact with do not pose a significant health risk as long as we handle them carefully. Chemicals that pose greater risks require following guidelines in order to protect ourselves. The same principles apply to inks and solvents. Chemicals should be handled according to the risks they pose. Some require only simple measures while others require greater protection. Health and safety issues for inks in the screen printing facility are addressed by two subjects: methods for exposure to chemicals and procedures for safe handling of inks and solvents.

Exposure

A reaction to inks or solvents may occur due to contact or exposure to that substance. There are four ways that contact can occur: inhalation, dermal, ingestion, and eye contact.

Inhalation

Inhalation is one of the most common ways of exposure to solvent- and water-based inks. Yet is is often overlooked since the fumes are colorless and sometimes odorless. Exposure to solvent fumes can lead to central nervous system disorders such as dizziness, drowsiness and headaches. Inhalation of fumes from UV inks are a less significant problem since they are low in volatility and do not evaporate at normal temperatures. However, the UV curing reactor produces ozone, a toxic gas.

Exposure to ozone affects the mouth, nose and throat. Minimal exposure creates a dryness in the mouth with more advanced symptoms including dry lips, sore throat, dizziness, headaches and nausea. This emphasizes the importance of an effective ventilation system for both UV reactors and shop ventilation.

In addition to proper venting, another precautionary measure that may be used is a respirator. There are various types from a simple filter type mask to more complex system using tanks with compressed air. Under most screen printing conditions a simple filter can be most effective. The choice of a respirator should be selected based on the hazard to which the operator is exposed. It is important that these devices are inspected and tested on a regular basis to insure they are functioning correctly. This is an important area that must be carefully evaluated to minimize employee contact with hazardous fumes.

Dermal Contact

Another primary route where inks or solvents can bypass the body's defense system is by contacting the skin. All organic solvents are potential skin irritants yet are mistakenly used to remove ink from hands or skin. Some solvents are more dangerous with skin exposure and can lead to liver and kidney damage, headaches, dizziness, drowsiness and other ailments to the central nervous system. In less extreme cases, exposure to solvents can lead to dermatitis or a skin rash or redness.

Solvents should be respected and not feared, however. If reasonable measures are taken to minimize skin contact few problems will occur. There is always the potential for some individuals to be more sensitive to various chemicals. It may take exposure over a period of time before a reaction occurs. This is further justification to be cautious and take reasonable measures to minimize contact.

UV inks pose a somewhat greater problem than conventional inks. Since the inks do not dry by evaporation they remain active. This increases the opportunity for skin contact. It is important for special attention to be taken to clean up ink spills as soon as they occur to prevent others from coming in contact.

UV ink formulations may contain chemicals with a greater potential for skin irritation than other inks. These additives are sometimes used for ink to achieve its desired properties and printability. It is important to consult the **Material Safety Data Sheet** (M.S.D.S.) on the ink manufacturer for proper handling procedures. A Draize primary skin irritation patch test is often conducted on inks to determine their potential for causing skin irritation.

The Draize patch test is a procedure where ink is applied to the skin of albino rabbits. After ink is applied to the skin it is examined for a reaction after given periods of time. It is rated on a scale of 0 (no reaction) to 8 (a severe reaction). As established by the Federal Hazardous Substance Act an ink must be marked with a cautionary note to avoid skin contact if the ink rates 5 or greater on the Draize scale.

When ink has come into contact with the skin (whether solvent base or UV) it should be removed to minimize contact. Soap and water should be used, never solvents or waterless hand cleaner that contains solvent. The use of solvents allows chemicals to break through the protective barrier of the skin. There are hand cleaners that are designed for removing inks. Use of a barrier cream may be useful in minimizing ink contact with the skin. If ink penetrates clothing, skin contact can occur. It is important to wear the proper protective clothing to prevent contact with the skin.

Ingestion

Ingestion is another possible route for exposure to inks and other potentially hazardous chemicals. Due to the nature of ink composition there is little fear of a person knowingly consuming it. Yet it may be taken indirectly into the digestive tract. They may be ingested if foods or cigarettes come in contact with ink or solvents. For that reason eating, drinking, and smoking must be done in separate areas isolated from contact with inks. Operators must wash their hands before eating. Smoking should not be permitted in areas where solvents are present. If inks or other chemicals are ingested medical assistance should be immediately contacted.

Eye Contact

All organic solvents will irritate the eyes if contact is made. Care must be taken to prevent ink or solvents from splashing onto the eyes. Protective safety glasses or a face shield should be worn to protect the eyes from accidental exposure. If solvent or ink comes into contact with the eyes they should be immediately flushed with warm water for at least fifteen minutes. There are several types of eyewash units or showers designed for this type of accident. Medical attention should be secured after a thorough washing to prevent more serious injury. A copy of the M.S.D.S. should be supplied to the doctor to assist in his diagnosis.

Safe Ink Handling Procedures

There is the potential for a reaction to occur when a person is exposed to various inks or solvents used in the the screen printing process. By following the proper handling procedures these materials need not pose a danger. The procedures are in the areas of equipment safety, personal hygiene, protective clothing, ink storage, spills and disposal.

Equipment Safety

One of the most important aspects with regard to safe use of inks is proper ventilation systems to minimize exposure to various solvent and chemical fumes. Ventilation is important in all areas where inks are handled. The degree of ventilation required for a specific facility must be assessed based on the types and amounts of inks and solvents used. Less ventilation may be required with low volatility UV inks than with evaporative solvent-based inks. Venting is also important with the UV reactor. It is important in removing harmful ozone and it also reduces heat from building up in the area of the reactor. Venting, ducts and motors required to achieve adequate ventilation should be carefully researched. The last item related to equipment safety with regard to inks is proper shielding of the UV reactor. It is important that operators are completely shielded from exposure to the lamp as injury to the eyes will occur.

Personal Hygiene

Employees should be encouraged to follow recommended procedures in personal hygiene that will minimize exposure to potentially harmful chemicals. This can be addressed by following two simple tasks. The first is to wear appropriate clothing to prevent accidental exposure. The second is to wash hands, arms and face as needed to remove any chemicals or contamination from exposed skin areas. It is important to wash using an approved soap and water before going on break or leaving for the day. It is of particular importance with UV inks since they can be more of a skin irritant. Waterless hand cleaners or solvents should not be used. Washing prevents inks from causing skin irritation due to prolonged contact and from ingestion. Contact lenses should not be worn when working with UV or solvent-based inks.

Protective Clothing

The most effective way to avert exposure is through the proper use of protective equipment and clothing. This approach limits possible routes of exposure within practical limits. Wearing the appropriate protective clothing prevents dermal contact from occurring. Such items as gloves, apron, shop coat or cap will cover exposed skin areas. Exposure by inhalation can be prevented by use of a respirator. Eye contact can be prevented by use of safety glasses, goggles or a face shield.

Selection of the protective equipment is based on the degree of risk to the employee. A simple respirator should not be used when handling inks or solvents that pose increased potential health risks. The selection of protective clothing should be based on the hazard that the ink or solvent poses. When using UV curing inks, plastic, neoprene, or rubber should be used for shop coats, gloves, and so on. If cloth is used the inks can penetrate the material and come in contact with the skin potentially causing a skin irritation. If UV ink is spilled on canvas or synthetic shoes the ink will be absorbed and cannot be removed. Plastic shoe covers should be used to prevent contamination from UV inks. Clothing that comes into contact with UV inks should be washed separate from other clothing to prevent the uncured ink from spreading.

Ink Storage, Spills and Disposal

Storage of inks following basic guidelines will give optimum performance and shelf life. Inks should be stored at temperatures between 60°-90°F. Some ink formulations will be adversely affected if allowed to freeze. Most inks will be harmed if stored at temperatures greater than 95°F. Inks should be kept in sealed containers. An air-space should be maintained between the containers lid and ink surface when storing UV curing inks (about 10%). This assists in stabilizing its shelf life. UV inks should be stored in light-proof plastic polyethylene containers. UV ink should not be exposed to bright light, heat, or allowed to be contaminated with chemicals (acids, alkalis, and so on).

The shelf life of an ink varies by its type and formulation. Many inks have a recommended shelf life of only six months while others have over 6 years. This does not usually mean that the ink cannot be used after this time. Best results are obtained with ink used within its recommended age. The ink's manufacturer should be contacted to determine a specific ink's shelf life.

All inks contain pigments, resins, and other additives that are not biodegradable whether solvent-based, water-based or UV curing. As such they may not be disposed of in any way that will allow them to seep into the water table. Disposal of inks are governed by local, state and federal regulations as with any industrial waste. Each locality has its own disposal regulations. These agencies should be contacted to determine what regulations apply before disposing of inks.

Practicing good housekeeping and personal hygiene by cleaning up spills as soon as they occur is only good common sense. When using water and solvent-based they dry in place after a period of time and will no longer be wet or tacky to spread. Yet since UV inks do not dry they stay active and will spread over much longer periods of time. Ink that is spilled can be spread several days later. A person could get ink on their hands without even working with it. That makes it important for ink to be cleaned up promptly once it is spilled to prevent further spread by employees.

INK ESTIMATING

Ink estimating is the process of determining the quantity of ink needed for a job and the cost of the job. Ink estimating is a complex issue made up of several factors. Chapter 4 discusses the effect fabric has on ink deposit and its use. Here we will discuss ink coverage related to its composition. Early ink formulations were evaporative in nature and were of a low solids content (up to 40%). Solids content relates to the pigment and resin content that remains after the ink has dried or cured. The remainder of the inks content (various solvents) evaporate into the air during the drying process.

Water-based inks have higher solids content than solvent-based inks. UV curing inks have 100% solids content since their formulations do not contain volatile solvents to evaporate into the air during the drying process. Higher solids content inks have greater ink coverage than lower solids content inks. A UV curing ink can cover up to 3500 square feet for each gallon on ink, while a poster ink has only about 1000 square feet per gallon ink coverage. Yet higher solids content inks are more expensive to manufacture since materials such as resin and pigments are more costly than many solvents.

Ink manufacturers provide product information sheets that include information on estimated coverage for each ink. These are only guidelines and vary under different circumstances. A chart gives general guidelines as to the coverage of various ink types. The chart is based on information from a number of ink manufacturers. The chart in Figure 8-22 gives a range from lowest to highest coverage for specific ink types.

Ink Type		Sq. Ft./ Gallon
Evaporative inks	Flat poster	1000–1500
	Fluorescent poster	1000–1500
	Gloss poster	1200–1800
	Vinyl	1000–1800
	Decal lacquer	1000–1200
	Industrial lacquer	1100–1800
Oxidation Inks	Enamel	900–1800
	Fast dry enamel	1000–1200
Water-based inks	Mulltipurpose	2000–3000
	Point of purchase	800–1800
Textile inks	Plasitsol	500–650
	Low bleed plastisol	300–400
Other inks	Epoxy	1000–1800
	UV curing	2500–3500

Figure 8-22 Estimated ink coverage

Here is a simple example of estimating ink usage for a job with a 10" x 10" print area for 7,000 printed sheets. The first step is to determine the number of square inches of print area for each sheet (100 square inches), then the number of square inches for the entire job.

7,000 x 100 sq. in. = 700,000 sq.in.

This is then converted to square feet of ink needed for the job.

700,000 ÷ 144 = 4861 sq. ft.

If a UV curing ink is used with a coverage of 3500 square feet per gallon, 1.38 gallons of ink are needed for the job.

4861 ÷ 3500 = 1.38 gallons

Printing the same job using poster ink with lower solids content (1000 square feet per gallon) requires 4.9 gallons of poster ink.

4861 ÷ 1000 = 4.9 gallons

With this fictitious example it shows the difference solids content has on ink coverage, with a poster ink nearly five gallons needed, and a UV ink only about 1.5 gallons are needed.

KEY TERMS

binder
blocking
catalyst inks
ceramic inks
clear base
colorant
conductive inks
corona discharge
dielectric inks
discharge inks
dye
evaporative inks
extender base
fast drying thinner
flame treatment
flattening agent
glitter inks
grinding
halftone base
ink grinding
Material Safety Data Sheet
milling
oxidation
pigment
plastisol inks
plastisol melt transfer
puff inks
resin
retarder
scratch-off inks
slow thinner
solvents
sublimation
thermal setting ink
thinner
topcoating
transparent base
UV curing inks
vehicle

REVIEW QUESTIONS

1. What is the difference between pigments and dyes used to add color to inks?
2. What is the primary purpose for grinding ink on a mill?
3. How is the milling operation evaluated for pigment dispersal?
4. How does a temporary conversion ink differ from a permanent conversion ink?
5. What are the five steps of ink drying?
6. Describe one method to evaluate ink curing problems.
7. Describe one method to evaluate ink adhesion problems.
8. What are the three basic UV curing ink problems?
9. What is the purpose of surface treatment such as flame treating?
10. What are the four routes of exposure for inks and solvents?
11. What steps can be taken to avoid dangerous exposure to inks and solvents during handling?
12. How much ink is needed to print a job using a water-based ink with a coverage of 2000 square feet per gallon? The customer desires 10,000 prints with an image area 5″ x 6″ in size.

NOTES

[1] N. Nazarenko, C.N. Lazaridis and D.M. Haney, *Polymer Thick Film Conductors and Dielectrics for Membrane Switches and Flexible Circuitry* (Fairfax: Technical Guidebook of the Screen Printing Industry, Screenprinting and Graphic Imaging Association International, June 1983).

[2] Nazarenko, Lazaridis, and Haney.

[3] Marvin Page, "Too Dry or Not Too Dry," *Screen Printing Magazine* June 1987: 70-73.

[4] Page, 70-73.

[5] Page, 70-73.

[6] Page, 70-73.

[7] Page, 70-73.

[8] Page, 70-73.

Screen Printing Presses and Dryers

Due to the diverse nature of the screen printing process presses must be designed to print on different substrate types. A different press is required to print on garments than to print directly on cylindrical containers. Screen printers purchase presses based on their product base, specializing in distinct sectors of the industry. Graphic printers, for example, rarely print garments due to the differences in equipment.

Once printing is complete a dryer speeds the drying process. Different types of dryers are needed based on substrates printed and ink type used. Dryers for curing plastisol inks on textiles are different than those used for curing UV inks. Dryer selection is important to insure productivity.

PRESSES

A printing press is a machine or device used to transfer images to paper or other substrates. There is a wide range of presses utilizing different image carriers which reproduce images in unique ways. This chapter is devoted to presses for screen printing use.

There is a diversity of different press types within the category of screen printing. Screen printing presses can be classified in a number of ways. They can be broken down by substrate use into either textile or graphic application. They can be classified by the type of printing base, flat bed or cylindrical base. They can be broken down by press configuration/printing head design, clamshell or vertical lift. They can also be classified by substrate format—either sheet or web. Another way to categorize screen presses is by degree of automation: manual, semi-automatic, three quarter automatic or fully automatic. A final category is one color or multicolor.

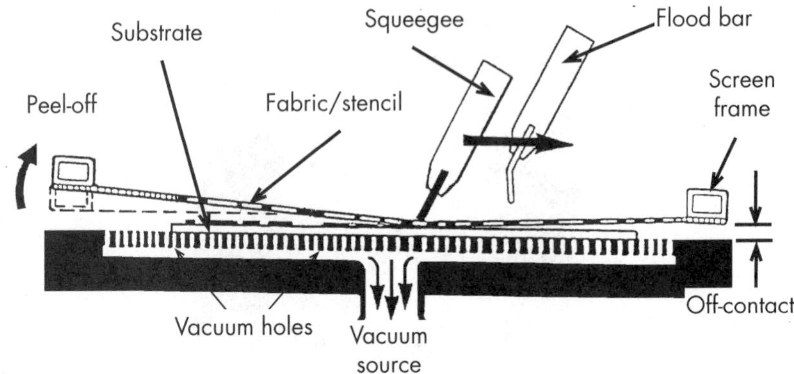

Figure 9-1 Flatbed press *(Mike Young)*

Graphic Presses

Screen printing presses are often used for graphic applications such as posters, signs, banners and other products excluding textiles. They are generally flat substrates but also include direct container decoration. The materials printed include paper, poster board, rigid and flexible plastics, metal and glass in addition to others.

Printing Base/Bed

Screen printing presses are designed to print on a wide range of substrates. Substrates are held on two types of printing beds: a flatbed or a cylindrical base. There are applications where each type of base has an advantage.

Figure 9-2 Flatbed press

FLATBED PRESS A **flatbed press,** as shown in Figure 9-1, uses a conventional flat printing screen that prints on a substrate placed on a flat printing bed. In order to achieve the best quality results the screen is held slightly above the surface of the substrate in an off-contact position. This assist the screen in cleanly separating from the substrate after printing. The screen is brought into contact with the substrate momentarily when the squeegee forces ink through the image areas of the screen. The screen separates from the substrate after the squeegee passes. Printing reverses with heavy ink coverage or use of low viscosity or tacky inks can be difficult using a flatbed press. This generally requires greater off-contact distance and the use of peel-off to assist the screen in separating from the substrate.

A flatbed press is very versatile with the ability to print on nearly any flat surface in a wide range of thicknesses from thin materials up to heavy board or wood. This makes it capable of printing a wide range of different jobs on one press type, small size jobs as well as large ones as long as they fit on the bed of the press without overhanging. See Figure 9-2.

CYLINDER PRESS A **cylinder press,** as shown in Figure 9-3, uses a flat printing screen that prints on a substrate that is wrapped around a cylindrical impression cylinder. The screen reciprocates as the impression cylinder rotates and the squeegee is held in a fixed position. Ink is forced through image areas of the screen during the print stroke using a different printing action than a flatbed press.

The cylinder press offers a number of advantages over a flatbed press. The substrate comes into contact with the screen only at its upper most point due to the cylindrical impression cylinder. This eliminates the need for placing the screen off-contact as with a flatbed press. The vacuum keeps the substrate positioned on the impression cylinder and causes the substrates to separate from the screen after printing. Eliminating off-contact reduces image distortion and registration problems. Cylinder presses are capable of printing at speeds of up to 5,000 sheets per hour although a more realistic speed is 2,000 to 3,000 sheets per hour. At higher speeds there can be more misfed sheets, less registration consistency and poor ink flow.

There are a number of disadvantages of this press type. A cylinder press can only handle a limited range of stock thicknesses, from 16 pound bond paper up to 50 point board. This limitation is due to the degree that the gripper fingers will open to allow stock to be held on the cylinder. Rigid material can be difficult to print since it is more difficult to conform around the impression cylinder during printing. Small size jobs are more difficult to set up and run on a cylinder press. See Figure 9-4.

Figure 9-3 Cylinder press

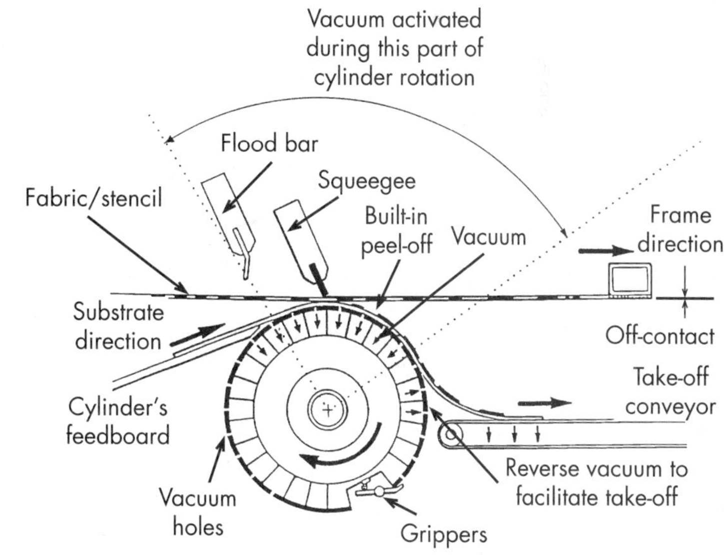

Figure 9-4 Cylinder press *(Mike Young)*

Cylinder presses are less suited to short runs due to the increased make ready time required over less sophisticated presses. Another factor is the suitability of a substrate for an automatic feeder. Some substrates that are often screen printed have a pronounced curl and do not lay flat. This is common with substrates such as pressure sensitive materials, made up of layers of adhesive, a liner and base material. A substrate with curl will be prone to misfeed and misregister when using an automatic feeder. A more effective approach might be to print using a three-quarter automatic press. Although the press speed is lower, press down time and spoilage would be reduced since each sheet can be controlled better by hand feeding.

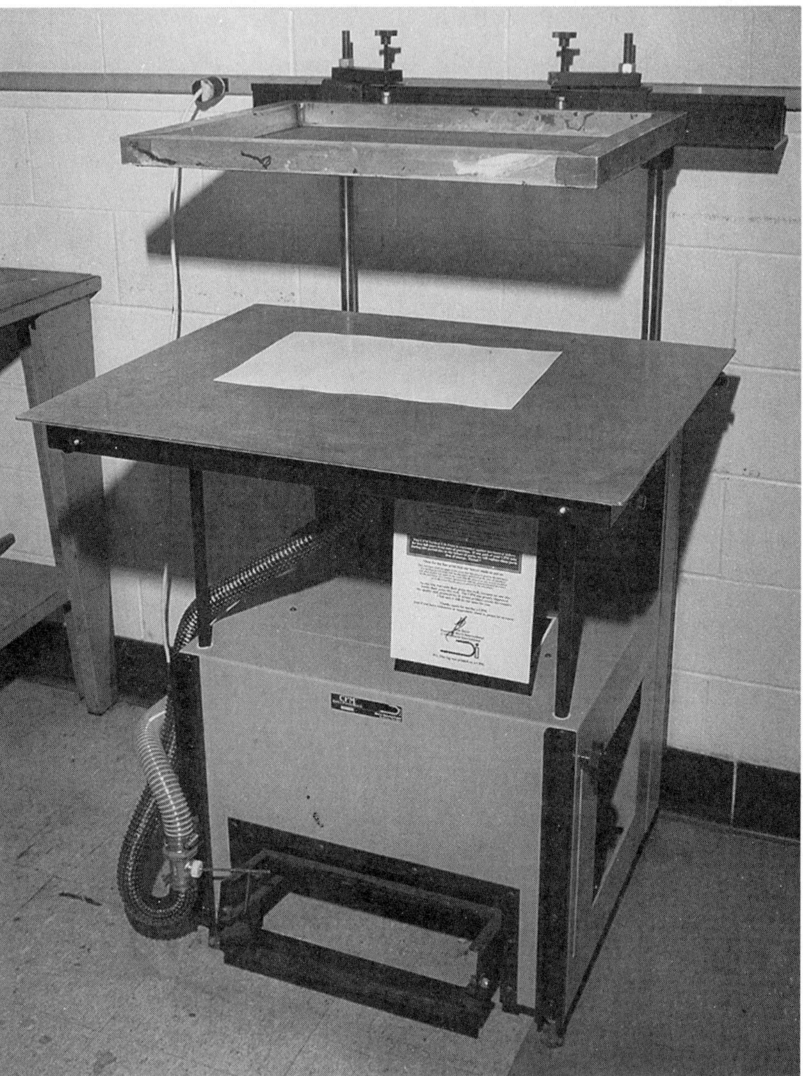

Figure 9-5 Manual press

Degree of Automation

Screen printing presses can be divided into different degrees of automation from manual to fully automatic. An automatic press prints at a higher speed than one that is less automated. Yet a press with the sophistication required for automation is significantly more expensive and requires greater time to set up for a press run. Manual and partially automatic presses are used for short runs and automatics for longer runs.

MANUAL PRESS/HAND TABLE

This is the simplest form of press. It is entirely manual in operation making no use of motors to power the device. It provides a system to hold the screen in position in relation to the substrate printed. The operator must manually load the substrate, lower the screen into position, apply pressure to the squeegee to print, raise the screen, apply flood coat and then remove the substrate. See Figure 9-5.

The simplest form of press uses a device known as "jiffy clamps." See Figure 9-6. These clamps have been widely used for a number of years. They are special hinge clamps that attach to a table or printing base. These hinges allow screen frames (up to 3" thick) to be clamped into the device. The clamps allow the screen to pivot up from the back so the substrate can be inserted for printing. The screen frame is held in place securely but also allow it to be removed for cleaning. Another type of hand table is known as a "one-man squeegee," as shown in Figure 9-7. This places the squeegee in a counter balanced holder that requires less effort to operate even with long squeegees.

Figure 9-6 Jiffy clamps

SEMI-AUTOMATIC As the name implies this press is partially automated. Printing functions are automated while both feeding and delivery of substrate is manual. Once the substrate is manually inserted and positioned in register the press is activated and the screen frame lowers into a slightly off-contact position with the substrate. The squeegee forces ink through image areas of the screen onto the substrate. Once printing is complete the screen is raised from the substrate and a flood coat is applied to the screen permitting the printed substrate to be

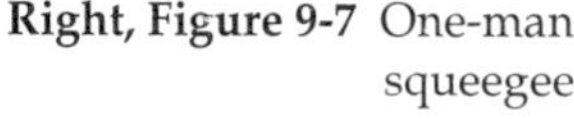

Right, Figure 9-7 One-man squeegee

removed and a new one inserted. See Figure 9-8.

Figure 9-8 Semi-automatic press *(Svecia USA Inc.)*

THREE-QUARTER AUTOMATIC
This press attains a higher level of automation than a semi-automatic press. Printing functions are automated. The screen is automatically lowered into position and the squeegee applies pressure to force ink through image areas of the screen onto the substrate. The substrate must be inserted manually and positioned in the register guides. After printing is complete a power take off device removes the substrate from the press and directs the sheet onto the conveyor belt of a drying device.

Three-quarter automatic presses are widely used by screen printers. They deliver a relatively high rate of production and can be used to print a wide range of flat substrates. They can use either jet air dryers or a UV curing unit. Hand feeding of stock can give greater control of substrates that are difficult to feed automatically due to curl or other irregularities. This allows the operator to guide each sheet into position in spite of substrate irregularities.

The power take off takes the sheet after printing and directs it into the automatic conveyor dryer and stacking system. The substrate must be positioned in a position on the bed where it can be picked up by the power take off after it is printed. Image position must be aligned or preregistered during the screen making operation. This can be done by using a ruler to measure position or using a jig to facilitate lineup of image on the screen. See Figure 9-9.

Figure 9-9 Three-quarter automatic press

Figure 9-10 Automatic press *(Svecia USA Inc.)*

FULLY AUTOMATIC This press achieves a full state of automation once the press is set up. The press automatically feeds the substrate into position, then the squeegee prints ink in image areas and the finished print is off-loaded into the curing unit.

There are several stages in press setup. The feeder must be set up based on substrate size, thickness and material. The screen is locked in position on the press and adjusted to print in the correct position of the sheet. Squeegee pressure must be adjusted to force ink through image areas of the screen after ink is placed in the screen without using excess pressure. The delivery system must be adjusted to remove the substrate from the printing unit into the automated conveyor system which dries and stacks the stock. Sheets may jam and misregister at a greater frequency when press speed is too fast. Press speed must be adjusted to achieve optimum print conditions. Also ink must have enough time to flow out before curing to achieve the desired quality standards. See Figure 9-10.

Press Speed Comparison

	Semi-Automatic	3/4 Automatic	Auto Cylinder	2-Color Web
Press Speed	700 i.p.h.	1400 i.p.h.	2150 i.p.h.	2250 i.p.h.
Press Time	27 hr. 40 min.	14 hr. 32 min.	9 hr. 20 min.	4 hr. 25 min.
Press Run Cost	$554.00	$286.00	$186.00	$88.00

Figure 9-11

PRESS SPEED COMPARISON It is clear that a higher speed press will print the job the most quickly. Let us look at a specific job and see how press speed affects its cost. We will look at a job requiring a quantity of 5,000 prints, printed four colors for a total of 20,000 impressions for the job. In the interests of keeping this example from becoming complex, we will not address the issue of makeready costs. We will also use an hourly press rate of $20.00 even though each press has its own hourly press rate *(Note:* The press speeds were supplied by the press manufacturer as a reference and cannot be assumed for all jobs). Refere to Figure 9-11. If a semi-automatic press is used, rated at 700 impressions per hour (i.p.h.) it would cost $554.00 to print the job and take 27 hours, 40 minutes. Using a three-quarter automatic press, rated at twice the speed of a semi-automatic (1400 i.p.h.) it would cost $286.00 and require 14 hours, 32 minutes to print. A fully automatic cylinder press run at a speed of 2150 i.p.h. could cost $186.00 and require 9 hours, 20 minutes to run. If a two-color web press were run at a rate of 2250 i.p.h. it would cost only $88.00 and require 4 hours, 25 minutes.

Press Configuration/ Print Head Design

With screen printing presses the screen must come into contact with the substrate. The screen is raised after printing to facilitate feeding of the substrate. There are two methods for raising the screen after printing based on the way the print head is activated: the clamshell and vertical lift press.

CLAMSHELL PRESS This is a press that has the printing head hinged to open in the same fashion as a clam. The printing head is in a raised position to allow insertion of the substrate into the registration guides. While the press is in this position the screen is at an angle with one end raised above the other. This allows ink to flow down the screen, especially with low viscosity inks (like water-based inks). It usually requires ink to be collected from the low side and re-distributed in the screen during the press run. It can also be more difficult to maintain an even flood coat. **Clamshell presses**, as shown in Figure 9-12, are available in both semi-automatic and three-quarter automatic models. They are built to print materials ranging in sizes up to 40″ x 55″.

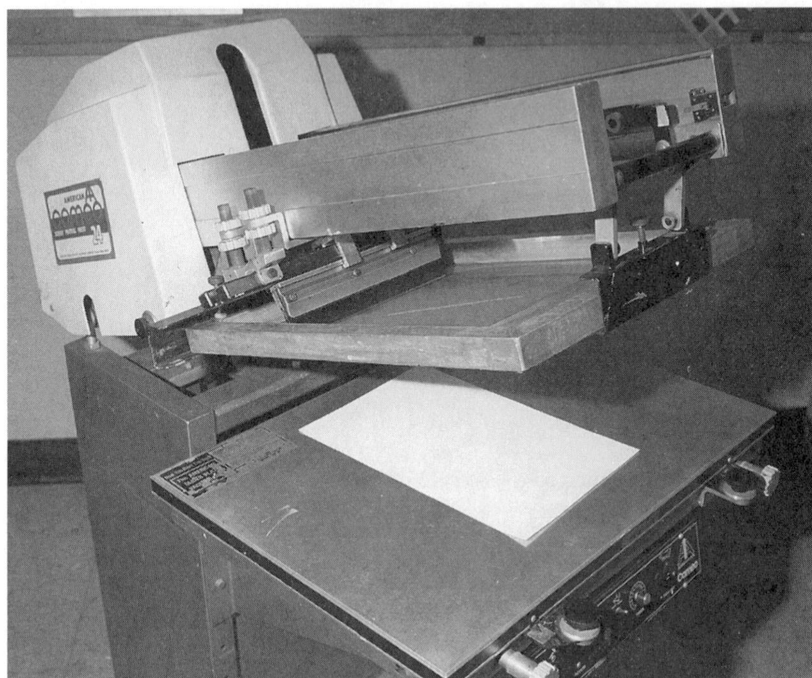

Figure 9-12 Clamshell press

VERTICAL FRAME MOVEMENT PRESS There are several different designs of presses that fall into

Right, Figure 9-13 Four post press

this category. The screen is kept in a horizontal position at all times during the process. It has the advantage of not having adverse problems when using low viscosity inks. A common press of this type is the **four post press,** as shown in Figure 9-13. The screen carriage is placed on four vertical posts. The printing bed (vacuum base) moves in and out for loading and unloading. They are available as semi-automatic and three-quarter automatic models. They are available in sizes similar to a clamshell press and also available for large format sizes, up to 68″ x 158″.

Substrate Format

Substrates are available in different forms. They can be paper, plastic or other compositions. After they are manufactured these materials are wound onto a core or spool. They are converted from web form if individual sheets are desired. Rigid materials such as poster boards and chipboard are manufactured in a flat state and thus may not be wound on a web. They would be printed sheetwise.

SHEET FED PRESS A **sheet fed press** moves sheets individually through the press for printing. The simplest flatbed presses are manually fed while more sophisticated flatbed and cylinder presses are automatically fed. Sheet fed presses are slower than web presses with lower registration accuracy since it is more difficult to feed and align individual sheets over a web. Sheet fed presses are less expensive and take up less floor space than web presses.

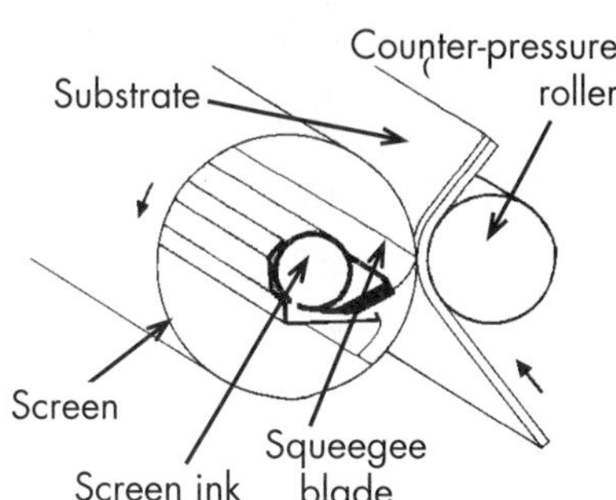

Figure 9-14 Stork rotary web press

WEB FED PRESS A web is a continuous sheet of flexible material that is wound on a central core. A **web press** can automatically feed the substrate from the roll into the printing units after it is rolled back on the core. There are two types of web screen presses. One type uses a rotary (or cylindrical) printing screen. While the rotary screen and impression cylinder rotate at a high speed the web passes between. This makes this press ideal for long production runs. See Figure 9-14.

A rotary press is made up of a metal screen material that has been formed into a cylinder with no seam. An emulsion is applied to the cylindrical screen, exposed and processed to create image areas in the screen. The squeegee is mounted inside the cylinder. The counter-pressure roller provides support for the substrate as it travels at the same speed as the rotary screen. As the rotary screen rotates the squeegee forces ink through image areas of the screen onto the web. Ink is pumped into the rotary screen as needed by the job requirements. See Figure 9-15.

Figure 9-15 Rotary screens *(Stork X-Cell)*

One primary manufacturer of rotary web screen printing presses is Stork X-Cell. See Figure 9-16.

A number of different models are offered. They have presses with web widths from 10 to 20 inches. They run up to 450 feet per minute. They are used to print labels, lottery tickets, decals, security printing, thick film printing, decorative products and packaging material. They can be used to print on nearly any substrate material with a wide range of inks or coatings.

A second type of web press uses a conventional flat screen. See Figure 9-17. The flat screen reciprocates back and forth as the web is transported through the print station. Its printing action is like that of the cylinder press. The screen moves at the same speed as the web and the impression cylinder while the squeegee remains in a fixed position. The primary difference in this press is that printing is done on a continuous web instead of individual sheets. There are a number of manufacturers of this type press. Web widths range from 10 inches or smaller up to 80 inches. They can be run at speeds of up to 4000 impressions per hour (or 100 feet per minute). They are used to print decals, posters, labels, ceramic transfers, membrane switches, printed circuits, and front panels for the automotive industry.

SHEET FED ROTARY SCREEN PRINTING PRESS The press is a rotary screen printing press that uses a sheet fed feeder system, the Stork Screen Rotation System. See

Figure 9-16 Stork rotary web press *(Stork X-Cell)*

Figure 9-17 Klemm web press *(Klemm)*

Figure 9-18. It uses the same rotary screen, squeegee and automatic ink feed system as the Stork Rotary Web Press. It allows more rigid materials to be printed than on a web press. It allows substrates to be printed ranging from 0.004″ up to 0.200″ in thickness, with a maximum sheet size of 30″ x 42″ and minimum size of 14″ x 16″. It will operate at press speeds up to 4,000 sheets per hour. Makeready time for changing the rotary screen and re-registration is 10 minutes. This press design allows for multiple colors to be printed in-line.

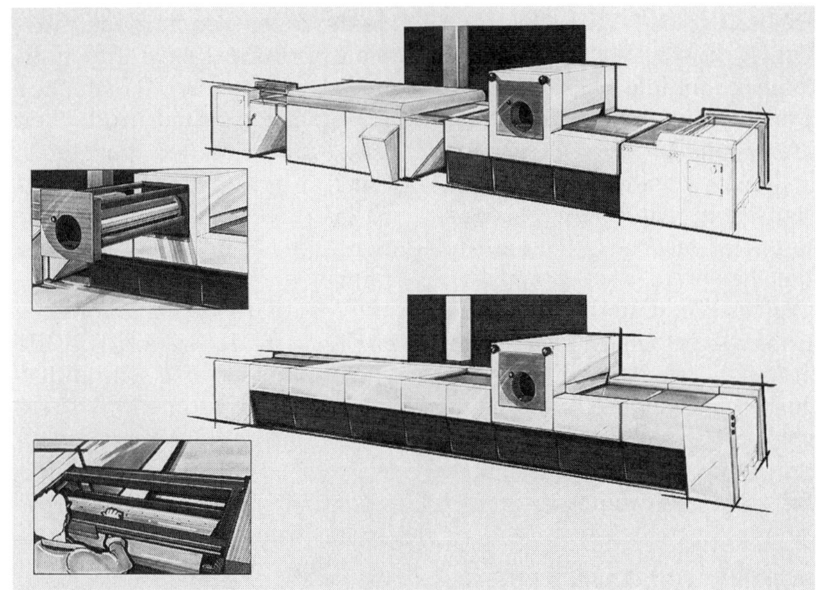

Figure 9-18 Stork screen rotation system *(Stork X-Cell)*

Multicolor Graphic Presses

A multicolor press is a screen printing device that can transfer more than one color of ink with one pass of the substrate through the press. The advantage of a multicolor press is its efficiency. It minimizes printing operations and handling by printing multiple colors in one operation. There are two basic designs of multicolor presses: circular (or carousel presses) and in-lines. See Figure 9-19.

Figure 9-19 In-line flatbed multicolor press *(Svecia USA Inc.)*

CAROUSEL PRESSES A **carousel press** has platens and print heads rotating around a central shaft. Carousel presses are described in greater detail in the section on textile presses. Although they appear to be identical to textile presses there are two differences. The first is a difference in the platens due to different substrate. A vacuum base is used to hold the substrate in place instead of gluing a garment on the platen. A second difference is curing procedures. A garment printer commonly applies ink, wet-on-wet, curing after printing is complete. A multicolor carousel press for graphics printing requires ink to be cured before the next color is applied. A UV curing unit is placed between each print station to set the ink. These presses print up to six colors in sizes up to 31″ x 54″.

IN-LINE FLATBED PRESSES
One of the simplest approaches is to place multiple presses in-line to print multiple colors. Curing units are required after each printing station as with the carousel configuration. Each sheet is registered, fed into the initial unit and then held in register through each print station until the last color is printed. It is then released into the automatic stacker. UV inks and curing units are used to speed the drying process. They are available for printing up to six colors, up to 54″ x 144″ maximum size.

IN-LINE CYLINDER PRESSES
This is very similar to in-line flatbed presses but is made up of two-cylinder presses that are made to run like one. Stock is fed automatically into the first press in register, printed and cured. The sheet is then re-registered a second time and fed in position to print and cure the second color and is then delivered into the automatic stacker. The two-color cylinder press requires a good deal of floor space.

Textile Presses

There are three ways to decorate textiles by the screen printing process. They are roll-to-roll, piece goods, or individual garments. Roll-to-roll screen printing is printed directly on a roll of fabric after which it is cut to size and sewn into finished garments. Piece goods is the practice of cutting fabric into individual pieces after which they are screen printed and then sewn into finished garments. The last type of textile decoration is direct printing. The garment that has been presewn into a finished garment is printed.

Presses are available for each method of decoration. Textile presses are available with different levels of automation. There are manual and automatic presses. Presses designed to print individual garments or piece goods are incapable of fully automatic operation. Both press types require the garments to be aligned by hand onto a pallet before they are printed. Both loading and printing operations are manual. A manual textile press (usually a carousel type) requires an operator to lower the screen into position and to apply force and motion to cause the squeegee to force ink through the image areas of the screen.

All printing functions are automated with an automatic press. It lowers the screen into position and applies force causing the squeegee to force ink through image areas of the screen. There are three different configurations for automatic presses: carousels, ovals and belt printers. They can also be broken down into three classes. The first class is an entry level carousel press. They are designed for start up businesses, low in cost, with smaller formats, limited to ten colors or less and designed for light duty use. They cost up to $80,000.

The next class is designed for high production, with heavy duty design for larger print sizes for up to 30 colors. They may be carousels or oval printers. They cost from $80,000 up to $500,000. The last class is belt printers, originally designed for roll-to-roll printing, but may also be used for cut piece goods or individual garments. They permit printing extra large sizes with edge-to-edge or total print coverage.

Printing speed is affected by a number of variables which makes it difficult to predict exact production rates. Automatic textile presses all run at rates from 60–80 dozen shirts per hour regardless of their configuration.

Manual Carousel

This is a manual multicolor screen printing press that has multiple platens (or pallets) and print heads that rotate around a central shaft. See Figure 9-20These presses are used for relatively short runs. Shirts are loaded onto pallets to keep the fabric from moving during the printing process. The garment is glued to the pallet to print each color in the correct position. Each individual print head (and screen) is rotated into locked position above the pallet and is then lowered to print in register on the garment. Each color is manually printed, wet-on-wet, under most

Figure 9-20 Manual carousel press *(Hopkins International)*

Figure 9-21 Automated carousel press *(M & R Printing Equipment Inc.)*

circumstances. After printing is complete the garment is removed and placed into the dryer. In some instances a flash dryer is used to spot cure between colors. Carousel presses are available in different models to print from 4 to 14 colors.

Carousel presses require a significant amount of floor space due to the circular design. The size, or diameter, of the press increases as the number of stations increase. For instance, an eight color carousel is approximately 15 feet in diameter while a sixteen color carousel is approximately 22 feet in diameter.

Automated Carousel

This is the same in principle as the manual carousel. Its operation is the same except that print functions are automated. Automated carousels are used for longer press runs. The printing heads are automatically lowered into position on the pallet and the squeegee is put into motion to force ink through image areas of the screen automatically. Loading and unloading of garments must be done manually. Automated carousels are available in models printing from 6 colors up to 16 colors. Automated carousel presses use two stations without print heads, one for loading and another for unloading. See Figure 9-21.

Automatic Oval/Modular

As carousel presses increase the number of stations the floor space requirement increases. At a certain point the size of the carousel press becomes excessive. The **oval press** design has the advantage of requiring less floor space. A oval press is two linear tracks that are lined up back to back with two end modules to connect the entire line. The pallets rotate on a track in an oval path from start to finish, like a simple oval toy train track. Print heads cannot be installed at the end stations, only along stations on the linear tracks. End stations may be used to manually load and unload garments. As many as twenty-eight print heads with thirty stations may be installed on an automatic oval. Printing operations will be increased significantly using more than two stations for garment loading and unloading. See Figure 9-22

Figure 9-22 Automated oval press *(M & R Printing Equipment Inc.)*

Belt/Roll-to-Roll

A **belt printer** unrolls a continuous roll of fabric to make contact with a printing belt fed into a series of in-line printing stations. As the fabric is transported by the belt it is indexed into position where it is printed one color at a time. Each successive color is printed wet-on-wet in position on the fabric until all colors are printed. It is then cured and directed onto a take-up roll.

In addition to its ability to print on a continuous roll it may be used to print pre-cut piece goods such as pants, aprons, towels, and so on, and for edge-to-edge printing on finished garments. When printing piece goods or finished garments they are positioned on the belt using a special alignment system. Glue keeps each piece in position on the belt. After printing and curing is complete a garment removal system strips individual pieces off the belt onto a secondary conveyor belt. A stainless steel washer removes lint, ink or other contaminants from the belt without removing the adhesive before the belt moves back to the in-feed position. A filtration system is used

Figure 9-23 Belt printer *(M & R Printing Equipment Inc.)*

to recycle the belt cleaning fluid.

A belt printer has a number of advantages over rotary printing systems for textile decoration. Shorter set up time is required over rotary presses. This results in less fabric waste and shorter run lengths are feasible. The overall job cost is lower since conventional flat screens are used. Greater control of quality is possible than with rotary printing systems. It also offers the versatility to print piece goods or roll-to-roll printing. Belt printers are available in models from four colors up to ten colors. Belt widths available are from 76″, 88″ or 100″ with image size for print stations up to 38″ x 90″. See Figure 9-23.

Container Printing

Printing or decorating is done directly on the container surface by the screen printing process. In addition to cylindrical shaped containers, three dimensional shapes such as conical, elliptical (one or both sides), spherical and tubular items can be printed. It can be used for rigid containers such as glass or with flexible materials such as plastic. Flexible containers are made rigid by inflating with air pressure to achieve high quality results. Containers as small as one ounce and as large as up to five gallons can be printed.

Container presses are available in manual, semi-automatic and fully automatic models. They are also available in single or multicolor models. A flame treater is placed in-line prior to printing to prepare the plastic for proper ink adhesion. Production rates of fully automated models are up to 4000 pieces per hour based on container shape.

Operation of an automatic model is as follows. Containers are loaded into a collection bin that feeds onto an infeed conveyor. A suction cup device picks up a container for transferal into a holder or printing station. The container is rotated into position using a registration indent, slot or lug at the container's base. This indent is especially important for multicolor printing. Once in position the container is moved in a rotary motion in synchronization with the linear movement of the screen frame. The squeegee forces ink through image areas onto the container as the screen and containers are in motion. The printing action is similar to that of a cylinder press. Once printing is complete a delivery system removes the container from the printing station into a conveyor system for drying.

DRYERS

After printing has been completed the ink deposit requires a period of time before it is dried or cured. This time period is based on the ink type in addition to other factors. During this time the ink film must not be touched or stacked or it will smear and not dry properly. There are several approaches to prevent this from occurring. The job with its wet ink film can be placed in a **drying rack** or in an automatic conveyorized drying system.

Manual Drying Racks

This is a rack made up of a number of wire grids spaced apart in a vertical arrangement to place a number of wet prints in the least area. The rack is made to flip up for storage and flip down to load as needed. This arrangement allows air to surround all sides of the print to facilitate air drying without damaging the printed ink film. These racks are relatively inexpensive, durable, and will last a long time. But the racks are time consuming to load and unload after drying is complete. This also requires more time for the wet ink film to dry by air. It is often used with inks (such as epoxy inks) that take longer to dry. See Figure 9-24, next page.

Drying Devices

A dryer is a device used to speed drying time of a wet material such as ink. This can be done by application of air, or heat or a combination of both. This is commonly accomplished using an automatic conveyorized drying system. It transports wet prints using a conveyor belt into a dryer, curing device or chamber and delivers the dried print into a stacking device.

Wicket Dryer

A **wicket dryer** uses conveyorized wire racks to transport sheets at a rate slow enough to allow air drying to occur before it is stacked. A greater number of prints may be transported in a vertical position rather than horizontally. This will allow the press to run at a reasonable speed. Since the wicket dryer is dependent on the time for the ink to air dry the press may not be able to be run at its greatest speed. It can only be run as fast as the sheets can be dried.

Dryers Using Heat

Heat may be used to speed the drying of evaporative and thermal setting inks. Heat may be transferred in three ways: conduction, radiation, and convection. **Conduction** brings the material in direct contact with the heat source for heat transfer to occur. Conduction is used to apply heat transfers to garments with a heat seal machine.

Heating by **convection** does not directly radiate on the substrate. Convection transfers heat through a flow of air or water onto the desired substrate. A hair dryer is an example of convection drying. A convection system generates heat by gas or electricity. Convection drying is commonly

Right, Figure 9-24 Drying rack

Figure 9-25 Heat element

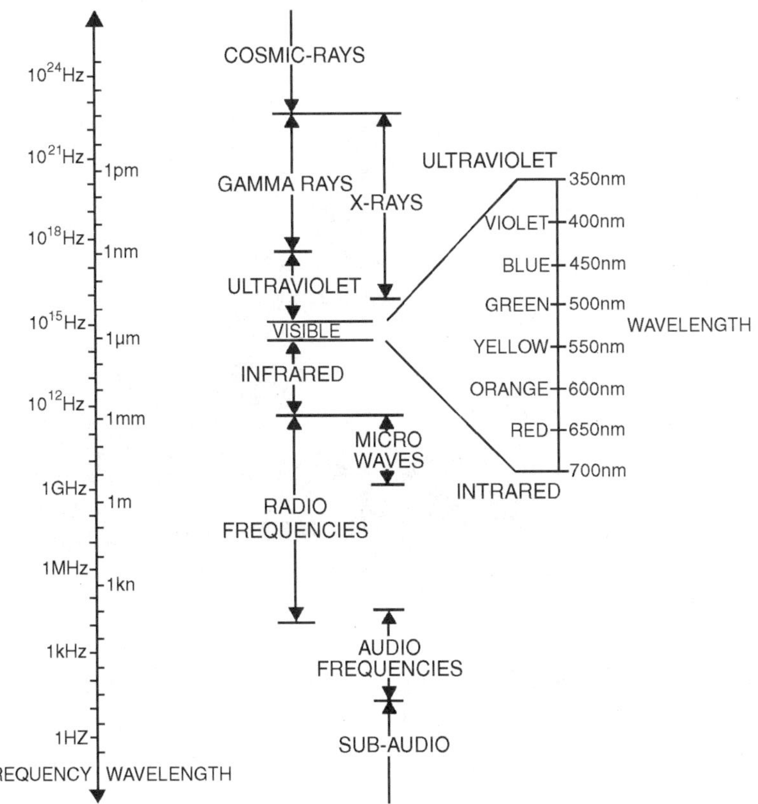

used to dry screen printing inks. Several oven and dryer designs use convection as a means to heat the ink film on the substrate.

Radiation is the means for energy to radiate or emit and is absorbed or reflected by a body in its path. Radiant heat may be produced from a heat panel. There are different types of infrared heating devices. See Figure 9-25 for one type of element. Some of them are tubular quartz, quartz plates, or ceramic types. A radiant heat source can generate high levels of heat energy in a short time. Due to its intensity a housing or enclosure is not essential to its function. Radiant heat is ideal for use with thermal setting inks (such as plastisols) used in the textile industry that require a significant level of heat to cure the wet ink film.

An **infrared** dryer can be used to generate heat for use in a drying system. It emits rays in the infrared portion of the electromagnetic spectrum (between 0.7 and 1,000 microns) between radio waves and visible light. See Figure 9-26. Heat that is produced speeds the drying of the wet ink film. Each ink or coating is most responsive to a specific wavelength of infrared rays. The greatest efficiency can be achieved by matching the infrared heat source to the specific coating. This will result in the ink or coating being

Left, Figure 9-26 Electromagnetic spectrum *(Autotype USA)*

cured at the most rapid rate. Infrared dryers are used in a number of different designs. Two common designs are the tunnel dryer and the jet dryer. Infrared dryers can be used with both tunnel and jet air dryers as a source of generating heat. Gas is more cost effective than generating heat with electricity.

There are two ways of regulating the dryer. By increasing the temperature of the dryer the ink's drying time is reduced. See Figure 9-27. Although this speeds the drying rate of ink it often causes the sheet to change in dimensional stability, especially with plastics. After the substrate is heated it may shrink in response to the heat and cause problems with registration during the press run. For this reason it is important not to exceed the optimum temperature for a given material.

Another approach is to change the speed of the conveyor belt. See Figure 9-28. Slow drying inks will require the conveyor speed to be reduced to allow more time in the dryer for the wet ink film to dry. It is important for the ink film to be completely dry before it is stacked, otherwise the ink will block or stick to other sheets in the stack. The proper procedure is to set up the dryer as follows. Enough heat should be used to dry the wet ink film while leaving the substrate dimensionally stable. The conveyor belt speed is then adjusted to achieve proper drying to allow stacking. The press should only be operated at a speed where the ink can be dried and no greater.

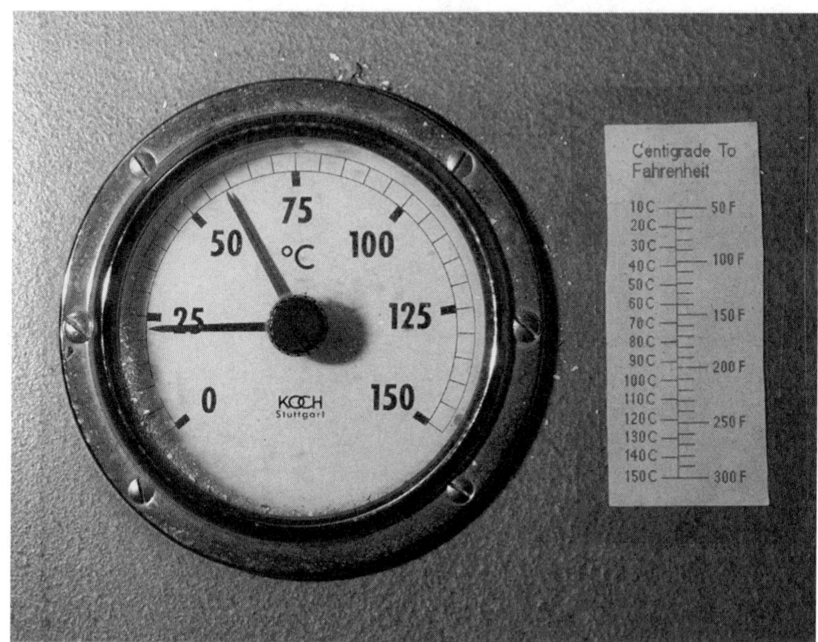

Figure 9-27 Dryer temperature

Figure 9-28 Conveyor belt speed

TUNNEL DRYER This device is made up of an enclosure much like a tunnel with a conveyor belt running through it. See Figure 9-29. The openings where the belt feeds through are just high enough to allow the substrate to pass. This is to prevent heat from escaping the tunnel, to maintain its greatest efficiency. A **tunnel dryer** allows for effective control of air circulation within the unit, and vents solvent fumes or moisture outside the plant. Tunnel dryers can be heated using an electric infrared source or gas fired heater.

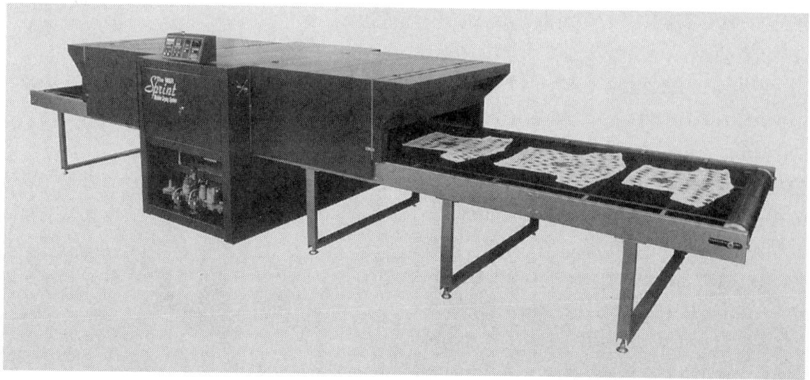

Figure 9-29 Gas dryer ((*M & R Equipment Inc.*)

JET AIR DRYER A **jet air dryer** is an example of a convection system. It uses a combination of heat and air flow to speed drying of ink. Jet air dryers are ideal for drying inks that dry by evaporation. It is called a jet dryer since it directs air flow through a grid or plate with small holes placed closely together. This causes air to be directed at a greater velocity which speeds the evaporation rate from the wet ink film. Early designs used a sheet of metal with holes drilled to create the jet air effect. Modern designs have improved on this initial approach with more sophisticated design forming individual nozzles for improved performance. See Figure 9-30. This has resulted in greater air flow and increased velocity for faster drying.

Figure 9-30 Jet air plates

There are two stages in a jet air dryer. A heated stage speeds evaporation of solvents or water from the ink film. A cool down stage is also used to complete the drying process. Jet air dryers are commonly used in screen printing shops due to their effectiveness.

FLASH CURING **Flash curing** is a technique used for drying textiles inks. An infrared heat panel is mounted in a stand to allow it to be used with a multicolor textile press. These devices are an example of a radiant heating device and are called spot curing or flash curing units. There are two primary uses for this device. Under most situations with textile printing, curing is done after all colors are printed. When it is desirable to print a color on top of a previous color, it is not advisable to print wet ink on top of an uncured ink film. Flash curing can be used to cure the surface of the ink film to permit overprinting. After all printing is complete the garment is cured to achieve a total cure. See Figure 9-31.

A second application for a flash dryer is a mobile unit to achieve a final cure of the ink on the pallet of the press. This may be used instead of a conveyor dryer as a cost saving measure for small shops or operations.

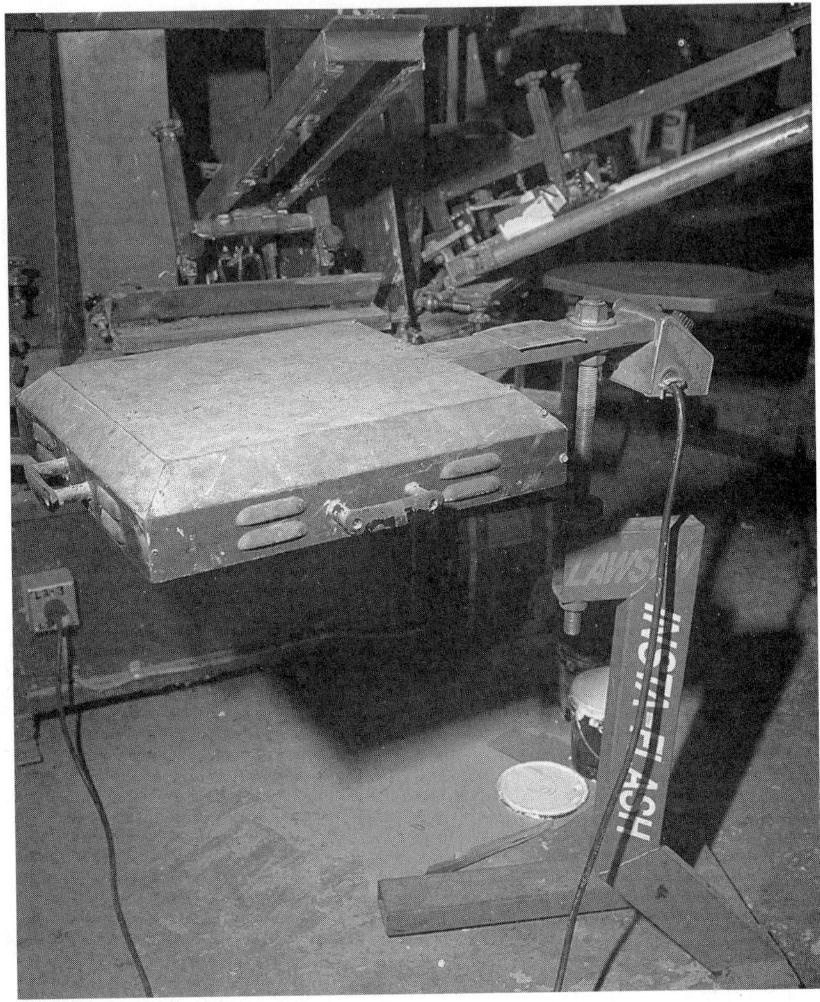

Figure 9-31 Flash dryer

Ultraviolet Curing System

An **ultraviolet curing** device is one that uses ultraviolet radiation to cause the ink to change from a wet liquid to a solid state. It requires a special UV ink that is formulated with an initiator or catalyst to trigger a reaction known as polymerization causing the ink to cure or harden. The reaction is different than other inks since it is instantaneous allowing curing to be done at a very rapid rate.

There are several components that make up a UV curing system. The lamp is the part of the system that generates light causing the ink to cure. It is similar to lamps used to expose stencil materials, mercury vapor or sometimes metal halide. It generates its output at the upper end of the visible light spectrum (about 300 to 400 nanometers) while infrared radiation is just below the visible light spectrum. Refer back to Figure 9-26.

A reflector is used to direct the ultraviolet rays onto the substrate

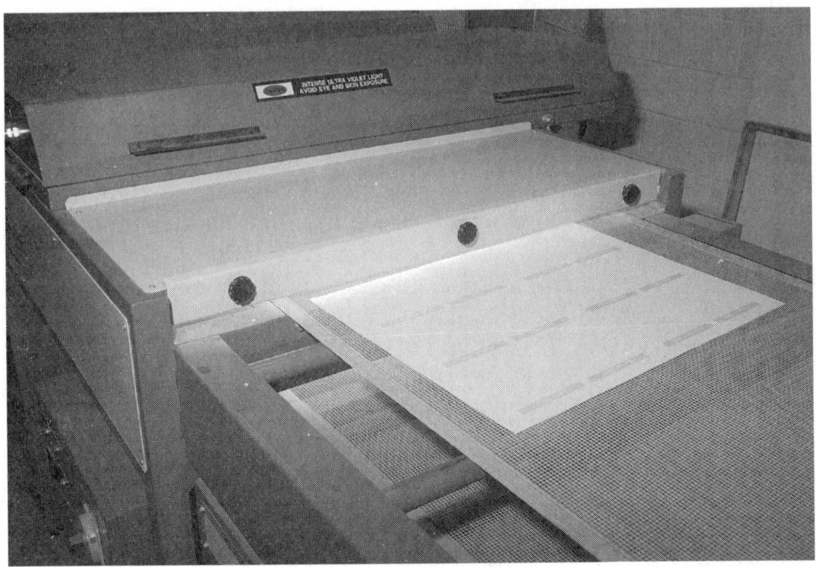

Figure 9-32 UV Reactor

to be cured. There are several different reflector designs. They can be classified into two types: focused or non-focused. There are advantages and disadvantages for each design for use with different applications. A focused reflector directs the rays into a small area creating greater intensity and faster curing. Non-focused reflectors direct the rays into a larger area which requires more time for the ink to cure. The reflector is also used as a heat sink to draw heat away from the bulbs using air or water circulation.

As with other drying systems a conveyor belt is used to transport the printed substrate through the unit. The exposure unit of the system is carefully shielded to prevent accidental skin and eye contact from the lamp as permanent damage can occur. An exhaust system is built into the lamp housing for several reasons. It is used to remove ozone that is generated primarily during lamp startups. It also creates an air flow through the unit that assists in removing heat from the curing unit. Excess heat can cause shrinkage of the substrate. There are multipurpose dryers available that combine both a UV curing unit anda jet air dryer. This allows either UV inks or conventional inks to be dried without purchasing two separate drying systems. See Figure 9-32.

Radio Frequency Curing

The principle of radio frequency drying, or **R.F. curing**, is by selectively removing moisture from the ink or coating without affecting the substrate. Radio frequencies relate to a band of frequencies used for broadcasting and other uses situated below infrared energy in the electromagnetic spectrum as discussed earlier in the chapter. Radio frequencies range from 10KHz (10,000 cycles per second) up to 900 MHz (900,000,000 cycles per second). Microwave is included as the upper portion of the R.F. band from 900 MHz up to 2.5 Giga Hz (2,500,000,000 cycles per second). There are four frequencies within the R.F. band that may be used for R.F. heating devices. The frequency that is often used with R.F. dryers for screen printing applications is 27.12 MHz.

The principle of using radio frequency waves for heat generation is simple. The sheet to be cured is passed through an R.F. electromagnetic field. Water molecules from the ink deposit align themselves within the electromagnetic field. The field alternates at a rate of 27, 120,000 cycles per second (27.17 MHz). Each time the field alternates the molecules realign causing heat to be generated within the water molecules of the ink film. Water evaporates from the substrate once the boiling point is reached.

Water has the greatest "loss factor" with regard to R.F. heating. This is ideal since evaporation of water does not damage the environment. The electromagnetic field only affects areas of the substrate with a significant moisture content. Other areas of the substrate are not affected during the heating process as with other dryers. This results in less distortion of the substrate with improved registration on multicolor runs.

The amount of energy required is based only on the area requiring drying. A small area of ink requires very little energy to cure. This results in significant savings over conventional drying devices with a constant need for energy. It does not take an extended time to warm up the dryer before it can be used. The process is fast, allowing greater productivity over evaporative solvent-based inks.

R.F. dryers require less space than conventional dryers, similar to UV curing devices. This will result in less floor space required. There are a number of reasons that make the R.F. dryer well suited to drying screen printing inks. Yet one primary factor prevents more widespread use: the higher cost of the drying unit. Curing of full ink coverages by R.F. curing will result in the substrate heated to a greater degree resulting in changes in dimensional stability similar to conventional dryers. Another limitation is that conductive substrates or inks cannot be cured using R.F. dryers.

KEY TERMS

belt prrinter
carousel press
clamshell press
conduction
convection
cylinder press
drying rack
fully automatic press
flash curing
flatbed press
four post press
infrared
jet air dryer
manual press
oval press
R.F. curing
semi-automatic press
sheet fed press
three-quarter automatic
tunnel dryer
ultraviolet curing
ultraviolet energy
web press
wicket dryer

REVIEW QUESTIONS

1. What are the advantages of a cylinder press over a flatbed press design?
2. What are the advantages of a four post press over a clamshell press design?
3. What are the differences between presses designed for graphics applications and presses for printing textiles?
4. What are the principles of a tunnel dryer?
5. What are the principles of a jet air dryer?
6. What is the principle of a UV curing device?
7. What are the advantages of a radio frequency curing device?

Glossary

These definitions are reprinted with permission from the Screenprinting and Graphic Imaging Association Glossary.

Abrasion Resistance
The inherent ability of a surface to inhibit deterioration or destruction by friction. Also called rub resistance, it relates to the toughness of an ink or coating.

Absorbency
That property of a porous material, such as paper, which causes it to take up liquids or vapors (e.g., moisture) with which it is in contact, and allow penetration into its bulk.

Actinic Light
Light rays capable of changing the properties of photosensitive materials on exposure to the light source emitting such energy.

Adhesion
A mechanical or chemically reactive bond between surfaces. Adhesion to a smooth surface may rely on polar adhesion.

Adhesion Test
Any of a variety of test methods used to determine the adequacy of ink or coating adhesion to a substrate. The cross-cut tape test is commonly used (ASTM D 3359).

Adhesive, Pressure Sensitive
A type of adhesive which in dry (solvent free) form is aggressively tacky at room temperature with the capability of inducing a bond with dissimilar surfaces on contact with slightly firm pressure.

Air Jets
The tiny holes in the sheet or plate (for similar configuration) within a drying system through which air is forced under compression, onto the surface of freshly printed substrates to accelerate drying.

Alligator
A term indicating the effect of a surface film contracting during drying to form small, irregular islands of color somewhat resembling the texture of an alligator skin. Any undercolor or coating usually shows through the very narrow lines between the islands.

Angle of Attack
The angle formed by the face of the moving squeegee blade and the plane of the screen, under pressure. Due to the flexibility of the blade, this angle generally differs from the squeegee angle, which is measured without movement or pressure.

Angle, Squeegee
The angle formed by the face of the squeegee blade, on the side toward the direction of the printing stroke, and the plane of the screen fabric, with squeegee in printing position but without pressure.

ASTM
Acronym for American Society for Testing & Materials, which is the world's largest source of voluntary consensus standards on the characteristics and performance of materials. Headquartered in Philadelphia, Pennsylvania.

Automatic Feeder
A device for picking up single sheets from a pile and moving them, one at a time into the printing area of the press to be printed.

Automatic Machine (Automatic Press)
A machine which completes partial or full operation cycles by means of energy other than human motion; i.e., a fully automatic screen press loads, prints, and discharges the print without manual effort on the part of the operator other than the switching on and off of the energy source, usually electricity, or controlling machine speed. In some presses, may include ink feeding.

Automatic Peel
A feature generally found on larger automatic screen printing presses, whereby the screen is lifted mechanically behind the moving squeegee, by a spring or cam device.

Backing Sheet
The plastic or paper support sheet of knife-cut stencil film, indirect photoscreen stencil film, camera film, and the support sheet of pressure sensitive laminations.

Back Lighted Display
A display printed and/or prepared on transparent material which can be illuminated from the rear to enhance attention value.

Base
1. A firm, true surface on which the substrate is placed for printing; 2. A modifying additive for screen printing inks-see Extender Base and Transparent Base; 3. A specific type of resin which determines the character of the ink in manufacture, such as acrylic base, oil base, synthetic base, vinyl base, and so on.

Belt Conveyor
A moving belt system for transporting prints from one processing stage to the next as from press to dryer, through dryer, from dryer to packing area, in almost any conceivable order. Belt may be made of metal, mesh, heavy cloth, web straps, wires, and so on.

Belt Speed
The rate of travel, usually measured in inches or feet per minute, of the belt of any conveyor dryer system.

Binder
1. That portion of the vehicle in an ink composition that, in combination with the pigments, forms the film; 2. In paper, an adhesive component used to cement inert filler, such as clay, to the sheet.

Black Light Fluorescent Tubes
Electrically activated light sources in tubular shape which emit rays in or very near the ultraviolet band of the spectrum. Such rays, high in actinic value, can be used for exposing photosensitive stencil films, before processing into stencils.

Blocking
An undesired adhesion between layers of material placed in contact under moderate pressure and/or temperature in storage or use. Usually occurs in a stack of printed material which is stacked prior to thorough drying.

Blocking Out
Sealing the fabric of the printing screen against leakage, in the areas between the design which is to print and the extreme edges (frames).

Blockout Solution (Blockout Compound) (Blockout Filler)
Liquid used for blocking out areas of the stencil fabric beyond the design to be printed.

Bond Paper
A light weight white paper stock widely used in the production of chain store window banners. It is also available in a few light pastel colors.

Book Paper
Term used to describe a group of papers, exclusive of newsprint, having common physical characteristics that in general, are suitable for the graphic arts. The basic size is 25" x 38".

Bottle Press
A screen printing press capable of printing on cylindrical or other three-dimensional shapes.

Bridging
The ability of a direct emulsion stencil material to "bridge the gap" between screen threads, and to retain solidity after exposure and washout.

Bristol
A solid or laminated heavyweight paper having a thickness of .006" or higher. The name is derived form the original rag board made in Bristol, England.

Bronze Powder
A metallic pigment added in printing inks consisting mainly of copper alloys in very fine flakes.

Bronzing (Bronze Dusting)
Printing with a tacky size or adhesive and then dusting with finely powdered metal particles to give the appearance of metallic printing.

Bronzing Adhesive
A varnish-like clear ink or coating on which dry metallic bronze powders may be applied—as opposed to bronzing liquid, into which the bronze powders are mixed for wet application to substrate.

Build-Up Layer
A layer or sheet of material such as glass, sheets of card stock, thin wood paneling, and so on, smaller than the inside dimensions of the printing frame but larger than the stencil area on which the finished stencil film is placed for adhering. Used to ensure pressurized contact with the fabric.

Butyl Acetate
Solvent used as a constituent of lacquers because of its low rate of evaporation.

Butyl Alcohol
A solvent high in strength for most natural gums, it is widely used in the formulation of nitrocellulose lacquers and synthetic resin inks and coatings.

Butyl Cellosolve
One trade name for ethylene glycol monobutyl ether, which is a high boiling point, high flash point, slow evaporating glycol ether solvent, sometimes used in lacquer inks or coatings based on vinyl, nitrocellulose and the like.

Calendered Fabric
Screen mesh that has been flattened on one or both sides, by passing through industrial rollers which have been heated.

Calendered Film
A term designating a film with a very glossy surface obtained by passing the film between polished rollers under pressure, and sometimes under elevated temperature conditions.

Calibration
1. The setting of dials of an exposure computer to know exposure elements such as film speed and/or shutter speed so that later adjustments will have repeatability; 2. The determining of absolute values for any graduated instrument.

Caliper
Term used to designate thickness, as of sheet material. The thickness is usually expressed in mils or points, both being terms expressing thousandths of an inch. (.050 is expressed as 50 point usually for paper stocks; or 50 mils when plastics are designated by thickness.)

Camera-Ready Art
1. All elements of the print set in correct size, mounted in proper place, including headlines, copy blocks, and screened prints; keylines showing exact size and position of halftones or four-color photographs to be stripped in; spot color elements mounted to acetate flips; properly registered over the black copy and marked for screen percentage and colors; 2. An original design, completely finished as it is to appear in the reproduction. May be in black and white, or full color (to be color separated).

Cap Printing Machine (For Garments)
A specifically engineered device for printing onto rounded surfaces of a cap. May use flat screens or flexible (curved) screens, depending on machine configuration.

Carbonized Thread
Monofilament screen fabric threads which have been treated to prevent the buildup of static electricity through friction. One variant has a carbon core.

Cardboard
Layers of paper laminated into sheets of varying thicknesses, generally 0.006 inch (0.15 mm) or greater.

Carousel
A multicolor screen printing device that typically has multiple pallets (platens) that rotate around a central shaft.

Cassette
A portable protective container for transportation of either exposed or unexposed photosensitive materials.

Cast Film
Plastic sheeting manufactured by the casting process as opposed to the extruding process.

Cast Vinyl
1. Vinyl sheeting manufactured by coating the liquid compound on to a substrate, usually a polished chrome plated sheet, where it remains until it sets to form the plastic sheet; 2. Vinyl compounds such as vinyl chloride, vinyl acetate or similar esters, formed or molded into specified shapes, sheets, or the like.

Catalyst
A substance which has the capability of initiating or accelerating the speed of a reaction between two or more substances when introduced into their presence, normally in relatively small quantities.

Catalyzed System
Chemical compound ink, coating, or the like which requires the use of a catalyst. A true catalyst is a substance which acts in a chemical system to increase the rate of chemical reaction.

Cellosolve
Trade name for ethylene glycol monoethyl ether, a solvent with toxic properties.

Centipoise
A unit of measure of viscosity equal to one hundredth (0.01) of poise. Water has an approximate viscosity of one centipoise at room temperature.

Central Processing Unit (CPU)
That part of a computer which contains arithmetic logic and control functions for accepting, decoding and executing instructions. See also Mainframe.

Ceramic Ink
An ink containing ceramic pigments and flux that is applied to a ceramic substrate, by screen printing or stamping.

Ceramics
Technology concerned with the manufacture of products from inorganic, non-metallic substances and materials, that are subjected to a high temperature during manufacture and/or use.

Ceramic Screen Printing
The decoration of ceramic articles by screen printing techniques.

CFM
Abbreviation for cubic feet per minute.

Chemical Resistance
The resistance of an ink film or imprint to deteriorating effects resulting from exposure to, or immersion in chemicals of specified type under specified conditions.

Chip Board
A paperboard made from waste paper.

Clamshell Press
1. A heat transfer machine/die cutting machine device with two platens, one directly over the other and hinged together on one side to open and close like a clam's shell; 2. Also may refer to a flatbed screen printing press designed with the screen carriage hinged to the printing table at one end.

Clean Room
An enclosed area in which airborne particles, temperature, relative humidity and pressure are controlled to specified requirements. One such specification is U.S. FED-STD-209B.

Clear Coat
Transparent protective coating applied to a screen printed imprint such as a finished decal or poster to ensure maximum durability.

Clear Frit
A frit that remains essentially transparent when processed into a porcelain enamel.

Clear Glaze
A transparent colorless ceramic glaze.

Cliché
A printing plate, usually photoengraved hard steel or plastic, used in pad transfer printing to supply the image.

Coater (Emulsion Applicator) (Spreader)
A tool with a rounded, sometimes slotted edge used for evenly spreading sensitized emulsion on the fabric of printing screens. See also Scoop Coater.

Cobwebbing
Fine filaments produced by the ink between the screen fabric and the substrate being printed, culminating in a cobweb-like appearance on the finished print. It may be reduced to a minimum by careful selection of solvents and proper adjustment of printing conditions.

Cohesion
1. The forces which bind the particles of ink or varnish film together. As distinct from "adhesion," which includes the forces binding the film to its substrate; 2. The ability of an adhesive to resist splitting.

Colorant
A substance used to modify the colors of a material, e.g., dyes or pigments.

Color Sequence
The order in which colors are screen printed onto a substrate; important to the correct trapping of colors.

Color Strength
In printing ink, the effective concentration of coloring material per unit of volume.

Conductive Ink
An ink for the screen printing of electronic circuits which contains materials that permit electric current flow through the printed line or pattern.

Consistency
1. The relative stiffness (body) of an ink or coating; 2. Describes the apparent viscosity of an ink or varnish when shearing forces of varying degrees are applied to it in various ways, e.g., when it is disturbed in the can, poured from one can into another, or printed through the screen.

Contact Films
A family of films used primarily for line work and the making of positives from negatives; negatives from positives; negatives from negatives; or positives from positives.

Contacting
One of the primary functions of the squeegee during screen printing, that of bringing the printing screen into contact with the substrate, so that ink transfer may take place.

Container Printing
A general term designating the screen printing of containers of various shapes with labels, directions, and/or ornamental designs, directly onto the surface of the container which may be glass or plastic, or depending on the fabricated shape, other types of substrates.

Container Printing Machine
A machine designed to accommodate various shapes of containers, holding them in position for imprinting. Container printers may be manual, semi-automatic or automatic.

Continuous Tone
Copy or image containing a range of tones from light to dark such as that found in photographs, in which the various tones blend smoothly into lighter or darker adjacent tones without visible boundaries, and without having been photographed through a halftone screen.

Convection Drying
The drying of screen printing in a convection oven.

Convection Oven
A heat chamber into which air of elevated temperature is introduced in static form, in which drying can take place under uncirculated heat. When the air is circulated, then force drying takes place.

Conventional Ink
Color mixed with vehicle for application in other than a dry state, except those containing frits or fluorescent pigments, or special purpose inks such as solder resists, conductive inks, and other designed for functional, rather than aesthetic results, usually.

Conveyor Dryer
An ink drying system which incorporates a drying chamber with a belt conveyor. Additional features may include an exhaust system, a cooling chamber, a UV lamp, and so on. Belting materials may be metal or heat-resistant synthetics.

Cooling Zone
That portion of a drying system in which dried products are cooled before removing from the system.

Copolymer
Mixture produced from a combination of two or more polymers or heteropolymers.

Copy
Art work, design, original or actual object to be copied for ultimate reproduction by screen printing or other printing methods. The subject to be photographed for ultimate multiple reproduction.

Copy Camera (Process Camera)
Generally a large camera consisting of lens, lens board, bellows, film holder and copy board for photographing art to be reproduced by printing methods.

Corona Discharge
An electrical, film treating method whereby the atmosphere (corona) around the substrate is ionized, encouraging oxidation and reducing surface tension for improved ink adhesion.

Corrugated Board
Laminate made of flat sheet paper stock and corrugated paper stock. Single face stock has one flat sheet laminated to one corrugate; double faced stock has a flat sheet on each side of the corrugate; double wall has a single faced sheet adhered to a double faced sheet, with flat faces outside.

Co-Solvent
One of two or more solvents in a mixture which combine to dissolve a solid.

Coverage (Mileage) (Spreading Power)
A term indicating the amount of area a given volume of ink will cover when applied to a given substrate. Secondary terms are also used. Not to be confused with hiding power, however.

Cover Papers
Similar to offset papers but with considerably more bulk. Indoor displays, signs and posters are popular uses of cover papers.

Cross Hatch Test
A method for testing ink adhesion to substrate using a sharp cutting blade and adhesive tape. Refers to ASTM D3359-78 Ink Adhesion Test.

Cross-Linking
The long chain, joining of molecules to form a change in the physical structure and properties of a polymer.

Cure
The resolving of coating material into a usable or specific state by heat or chemical action other than baking in the usual sense, or firing. See Curing.

Cure Time
The time/temperature combination required to bring organic decoration to the desired level of hardness, caustic and chemical resistance, and so on.

Curing
1. A drying process usually requiring elevated temperature of a film that can not be dried by oxidation; 2. In textile decoration, the application of heat to remove volatiles and set the emulsion of pigment dye into the textile fibers; 3. A two (or more) part chemical reaction that, when completed, resembles a dried appearance. Photopolymerization of UV curable coatings is one example.

Curing Agent
An additive which promotes the curing of a film.

Curing Oven
A chamber in which drying and/or some change of a freshly printed ink surface takes place during the drying process, to improve adhesion, solidify the film or otherwise convert film characteristics by means other than by solvent evaporation.

Curing Unit
A UV curing reactor that houses a UV energy emitter used for the polymerization of ultraviolet curable inks, coatings and adhesives.

Cyan
Blue green color, complimentary to red and one of the three primary subtractive pigment colors, the other two being yellow and magenta. Cyan reflects blue and green light, while absorbing red.

Cycle
The mechanical action of a screen printing press required to complete one print sequence.

Cycle Time
1. An amount of time, expressed in nanoseconds, required for a computer to access data in its memory; 2. The time it takes for a screen printing press to complete one print cycle.

Cylinder Press
1. A screen printing press so constructed that the substrate, wrapped around a rotating drum, contacts the printing surface of a moving printing screen, being discharged onto a conveyor after printing; 2. A press used for die cutting.

Cylindrical Printer
A mechanical arrangement for screen printing cylindrical forms such as bottles, metal drums, and so on.

Daylight Fluorescence
The phenomena of increased color brilliance of materials by conversion of wavelengths of other colors in the spectrum.

Decal
Originally an abbreviated form of decalcomania, the French designation of a design printed on special paper for transfer to a substrate. Current usage includes pressure sensitive markings as well as water-slide transfers, or any or all designs that are externally processed prior to application to end product or surface.

Deep Well Exposing Unit
A table or bench mounted unit equipped with a flexible, transparent top instead of glass which can be molded around a direct printing screen by vacuum for exposing.

Definition
1. A subjective measure of the overall quality, resolution, and acutance of a printed shape against the substrate or background; 2. Clarity of detail.

Degrease
Term used to indicate the act of removing the grease film from metal parts for printing or from screen fabrics prior to stencil application, using appropriate chemical means.

Densitometer
An instrument which measures either photographic density, or density of printed color by either reflected or transmitted light.

Density
1. The opacity of a halftone dot or solid subject on a transparent film which will not permit the passage of light; 2. The density of a fiber is its weight expressed in grams per cubic centimeter; 3. The mass of any unit volume of a material.

Density Range
The range of tones in a developed negative or positive measured in gamma units.

Diazo
A photosensitive chemical or process by which screen printing emulsions can be made sensitive to actinic light. Images are formed by a molecular dye process.

Diazo Emulsion
A light sensitive emulsion for making a screen printing stencil that is sensitized with diazo chemicals rather than bichromates.

Dielectric
A non-conducting medium or a material which does not permit electric energy to flow through or pass through, e.g., glass, porcelain, plastics, air, and so on. An insulating material.

Diffusion Transfer
Photographic method of processing an exposed sheet of sensitized paper in contact with a receiver sheet.

Diffusion-Transfer Base Stock
A paper with a high degree of wet strength and smooth surface used for application of a silver halide-gelatin emulsion. Made of stock free from iron, copper, and sulfur and resistant to yellowing when exposed to a caustic solution.

Diluent
A volatile liquid which extends a solution but weakens the power of the active solvent, and reduces the concentration of resin.

Dimensional Stability
That property of a material which enables it to resist length, width, or thickness changes under varying conditions of heat, cold, moisture, and other influences.

Direct Emulsion
A liquid polymer emulsion used as a screen printing stencil after being photosensitized, coated onto a stretched screen, exposed to actinic light, developed and washed out.

Discharge Printing
The pattern printing of darkly-dyed textile substrates with a color-removing chemical to provide a design into which lighter hues may be printed.

Dose Rate
In ultraviolet curing, the energy absorbed by the ink or coating per unit mass per unit of time. Usually expressed as Megarads per second.

Dot
The individual element of a halftone which may be square, elliptical or a variety of shapes.

Dot Area
The sum of halftone dots in relation to a given unit area. Twenty-five percent dot area means 25% of the given area is covered by dots, with 75% representing the uncovered areas.

Dot Gain
The tendency of the printed halftone dot to change in size at the moment of ink imprinting, thus changing the overall visual quality of the print. Due to a number of variables, the printed dot will be larger than its film counterpart. Also called "dot growth" or "dot spread."

Dot Pattern
The pattern formed by the dots in a halftone screen for use in camera or for use as a stencil in screen printing, which represents the original art or subject, in light and dark tones produced by varying size of dots which make up the whole image.

Dot Size
A term indicating relative area occupied by each dot composing a halftone negative, positive or print in relation to respective highlight and shadow areas in the image.

Draize Test
A method for estimating the skin or eye irritation due to contact with a chemical substance.

Dryer
Essentially a conveyor or static oven used to hasten drying of a wet material by subjecting it to heat generated by gas flame, electricity, and so on, or by circulated air at ambient temperature. May also be used to cure solid inks, such as plastisols.

Drying
The multistage conversion of a material from a wet, liquid, or semi-liquid state to a dry, solid state typically be removal of volatile solvents and/or water. In screen printing this normally refers to ink or coating applications on substrates.

Drying Rate (Drying Time)
The relative length of time required for a freshly deposited ink imprint to be changed from a wet to a dry state.

Durometer Gauge
An instrument for measuring the degree of hardness of an elastomer or rubber, such as used in squeegee blades. See also Shore Hardness.

Dwell
Time lapse or pause between cycles of an automated press to allow feed of printing stock and take-off of prints.

Dye Pigments
Dyestuffs that, by nature, are insoluble in water and can be used directly as pigments without chemical transformation.

Dyes
1. Coloring materials which are soluble in a vehicle or solvent as opposed to pigments which are insoluble; 2. Non-pigment coloring agents of mineral or vegetable origin, with high penetration capability, used mainly in decorating of textiles.

Elliptical Dots
The shape of the dots forming a halftone image which are not of the conventional round shape. Elliptical dot structure provides joining to form denser areas at the ends of the dot first, then as density increases, at the side of the dot shapes. Also called "chain dots."

Elongation (Stretch)
The increase in length or width of a material produced by extending it to the point of rupture. Not to be confused with conformability.

Emulsion
A liquid or semi-liquid compound type used in (a) silver halide photographic film, (b) photostencil process, or (c) textile inks. The compound is usually made from two or more ingredients, (such as oil or lacquer and water in ink manufacture) which do not intermix readily in their primary state.

Emulsion Coater
A tool, typically a smooth metal trough, used to spread thin layers of direct emulsion on a prestretched screen. Also called a "scoop coater."

Emulsion Side
The side of the indirect photosensitive stencil, or photographic film, which is coated with the emulsion.

EPA
Acronym for the U.S. Environmental Protection Agency, formed in order to implement the Federal Water Pollution Control Act of 1972 and subsequent environmental legislation, including the Clean Air Act and Solid Waste Amendments.

Epoxy
Generic term for a group of thermosetting resins having strong adhesive qualities, also capability of forming a very tough ink film with excellent chemical and environmental resistance. Epoxies exhibit good adhesion properties to hard surfaces, such as metal and glass.

Ergonomics
The application of biotechnology and engineering principles to improve the work environment with regard to safety, efficiency and precision.

Exposure Time
The relative amount of time in seconds or minutes during which a photosensitive material is acted upon by light.

Exposure Unit
The light source or system used in exposing photostencil materials.

Extender Base (Extender)
A non-pigmented compound used in screen printing to increase ink volume without reducing viscosity. Ordinarily, it is a buttery semi-paste that has no effect on ink color except to reduce its intensity of hue.

Fabric (Cloth)(Textile)
A comprehensive term denoting a product resulting from weaving, knotting, felting, knitting, binding or otherwise combining natural or synthetic fibers or filaments.

Fabrics, Stencil (Fabrics, Screen Printing)
Woven web materials manufactured for screen printing purposes of silk, man-made fibers or strands of fine wire, usually stainless steel.

Fabric Stretcher
A mechanical device for tensioning screen printing fabrics over the screen frame, accurately and correctly.

Fabric Tensioning
The act of imparting stretch in warp and weft directions to screen printing fabrics, preparatory to securing the fabric to the screen frames.

Fabric Thickness
Term used for the total average height of two crossing threads in a woven screen fabric, measured under tension.

Fade Resistance
That property of a color or ink film that inhibits deterioration that may be caused by environmental influences.

Fading
Partial or complete loss of color due to excess heating or environmental influences; a gradual "bleaching out" appearance of a color from a print, common causes: (a) intense sun exposure; (b) too much "watering down" of ink with solvents during printing; (c) lack of wash resistance of garment inks or dyes.

Fiber
A thread-like filament, many times greater in length than its diameter.

Filler
1. An inert substance added to plastic or ink formulations to reduce cost and/or to provide bulk; 2. A material, generally nonfibrous, added to a paper mixture to increase smoothness or opacity.

Film
A term applied variously to: 1. Transparent support sheet coated with light sensitive emulsion for use in a camera; 2. Indirect photoscreen stencil film; 3. Any of the various thin sheet materials transparent, translucent, or opaque, used as the face material in manufacturing pressure sensitive stock, and having a thickness usually not greater than 0.01 in. (0.25 mm).

Film Backing
1. The transparent sheet which carries the sensitized emulsion layer of photographic films; 2. The plastic or paper sheet which carries the photosensitive emulsion layer of a photographic screen printing stencil film, or the transparent plastic or semi-transparent paper sheet on which knife-cut stencil film is temporarily mounted.

Film Base
The transparent support for the emulsion or gelatin coat.

Film Emulsion
The light sensitive layer of the film which is coated onto the film base and which, on exposure and developing, forms the photographic image.

Film Negative/Reverse
A negative image made on photographic film.

Film Positive
A positive image made on photographic film.

Film Solvent
Solvent to be used in removing knife-cut stencils or paper stencils from the fabric of the printing screen.

Fineness of Grind
1. The degree of dispersion of a pigment in a vehicle; 2. The fineness of pigment particle size.

Fish Eye
A flaw in a screen printed ink film consisting of a generally circular defect caused by slight bubbling of the ink with resulting dispersion of the pigment within the immediate area, causing non-uniformity of color.

Flat
The stripped-up film positive or negative used to make a photostencil.

Flatbed Press
A screen printing press in which the substrate is placed on a flat surface prior to printing in contact with a flat printing screen which is attached by a carrier held on vertical posts or in clam-shell fashion.

Flatting Agent
Any material added to reduce the gloss level of an ink or coating.

Flat Screen Printing
Screen printing on any substrate which is not normally shaped or contoured on its surface.

Fleet Markings
General term applied to decals or pressure sensitive applications designed and produced for customers having more than one company owned vehicle for business use, delivery transport use, and so on. Usually produced to identify and promote the company owning the fleet, or its products.

Flexographic Printing
Formerly called aniline printing. A method of rotary printing utilizing flexible rubber plates and rapid drying fluid inks.

Flood Bar
The device on a screen printing press comprised of a thin metal (or plastic) blade, which has the function of spreading a thin film of ink uniformly over the printing screen, in the opposite direction of and preceding the printing stroke.

Flood Coat
Thin coating of ink applied to top of printing screen by the flood bar or, in manual operations by the squeegee, prior to the printing stroke.

Flooding
The application of an ink coating on top of the printing screen without printing. Also called "flood coating."

Flood Stroke
The mechanical action involved in flood coating a printing screen.

Flow Agent
An additive used to disturb the surface tension and increase the ink flow, when bubbles or orange-peel occur.

Flow Out
The capacity of a screen printing ink to spread on deposit for the purpose of covering the intersections left in the printed film by the threads or strands of the printing screen at the instant of printing. This provides a top surface, on drying of the film, that does not show mesh marks.

Flow Rate
Actual speed or velocity of the fluid movement.

Fluorescence
The emission of visible light by certain substances under the influence of ultraviolet radiation.

Fluorescent
A pigment which not only reflects a visible wavelength but is activated by most of the remaining absorbed light to re-emit it as color of a longer wavelength, which results in reinforcement of the reflected color.

Fluorescent Exposing Unit
A self-contained unit consisting of a bank of fluorescent lamps of high actinic value for evenly exposing light sensitive materials such as photostencil film or emulsion, and a vacuum blanket for holding the stencil film or screen frame.

Fluorescent Ink
An ink formulation in a range of colors containing pigment which has the property of increasing apparent brilliance when coated over a white or light-colored substrate. The phenomena involves the changing of light wavelengths of certain portions of the light spectrum to the base wave-length of the color of the pigment in each case, thus, adding to the intensity of the light reflected from the colored surface. This phenomena increases the brilliance up to four times that of conventionally formulated screen printing inks of the same base color.

Foam Board
A family of rigid, foam centered sheet and boards, made of a variety of laminate materials.

Footprint
The edge of the squeegee which comes into contact with the screen fabric, usually no more than a few mils in width, and the length of which will equal the overall width of the squeegee blade. Rounded-edge squeegee blades will have a larger footprint than sharper ones.

Force Drying
Any system of drying of screen printing inks, industrial coatings, etc., by application of influences beyond normal atmospheric conditions, e.g., forced air flow at ambient temperature, heated air, and so on.

Four Color Process Printing
A system of photographically reproducing an illustration or design to produce all colors in the original by using magenta, cyan, yellow, and black ink printed through color-separated halftone printing screens.

Four Post Press
A flatbed screen printing press in which the screen carriage is mounted on four vertical posts. Typically, the vacuum bed moves forward for loading.

Frit
A smelted mixture of soluble and insoluble materials forming a glass which when quenched in cold water shatters into small friable pieces. Used in aluminum enamels, glass colors and overglazes.

Garment Discharging
A process which allows the printing of dyed-dark textiles with light colored designs, by using sulfoxylate reducing agents with special dyes. See also Discharge Printing.

Generation
Each successive stage in reproducing an original is one generation.

Ghost Image
Ink stains on screen fabric which have not been removed during screen cleaning and reclaiming, and which generally require caustic agents to eliminate.

Glaze
A thin vitreous coating, either colored or clear, that attaches itself formally to the body of ceramic ware, imparting a gloss and smoothness to the surface.

Glitter
Small decorative flakes of a high gloss material added to plastic or pastisol ink to achieve a sparkle appearance in the final product or print.

Gloss Ink
An ink that dries with minimum penetration into the substrate surface and which yields a high luster.

Gravure Printing
An intaglio printing process in which the ink is carried in minute etched "wells" on the plate, the excess being removed from the surface by a doctor blade. Rotogravure printing is done on web stock with cylindrical plates. Sheet fed gravure printing involves the feeding to the printing plate of individual sheets of substrates.

Gripper Edge
A narrow area along the edge of a printing sheet which allows space for mechanical fingers or suction cups to attach to move the sheet through the printing operation and/or to remove the sheet from the press to the dryer conveyor. Also called "gripper margin."

Grippers (Gripping Fingers)
Mechanical fingers on a press, or small vacuum suction cups, designed to pick up substrates from the stockpile and move them to printing base or from printing base to dryer or other conveyor. The attachment of the fingers to the substrate is temporary and releasable. See also Suckers.

Guides, Register
Stops on the printing base against which edges of substrate may be placed for printing to ensure all substrates being printed in identical areas or positions of print.

Hairline Register
Very tight register of color to color, or dot to dot. In halftone printing, it is within one-half row of dots in tolerance.

Halftone
A print in which details and dark and light tones are represented by dots of varying sizes in relationship to the tones or shades which they must portray. Small dots form light tones, larger dots form darker tones.

Halftone Line Count
A means of determining the fineness or coarseness of a halftone screen, negative, positive, or stencil. The halftone dots, regardless of size, are equidistant from others on their centers, thus, located in parallel lines. A count of lines per inch indicates fineness, i.e., a screen designated as 65 line has 65 lines of dots per inch is a coarse screen, while a screen designated as 150 line (150 lines per inch) is relatively fine.

Halftone Printing
A technique by which an image which has been broken up photographically into a structure of tiny dots, each equidistant from others on centers, but varying in size in relation to light and dark areas, can be printed to preserve the gradations of tone by virtue of larger dots producing darker tone areas. The dots are smaller than can be normally noticed by the unaided eye.

Hand Fed
Term used to designate the need for manual, as opposed to automated feeding of a screen printing press or unit.

Haze
1. Undesired cloudiness generally found in transparent areas, sometimes in the base substrate; 2. Residue of ink and/or stencil material remaining in a screen following stencil removal. Often requiring caustic detergents for complete removal.

Heat Transfer Application
The process of image transfer to substrate by application of heat. Manufacturers recommend the following for correct application of most plastisol transfers: (a) temperature—375 degree; (b) pressure—60 pounds (medium pressure for manual machines); (c) sealing time—12 to 15 seconds; (d) allow garment to cool before removing backing paper.

Heavy Metals
Generally toxic metallic elements contained in some pigments, e.g., chromium, cadmium, lead, and so on.

Highlight Density
The density in that portion of a halftone negative or positive which ultimately results in the printing of the highlight area.

Highlight Dot
Normally the largest dot in the film negative, or the smallest dot in the film positive and photoscreen stencil that defines a highlight area in the reproduction.

Highlights
The lightest areas of original copy or reproduction with respect to depth of color.

Hot Stamping
A method of printing which uses hot metal types to impress an adhesive-backed film or foil on the surface to be printed.

Image
An original design of any kind; the reproduction of an original design or pattern.

Image Area
The live area or area that is to be reproduced or printed.

Indirect Printing Screen
1. A printing screen made by exposing a photosensitive emulsion which has been coated onto a plastic support sheet through a positive, developing the stencil on the support sheet, then adhering the emulsion side to the fabric. The support sheet is removed when the stencil is dry; 2. A printing screen made with the use of a hand-cut (knife-cut) stencil, prepared prior to adhesion to the stretched screen fabric.

Indirect Stencil
A photosensitive stencil made from a light sensitive gelatin emulsion coated onto a polyester carrier or backing sheet which is exposed to a film positive and chemically processed into a stencil before adhering to the stretched screen fabric. After adhesion, the support or backing sheet is removed. This opens the portions of the stencil which are to print.

Infrared
An area in the electromagnetic spectrum extending beyond red light from 760 nanometers to 1000 microns (10^6 Nm). It is the form of radiation used for making non-contact temperature measurements.

Infrared Dryer
A drying system for screen printed sheets or three-dimensional items utilizing infrared emission as a heating source.

Ink
A general term applied to any screen printable composition, usually a liquid, whether used for aesthetic or functional purpose.

Ink Adhesion Test
1. Any of several controlled tests for the long or short-term adhesion properties of an ink; 2. A surface treatment test method concerned with determining the degree to which a standard or designated ink will adhere to a treated polyolefin surface.

Ink Deposition (Ink Deposit)
The actual ink placed on the substrate by screen printing techniques. Usually used in relation to thickness of the ink film when printed, but without inference as to actually what has been printed.

Ink Flow
The ability of imprinted ink deposits to spread minutely in order to provide a solid coating. See also Flow Out.

Ink-Jet Printing
A printing process whereby small computer-initiated jets of ink form printed images on a moving web. Used to some degree in label printing.

Inks, Halftone
Screen printing inks specifically designed for the screen printing of halftones. Such inks are usually translucent and thixotropic.

Inorganic
Descriptive of any substance that is not derived from hydrocarbons, generally structured through ionic bonding.

Inorganic Pigments
Pigments which are derived from mineral sources, some containing metal.

Insoluble
Describes a condition in which a solute will not dissolve in a particular solution.

Intaglio
A method of printing by means of ink carried in depressions etched into the printing plate.

Intercoat Adhesion
The adhesion of one ink to another with regard to the compatibility, strength and quality of the bond.

Jet Dryer
A mechanical unit consisting of a conveyor belt for transporting wet prints under a plate having numerous very small holes (or similar aperture) at close intervals through which compressed air at elevated temperature can be discharged onto the surface of the print to hasten evaporation of the volatile solvents from wet ink films.

Knife-Cut Film
A lacquer or similar film temporarily affixed to a clear support sheet, into which designs or images may be cut either mechanically or manually with a sharp knife, for making a screen printing stencil or a detailed photographic mask or positive from which a photographic stencil can be made.

Knife-Cut Positive
A design or image cut into masking film which is usable in the same way as a film positive made by camera, for making a screen printing photostencil.

Lacquer Stencil
A knife-cut stencil made of a lacquer-like material laminated to a thicker temporary support.

Lacquer Thinner
Generally solvent mixtures used with lacquer inks, paints, and stencils.

Lamp Black
A carbon black pigment produced by incomplete combustion of vegetable oils, petroleum, or asphalt materials.

Layout
1. The drawing or sketch of a proposed printed image area; 2. The plan view of a printing plant or manufacturing area.

Lead-Free Ink
Inks formulated for special purposes where the presence of lead would constitute a danger, e.g., in food packaging, and on children's toys and garments. In the U.S. "lead-free" surface coatings must contain less than 0.06% lead by weight measurement.

Letterpress Printing
A process in which ink is applied to paper or other substrate by means of raised portions of printing plates or type. A variant of the process is rotary letterpress printing.

Light Integrator
A light sensitive device that measures units of light, used for maintaining consistent exposure of film or stencil.

Light Source
Aside from the sun, which is the prime point of origin of light energy, any device capable of converting electrical or mechanical or chemical energy into light-emitting form.

Light-Source Geometry
The effective increasing of undercutting angle that occurs as the light source gets closer to the copy.

Line Art
Original art rendered in poster style, i.e., solid areas without gradations in tone. Examples—lettering, outlined drawings without shading, and so on.

Line Count
The number of lines of halftone dots per linear inch.

Line Drawing
Art work, originals, or printed matter consisting of lines or solids or dark and light tones. These can be reproduced by photographic printing screens or by hand-prepared screens, depending on the detail to be reproduced.

Line Image
A photographic image that is composed of fine, solid lines or dots or other shapes, all solid black or color, with no graduations of tones as in a continuous tone image.

Litho Film
A common term used to describe high contrast photographic film, which after exposure develops out to either black or transparent areas, with no intermediate gray tones.

Luminescence
A phenomena of light emission by a chemical composition which is film-forming and which absorbs light, releasing it when extraneous light sources have been removed. A "glow-in-the-dark" capability.

Make Ready (Set Up)
The procedures necessary to properly mount and register a printing screen for printing. The act of making ready or setting up to print.

Membrane Switch
A series of thermally stable films containing a backer board, spacer, circuit sheet(s) and graphic overlays, which together perform the function of an electronic switch.

Memory
1. The capacity of a plastic to return to an original state after applied stress; 2. In computer technology, the ability to store input data for later use.

Mercury Vapor Lamp
A type of illuminant high in actinic value; used in camera lighting systems and in UV curing reactors.

Mesh
The open space between the threads of a woven fabric; also, the threads collectively on the fabric itself.

Mesh Marks
1. A fine, cross-hatch pattern left by the mesh of the screen printing fabric, due to printing with an ink that does not have sufficient flowout, after the ink film has been dried; 2. A condition occurring when certain areas of the screen do not properly separate from the substrate, due to poor tensioning of the fabric or insufficient off-contact distance. See also Screen Marks.

Mesh Number (Mesh Count)
The number of openings per linear inch in any given screen printing fabric; the higher the mesh number or mesh count, the finer the weave.

Mesh Opening
A measure of the distance across the space between two parallel threads, expressed in microns.

Metal-Halide Lamp
A mercury light source enhanced by the addition of metallic elements to increase emission spectra and output energy.

Metallic Inks
Inks for screen printing compounds made with metallic powders, usually bronze or aluminum, binders, solvents, and so on, which when printed and dry, present an appearance of metal, such as gold, silver, or copper.

Metallized Fabric
Screen fabric woven of polyester threads that have been totally encased in nickel by an electrocoating process.

Metal Screen Fabric
A screen printing fabric of fine mesh woven from wire strands of stainless steel, phosphor bronze, nickel or copper. Usually used for very close tolerance screen printing and where abrasive inks such as frit for ceramics and glass are used, and where rough substrate edges would quickly destroy silk or synthetic screen printing fabrics.

Micron
A term used to express the wavelength of light or the size of the pigment particles; one millionth (1/1,000,000) of a meter, or 0.000039 inch. Used as a measure of stencil thickness. Represented by the symbol μ.

Modifier
In chemical terms, an inert ingredient which can change the properties of a resin mixture when added.

Monitor
1. A display screen for viewing information inputted or retrieved from a computer; 2. A device for continuously measuring a pollutant or effluent.

Monofilament
A strand composed of a single thread or filament, usually produced by extrusion.

Monofilament Polyester
Screen printing fabric woven from single strands of extruded polyester plastic.

Mottle (Ink Mottle)
The spotty or uneven appearance of printing, which becomes most pronounced in solid areas. It is usually caused by variances in absorbency of the paper or other substrate in various areas of the surface.

Mouse
A mechanical device that transmits electrical impulses to a specific location or coordinates on the CRT screen.

Multifilament
A term used to describe a yarn or thread composed of a number of filaments or fibers twisted together.

Newsboard
A paper board used primarily in the set-up box trade, also used as a core for lining one or both faces with a higher quality paper. Made from reclaimed newspapers.

Nylon Monofilament
1. A single strand or thread of nylon of even diameter and smooth surface; 2. Generally, the term indicates nylon screen printing fabric.

Off-Contact Printing
Screen printing accomplished with the printing screen adjusted above the substrate so that in the printing position it does not make contact with the substrate except at the line of the squeegee edge while printing. The space between stencil and substrate may range from near contact to as much as ⅜ or ½ inch in some instances, but normally varies from 1/16 to ⅛ inch (1.5 to 3.0 mm), approximately.

Offset
1. An indirect form of printing; 2. The transfer of a freshly screen printed image to the bottom of the printing screen, the back of a succeeding print, or other undesired surface.

Offset Printing
A method of printing in which the design is printed on the surface of a temporary carrier before transfer to the substrate. The carrier with the design is placed in contact with the substrate to transfer the design to its final position.

One-Man Squeegee
A squeegee mounted on a counter-balanced carrying device so that the operation of very large squeegees can be accomplished with a minimum of effort. Same as the one-arm squeegee.

Opacity
A state in which a printed film or a substrate does not permit the passage of light. The opposite of transparency as a characteristic.

Opaque
1. Not able to transmit light; not transparent and not translucent; 2. (v.) To apply an opaquing fluid to a negative.

Opaquing
Making portions of positives or negatives lightproof so that no light will pass through the portion; blocking out or stopping up pinholes in negatives and positives before exposing.

Orange Peel
A term describing the surface of a dried ink film which failed to flow out to a perfectly smooth surface, thus retaining very small elevations and valleys resembling the texture of an orange peel.

Organic
Term applied to pigments or any other materials compounded of raw materials of animal or vegetable origin, but not of mineral origin. A compound of ink, for example, may have both mineral pigments and organic compounds in the vehicle. Term refers to chemical structures based on the carbon atom.

Overexposure
The subjection of photosensitive material to light for a longer period than is necessary to accomplish the desired result.

Oxidation
The effect produced by contact with oxygen, either in the atmosphere or introduced in more concentrated form, which produces drying in some screen printing inks, deterioration of photographic developers in open trays, and so on.

Oxidizing Inks
Those screen printing inks which are caused to change from wet to dry state on contact with atmospheric oxygen.

Ozone
Gaseous form of oxygen containing three atoms to the molecule (O^3); may be generated by a high-voltage discharge across a stream of air. Causes oxidation of metals, other materials.

Pad Transfer Printing
Method for transferring images from a photoengraved plate, made of steel or plastic, to a round or irregular surface via a silicone rubber pad. The plate, or cliché, is filled with ink between each impression.

Paperboard
One of the two broad subdivisions of paper (general term). The distinction between paperboard and paper is not sharp but broad. Heavier in basis weight, thicker, and more rigid than paper, it is generally 12 points (0.012 inch) or more in thickness.

Paper Stencil
A screen printing stencil made of thin paper which is adhered to the fabric by one of two methods: (a) with the first imprint of ink; (b) by coating the paper with shellac, then after the shellac has dried, attaching the stencil to the fabric with a moderately hot electric iron.

Paste Up
Copy consisting of type characters and designs which are pasted in position for reproduction by means of photography or by hand screen separation.

Percent Open Area
The relationship between that part of a screen fabric that is blocked by threads, and that part that is open, or between threads.

Phosphorescence
A property of a certain class of films or coatings which utilizes the effect of heat or light on certain chemical elements (phosphors) within the structure of the product to provide a visible color in the absence of a normal light source.

Photoinitiator
A substance which absorbs light and is directly involved in the production of initiator radicals for polymerization (as in UV curing).

Photopolymer
A type of polymer that undergoes a distinct change such as depolymerization, on exposure to light. When used as a photostencil material, requires no addition of photosensitizer.

Photostencil
Any light sensitive system which utilizes original or photo-generated artwork to produce a stencil. A thin layer of photosensitive gelatin material, precoated onto a support or backing sheet of clear film, is one common type of photostencil.

Pigment
Substances that impart color, including black and white. Finely divided solid, organic or inorganic coloring material insoluble in the medium in which it is applied. Pigments must be bound to the receptor surface by dispersing in a vehicle or binder, such as resins in screen printing inks.

Pigment Dyes
Textile dyes formulated from appropriate vehicles and pigments of mineral or synthetic origin.

Plain Weave
A pattern of weave whereby fabric threads are woven over one and under one, as opposed to twill weave whereby threads are woven over one, under two.

Plastisol
A dispersion of finely divided polyvinyl chloride resin or resins in a plasticizer or series of plasticizers. This system is usually 100% solids with no volatiles. (When volatiles exceed 5% of total weight, this system is called a PVC organosol.) When the screen printed plastisol film is heated, the plasticizer solvates the resin particles and gelation occurs. After complete gelation or fusion with sufficient heat, a thermoplastic continuous PVC film is achieved.

Plexiglas
Trade name for acrylic plastic sheets, which through long usage, is incorrectly regarded by many as a generic term.

Ply
A term used to indicate thickness of cardboard by number of plies or layers used in the laminate. Plies are converted into points (a point is 1/1,000 inch) since ply gauges are non-existent for measuring purposes.

P.M.T.
Abbreviation for photomechanical transfer. A diffusion process whereby positive, reversal or negative prints can be made without an intermediate negative process step.

Pneumatic Stretcher
A compressed air-actuated stretching device used for tensioning fabric before it is attached to the frame.

Point Light Source
A light source for use in photomechanics from which light rays are emitted in nearly parallel arrangement to avoid undercutting during exposure.

Point of Purchase Displays (Point of Sale Displays)
Displays or merchandising units designed for use at the point of purchase, as in a retail store. Abbreviated as POP displays.

Polycarbonate
A thermoplastic material with high impact strength, low water absorption and good electrical and optical properties.

Polyester
A thermosetting plastic composition with the capability of being drawn into extremely fine strands or threads which can be woven or knitted into many types of textiles including screen printing fabric. A common trade name in the general textile field is Dacron.

Polymerization
A chemical reaction initiated by a catalyst, heat or light, in which monomers and/or oligomers combine to form a polymer. Monomers are simple molecules which unite in numbers of two to thousands to form a polymer or macro molecule. Ethylene molecules under proper reactive conditions will react with themselves to form polyethylene resin (a monopolymer). Styrene and butadiene monomers react to form SBR synthetic rubber (a copolymer).

Polypropylene
A polyolefin material similar to polyethylene, and sometimes used to manufacture plastic bottles.

Polystyrene
A clear plastic material with capability of molding into objects of contoured design or flat sheets.

Polyvinyl Chloride (PVC)
A common and widely used synthetic thermoplastic resin used in both solution and dispersion coating systems.

Poster Board
A specific weight of cardboard beginning with caliper 0.024 (24 point). Standard sheeted sizes are 22 x 28 inches and 28 x 44 inches.

Pot Life
A term indicating the length of time during storage in a specific container under normal storage conditions, that chemical composition will not lose usefulness through deterioration in the original container. Also called "working life."

Pressure Sensitive
1. A tacky adhesive which can be applied to sheet material to enable the sheet to be adhered to an unrelated surface by contact and light pressure without the use of water or solvent; 2. A sheet material that has pressure sensitive adhesive applied either at the factory or in the screen printing plant.

Pressure Washer
A screen cleaning unit consisting of a device for multiplying tap water pressure through a hose and a spray-type nozzle under high pressure.

Pretreatment
Preparing the screen fabric; i.e., degreasing, abrading, and so on, before adhering the stencil.

Puff Ink
An ink that when heated to a specific temperature for a definite period of time, achieves a characteristic of three-dimensionality by expansion.

Pulsed Xenon
Describes a type of actinic illuminant (xenon gas) which has been incorporated into photographic exposing systems, camera light units, or UV curing reactor.

PVC
Abbreviation for polyvinyl chloride, a plastic used in the manufacture of some screen printing materials. Plasticized PVC is generally known as "flexible vinyl."

Rack Drying
The drying of screenprinted sheets in racks, usually in ambient temperatures, but also placed in a room where temperatures are elevated.

Radiometer
An instrument, usually self contained, for measuring UV energy inside of curing units.

RAM
Abbreviation for Random Access Memory, the working component in a computer.

Reclaiming
1. The process of removing both ink and stencil from the screen fabric after a printing run in order to reuse the fabric for a later job; 2. The process of distilling used solvents to obtain a reusable, cleaner solvent for cleaning screens.

Reclaiming Solution
A solution used to remove screen printing films and coatings from screen fabric in order to make the fabric useful again.

Reflection Densitometry
A technique of measuring the density range of a film positive or negative by means of a light sensitive cell, capable of converting the light energy to mechanical energy to move an indicator on a scale, and showing varying degrees of density of the film under examination.

Register Guides (Guides)
Physical stops, usually three in number, and so placed on the printing base in relation to two adjacent edges of the printing sheet to ensure proper positioning for printing when the two edges of the substrate come into contact.

Register Marks
Crosses or other image devices applied to original copy prior to photography. Used for positioning negatives in perfect register or for color register of two or more colors in printing.

Relative Humidity
The amount of water vapor present in the atmosphere expressed as a percentage of the maximum that could be present at the same temperature.

Resin
A solid or semi-solid material of vegetable origin, or obtained synthetically by solvent extraction, which can be dissolved to a liquid state, suspended in a vehicle to make an ink or coating, and which, on drying, forms the solid part of the dried, printed film. Resins tend to flow under stress and have no fixed melting point.

Resolution
The relative ability of a stencil to form line pairs of acceptable acutance, at a minimum separating distance. Expressed in line pairs per inch.

Retarder
An additive for screen printing ink that slows down drying time. Usually composed of slower evaporating solvents.

Right-Reading
Refers to copy on a film positive (or negative) which reads from left to right, when the film is placed emulsion side up.

Rotary Screen Printing
The screen printing of web or sheet materials using a semirigid cylindrical metal screen, which revolves on its axis and includes a squeegee blade mounted within the screen. Ink is pumped into the rotating cylinder during printing.

Roughening
A treatment for abrading the smooth surface of the strands of monofilament screen printing fabric, for better adhesion of stencil films. A 600 silicon carbide powder is one abradant commonly used.

Rubylith
A red plastic film used in pasteup work which exhibits sufficient opacity to serve as a mask for stencil making.

Sawtooth
The effect of stencil material which tends to conform to the meshes of a screen printing fabric rather than the cleaner contours of the design on the film positive from which the stencil is produced. Both insufficient bridging and filling-in of the meshes produce a notched effect where lines of the design cross the fabric mesh diagonally.

Scoop Coater
A tool for coating screen printing fabrics with photosensitive emulsions for making printing screens. Also called "emulsion coater."

Screen Fabric
Woven fabrics for screen printing made of silk, synthetic polyester or nylon fibers, or finely drawn wire, the latter usually stainless steel.

Screen Ink
Ink, usually quick drying, full bodied and formulated for screen printing. There is a tremendous variety of screen inks made or adjusted for adhesion to a variety of substrates.

Screen Marks (Mesh Marks)
Marks left by the fabric in the surface of the screen printed imprint, due to lack of flow capability in the ink or color, or to insufficient snap-off.

Screen Mesh
1. A term generally indicating screen printing fabric; 2. That portion of the screen printing fabric which can be counted or measured to identify fineness or coarseness of the fabric.

Screen Printing
A commercial and industrial printing technique which involves the passage of a printing medium, such as ink, through a taut fabric to which a refined form of stencil has been applied. The stencil openings determine the form and dimensions of the imprint thus produced.

Screen Ruling
The number of lines or dots per linear inch in a halftone screen.

Screen Washer
A unit in which printing screens can be washed out to remove ink residues after printing, or be reclaimed completely by removing the stencil, usually by high pressure spray. Automatic units are also manufactured.

Scum
A colorless or nearly colorless residue derived from the processing of photoscreen stencils which may lodge in the stencil openings, thus blocking those areas of the printing screen when improper or incomplete washing out of the stencil occurs.

Selvage
The edges of woven fabric finished to prevent raveling of the threads. Weft threads cross the warp from selvage edge to selvage edge.

Semi-Automatic Flatbed Press
A screen printing press of the flatbed type which must be hand fed and the printed sheets must be manually removed. Only the printing action is automatic.

Semi-Automatic Machine (Semi-Automatic Press)
A machine which requires manual operation of one or more of its functions, i.e., a semi-automatic screen printing press requires manual register of substrate and manual take-off of printed sheet.

Sensitivity
Degree of response of a sensitive photographic substance to exposure.

Sensitizer
1. Photosensitive chemical, usually potassium bichromate, aluminum bichromate, or diazonium compound used for sensitizing photographic screen printing stencil films or emulsions; 2. Any chemical substance or mixture that causes a substantial number of persons to develop a hypersensitive reaction upon re-exposure to the chemical substance or mixture, through an allergic bodily reaction.

Serigraphy
A term used by fine artists to denote the result of the screen printing of original art. Used also to denote the fine arts reproduction phase of the screen printing industry.

Shadow
The darkest areas of a design or illustration or in a photograph, those portions of the print that do not show the effects of light as it reaches the subject.

Shear
1. The relative movement of adjacent layers in a liquid or plastic during flow; 2. A cutting machine for printed plastics, laminates, printed circuit boards and the like.

Shear Force
The internal force acting along a plane between two adjacent parts of a material when two equal forces, parallel to that plane, act on each part in opposite directions.

Shelf Life (Storage Life)
The period of time during which a product can be stored under specified conditions and still remain suitable for use. See also Pot Life.

Shore Hardness
A scale for measuring the relative indentation hardness of the material used to make squeegee blades, as determined by tests made with a durometer gauge or scleroscope.

Sign Board
Paperboard made of wood pulp and reclaimed paper stock, usually 0.020 to 0.040 of an inch in caliper which may be white patent-coated or clay-coated. It is not susceptible to warping and is frequently treated for water resistance.

Silk
A natural fiber with the high tensile strength produced by silk worms used in the manufacture of multifilament threads for use in weaving fine textiles and, historically, in printing screens.

Silk Screen
Archaic designation for printing screen, now largely obsolete since, in most instances, printing screens are made with other fibers than silk.

Silk Screen Process (Silk Screen Printing)
Archaic term, now obsolete, to denote screen printing.

Sketch
Unfinished rough drawing on any kind of paper, usually in pencil or felt marker, primarily to convey the idea of the projected design.

Skew
Occurs when a squeegee travels with its lengthwise dimension at an angle that is not perpendicular to the direction of its travel. Also called "snowplow."

Slur
1. A printing defect caused by slippage or movement of screen, substrate, or stencil at the moment of printing; 2. Also may be caused by a highly elastic ink splashing onto the substrate following ink shear.

Solid
The area of a print that is covered uniformly and entirely with ink and containing no halftones. Also called "solid print."

Solids
The components of an ink formulation other than the vehicle which are not removed from the film by the drying process.

Solids Content
The percentage weight of non-volatile components in an ink or coating, under specified conditions.

Solution
A uniform liquid mixture which consists of a solvent or liquid and a solute, or that part which dissolves in the solvent.

Solvent
A dissolving, thinning or reducing agent. An additive used to reduce viscosity of a screen printing ink, generally. Specifically, a solvent is a liquid that dissolves another substance, such as a resin.

Solvent-Evaporating Inks
Inks which may be dried after printing by allowing the solvents to vaporize either in ambient or elevated temperature conditions.

Solvent Evaporation
Vaporizing of liquid solvents, resulting in their removal from a printed film, hence drying of the ink film.

Squeegee
A tool used to force ink through the openings of a screen printing stencil when in contact with a substrate, consisting of a rubber or plastic strip or blade held in the edge of a wooden or metallic handle. A variety of blade shapes and hardnesses are available

Squeegee Angle
The angle formed by the near-vertical axis of the squeegee and the plane of the screen, measured when the squeegee is in position, but no force or movement has been applied. See also Angle of Attack.

Squeegee Holder
That part of a screen printing press or manual screen printing unit to which the squeegee is attached for printing.

Squeegee Pressure
The force exerted by the squeegee on the printing screen to bring it into contact with the substrate and press ink through the open screen apertures.

Squeegee Profile
The cross-sectional shape of the squeegee blade, e.g., rounded, square-edged, and so on.

Squeegee Sharpener
A mechanical device usually in the form of an abrasive roller, belt or wheel, to restore sharpness to squeegee edges.

Stainless Steel Screens
Printing screens made of stainless steel screen printing fabric, also called "wire cloth."

Static Electricity
A built-up electrical charge on the surface of a substrate, or other surfaces, usually induced by friction, and most evident under low atmospheric humidity conditions.

Static Eliminator
An electrically activated unit capable of reversing positive or negative static electricity charges thus negating the attraction effects produced by the static.

Stencil
The component of a printing screen which controls the design to be printed. See also Knife-Cut Stencil and Photostencil.

Stencil Knife
A tool for cutting screen printing stencil film usually with a small diameter, round handle to facilitate "twirling" in the fingers to trace very small curves, and with a blade about ⅛" wide, sharpened to a bevel to form a cutting point, usually beveled on both sides of the blade.

Stencil Thickness
The actual thickness of the stencil portion of a printing screen, measured in mils.

Step and Repeat
A technique of repeating a single image exposure onto photosensitive material through a negative or positive as may be required, in accurately arranged and spaced increments, to obtain multiple exposures of the same design on a single sheet of film.

Step Exposure
The progressive exposure of a piece of sensitized material by using a number of uniform increments of time to determine the correct exposure time under that given set of conditions. Also called "step test."

Step-Wedge
A scale of density steps increasing from transparent or white to opaque or black. It is used in exposing separation negatives, establishing correct filter factor and development, and establishing correct exposures for printing screens.

Strand
Individual component of a thread, which is normally made by twisting a number of strands together.

Stretch
(n.) The degree to which a material can accommodate deforming tension; (v.) The tensioning of screen printing fabric preparatory to securing it to the printing frame, or by self-stretching frame.

Styrene
A usually colorless plastic used in the manufacture of indoor and outdoor displays and signs.

Sublimable Dyes
Dyes that can be vaporized (from a solid directly to a gaseous state) by the application of heat. They are then condensed and absorbed by synthetic textile fibers. For heat transfer printing, this must occur within a temperature range that will not damage the fabric.

Sublimation Transfer
A process of image transfer to fabric containing high polyester content, by the application of heat and pressure; the dye in sublimation ink will become trapped within the polyester fiber of the garment.

Substrate
A term meaning, generally, a surface to which something adheres, the base material to be printed on, or the surface to which a pressure sensitive decal is adhered. In particular, any surface on which screen printing is applied.

Suckers
Rubber suction cups used as grippers on some three-quarter and fully automatic sheet fed presses.

Surface Tension
The property, due to molecular forces, by which all liquids through contraction of the surface tend to bring the contained volume into a form having the least area. If an ink is to be compatible with a substrate, the surface tension of the ink must approximate that of the substrate surface. Measured in dynes/cm.

Synthetic Fabric
Any fabric make from man-made fibers, strands, or threads.

Synthetic Resin
Complex chemical resins produced through reactions of simple molecules.

Tag
A device made of card, paper or plastic and used to convey a message, such as to identify a dangerous condition.

Tag Stock
Thin flexible cardboard available in white and a range of colors, widely used for screen printed tent cards due to good folding ability and tear resistance.

Take-Off Device (Take-Off)
A mechanical device for removing freshly printed substrates from the press, usually consisting of grippers and/or belts.

Tension
The stress caused by a force or forces operating to extend, stretch, or pull apart a material, such as in a taut screen fabric.

Tensioning System (Tensioning Machine)
A mechanical device for stretching screen printing fabrics to correct tension before adhering or otherwise securing fabrics to frames.

Tensionmeter
An instrument used to measure surface and interfacial tensions of liquids, or tensile strength of solids. When measuring screen tension, deflection forces are expressed in Newtons per centimeter (N/cm). Also referred to as "tensiometer."

Textiles
Cloth, woven or bonded, made of natural or synthetic fibers, usually those suitable for apparel or other utility purposes. Screen printing fabrics are textiles actually but in screen printing terminology, they are categorized as fabrics.

Thermal Setting
The use of elevated temperatures in setting or curing to obtain a usable form of product.

Thermoplastic
Having the property of becoming liquid under the application of heat, while rigid, semi-solid, or solid at normal or ambient temperature and regaining elasticity under heat applications, repeatedly.

Thermoset
A type of plastic that can be shaped to desired form by heat, that hardens on cooling, and then is substantially infusible and insoluble.

Thermosetting Ink
Inks which polymerize to a permanently solid and infusible state upon application of heat.

Thinner
A liquid which can extend a solution but which does not materially impair the power of the solvent.

30 Sheet Poster (Billboard)
Larger outdoor poster which can be approximately 117" x 261", usually consisting of 12 sheets or less. See also Poster Board.

Thread
1. (n.) An individual fabric strand or fiber; 2. (v.) To insert the web through the various stations of an inline screen printing press, and onto the rewind mechanism.

Thread Diameter
The measurement across the center of a thread or strand of fiber.

Three-Quarter Automatic
Refers to an automated press in which substrate feeding is done manually, but printing and substrate removal functions are automatic.

Toxic Chemicals
Those chemicals which have been demonstrated to possess the potential to cause death, cancer, or genetic defects through exposure to living organisms.

Transparency
1. A film positive, either black and white or in color; 2. A screen printed piece printed on clear or transparent sheeting with transparent or translucent inks, for backlighting in a display; 3. A positive image on photographic color film; 4. A manually produced design on transparent sheeting.

Transparent Base
A semi-paste compound used as an ink additive to make the ink/base mixture "shorter," i.e., less sticky or tacky, and to improve release of printed substrate from the printing screen.

Transparent Inks
Screen printing inks which, when printed, permit sufficient number of light rays with minimal diffusion, that the reflecting design or object can be identified. Such inks are more correctly identified as "translucent."

24 Sheet Poster (Billboard)
Larger outdoor poster, approximately 109" x 238", usually consisting of 10 sheets or less. See also Poster Board.

Twill Weave
A pattern of weave whereby threads are woven over one and under two. Most screen fabrics of 305 threads per inch and finer are twill weave. The area in which one thread crosses over two threads is called a float.

Ultraviolet Curing
Polymerization effected by the presence of ultraviolet rays.

Ultraviolet Drying System
Any system which utilizes ultraviolet rays to affect the drying or curing process of inks, coatings or adhesives. More correct term is ultraviolet curing system.

Ultraviolet Light
Highly energetic part of the electromagnetic spectrum of rays falling between 200 and 400 nanometer wavelengths, which are shorter than that of visible light. Carbon arc lamps, black light and mercury vapor lamps are examples of artificial sources of ultraviolet light used by the screen printer.

Undercutting
Unwanted exposure of photosensitive material beyond the limits of the positive image by slanted or reflected light rays.

UV Ink
Refers to screen printable inks which are chemically formulated to polymerize under exposure to intense ultraviolet light.

Vacuum
1. Air removal system fitted to printing base to create a vacuum between substrate and base to hold the substrate in printing position; 2. Air removal system to draw heat softened plastic sheets to mold or die for vacuum forming.

Vacuum Frame (Vacuum Printing Frame)
A unit consisting of a supporting base covered with heavy glass, between which a film positive is "sandwiched" with a piece of indirect photographic stencil film or emulsion coated printing screen. Air is exhausted from between the glass and stencil by vacuum, insuring as nearly perfect contact as possible between the film positive and the stencil film or emulsion for exposure through the glass.

Vehicle
The fluid portion of screen printing ink which acts as a carrier for the pigment.

Ventilation
The circulation of air with the object of replacing existing air with new, usually fresher air, to remove vapors, odors, and so on.

Vertical Camera
A camera in which the film holder, lens and other head components are positioned directly above the copy board.

Vinyl
Synthetic plastic product which can be made in film, sheet, and other forms. Sheets can be manufactured in either rigid or flexible constructions. Generally more flexible and formable than polyesters, they are resilient and abrasive resistant. A tough, virtually unbreakable plastic formed by polymerization of compounds, suitable for indoor or outdoor displays, signs, screen printed inflatable toys, and other 3-D fabrications.

Viscometer
An instrument for measuring the viscosity of liquids at specified temperature and atmospheric conditions, by measuring the force required to move one layer over another without turbulence. Also called "viscosimeter."

Viscosity
A term used to designate the degree of fluidity, or internal resistance to flow, of a compound ranging between liquid and heavy paste conditions.

V.O.C.
Abbreviation for Volatile Organic Compound, which refers generally to organic solvents.

Volatile
Subject to evaporation at a relatively low temperature.

Warp
1. The forming of curvature in a flat sheet due to moisture absorption on one side, or continued stress or bending action; 2. The lengthwise direction of threads in a woven fabric; 3. Distortion in any material, as caused by a nonuniformity of internal stresses.

Water-Based Inks
Inks containing a vehicle whose binder is water soluble or water dispersible.

Weatherability
The inherent resistance of a product to weather influences when subjected to exterior exposure conditions.

Weathering
The effect on a printed piece of atmospheric elements when exposed out of doors. Natural outdoor weathering tests are normally carried out at selected exposure sites, on printing panels, exposed either vertically or at 45 degrees facing south in the Northern Hemisphere. Artificial weathering tests are conducted under laboratory conditions.

Web
A continuous sheet of pliable manufactured material; may be paper, cloth, film, and so on.

Web Fed
1. An automatic feeding system that feeds substrates from a continuous roll, synchronized to a stop motion arrangement which stops movement for printing; 2. A term to indicate a type of screen printing press that feeds the substrate from a bulk roll or bolt (as in textiles).

Weed
Disposable portion after die cutting; that portion of a die cut sheet that is waste. Also called "matrix."

Weft
The horizontal threads or fibers that cross the warp from selvage to selvage. Also called "woof."

Wet Film Thickness
The depth, expressed in mils, of an applied coating measured immediately after application.

Wet-On-Wet
Describes the printing of multiple colors onto a substrate before the previously printed colors have dried, used in the screen printing of absorbent substrates, such as textiles.

Wetting Agent
A chemical additive which reduces the surface tension of a fluid, inducing it to spread readily on a surface to which it is applied, thus causing even "wetting" of the surface with the fluids.

Wicket Dryer
A conveyorized system of wire forms, trays, or racks designed to hold sheet substrates in a near-vertical position while drying.

Work Harden
To gradually harden synthetic screen fabrics through repeated tensioning, by the use of certain self-stretching chases or devices, between print runs, reclaiming and so on.

Wrong-Reading
A film positive that is not right-reading, i.e., has emulsion-side down or copy which is reversed. Such positives are useful for screen printing in reverse. Also called "reverse-reading."

Index

H

I

J

K

L

M

N

T

U

V

W

Colophon

AUTHOR MANUSCRIPT PREPARATION

Digital Photographic Conversion

Nearly all the photographs in the text were taken by the author. A Nikon F3 camera body was used with various focal length lenses. Kodak Royal Gold Film (ASA 100 and 200) and Kodak Lumiere Professional Slide Film (ASA 100) were used to take photos.

Color negatives and slides were converted to Kodak Photo CD or Kodak Pro Photo CD format.

Kodak's Photo CD Access Plus software was used on a Macintosh computer to view each image and export in the following settings: Millions of colors; 1024 x 768 pixels; TIFF-YCC; TIFF 300DPI.

Images were reopened using Adobe Photoshop software. Each image had its channels split; the red channel was cropped and saved as a tiff, and the green and blue channels were discarded.

The highlight and shadow areas were adjusted by increasing contrast, and brightening or darkening the midtone. Images were sharpened using the unsharp mask filter (usually between 150% and 300%, radius was .4 to .9, and threshold was always at zero). Each image was then saved in TIFF format.

Further adjustments were made at RR Donnelley to optimize for their press.

Computer Hardware

Macintosh 9500
Macintosh Sytem 7.53
32mb RAM
NEC21: MultiSync Monitor

Computer Software

Photoshop 3.0
DeltaGraph 4.0
FreeHand 5.5
Kodak Photo CD Access Plus
Quark XPress 3.31

PRODUCTION

Pages were designed and composed at Stillwater Studio, Stillwater NY.

Text: Palatino 10/12
Display: Futura

Design and Composition: Power Macintosh 8100/80, with 172mb RAM, Quark XPress 3.32, Adobe Photoshop 3.0, Adobe Illustrator 5.5
Printer: RR Donnelley & Sons Co., Harrisonburg VA Division
Press: web offset

Paper: 50 lb. Restorecote
Cover Films: The Color Shop, Clifton Park NY
Cover Printer: Phoenix Color Corp., Hagerstown MD
Cover: Kivar 6, printed four process colors with film lamination